THE DEVIL'S OWN DAY: SHILOH AND THE AMERICAN CIVIL WAR

ISBN 978-1-60910-661-4

Printed in the United States of America.

Maps are extracted from *Staff Ride Handbook for the Battle of Shiloh, 6–7 April 1862* by Jeffrey J. Gudmens; Combat Studies Institute Press, Ft. Leavenworth, KS. [Electronic version downloaded 2008].

Portions of this book have appeared in the *General Orders* of the Civil War Round Table of Milwaukee, Inc.

Booklocker.com, Inc.
2011

The Devil's Own Day:
Shiloh and the American Civil War

John D. Beatty

"CRANBROOK! THY NAME, A GLOWING SYMBOL LIVE!

"TO FUTURE SONS, AN INSPIRATION GIVE;

"'THO EYES GROW DIM, 'THO STRENGTH BE PAST, YET WE

"'TILL LIFE IS DONE, SHALL EVER CHERISH THEE."

FOR KURUSH BHARUCHA-REID

CLASS OF '73

COL, USA

RIP

Table of Contents

Introduction

Shiloh has taken a back seat to nearly every other Civil War battle for a number of reasons, but all of them, I submit, start with misinterpretation. Battles are more than just slugfests between men with guns and swords: they are contests of wills, of personalities, of position, geography, weather, timing, training, climate, ordnance and logistics and, to a certain extent, that elusive sum of preparation and opportunity called luck. In the spring of 1862 two forces clashed in the piney wilderness of south central Tennessee. For two days they fought around a small river landing that changed the fate and the direction of the United States in 48 hours. There was so much at stake at Shiloh--far more than was known when the battle was joined—and because this one campaign had so great an effect not only on the war but on the entire country, controversy after the fact was inevitable. The view that I put forward here will be rejected by a few readers. So be it.

This is a work of exploration. The reader will find some in the way of traditional American Civil War history here. There is a little background on the principal players, but long and quoted excerpts from diaries and letters are absent because others do that much better than I can. I hope the reader will find the connection of cause and effect at Shiloh in a greater context than most books on the American Civil War.

There have been several Shiloh books over the years, each with a slightly different message. Despite this, Shiloh has always defied rational battle analysis. The major works on Shiloh whose descriptions I use here--including those of James Arnold, O. Edward Cunningham, Larry Daniel, David Martin, Lee McDonough, David Reed, Wily Sword and George Witham--are brilliant interpretations of the evidence that I have shamelessly picked apart and have tried to build on. Each has provided new pieces of the historical puzzle that I'm putting together to create yet another image.

A Word on Organization

The chapters leading up to the battle itself are an attempt to give the reader some appreciation for how the armies were led, equipped, trained, organized and motivated, and of how the course of the war immediately before the shooting started affected the battle. Since the two halves of Shiloh only connected intermittently on Sunday, the battle narrative is built up from different essays on the Federal right, the Federal left, leadership before the battle and during, the last fighting on Sunday, and the second day of the fighting. Other events, including Buell's approach and Lew Wallace's experience, were important but far from the fighting and defy casual insertion, so they appear separately. The last chapter tries to place Shiloh into a larger context of history.

The Appendix, "The Steamboats of Shiloh," is a foray into the shadowy world of river steamboat information sources and the disparity of hard information derived thereof. There is a lack of hard information on the steamboats in general, the contracts they used, their conditions and their crews because there was simply no central records depository for the industry that was built as it went along, nor has there been the inclination to create a record collection since. Most steamboats were built without drawings as we now know them; specifications were only vague guidelines such that modern scholars rely on underwater archaeology for steamboat dimensions. The histories of the inland rivers have a surplus of romantic stories of gamblers and wrecks, but not much else for the practical historian to work with. I encourage the ambitious reader to do further research on this little-explored aspect of the Civil War and America's past.

A Word on Rank and Nationality

Most Civil War books spend a great deal of time and space on making sure that the reader knows what specific rank a person held at a given time. While I have respect for my fellow historians and a great deal of respect for how rank is achieved (not necessarily for how it is sometimes simply bestowed) I do not share other historian's concern with it. For reasons explained in Chapter 1, rank and seniority were very contentious issues in the Civil War: rank could be conferred from sources at the local, state or national level, or even by election by the units themselves. The feuds that sometimes followed were prodigious; commissions were routinely backdated to assure seniority to political friends over foes; officers sometimes refused to serve under this officer because his commission came from the wrong state or was once outranked by another; and on and on. In this book I am far more concerned with the larger, deadlier fighting than with the machinations of the influential. Except where it is important to the story, rank is omitted.

The Confederate States of America in 1861 was as lawfully constituted a nation as the United States of America was in 1776. Members of the armies of that country are called "Confederates;" members of the armies of the Federal Union are called either "Federals" or "Unionists." My deepest apologies to anyone that I offend with my choices.

Credit and Blame

For more than two decades the members of the Civil War Round Table of Milwaukee have enlightened, frustrated, entertained and inspired me to think of the American Civil War as something other than a distraction. Most especially, Lance Herdegen's yeoman work on the Iron Brigade (which regrettably played no role at Shiloh, but Lance lost an ancestor there), and David Eicher's inspiration and painstaking researches have been encouraging and helpful in my endeavors. The Board of Directors of the Round Table that suffered my inattention and irritation for far too long also deserves my heartfelt thanks, and my apologies for neglecting my duties to them.

Frank Devoy, my long-suffering editor, foil, intellectual sparring partner and good friend of many years, struggled with me through this manuscript, learning about American military history and the peculiarities of the Civil War as he suffered my distain at his ignorance of the subject matter. But his responses drove me to think of the wider audience (of which, after all, he is one), and made me rethink much of the "everyone knows" kinds of usage that Civil War aficionados expect to see in their books. And through all that, Frank's wife Joanne still puts up with him, and with me from time to time. I have to express my deepest thanks to both.

But my deepest and most heartfelt thanks, adoration and love go to my long-suffering writer's widow, Evelyne. No spouse should ever have to suffer as much for a book as she has, twice now. But now that this is done she won't be as alone as I have left her in the past…for a while anyway.

For blame I have to look to the US Army's dysfunctional non-commissioned officer education system of the 1980s and '90s. I tried, but whenever one milestone towards promotion was reached, it moved--a perverse carrot-and-stick game called "catch the school slot and get the promotion before we change the requirements again." While it was happening, fellow sergeants reminded me that I wore the stripes not for myself but for my people, officers included. This constant reinforced my appreciation that the NCO's lot is to be a middleman; his duty is to others, not himself. My experience as a member of the NCO corps of the United States Army in part triggered my critical examination of Shiloh and how Civil War armies worked, and what both have meant to America.

JDB

West Allis, Wisconsin

January 2011

Prelude:

Forts Henry and Donelson, February 1862

Gun smoke lingered over the frozen fields, held down by an eerie ice-fog that blanketed the battlefield as the sun set and the snow stopped. Lacking winter coats, the weary Federals quickly gathered kindling and firewood. Everything was covered with a thin sheet of ice, beautiful in the sunset; the men had to crack the ice off their firewood with musket butts and bayonets, burning gunpowder to get kindling dry and warm enough to light. The dead were ignored on the field; many were covered in snow and ice after a battle in a blinding snowstorm. The wounded cried piteously in the fog and smoke, their hot breath rising in steam for the litter teams to follow under white flags of truce.

The Confederate bastion on the Tennessee River called Fort Henry had fallen to the Navy just over a week before, when the weather was warm. The Federal army unloaded the men from the hired steamboats to take possession of that fort, only to find that much of the garrison had fled to Fort Donelson just ten miles east. The Unionists set out cross-country east as if on a lark; a bunch of boys playing dress-up, hiking in easy camaraderie in unfamiliar country. As the Tennessee climate was warm, the volunteers from Illinois and Ohio, Wisconsin and Indiana discarded winter coats, and their packs with their shelters and blankets. Few of these volunteers had been more than twenty miles from the places where they were born. Everyone knew the rebellion would be over soon.

The weather turned cool, then cold. First it rained, then it sleeted, then it snowed, then it froze, and then came the cold that gripped sentinels too weary to stay awake. Men glazed in sweat under unfamiliar blue uniforms froze to death on picket duty, giving their messmates a ghastly introduction to the realities of war. Inexperienced staff officers didn't get food and ammunition landed, and very few wagons with horses or mules managed to get off-loaded before there was another rise in the river. Cannon ammunition arrived, but not musket cartridges; most regiments had only what the men carried when they reached Fort Donelson. Food was in short supply; horses starved to death in teams. The men were on half-rations for a week, then on no rations at all.

The Navy shelled Fort Donelson in vain. Fort Donelson was much better sited than Fort Henry had been, better manned and better gunned. When the Navy gave up the Army tried a siege, but with only a handful of field guns with ruined horses to move them it wasn't easy. When wagons finally arrived they brought only a handful of picks, shovels, axes and saws. Without enough tools for digging trenches, felling trees for firewood, and building abatis to defend against attackers was time-consuming. And there was always a threat of a Confederate relief army from Nashville just two days march away.

As skillful and as well-placed as their artillery was, and as miserable and nervous as the Federals were, the Confederates at Fort Donelson were on the end of a very long and even more tenuous supply line, and had similar problems feeding their animals. Their officers had even less experience at war than their soldiers did. Realizing that the Unionists would eventually be able to overwhelm or starve the fort, the Confederates tried to escape on 15 February. The fight could have gone either way, but eventually command confusion and misunderstanding of the battle overcame a near Confederate victory, and they went back into their lines. It was a near-run thing for the Federals, but a victory is a victory.

The next morning a stern and crusty Union Army campaigner named Charles F. Smith handed the senior Union general a note from Fort Donelson, saying, "Here's something for you to read."

> HEADQUARTERS,
> Fort Donelson, February 16, 1862.
> SIR:
> In consideration of all the circumstances governing the present situation of affairs at this station I propose to the commanding officers of the Federal forces the appointment of

commissioners to agree upon terms of capitulation of the forces and post under my command, and in that view suggest an armistice until 12 o'clock to-day.

I am, sir, very respectfully, your obedient servant,
S. B. BUCKNER,
Brigadier-General, C. S. Army.

Ulysses Grant, one of Smith's former West Point pupils, probably read Simon Buckner's message with some dejection, and with more than a bit of sorrow. In 1854 Grant had been dead broke and was stuck in California, having resigned his captain's commission under unclear circumstances. He borrowed money from Buckner, with whom he had served in Mexico, so he could go back to his wife and family near St. Louis. Eight years later, Grant was going to have to kill or capture one of his best friends.

If he had wanted to comply with the spirit of the note, Grant would have selected a few of his officers to meet with a similar number of Buckner's. They would have met in a tent near the front lines, exchanged pleasantries, and negotiated the timing for what boiled down to a parade. At a time these commissioners agreed on, the Confederates would march out of their fort with their flags flying and drums beating, past the ranks of Union soldiers, who might be expected to salute as their opponents marched away. The Confederates would be expected to leave most of their artillery and supplies behind when they marched to Nashville, from there to fight again. Grant likely knew this "honors of war" ceremony was what Buckner expected, but Grant also knew it would not be possible.

Grant asked Smith, his principal subordinate, how he should reply. "No terms to the damned rebels," Smith snapped. Perhaps with a tinge of guilt, Grant wrote:

HEADQUARTERS ARMY IN THE FIELD,
Camp near Fort Donelson, February 16, 1862.
SIR:

Yours of this date, proposing armistice and appointment of commissioners to settle terms of capitulation, is just received.

> No terms except unconditional and immediate surrender can be accepted. I propose to move immediately upon your works.
> I am, sir, very respectfully, your obedient servant,
> U.S. GRANT,
> Brigadier-General, Commanding.

"It's the same thing in smoother words," Smith grunted.

At Fort Donelson, shortly after Grant's note was passed through the lines, a bizarre change-of-command meeting was held between John B. Floyd, the senior officer at Fort Donelson who had been United States Secretary of War just a year before; Gideon Pillow, a politically-appointed bungler of a general who was next in line of seniority; and Buckner, a professional in the antebellum US Army and last. Floyd and Pillow passed the command in succession to Buckner.

Buckner must have felt a tinge of indignation at Grant's reply, but he already knew his army was in a losing position. As Buckner sent his reply to Grant, Floyd and Pillow were escaping across the Cumberland with small groups of supporters.

> HEADQUARTERS,
> Dover, Tenn., February 16, 1862.
> SIR:
> The distribution of the forces under my command incident to an unexpected change of commanders and the overwhelming force under your command compel me, notwithstanding the brilliant success of the Confederate arms yesterday, to accept the ungenerous and unchivalrous terms which you propose.
> I am, sir, your very obedient servant,
> S. B. BUCKNER,
> Brigadier-General, C. S. Army.

Over ten thousand Confederate soldiers fell into Union hands the next day, the largest single surrender of any American force up to that time. More men surrendered at Fort Donelson than had fought with

George Washington in the first year of the Revolution.[1] The news of Fort Donelson reached Richmond on the same day as Jefferson Davis was sworn into office as the Confederacy's first president. Buckner's hurt feelings and the huge loss of men, supplies and arms would soon be the least of the Confederacy's problems.

Before the first shots were exchanged in the wet darkness between Confederate and Federal troops near the flatboat landing on the Tennessee River on a Sabbath morning in April, the war had been an indecisive mobilization of barely trained militiamen blundering into each other, led by a few Grants, Buckners and Smiths, and a huge number of Floyds and Pillows. This was a war no one was ready for, under conditions that few Americans had ever seen. In 1862, former friends faced each other with menace and threat across a cultural and military divide that could not have been wider.[2]

---

1. Somewhere between 8,000 and 15,000 Confederates were captured at Fort Donelson. Since they were to be exchanged shortly, no one seems to have bothered with accurate numbers. As at Stalingrad generations later, there may not have been time or resources to sort and count them.

2. Edward H. Bonekemper, *A Victor, not a Butcher: Ulysses S. Grant's Overlooked Military Genius* (Washington D.C.: Regenry Publishing, 2004), 35; Jack D. Coombe, *Thunder Along the Mississippi: The River Battles That Split the Confederacy* (New York: Sarpedon, 1996), 71–2; James L. McDonough, *Shiloh--in Hell Before Night* (Knoxville: University of Tennessee Press, 1977), 28; Brooks D. Simpson, *Ulysses S. Grant: Triumph Over Adversity, 1822–1865* (New York: Houghton Mifflin Company, College Division, 2000), 117–20; War Department, "Shiloh, Corinth Series I, Volume VII," in *War of the Rebellion: Official Records of the Union and Confederate Armies* (Washington, D.C.: U.S. Government Printing Office, 1911 (Electronic version 1999 by Guild Press, Indianapolis, IN)), 160–1; Joan Waugh, *U.S. Grant: American Hero, American Myth* (Chapel Hill, NC: University of North Carolina Press, 2009), 41, 54.

CHAPTER 1
A NATION DIVIDED: AMERICA AND ITS WAY OF WAR BEFORE SHILOH

Whatever it was that started the American Civil War had to be enough to drive three armies--with some hundred thousand men between them--to two days of horrifying battle in a lonesome wilderness in western Tennessee, and inflict more casualties than America had seen in its entire history up to that time. Shiloh was the second major land battle of the Civil War, and the second American battle since 1846 that lasted more than eight continuous hours.[1]

After a century and a half of discussion there should be a simple, single explanatory theory for the secession of the slaveholding states and the war that followed that a majority of scholars can accept, but at this writing there really isn't one. However, for all their vision, the framers of the Constitution failed to foresee that any part of the Union would feel that their needs trumped those of the rest of the country and would want to leave the Union. This lack of imagination practically guaranteed that any attempts to separate the states or nullify the Union might be a nasty proposition, but the framers couldn't imagine anyone wanting to do it. Their failure ensured that if a part of the country just didn't want to be associated with the others any more, there *could* be a genuine crisis.

Slavery just made things worse. The framers felt it was going to be hard enough to get their creation ratified without addressing the logical disconnect between the "all men are created equal" phrase in the Declaration of Independence and the deeply entrenched, cruel reality of the slaves. The "peculiar institution" was a name not just for chattel

---

1. Joseph Allan Frank, and George A. Reaves, *"Seeing the Elephant:" Raw Recruits at the Battle of Shiloh* (Chicago: University of Illinois Press, 2003).

slavery, but for the political, economic and social system that built, supported and advocated the practice and business of slavery: it was a whole outlook on life, wealth and social status, of which the slaves were only the most visible, and the practice the most vilified. The slave population was immense before 1787, making up as much as 20% of the national population. Article V of the Constitution prohibited the states and the Congress from stopping slave importation before 1808, but even this was delayed for a decade, until the slave population was orders of magnitude larger than it had been in 1788. If politics are rooted in compromise, American politics had failed completely by 1860. The 1861-65 conflict was a symptom of the breakdown of the American political process.[2]

This Constitutional explanation may be adequate for parlor discussions, but would not have been enough to explain why the soldiers kept fighting after the first few minutes of panic and pain. Grand speeches and thundering editorials might get the men (and women) to march to the battlefield, but were not likely enough to keep them there. To get people to march through drenching rain and gelatinous mud on empty bellies with raging fevers, to get them to suppress their fight-or-flee response while friends, families and neighbors are shot to pieces in storms of buzzing metal and choking smoke requires drives much deeper.

---

2. Bruce Catton, *Reflections on the Civil War* (Norwalk, CT: Easton Press, 1987), 29–31; John Ellis, *Founding Brothers: The Men of the Revolutionary Generation* (Cambridge: Yale University Press, 2004); Max Farrand, *Fathers of the Constitution: A Chronicle of the Establishment of the Union* (New Haven, CT: Yale University Press [Project Gutenberg], 1921 [Electronic edition 2006]), Ch. III, P. 1; Woody Holton, *Unruly Americans and the Origins of the Constitution* (New York: Hill and Wang, 2007); John G. Nicolay, *Outbreak of the Rebellion*, Campaigns of the Civil War (New York: Charles Scribner's Sons [Guild Press of Indiana], 1861 [electronic edition 1999]), 6, 17; Albert A. Nofi, "The American Civil War, 1861–1865," *Strategy and Tactics Magazine #43* (1974).

"Civil wars" are said to be more relatively savage than other conflicts. Judging by the relative ferocity and duration of the 1861-65 war, the justification for fighting this civil war the way it was fought must have come from a combination of desire for adventure on the behalf of the soldiers, belief in the correctness of the causes that got them to join up, and a generations-old section/tribe/clan animosity as deep and ugly as any ancient feud that keeps any society fighting another. Multicultural 19th Century American society was no more immune from distrust of the "other" than any other society at any other time.[3]

Worse, by 1860 the North and the South had grown so culturally, politically and economically separate that the entire edifice of the Union was sundered by a single national election. Given some of the antebellum rhetoric, one might wonder how the country stayed together that long. Philosophical disagreement over the value of land over the value of labor as the source of wealth may have been the very heart of the problem, and may have come to the New World from 17th Century England. By 1775 Tory land-first political economy was dominant in the South--where land was fairly plentiful. Whig labor-first political economy was dominant in New England, where land was harder to come by, and competitive in the Middle Colonies, where labor was cheaper but slavery generally not economical.[4]

The motive for the war among Unionists both in the North and the South was a desire to keep the country together for its own prosperity and security. The doctrines of "manifest destiny" that had driven the exploration and colonization of the continent in both the North and the South were forged with an understanding of collective security by a

---

3. Grady McWhiney, and Perry D. Jamieson, *Attack and Die: Civil War Military Tactics and the Southern Heritage* (University, AL: University of Alabama Press, 1982), 172–3; Robert Penn Warren, *The Legacy of the Civil War: Meditations on the Centennial* (New York: Vintage Books, 1961), 4–5.

4. Steve Pincus, *1688: The First Modern Revolution* (New Haven: Yale University Press, 2009).

single, powerful country, not a hodgepodge of smaller and easily cowed ones. Divided, its further expansion or even survival was perceived as doubtful. It was feared by some in both North and South that European powers would take advantage of any weakening of American unity.

While the North held for Union, they stood for other cultural values, such as courts, constables and prisons, factories and fertile farms, and labor for making finished durable goods--the value of labor and manufactured goods was above that of land. The North held that the Union forged by the Founding Fathers was more important than the mere preference for what they saw as the South's old-fashioned and romantic social/economic order.

The South valued cash crops like tobacco and cotton, and only enough manufactured goods to fulfill local needs. As a people, Southerners treasured the value of land owned by a few, believing that any rude peasant or slave could provide infinite labor. The plantation owner/planter was seen as a hereditary lord of the community, a class of landed gentry regarded as the natural superior to all others. The "state's rights" that the South was trying to uphold was a moonlight-and-magnolias-juleps-on-the-veranda-slave-in-the-fields Utopia that only few *very* wealthy people enjoyed. The South had come to believe that the preservation of their way of life was not just a matter of social preference, but was sanctioned by the Almighty; Southern churches maintained that it was by God's holy ordinance that the black man was enslaved. Rather than courts, Southern gentlefolk preferred to settle their differences using the *Code Duello*, the ancient rules that "controlled" dueling.

Cotton typified the challenges to this system, but was in no means the only challenge. It provided so much revenue that some planters had sold their crops two years in advance. Its cultivation sucked the life out of the soil faster than the antebellum planters knew how to restore it, requiring them to expand their holdings or keep moving to maintain the capital flow. It defied 19th Century mechanization and required prodigious manual labor to produce.[5]

While a majority of Southerners did not own slaves, such was the South's fear of losing their version of civilized society that they felt that to it they had to rend the Union apart. This to-save-the-village-we-must-destroy-it logic made perfect sense to many in the Southern Confederacy. The South reasoned that since the federal Union was entered into voluntarily, it could be sundered voluntarily, departing peacefully and as friends. But the Declaration of Independence had been written with similar sentiments, and the global war fought to enable it lasted eight years.[6]

A peaceful separation may have been effected if the war hadn't started in such a dramatic fashion. Once the states started to secede in 1860, they began to seize Federal assets that they believed became theirs as soon when they pulled away. The seceding states believed that everything within the boundaries of their state belonged to them regardless of origin. There was simply no time for the small and scattered Regular Army to secure the arsenals, since most antebellum

---

5. Nicolay, op. cit., 138; Brian Tyson, *The Institution of Slavery in the Southern States, Religiously and Morally Considered in Connection with Our Sectional Troubles* (Washington, D.C. [Chapel Hill, NC]: H Polkinhorn, Printer [University of North Carolina at Chapel Hill], 1863 [electronic edition 2001]), 1–6; Stephen Yafa, *Big Cotton: How a Humble Fiber Created Fortunes, Wrecked Civilizations, and Put America on the Map* (New York: Viking Press, Inc., 2005), 158–60.

6. Peter S. Carmichael, "New South Visionaries: Virginia's Last Generation of Slaveholders, the Gospel of Progress, and the Lost Cause," in *The Myth of the Lost Cause and Civil War History* (Indianapolis: Indiana University Press, 2000), 112–15; John Patrick Daly, "Holy War: Southern Religion and the Road to War and Defeat, 1831–1865," *North and South*, September 2003, 35–46; Nicolay, op. cit., 49–50; Stephen Yafa, "The Man Who Made Cotton King," *Invention and Technology*, Winter 2005, 37–8.

posts east of the Mississippi were garrisoned by less than a hundred men. Since all but a few Federal arsenals and forts were seized by Confederate mobs and orderly militia units without violence this was not regarded as particularly dangerous. Until Fort Sumter.

The blockade and bombardment of Fort Sumter in Charleston Harbor could pass for a scriptwriter's final draft for the dramatic opening act of an epic tragedy. All the most dramatic elements are present: the midnight movement of a handful of soldiers through hostile territory to an unfinished island fortress with guns facing the wrong way; heroic defiance uttered by Robert Anderson, the long-in-the-tooth major commanding the garrison; rescue missions driven off with cannonballs whistling overhead; defiant messages from the fort to the press. The finale was the gallant little band defending their flag against a storm of shot and shell for 34 hours, marching out with the full honors of war when their supplies were exhausted. The North could not have asked for a better motive or visual image to go to war.

Union President Abraham Lincoln saw it this way: a combination of states that had fired on unarmed vessels trying to provide non-military supplies to a lawfully constituted force on Federal property. To him this was a rebellion, and believed it was his Constitutional duty to call out the militia to suppress it. Regardless of why it happened, firing on the flag at Fort Sumter was enough provocation for war, just as any other insult might occasion a furtive meeting in a secluded meadow at dawn. South Carolina claimed it "owned" the manmade island that Sumter sat on, and that "Southern honor" made its possession a matter for guns to decide, not courts, thus making it an exaggerated extension of the *Code Duello*. The American Civil War, in this view, began when the South resorted to their preferred means of settling disputes. Social revolution, human equality, political economy, and the end of the slavery system were simply not a part of the calculus of the war until two years of bloodletting made it so.

Presidential Dilemmas

Lincoln, a railroad lawyer from Illinois, was unfamiliar with the requirements of both war and presidency and accepted military advice from all sides, acting on some. He and his Secretaries of War had to learn as they went along, reading the works of the most popular English language works in military thought of the time. These included the leading European military theorist, Henri Antoine Jomini, who was popular because he had once worked with Napoleon I, and Henry W. Halleck, an American disciple of Jomini who had quit the Army and become a prosperous attorney in California. Jomini and Halleck wrote about huge, largely professional armies. American strategic theory, in the books anyway, was essentially French.

Of all the battles fought in July 1861, none had held a candle to the scale of the Confederacy's apparent success at Manassas, or Bull Run, the first major ground action of the war. This was a showy and morale-boosting fight for the Confederacy, and an embarrassing spectacle for the Union watched by hundreds of Washington civilians and foreign diplomats. But it was a strategically meaningless victory that had not been exploited. Soldiers on both sides fought better than they were led; the Southern victory was more due to Northern inexperience and bad timing than to Southern brilliance. The lack of follow-up by the winners was something that few spoke of at the time, but showed that the Confederate forces were perhaps not the indomitable host that they made themselves out to be.[7]

The strategic situation for the Union was a jumble of "needs" from governors of states bordering the Confederacy who were pleading for troops to protect them from real and imagined invasions by Confederate hordes. Lincoln's armies did not seem to be losing any ground or appreciable numbers of troops in the first year of the war, though the death toll from disease in the first winter was appalling. The North's losses could be made up quickly because, at that moment, men seemed to be tumbling from the sky to volunteer.

What Lincoln needed was a general in command of an army that could win, and win consistently. Lincoln's generals were mostly political appointees or overaged remnants of earlier wars; those healthy

---

7. Jeffry J. Gudmens, *Staff Ride Handbook for the Battle of Shiloh, 6–7 April 1862* (Ft. Leavenworth, KS: Combat Studies Institute Press, n.d. [Electronic version downloaded 2008]), 2.

enough to take field commands were well-meaning but incapable of handling large forces. They had a habit of stopping to catch their breath after victory, and demanding massive reinforcements after a setback. It was this dearth of men who could lead troops into reasonably decisive action and keep pushing that would be most severely felt in the North.

There was concern in the North and hope in the South about what Europe would think of America's troubles, but the Great Powers of Europe had other things to concern itself with than a civil war in America. The end of the Crimean War (1854-56) left very bitter gall in both French and British throats, with the two allies nearly going to war with each other. Neither France nor Britain would trust the other enough to either cooperate in another major foreign venture, nor would they sit placidly by while the other undertook a solo project. France and Britain tag-teamed Confederate diplomats, pointing at each other and saying "I will if he does," while knowing that neither was much interested in either recognition of the Confederacy or participating in the fighting (which were not the same thing). The Confederacy held out the fervent hope that Britain and France would become involved in the conflict, and withheld their cotton for nine months early in the war. They concluded that without cotton to keep the mills running, Europe would soon intervene against the North, just as France had against Britain in 1777. Europe wanted to see America's expanding commercial power reduced, but was not going to do much more than sell arms to both sides. The abysmal failure of France's Mexican foray of 1862-65, weakly backed by Britain and Spain, was a stark example of how unready the Old World was to fight in any part of the Americas in the 1860's.[8]

Confederate fortunes had plummeted much faster than Union fortunes had risen, and Confederate President Jefferson Davis, a senator from Mississippi until 1861, accepted advice from few and acted on even less than Lincoln did. By early 1862, Confederate forces were pulling back everywhere. Governors of all the states in Davis' new

---

8. Brian James, "Allies in Disarray: The Messy End of the Crimean War, *History Today* 58 (March 2008): 21–34.

country were clamoring for arms, munitions, men, ships, supplies, and salvation from threats real and imagined. From Tennessee to Florida, from Virginia to Texas, the Union army and navy seemed to be everywhere, and each governor was certain that his state would be invaded next. Maryland was almost entirely occupied by Federal forces, Virginia was partly Union-held, and the Carolinas and Chesapeake Bay region were under a developing blockade.

There was some fatalism to Davis' strategy and goals. He felt that once Southern slave-holding territory was lost to the Northern "forces of abolition," it would be worthless to Southern slave-holding interest forever after. Yet, the forces that Davis could use to hold the country were always limited. Such was the fear of slave revolt that some in the Confederacy felt they were doomed if the war lasted beyond a few months. There had been four major slave-related disturbances--Wat Tyler's and John Brown's being the best known--between 1787 and 1859, each more terrifying to the slaveholders than the last. Because of this, the Confederate states kept large state militias which, by law, could not leave their state, and exempted large numbers of able-bodied men from the Confederate draft. There was nothing much more Davis could do than give many governors his best wishes, a few officers, and what little equipment he could spare.[9]

Even though Confederate resources were stretched so thin in places as to be non-existent, Davis had to resist the temptation to abandon any state or area. When he shifted the seat of the Confederate government to Richmond, he called on the states to send troops to protect the capitol, only 90 miles from the main Federal forces near Washington. All the states responded to the call, including faraway Texas and Arkansas. If Davis wrote off regions that had sent so many troops to protect Richmond they might feel perfectly entitled--under state's rights theory--to just return to and defend their homes. If abandoned by Richmond, undecided Missouri would never officially leave the Union,

---

9. Holton, op. cit., 222; Archer Jones, *Confederate Strategy from Shiloh to Vicksburg* (Baton Rouge, LA: University of Louisiana Press, 1991), 19–20.

teetering Kentucky would be permanently lost, isolated Texas and Arkansas might rethink their positions, and East Tennessee and northwestern Virginia might become even more unmanageable havens of pro-Union sentiment--and there were more pockets of Unionists in nearly every Confederate state. Davis couldn't afford to make more enemies by abandoning friends.[10]

If Davis believed he was no better off than the Union in this regard, he also had to have known that the situation could not last. He must have known that the side with the biggest battalions in the right place at the right time was going to dictate what the solution to the primary problems of the conflict would be. The Confederacy as a whole didn't have enough powder on hand in the spring of 1862 to fight more than two Manassas-scale battles. Most of the ammunition that had been captured in earlier fights had already been distributed. New powder and shot had to be made from painfully sparse resources, captured, or brought from Europe. The South's main advantage was believed to be, if not in numbers, in martial ardor. In the South it was widely accepted that the Southern soldier was naturally superior to his Northern counterpart. Southern officers were said to be more universally loved, courageous and skilled, and the marksmanship and fighting spirit of the men in the ranks was said to be far better than those of the Northerners.[11]

The Confederacy was like an island--surrounded by water, but they had no navy with which to defend their long seaward frontiers. Despite captures of vast naval stores and stacks of ordnance, there just were not enough hands or machinery to build the vessels needed to either get the cotton to markets, damage Union trade, break the blockade for a

---

10. William C. Davis, *The Orphan Brigade: The Kentucky Confederates Who Couldn't Go Home* (Garden City, NY: Doubleday & Company, 1980), 12; Alan Hankinson, *First Bull Run 1861: The South's First Victory* (London: Osprey Publishing LTD., 1990), 87–8; Archer Jones, op. cit., 19.

11. John H. and David E. Eicher, *Civil War High Commands* (Stanford, CA: Stanford University Press, 2001), 886–92.

meaningful period, or support the army. The Norfolk Naval Yard had yielded a bonanza of material, but the Confederate Navy lacked the manpower to do much more than arm an ironclad ram based on the hull of the screw sloop *Merrimack*—called *Virginia*—but it could not leave the Hampton Roads. On its many river highways, other Confederate warships were being built that had neither engines, nor armor plate, nor guns, nor seamen. Confronted with a sea frontier longer than that of the first thirteen colonies and no realistic way to make a navy, Davis despaired of his country's future. Without a navy, coherent army policy, transport, adequate munitions or food, shoes, field equipment, medical supplies or even horses, the Confederacy needed a plan to defeat the Federal armies approaching so swiftly and so relentlessly, or they needed the war to end once and for all.[12]

The American Militia Tradition

The unspoken reason that the Americans kept no large standing forces from its founding until the Cold War was that they really didn't need them. American defense strategy since Washington's time depended on the militia, in keeping with the ancient English traditions of the yeoman-farmer/citizen-soldier, and who made up a bulk of American armies before 1917. Resisting any invasion was the responsibility first of the militias that had nowhere to run without abandoning families and hard-won land. To allow the rest of the country time to build needed forces to repel any invasion, the militiamen would be the first to engage any interlopers. The vast expanses of North America between Canada and the Rio Grande were under the nominal ownership of one person for every three square miles of territory in 1860; too much space to protect and hold. Enabled by the Rush-Bagot Treaty with Great Britain and by politico-economic chaos in Mexico, both the northern and southern borders of the United States were demilitarized. Defense did not eat up every 19th Century

12. R.W. Daly, *How the Merrimac Won: The Strategic Story of the CSS Virginia* (New York: Thomas Y. Cromwell, 1957).

American budget as it might have without the dirt-cheap militiamen with their muskets over the mantle.

Since the Pequot War (1634-38), organized and unorganized militiamen had been facing real and potential menaces including the Apaches, British, Canadians, Cheyennes, Comanches, French, Iroquois, Japanese, Mexicans, Russians, Seminoles, Sioux, Spanish or anyone else that might have had a taste for trouble in North America. The amateur fighting men at King's Mountain in the Revolution, New Orleans at the end of the War of 1812, and the Alamo in the Texas War for Independence were a part of a long militia tradition, fighting for as long as they could hold a weapon, until the Regulars could come up.

In America's five foreign wars before 1860 (the Revolution, the Quasi-War with France (1799-1800), the Barbary Wars (1803-07), the War of 1812 (1812-1815) and the Mexican War (1846-48)), the militias had been called up three times by the President. The mechanics were simple: the states, towns, cities and territories chose from among themselves those they felt best suited to lead, and commissioned them to fulfill their duty. These officers gathered their friends, retainers and trusted neighbors about them, and raised enough money and supplies to get themselves and their people to where the army gathered. Early in the Civil War the units were somewhat self-organizing; they were often composed of men from the same locale, professions, church or social group. Officers, replacements and ammunition were the responsibility of the states, not the Regular Army.[13]

Socially, this was quite unlike any army anywhere else in makeup and in attitudes. A Private had been a neighbor to the Captain; another had once sold a crop to the Colonel; they all felt fully entitled to share their thoughts and a chaw of tobacco with the General, who once served them in Congress. It was completely within the 19th Century American soldiers' mindset to loudly protest martinets who tried to bark orders and to thrash blockheads who they believed needed it. Soldiers know a lot more about how their army works than officers like to admit, and it's not easy to put anything over on an American soldier

13. Nofi, op. cit., 9.

for very long. Since Baron de Steuben first drilled the Model Company at Valley Forge, American soldiers have had to have a good reason for what they are told to do and for what happens to them or they simply don't perform.

To these militiamen, when in quiet repose in their parlors and taverns, the thought of running away was repulsive, of shirking any duty dishonorable. This is not to say that they would not run off if they thought it necessary--when they got too tired or too few to keep fighting or they didn't have anything left to fight with. When these men "broke and ran" in any battle, at core they performed a time-honored militia maneuver that in modern military terms might be called a tactical withdrawal. When fighting Indian raids these militias often withdrew to a fortified house or a stockaded magazine: in stand-up battle against soldiers or other militiamen, doing this looked a great deal like simply bugging out.

Both the Union and the Confederacy built their forces based on the same tactical building block: the regiment. Regimental cohesion relied on both command effectiveness and something else. The men could have unswerving loyalty to their regiments and their commanders--for a time. When the horrific realities of battle, isolation, privation, bone-bending toil, short rations and disease beat on them without letup, the cause for which they served had to be convincing enough to keep the nuclei of these units--the persuasive at any level in any social group--to hold the despondent in camp for just a little while longer. Often the steadying voices around the mess fire were sergeants, but not always. The steadying voices that survived long enough nearly always ended the war with at least three stripes, and sometimes with commissions.

Regimental colonels were prominent citizens who sometimes helped pay the myriad expenses required to build the regiments, and sometimes for arming them. The men frequently voted on their own company officers (lieutenants and captains), and selected their NCOs (sergeants and corporals) by diverse means, from votes of hands to games of chance to fistfights. When an officer was imposed on a regiment from the outside, the men had to find his command style acceptable or they simply would not perform, and in the extreme would not muster in enough men to be sworn to service, or would simply desert the regiment to nothingness. These leaders with chevrons, shoulder straps and collar patches were neither fathers, brothers, pals nor tyrants, but a bit of all of these. The worst officers tried either to be buddies or slave drivers, and the men responded in kind. The best officers knew that their people were neither slaves nor buddies nor cannon fodder, and worked diligently to provide what they needed, punished men only where necessary, and tried to be as good an overlord as they could within American traditions. They also knew that soldiers are like musket cartridges: expendable but impossible to reuse once fired, deadly in the right hands, useless in the wrong ones, hard to find when they run short, and tedious to remake once damaged.

Any losses were made worse by the fact that there was no regimental replacement system for any but one state (Wisconsin), so once a regiment was sworn in its head count was only going to get lower until it went back home to recruit or managed to snag men along the way. Civil War armies were generally rebuilt by adding new regiments created by the states with new men and commanded by new appointees. The thinner the regiments became the more effective they became, man-for-man, because the weak, sick and otherwise unsuitable were winnowed out early. Since the same attrition affected both sides in the same way, the regiments were thinning at about the same rate. The differences were that the North had more resources to start with and could build more, and the South suffered more desertion; it was a great deal easier for the Southerners to just walk away since most of the war took place in the Southern states.

There was a long-standing divide in the American military policy debate between the professionalist philosophy and the volunteerist. The professionalists, in the minority, held that “real” soldiers required years of steady drill to be able to accomplish anything at all without catastrophic losses. They favored a large standing army constantly exercising, growing and evolving with those of the Great Powers in Europe, who were the likeliest “real” opponents in future conflicts. But their small, professional, antebellum army operated mostly as companies of less than a hundred men, and primarily against the Indians, who usually fought in small and disorganized bands. Some professionals regarded fighting Indians as being something other than "real" war since they didn't form up and die in quite the same way as "real" armies did.[14]

The volunteerists, whose natural habitat was the militia drill field and the occasional foray against marauding Indians, were enamored of the romantic model of the yeoman farmer, forsaking his fields to take up the musket to thrash the enemy in *ad hoc* units and militias, and then returning to his more pacific and humbly constitutional occasions. They felt that an army could be built to fit each situation as it arose, and that even uniform training of militias was symbolic of impending dictatorship. In this view, extravagances such as the United States Military Academy at West Point were wrong-headed blots on the American landscape. They pointed to European standing armies, their tyrannies and costs, and again pointed wistfully to the Revolution and War of 1812, assured that these examples were proof of the successes of their militia models, and was the only Constitutional, "Jeffersonian" way Americans went to war. They downplayed Washington's disdain for militia he expressed even before the Revolution, and his hard work to develop the Continentals. The volunteerists also overlooked the fact that the United States had survived the Revolution and the War of 1812 on land, not actually won them, and that most militia victories in those conflicts, such as Yorktown and New Orleans, were from behind ramparts and backed by good artillery manned by those for whom big guns were a livelihood. The volunteerists also glossed over the fact that the Mexican War was won by a small body of Regulars with the most

---

14. William T. Sherman, (Peter Cozzens, Ed)., "We Do Our Duty According To Our Means," in *Eyewitnesses to the Indian Wars, 1865–1890* (New York: Stackpole Books, 2005), 2–3; Russell F. Weigley, *History of the United States Army* (New York: Macmillan, 1983), 266–70; Russell F. Weigley, *Towards and American Army: American Military Thought from Washington to Marshall* (New York: Columbia University Press, 1962), 59–60.

effective field artillery park in the hemisphere. The two camps had been arguing since Washington's day.[15]

Both camps had a point, but the professionalists had the ordnance and the training. In all the conflicts between 1783 and 1861 American forces never wanted for arms, powder and shot, but they were often wanting in leaders who understood the field engineering and reconnaissance that the West Point-trained junior and mid-grade officers provided in abundance in Mexico. It was the Mexican War that, for good or ill, probably saved West Point for future generations.[16]

As a result, there was a thoroughly professional but tiny Regular Army spread across the continent led by an aging officer corps. This force was joined by a bizarre array of militia organizations with little uniformity, and mobs of volunteers with no sense of drill or fire discipline, and little practical knowledge of tactics or fieldcraft. Worse, there was no unifying theory for the Regulars, the militias and the new volunteers to operate in concert. On both sides the public and government thundered that the generals should march to the sound of the guns and "win the war," though everyone from president to private was short on exactly how.

National Mobilization and Army Administration in 1861

Lincoln's first military problem after Fort Sumter wasn't just finding a field leader, finding a way to get the South to rejoin the Union, or even how to organize the militias into an army. He first had to figure out how to manage the avalanche of resources that were suddenly at his disposal, with more coming in all the time. The flood of volunteers revealed some real shortages of materiel and organization that the

---

15. Brent Nosworthy, *Bloody Crucible of Courage: Fighting Methods and Combat Experience of the Civil War* (New York: Carroll and Graf Publishers, 2003), 131–2; Weigley, *Towards*, 28, 29.

16. Weigley, *Towards*, 52; Geoffrey Perret, *A Country Made By War: From the Revolution to Vietnam--The Story of America's Rise to Power* (New York: Random House, Inc., 1989), 133.

Army was poorly disposed or organized to handle, and no other branch of government was any better off.

The Civil War took place on the longest hostile frontier in the history of warfare in North America, on a geographic scale greater than Europe's. The distance between the Chicago Loop and the French Quarter of New Orleans (a little over 800 miles) is a fortnight's march farther than that between Napoleon's Paris and the throne of his most persistent continental enemy in Vienna (about 650 miles); a foot march between Berlin and Moscow would have taken any army on Earth a month less than a similar march between Kansas City and Charleston. Both sides were "green together," in Lincoln's words, and were stumbling and fumbling with different technical means.

Early in the war no one was sure what the "elephant" of combat was going to look like. American Civil War mobilization was proportionally faster even than that of WWI or WWII. If more arms and equipment had been available, both sides might have fielded twice the men they did in 1861. But once these huge armies were built, there was no agreed-upon plan to deploy them and no notion of what real "victory" would look like. Bombasts made grand speeches and wrote thundering editorials about vanquishing the enemy for the "restoration of the Union" or "achievement of our independence," but no one knew how.[17]

This lack of strategic direction was rooted in a decades-old question: who held command of the Army in the field; the President, the Secretary of War or the senior Army officer? The Secretary of War was a political appointee whose function was to assist the Commander in Chief (the President) in military affairs--a sort of civilian chief of staff. This casual definition worked well enough when the Secretary and the President were old Revolutionary War buddies Henry Knox and George Washington, but in the real test of the War of 1812 it failed rather miserably. In 1821, after the many command and administrative debacles of the last war against Britain, Congress created the position of Commanding General of the Army. The idea was that the Army's

17. Gudmens, op. cit., 3; Weigley, *Army*, 200–1.

senior officer was to take up the administrative load from the Secretary, but Congress drew no clear line as to where the general's authority began and any other's authority ended. Each Secretary of War or President could do with the Commanding General whatever they wished, and the Commanding Generals could do whatever they could make happen.[18]

At the beginning of the Mexican War (1846-48) "Old Fuss and Feathers" Winfield Scott, self-educated hero of the War of 1812, had been Commanding General for four years. His animosity with James K. Polk's Secretary of War William Marcy had driven him to move his headquarters to New York. Polk had wanted Thomas Hart Benton to lead the army into Mexico, but Scott personally commanded the expedition that landed at Vera Cruz and marched to Mexico City and victory, further alienating his boss. Between 1848 and 1861 Scott stayed as Commanding General, and had grown great (literally) in the job. He held great prestige and weighed in at nearly four hundred pounds by 1861. He could no longer mount a horse and could barely walk because of gout, but he still had the ear of many a Congressman and had a keen mind for cutting through bureaucratic nonsense. As throwbacks to earlier eras went, Scott was something of a treasure.[19]

The Army that Scott was supposed to be in charge of used an administrative system that didn't even answer to him: the Army's bureaus answered directly to the War Department and the Secretary. They were run by senior officers who were in the twilight of long, predominantly bureaucratic careers; six of the 10 bureau chiefs were over 70 years old in 1861. The bureaus and branch chiefs gave the Secretary of War a tremendous base of patronage-like support. Montgomery Miegs, Quartermaster General of the Army who *did* answer to Scott, formed a War Board in 1861 to help with the mobilization, but this made for a great deal of redundancy and little clarity. This antiquated system doomed any thought of creating a general staff in America for generations. The Confederate government,

---

18. Weigley, *Towards*, 164–5; Weigley, *Army*, 117–33.
19. Weigley, *Towards*, 36.

forced to start from scratch, established a parallel structure to the bureaus--many important figures in Confederate bureaus had served in one of the prewar bureaus.[20]

The peacetime bureaus totaled no more than a hundred men altogether, and were not equipped to assess new contracts for goods or evaluate the host of new technological innovations. Gifted and patriotic inventors, notorious swindlers and all shades in between approached anyone in Washington wearing a top hat or a uniform, pleading for a contract. Practically everyone with a useful tool, gimcrack, sound idea or harebrained scheme absolutely had to have Lincoln's or Davis' ear immediately, which for political reasons they often had to give. In the Confederacy, plagued from the beginning with disorganization and resource shortages, the situation was worse. Many well-meaning Southern contractors, especially in the West, made equipment that was never used under contracts that were never honored. The result was not only wasted acquisitions, but false progress towards building an organization capable of achieving national goals. It made for a false sense of military capacity; and the cornucopia of ineffective equipment fueled the assumption that conflict could be resolved quickly.[21]

This lack of logistical coordination combined with a lack of large-unit operational experience made for a deadly combination when they combined at the sufferance of a key element in 19th Century warfare: draft animals. The cavalry, artillery, and infantry all needed huge numbers of the tactical prime movers of the age; without them the supply and ammunition wagons, ambulances, even the general's dining set didn't go anywhere beyond the dock or railroad tracks. Once the armies began to mobilize and move, tens of thousands of horses, mules and oxen had to be acquired, trained, fed, harnessed, cared for,

---

20. The German/Prussian General Staff system was becoming increasingly popular in Europe and was discussed in American military circles, but was not taken seriously in the US until after the Spanish-American War of 1898, and not adopted until after the retirement of the last Civil War-era veteran Commanding General in 1912.

21. Gudmens, op. cit., 1–2.

disposed of and replaced every season, and there was absolutely no system in North America to do any of it in 1861.[22]

The Confederacy inherited this confusion whether they wanted it or not. They would not have a Commanding General or its equivalent in authority until early 1865, but they did have a President who had quarreled with one extensively: Jefferson Davis (United States Military Academy (USMA) class of 1828) had been Secretary of War under both Polk and Buchanan, leaving office in 1857. His loathing of Scott was the stuff of legends; they barely spoke and corresponded only through others. Davis was chiefly responsible for the enlargement and strengthening of the bureau system before the war. As experienced a military administrator as he may have been, as President of the Confederacy Davis lacked the resources and the political support for making the Confederate militia systems work together to even supply themselves, and the Confederate Regular Army never had enough officers to spare to support an effective military administration.[23]

The Confederate Provisional Army was structured on the "assembled militia" model used in the early republic. It was created because the Founding Fathers' grandfathers so abhorred Cromwell's military rule in England--and James II's huge standing army that followed it--that they replaced it with the decentralized mob that Washington had little regard for. Some states even provided strategic direction by forbidding their militiamen from going any further from home than they could walk in a day.

This kind of militia mobilization had been largely abandoned by the US Army in favor of a "build as you go" philosophy, where the Regulars took operational control of units and forged them into a national army. In both models it was the states, not the central government, that put troops in the field, and that were responsible for supplying them with men and ammunition. Further, both sides limited

---

22. Spencer Jones, "The Influence of Horse Supply upon Field Artillery in the American Civil War," *The Journal of Military History* 74, no. 2 (April 2010): 360–1.

23. Weigley, *Towards*, 62, 165; Weigley, *Army*, 193–4, 216–26.

the duration of military service; some units were sworn into service for as little as ten days, very few were enlisted for more than three years.[24]

The sum of this situation was that early Civil War armies were supplied well enough to last no more than a few hours before ammunition became a serious problem, usually fed well enough to avoid mass starvation, equipped well enough to avoid having to live and fight stark naked in winter (though not always in summer), and organized at least well enough to survive the first few volleys of battle. After mustering in, the first months of training, uneven rations, and the first battles took their tolls, unit combat power dropped like a stunned duck, and unit organization inevitably broke down even if the men stuck together. Cohesion without organization, anathema to military professionals because of its tendency to inflame panic, was going to be the best that most Civil War units were going to be able to manage for a while.

In the first year of the war the only issue that had been decided was that the new armies were good for consuming supplies and dying of disease. Malaria, typhoid, yellow fever, chickenpox, measles, pneumonia, mumps, influenza, scrub typhus and any one of a score of diarrheas swept through the camps and persisted with the armies as long as they were together, killing three times as many men as combat did. At any one time at least half of all Civil War armies were sick enough to have been on 21st Century bed rest, yet normally only 10 percent or so usually were. Having lived with such miseries all their lives, most men suffered in silence or simply died in ranks. Many simply didn't bother to go to practitioners who were unable to effectively treat, let alone cure, most diseases. Many treatments available were as bad as or worse than the maladies themselves. Early in the war, the longer the armies stayed in contact with the enemy in battle, the more the men suffered, and the less energy they had.[25]

---

24. Weigley, *Army*, 30.

25. Andrew M. Bell, "'Gallinippers & Glory: The Links between Mosquito-Borne Disease and US Civil War Operations and

Strategic military thought, commonplace in the 20th Century, didn't exist in 19th Century. The Union and the Confederacy were creating some of the largest armed bodies since Napoleon's day. Both sides still hoped for some reconciliation, though neither had any idea how to achieve it without giving in to one side's demand or another, which after Fort Sumter was unlikely. Butting into each other along lines of march that senior commanders took a fancy to would win no objectives other than great casualty lists and the exhaustion of public patience. But, there was no individual or group in either the North or the South that knew how to plan a strategic mission (one intended to result in, say, securing a state or an enemy capitol), or to determine how many men, horses, guns, biscuits and days were needed to do it. In early 19th Century America, tactics was the only subject resembling an organized body of theory, but tactics alone can't show how to exploit a battlefield victory. "Grand tactics" fell in between tactics and strategy, and the meaning and use of the concept in the mid-19th Century is disputed and unclear. Strategic planning, grand or otherwise, was generations away as an organized body of thought anywhere but Prussia.[26]

In 1861, Scott proposed a blockade of the principal Southern ports, to be followed by an offensive down the Mississippi River to isolate Texas, Arkansas, and Missouri from the Confederacy. From there, Scott surmised, the South would slowly starve to death over the course of years. Derided by many as the "Anaconda" plan, it was more strategic concept than a "plan" (in the sense of a "D-Day" scale plan that needed its own staff just to do the filing). While the "slowly starve" part was politically unworkable (Northern voters would not

---

Strategy, 1862," *The Journal of Military History* 74, no. 2 (April 2010): 379–405.

26. Perret, *Country*, 175–77; Jon Tetsuro Sumida, *Inventing Grand Strategy and Teaching Command: The Classic Works of Alfred Thayer Mahan Reconsidered* (Baltimore, MD: The Johns Hopkins University Press, 1997), 2–3, 5–7; Ibid., 154–56, 243; Weigley, *Towards*, 158–9.

wait that long), it was something more than nothing, and was one more overall strategic plan than the Confederacy ever came up with.[27]

The Killing Trade in the Mid-19th Century

The responsibility for having to perform the ill-defined national missions fell to the senior officers. In addition to a shortage of strategic ideas, there was also a shortage of consensus on everything else having to do with the troops, and the quarrel was by no means exclusive to one side. Fundamental to this was the minor question of what training would best turn green troops into soldiers good enough to achieve whatever the generals and politicians finally agreed on.

"Training" meant different things to the different branches of service. To the infantry it meant marching in squads, platoons, companies, and occasionally regiments, then doing it again. To the cavalry it meant a lot of riding, grooming and stable-cleaning, then doing it again. To the artillery it meant the back-breaking work of hauling the guns and equipment around, pointing the pieces in an appropriate direction, firing salutes with bang and smoke while the crew performed its choreographed duty, then doing it again. There was a great deal of repetition and not a lot of realism, tactical training, or thought of combined arms exercises.

The tactics of Napoleonic linear warfare taught in 1861 worked perfectly well with the weapons technology of a generation before, but were obsolete by Bull Run. At the height of the smoothbore musket's dominance in 1815, infantry battles had become somewhat formulaic in Europe, but those tactics were unknown *in that form* in the Americas. In European-style warfare, the infantry would exchange volley fire while the flank companies, skirmishers and riflemen picked off the officers and NCOs, and the cavalry dashed about making sure the intended targets were bunched up. The artillery and musket barrages would then slay the leaderless foot soldiers in large clumps, and the bayonet would turn them into running rabble. The picture was

---

27. Nofi, op. cit., 6, 9; Geoffrey Perret, "ANACONDA: The Plan That Never Was," *North and South* Vol. 6 # 4 (May 2003): 36–42.

changing, but this is what many theorists before 1861 knew of land battle.

The US Army adopted a rifled musket in 1855, which greatly increased the infantry's range and accuracy. In a generation half the artillery was out-ranged by at least half of the infantry battle line who had some training or skill. More, the infantry's fussy flints had been replaced by far more reliable percussion caps at around the same time. The differences between percussion cap muskets of Bull Run and the flintlocks carried by most troops in Mexico were like the differences between a horse and an ox: they could do each other's job, but not under the same conditions and not as well. Percussion cap weapons increased the casualty count regardless of rifling by raising the number of balls by a factor of ten--accurate or not--sent downrange, which meant even nervous and unaimed fire often hit *something*. The conical bullet amplified the reliability, increasing infantry range and accuracy enough to put the artillery at greater risk, and kept the cavalry far out of charging range. American troops took the tactical offensive in most Mexican War battles with great success, and suffered fairly light losses. Mexico did a lot to empower American leadership and artillery, but infantry lessons were muted by the ineffectiveness of their Mexican counterparts. By the beginning of the Civil war, large numbers of units on both sides had good-quality rifle muskets except in the West, where old militia arms and hunting weapons had to do for at least a third of the Federals and more than half the Confederates for much of the first year of war.

American tactical doctrine didn't recognize the potential of the new musket. Before 1855 the most influential tactical guide was Scott's three-volume *Infantry Tactics* of 1835, based on tactical models of Napoleon's time. William J. Hardee published a two-volume tactical manual, *Rifle and Light Infantry Tactics* to coincide with the introduction of new rifled musket, but it failed to recognize the tactical battlefield balance shift in favor of the defense.

If Scott's and Hardee's works were behind technological innovations, at least the infantry had two slightly more realistic manuals to start with than the other two main branches did. Cavalry and artillery fell even farther behind in recognizing the shift in favor the infantry. The cavalry's "latest" manual, published in 1841, was based on French sources that focused on close-order offensive tactics, favoring cavalry attacks in two ranks of horsemen armed with sabers or lances that looked like the Charge of the Light Brigade. It took no notice of the rifled musket's potential and gave scant attention to dismounted operations. Similarly, the artillery had a basic guide describing crew drills, but it had no tactical manual. Like those for the cavalry, artillery theorists showed no concern for the tactical changes the rifle required. Both North and South went to war with tactical manuals for two of their principal arms that were more useful to throw at the enemy than they were as guides for training.[28]

Most Civil War units were infantry: inexpensive, easily organized, foot-tired and mud-spattered line soldiers, the lowest common denominators of land warfare. Militia infantry drilled to suit their families, friends and neighbors out for sociable afternoons with gaudy parades. The professionals derided their fancy uniforms, old weapons and comical and tactically useless maneuvers. There wasn't a great deal of uniformity in militia drills; infantry companies infrequently got together until after they had been fairly thoroughly drilled by squad and platoon. Sometimes, when a regiment finally drilled as a unit, companies would "evolve" (transition from one formation to another, such as from a marching column to a firing line) differently, sometimes at odds with their neighbors. This occasionally resulted in messy debacles and the odd fistfight. Many West Point-trained officers were promoted above regimental command fairly early, so that most of the elected and appointed officers watching these spectacles had no idea what it should have looked like. But the men knew the basics of drill, and that counted for a lot. Once the rudiments of the marching maneuvers were learned, they were adaptable to any other infantry outfit from squad on up. Men from broken infantry regiments could be cobbled together to form a respectable battle line by nearly any officer

---

28. Gudmens, op. cit., 19–20.

with a commanding enough presence to get the men to obey orders and NCOs to make sure they paid attention.[29]

For the infantry, not much visually changed between the battles of Breitenfeld in 1631 and Bull Run in 1861. Both battlefields consisted of blocks and lines of infantry studded with artillery, occasionally seeing an odd horseman or two between the shoals of noxious smoke through which the shadowy figures on the other side noisily launched buzzing metal that delivered sudden death and dismemberment. This marching and standing in battle has been derided as silly and dangerous, bordering on suicidal. It may have been for any *but* the rifled musket-armed nominal civilians fresh from the shops, farms and factories of the mid-19th Century. Without any means of tactical signaling, keeping the men moving and fighting together through constant drill offered them their best chances of success and survival.

There wasn't a great deal of shooting practice for most infantry units: dumb show was the norm in most places. Target practice was thought to be wasteful. To be effective, infantry gun power had to be tightly controlled using a technique known as "locking" that came from the British. When the line was ready and the muskets were at the "present" position, an NCO shouted "lock," and a group of 16 to 24 men stood as close to each other as they could, aimed at a point at their most effective range (two to five hundred yards), and fired as one. The Americans didn't lock in quite this way, but they knew to create a sudden blast of lead and smoke on a small area that, repeated every twenty paces or so three times a minute down a hundred-pace line, was often enough to break the line of those they were shooting at. Most important, it gave the infantry cohesion to receive (or execute) a bayonet charge.[30]

---

29. Francis Alfred Lord, *They Fought for the Union* (Harrisburg, Pa.: Stackpole Co., 1960), 20, 23–6.

30. Brent Nosworthy, *Battle Tactics of Napoleon and His Enemies* (London: Constable and Company, Ltd., 1995), 86–90; Perret, *Country*, 11–17.

The bayonet charge had been called an anachronism by the Civil War. It is said that, since there were so few casualties caused by bayonets, they were rarely used in combat. While they may not have drawn much blood, that's not the point: bayonet charges were regarded as at partially failed if they did result in the kind of musket-swinging brawl that moviemakers love to stage since it was too hard to get the men back in control afterwards. Civil War-era tacticians knew that "resorting to cold steel" worked best when attacking already shaky opponents. A phalanx of steel spears borne by men whose faces have been blackened by powder and smoke invokes an immediate threat of pain and death, much more real than the bullets and shells they could rarely see. Giving people time to think about what will happen to them is the best way to amplify fear, not unlike what serial killers are said to relish when torturing their victims. In this way the bayonet acted like the flamethrower of the 20th Century, causing more casualties by fear than by contact. In some circumstances, however, there was nothing left for the infantrymen to fight with but their bayonets, their muscles and their nerves. The bayonet was still an important weapon by 1861, a generation or more from being discarded, even if it was more frequently used as a candleholder or a roasting spit.[31]

Infantry unit structure was generally the same for Union and Confederate units, reflecting the common roots for both armies. Each of the ten prewar US Army infantry regiments consisted of ten 87-man companies, with a maximum authorized strength of from 866 to 1,046, depending on locale. The Confederate Congress fixed its 10-company infantry regiment at 1,045 men. Both sides used variants of these organizations for their volunteer regiments. Rarely were more than a half these numbers seen in the regiments in the field.[32]

Artillery had evolved differently than infantry. 19th Century field and horse artillery pieces were not simply scaled-down versions of the

---

31. Paddy Griffith, *Battle Tactics of the Civil War* (Mansfield, England: Fieldbooks, 1986), 40–1; Nosworthy, *Napoleon*, 230–1; Nosworthy, *Crucible*, 599–601.

32. Gudmens, op. cit., 4.

equipment used to defend seacoasts; they were completely separate developments. It had always been an American desire to win with a minimum of American bloodshed, and making their artillery the best on the continent was one way of ensuring that. Artillery backed by musket-toting infantry was the dominant means of American land warfare. American artillery had reinvented itself twice in two generations before 1846. Before Mexico, they had standardized the wheels, carriages, equipment and calibers for the Regular Army's artillery. Rifled guns had begun to make an appearance in the 1840s, and were rapidly being added to the Regular Army's artillery regiments. As the Regulars discarded their old guns, the militias were more than happy to snap them up. Further, since there was nothing stopping any iron founder from casting cannons, local entrepreneurs sold entire batteries to wealthy patrons who fancied militia commissions and patriotic organizations that wanted to "do their bit." By the beginning of the Civil War there was a dizzying array of artillery calibers in the militia units. More than half the guns in most Confederate batteries in 1861 were 6-pounder smoothbores, and less than 20% were rifled guns; there were field guns of up to 24-pounder size in the Union Army, about a third of their batteries were rifled, and more than half were 10-pounders or larger.[33]

The artillerists' crew drill had to start from someone with real training if no one was to get hurt. Unlike the infantry, artillery crew drill wasn't just dumb show and parades around larger cities and towns. They fired salutes with blank cartridges on holidays, where every member of the crew had his precise place to be and a satisfying BOOM followed. Safety precautions also had to be taken for the very same reasons that they were in battle: doing it wrong meant preignition, where a confined black powder blast will rip an arm or a head off as well as a cannonball would. Any militia-trained gunner was a drilling equal to his Regular counterparts. One trained gunner could teach an

---

33. Philip Katcher, *American Civil War Artillery 1861–65* (Oxford, UK: Osprey Publishing, 2001), 8–9.

entire battery of recruits enough of the basics to keep from hurting themselves. Aiming these guns took practice, but few had a great deal of that. Adequately trained and supplied, a hundred men in a battery of six 12-pounder howitzers could deliver a man-killing metal storm in an area about a hundred yards wide and two hundred deep, and could effectively disable a thousand men and animals a minute.

Militia artillerymen also learned that there was great danger in firing all their guns at once. They tried to space each shot 10 to 30 seconds apart by counting repetitions of the phrase "if I wasn't a gunner I wouldn't be here" and many variations. Artillery silence--when the guns were being reloaded all at once--was the undesirable alternative, which was the infantry's opportunity to rush the guns. The more pieces in a position the closer together the guns could fire. Massing artillery fires from more than one battery was difficult because infantry commanders often controlled their own artillery or left it up to inexperienced battery officers who were as tactically clueless as anyone else.[34]

The artillery could do as much damage with a near miss as the infantry could with a direct hit. The psychological effects of seeing a human being torn apart by an exploding shell or blast of canister balls are incalculable. The effects of high intensity noise on the central nervous system--acoustic pressure--that doesn't cause hearing loss may have an unmeasurable effect. Having one's own breath pulled out by a close-passing round ball or a nearby shell explosion--negative air pressure--is just as exhausting as running up a hill in full combat gear.

---

34. O. Edward Cunningham, (Gary D. Joiner and Timothy B. Smith, Eds.), *Shiloh and the Western Campaign of 1862* (New York: Savas Beatie, 2008), 168–9; Griffith, op. cit., 26–7; Philip Katcher, *The Confederate Artilleryman* (Chicago: Raintree/Reed Elsevier, 2003), 10–15; Wiley Sword, *Shiloh: Bloody April* (New York: Morrow, 1974), 174; Harold L. Peterson, *Notes on Ordnance of the American Civil War: 1861–1865* (Washington, D. C.: American Ordnance Association, 1959), 10.

Cannon balls and rifled artillery bolts (solid rifle rounds) not only have longer effective range than musket balls, they create larger pressure waves as they pass a soft target, like a person. Pressure waves of any kind on the human body, especially on the soft tissue like brains, lungs and eyes, will eventually cause sufferers to want to either run away or do nothing at all until the waves stop or the sufferer expires. Modern battlefields are much more subject to these unseen forces, but the 19th Century soldier had to have suffered from these of casualty creating effects--pressure and noise--just as modern soldiers do, if on a smaller scale. Early in the war, when nearly half of the Confederate artillery pieces were 6-pounders and 2/3rds of the Union's guns had a throw weight of more than ten pounds, the Confederates got a worse beating by noise and pressure than the Unionists did.[35]

The artillery didn't form field regiments like the infantry or cavalry, but made up batteries of as many as seven guns, and occasionally battalions of several batteries. A Federal battery usually consisted of six guns of one caliber, and had an authorized strength of 80 to 156 men. A battery of six 12-pounders could need 130 horses and more. If organized as horse or "flying" artillery, the gunners were provided with their own mounts. Confederate batteries, plagued by draft animal shortages and available manpower, often had to be content with four-gun batteries; more frequently their batteries were of mixed weapon types and calibers. Confederate batteries seldom reached their authorized strength of 80 men. The limiting factor for battery size was the availability of horses, not of ordnance. Six-pounder guns needed four horses for each limber and caisson; 12-pounders needed six; larger pieces needed eight or ten, and more for the forge wagons, ammunition wagons, baggage and food: each horse needed a minimum of twenty to thirty pounds of fresh grain and hay forage every day; each man needed at least three pounds of food. Because no one had any organized means

35. David G. Martin, *The Shiloh Campaign: March - April 1862*, Great Campaigns (Pennsylvania: Combined Books, 1996), 50–4.

of providing horses or food for them (or even curry combs), the artillery suffered tremendously.[36]

The most romantic units were those that were the most desirable for Southerners to join but that the North couldn't get enough of: the cavalry. By the middle of the 19th Century the simple glories and unbounded successes of mounted charges were at an end, for the rifled musket and longer-ranging artillery made Balaclava-like charges too risky. Despite the dash and *élan,* there wasn't a lot of room for cavalry in 19th Century American military theory. Cavalry was expensive, and considered by many Americans to be a symbol of oppression ("dragoon" was an insult at the same level as "Hessian" in Revolutionary War-era America). Washington didn't understand cavalry, never worked with it in his militia career, and could barely afford to feed his men and draft animals for most of the Revolution, let alone cavalry mounts. As a result there was very little interest in cavalry in Revolutionary armies except irregular raiders and a handful trained late in the war. Even so, there weren't a lot of saber-armed and trained cavalrymen opposing American horse soldiers before 1861, so gradually they became mounted infantry. The militias used horses for mobility and little else. Though the Regulars knew European-style cavalry theory and had small mounted units that drilled in traditional roles and combat, there just wasn't a lot of use for heavy cavalrymen in antebellum North America.

The cavalry looked for the enemy; raided enemy territory occasionally, protected friendly troops from other cavalry, and herded stragglers on the march. They fought each other more than they did the infantry, but mounted combat with slashing sabers was physically exhausting, and nearly impossible without trained mounts. Fighting side-by-side in ear-splitting noise amid the stench of blood and smoke while carrying two hundred pounds and more of deadweight is an unnatural act for a horse, and early in the war there just wasn't time for training war horses. Mounts for the cavalry were lower on the demand scale than for swift, surefooted mounts for the officers and couriers,

---

36. Gudmens, op. cit., 4; Spencer Jones, op. cit.

and for the draft animals needed for the artillery and supply wagons. Each horse needed the same grain and forage every day as their artillery stablemates did, a demand that could only be met close to the supplies. Winter campaigns restricted cavalry operations simply because long forage was generally unavailable in the field.

The leading American theoreticians of the day emphasized infantry shock and artillery bombardment, not cavalry charges. Geographic locations were the objects of war, not armies. Doctrine expected pursuit only when an enemy is clearly fleeing, and that wasn't very often caused by firepower alone. American doctrine thus did not expect anything like a Napoleonic pursuit from its horse soldiers.[37]

Cavalry units were generally smaller than their similarly named infantry brothers. Ten cavalry companies of about 80 troopers comprised a Union cavalry regiment early in the war; Confederate cavalry units authorized ten 76-man companies per regiment. Although the term "troop" was used, most cavalrymen kept the more familiar term "company" to describe their units throughout the war. Some volunteers on both sides formed small cavalry battalions and independent companies. The Federals sometimes grouped two companies or troops into informal and impermanent squadrons. Like the artillery, the cavalry suffered from horse problems throughout the conflict.[38]

Strategic Unit Organization and Staffs

The brigade was the smallest strategic unit used in the Civil War, and its composition was extremely flexible from a few loose battalions to a score of depleted regiments. The brigades, divisions and corps were made by local commanders to simplify their jobs in reducing the number of orders needed to get the regiments into position. They also provided a headquarters to which a commander could attach supporting units like cavalry and artillery. But the regiments--living, marching and

---

37. James R. Arnold, *The Armies of U.S. Grant* (New York: Arms and Armor Press, 1995), 58.

38. Gudmens, op. cit., 4–5.

training together for months--often knew very little about any higher organizations. Early in the war, if a soldier's brigade had a number he often didn't know it, even if he knew who the commander was. If his brigade was a part of a division, this fact was often transparent to him. He frequently knew whose corps he was in if he was in one, but not always the formal designation; he might know the army commander's name but not always what the army was officially called, if it was officially called anything.

Then there was the "other army" that followed the one with the weapons. Prewar regulations allowed one laundress, cook or seamstress to draw rations from the Army for every seventeen privates—about three to a company. They were the responsibility of the regiments, and were often wives of men in the ranks. But there was a host of other women (and men, and children) who were not supported by the regiments but who were informally attached to the army. Sutlers, the earliest form of Post Exchange, were contracted by the regiments, but there were also blacksmiths, card sharps, carpenters, embalmers, horse dealers, loan sharks, reporters and wheelwrights, as well as the unofficial laundresses, cooks and seamstresses, a few ladies of negotiable virtue and their business managers, and a host of others. Many camp followers had breadwinners in the ranks but couldn't get on the mess rolls for whatever reason; these may have included a colonel's wife, a sergeant's children, a corporal's parents, or a private's siblings. All of these had to be corralled and controlled, like the others, by the overworked staff officers.[39]

Commanders personally handled some modern staff functions like intelligence analysis and operations planning, but there was just too much for one man to do, so they had staff officers. Officers came in two flavors during the Civil War: officers "of the Line" were the combat leaders; officers "of the Staff" included engineers, doctors, supplymen, and the few signalmen there were at the time. Staff officers

---

39. Linda Grant De Pauw, *Battle Cries and Lullabies: Women in War from Prehistory to the Present* (Norman, OK.: University of Oklahoma Press, 2000), 160–5; Lord, op. cit., 110–35, 244.

had to help with the paperwork, conduct reconnaissance, run messages as needed, and direct the various departments to find whatever the army needed, from sewing equipment and river transportation, hay and opium to new staff officers, new recruits and common laborers. They also had to ensure justice in courts martial, fair dealing in sutlers, moderation in chaplains, cleanliness in prostitutes, and honesty in the rest of the contractors. Sometimes they were also expected to tell the commander how to win the war.

The staff at army level consisted of about a score or so officers of field grade (majors and colonels) and lower, and volunteers like Isham Harris, the Confederate Governor of Tennessee who was on the staff at Shiloh. There was no formal training for staff work in the United States. West Point did teach administration, but the USMA had no notion of the sheer scale of wartime demand. Without specialized training for staff officers, especially in supply, the line officers who had to step in to do the various jobs that further depleted their energy and time; Ulysses Grant had worked in supply for much of his Army career. The chief of staff and most other positions were used as the commander saw fit, making staff responsibilities different under each general. The chief of staff was not used in any uniform way by either side, and seldom did the man in this role have any central coordinating authority. Staff officers sometimes had their own commands (Braxton Bragg, the Confederate army's Chief of Staff at Shiloh, commanded a corps, but his Union counterpart, William Webster, did not).

The staff officer's most visible function in 19th Century battle was the heart and soul of command control--liaison between commanders. Staffs were sent off to find whoever was in charge of a unit the commander wanted to control and told them to perform a required action. These staff runners had to know their intended audiences by sight, and had to be able to find them before the orders became obsolete. None of the division commanders at Shiloh had more than a dozen such officers at their disposal at once, and brigade commanders often worked with less than half that. Liaison procedures were ill-defined, with the various staff officers or soldiers performing this function with little formal guidance, if any at all. Inconsistency was among the most important shortcomings of staff work. In two forces thrown together as quickly as they had been in 1862, this created great potential for catastrophe.[40]

Rank and Leadership

In 1861, Lincoln appointed 126 general officers, of whom 82 were or had been military professionals. Davis appointed 89, of whom 44 had received professional training. The remaining officers were political appointees, but 16 Union and seven Confederate generals had no military experience at all. The rank and seniority situation was exacerbated in the North by a Union Congressional resolution that stated that the President could appoint a field commander regardless of his seniority. This offended officers who had worked hard for their positions and thought their replacements were unqualified interlopers. Although the Confederacy managed to avoid the kind of a mess the Union suffered, Davis had favorites that he kept in important posts far beyond their demonstrated usefulness.[41]

Few generals anywhere had commanded troops armed with rifled muskets in combat. The French Wars (1792-1815) and the Mexican War were fought primarily with smoothbore flintlocks. The Crimean (1854-56) and Piedmont Wars (1859) used the new technologies, but gave mixed signals as to their effectiveness compared to bayonets and artillery. Much of the military lesson of the latter two conflicts seemed to concentrate on lengthy marksmanship training and steely nerve to work under fire, both of which required a great deal more time and resources to drill into the troops than the generals thought they had. Public opinion in neither the North nor the South would wait the years needed to build European-grade forces.

As a result, much of the senior leadership in 1861 was unsure of the capabilities of their forces; uncertain of what was to be done with them other than to defeat other armies, had no clear impression of the

---

40. Gudmens, op. cit., 7–8; David W. Reed, *The Battle of Shiloh and the Organizations Engaged* (Knoxville, TN: University of Tennessee Press, 2008), 37–44.

41. Eicher, op. cit., 19; Gudmens, op. cit., 6.

lethality of their equipment and training, or how to use them in combination with the needs of the linear combat formations required for command control and optimum firepower. Few officers had seen major actions like Bull Run, especially on the Confederate side, and those who had didn't have time to drive home any lessons to the men in the West.[42]

In the period between the end of the Thirty Year's War in 1648 and the defeat of Napoleon in 1815, national armies became so large, expensive and spread out that no gentry in any country or empire was large enough to provide sufficient "gentlemen" to lead or administer--let alone pay for--the huge armies that industrialized warfare made. It came to be expected that "commoners" were to somehow be ennobled by great deeds on the battlefield, learning leadership and command as they went along. By the mid-19th Century, those who had made their fortunes and had exalted themselves in government or civic life were expected to be able to perform heroic and brilliant deeds in uniform. History's record of this great untrained group is spotty.

Commanding an army has never been and will never be easy, but the challenge of senior command in the mid-19th Century was becoming especially daunting. An observer from the 21st Century might conclude that people of the 19th expected military leaders to just shrug off a business suit and put on a uniform. Some cases have been made for the idea that most liberal educations imparted some military knowledge to all young men who finished university, but the evidence for this is reed thin. The Prussian military educational system, which began in 1810, had begun to institutionalize staff procedures, but only the rudiments of this method had reached America by 1860, and no Americans attended a staff school anywhere until after the war.[43]

---

42. Nosworthy, *Crucible*, 40–60, 77–95.

43. Robert M. Citino, *The German Way of War: From the Thirty Year's War to the Third Reich* (Lawrence, KS: University of Kansas Press, 2005), 115; Russell F. Weigley, "American Strategy from Its Beginnings Through the First World War," in *Makers of Modern*

The Union's Volunteers (United States Volunteers or USV) were a patch between the traditional militias and the Regular Army. The USV was, legally, another army under the control of the Regular Army that was only intended to exist for the duration of the emergency. The Confederacy made a similar distinction between their Provisional Army of the Confederate States (PACS) and the Army of the Confederate States of America (ACSA).[44]

Though the volunteer/provisional organizations and their professional counterparts worked seamlessly in concert and under fire, deciding who was in charge was more complicated. For example, by August 1861 Ulysses S. Grant wore a Brigadier General's star in the Volunteers, but his rank was backdated to before he was a Colonel, to take effect from May 1861. When he was promoted to Major General in March 1862, it was in the Volunteers and backdated to February. But John A. McClernand and William H.L. Wallace were also Major Generals of Volunteers, and both had their commissions in their hands (though unconfirmed by Congress) before Grant had his, but with dates of rank *after* Grant's, which made them subordinate to Grant.

This situation was further complicated by the "brevet" affliction, or honorary rank. Brevets were awarded for a number of reasons, with the best known for valor or distinguished service; there were no active medals in the U. S. military before 1862. The second kind of brevet was *sometimes* awarded for ten years of service, a way for officers with influence to get around the glacial promotion system (known in the Navy as "waiting to fill dead men's shoes"). The last use of the brevet was to give new officers rank when there were no vacancies in the regiments, such as in the case of the entire West Point graduating class of 1861. Article 61 of the Articles of War, the regulation controlling brevet rank that dated from 1806, was vague beyond comprehension and subject to bizarre interpretations. Simply put, a brevet promotion gave an officer the authority (technically) without the pay of the higher

---

Strategy, Peter Paret (Princeton, New Jersey: Princeton University Press, 1986), 413, 417.

44. Eicher, op. cit., 17, 23.

grade. In practice, Regular Army officers who were promoted by brevet were of higher rank than others, and the higher the Regular grade the more seniority an officer had. William Sherman outranked Grant when they were both brigadiers because Sherman's captain's commission predated Grant's. It got a great deal more complicated in the volunteers. One argument over brevet seniority was informally decided because the winning officer was from Vermont, which had been a state before Ohio was, the losing officer's home. No wonder Civil War generals in their portraits often look grumpy.[45]

Both sides suffered from the same lack of realistic officer training. West Point produced some splendid platoon-leading civil engineers, but wasn't set up to do much more. If the twentysomething graduates stayed with the Army, they were fortunate to see any promotions at all before they were thirtysomething. Any further training had to come in the furnace of battle or the tedium of routine. No one anywhere was training generals to lead armies, and no one in America was training staff officers to organize and run them. Without administrators and commanders who appreciated the needs of national-scale warfare there would be no consistent strategic direction, just a collection of men with no greater purpose than to survive a battle fought because someone thought it was a good idea at the time.[46]

But the leaders were merely creatures of their time who were asked to perform a job under conditions no one had ever seen, on a scale unknown since the Khans ranged the steppes of central Asia.

---

45. Ibid., 16, 18; Dale E. Floyd, "Brevet Rank," in *Historical Times Illustrated Encyclopedia of the Civil War* (New York: Harper & Row, 1986), 79; Mark M. Boatner, "Brevet Rank," in *The Civil War Dictionary* (New York: David McKay & Company, 1988), 84.

46. Weigley, *Army*, 229–30.

CHAPTER 2
LEADING THE CHARGE: SENIOR LEADERSHIP AT SHILOH

The senior officers described here--the senior Army and Navy officers involved with Shiloh--fall into four broad groups: Professionals, Former Professionals, Militiamen and Amateurs. Their abilities were just as mixed and though earnest and well-meaning they were all inexperienced at higher command. The Professionals were those who were in the US Army or Navy in 1860. The Former Professionals had been trained in the Army and some had some experience at soldiering, primarily in the Mexican War, but who had left the Army before 1860. The Militiamen were those who were serving militia units when the call-ups came; while some had formal military training or experience, most did not, but they did have the respect of their communities. The Amateurs had little or no prewar military training or experience.

Most of the leaders knew somebody with power and influence, who knew someone who knew someone in state or national government who could arrange for a commission, either as a political favor or in an effort to win support of a voter bloc. The mix was typical of the Western theater in the spring of 1862, but there were far fewer political appointees among them and far more experienced Regulars, former Regulars and militia leaders than in the Eastern theater. Few were in their positions because of demonstrated merit because the war was too new, and the prewar army was too small to have many real standouts. Only a few had ever seen a battle. None were stupid, but all were fumbling.

Department of the Missouri, United States Army

This command, created on 11 March 1862, encompassed all the Union's armed forces between (roughly) the Appalachians and the Rockies, Canada and the Louisiana/Texas border. It was commanded by Former Professional Henry W. Halleck of New York (USMA 1839), a brilliant if dour military theorist who was first commissioned in the engineers and had won a brevet in Mexico. He had worked on fortifications, taught at West Point, and studied the French military extensively. His writings included *Report on the Means of National Defense*, *Elements of Military Art and Science*, and a translation of Jomini's *Vie Politique et Militaire de Napoleon.* Due to his high sloping forehead the men knew him as "Old Brains." His antebellum scholarly pursuits make some researchers think his nickname was given before the war, but this is unclear.

Halleck left the Army in 1854 to practice law in San Francisco, and became one of the wealthiest men in California, a leader in the California militia, and one of the most respected legal minds in the world. Winfield Scott recommended him for the District of Missouri at the outset of the war, which he accepted. Soon after reaching his headquarters in St. Louis in June 1861, he straightened out the mess that had been left behind by John C. Fremont, and was rewarded with command of the Department of the Missouri when it was created that November. After Fort Donelson fell his department was joined to the Department of the Cumberland to form the Department of the Mississippi. Halleck had three field armies in his vast department: the Army of West Tennessee under Ulysses S. Grant, the Army of the Ohio under Don C. Buell, and the Army of the Mississippi under John Pope. Although he was a tireless and painstaking administrator, Halleck resisted being held responsible for the conduct of his subordinates, and often refused to give direct orders to them.[1]

---

1. Civilwarhome.com, "Halleck, Henry Wager," http://www.civilwarhome.com/ halleckbio.htm (Accessed October 2008); Fredrick H. Dyer, *Dyer's Compendium*, reprint, (Electronic Version 1996 by Guild Press) (Des Moines, IA.: The Dyer Publishing

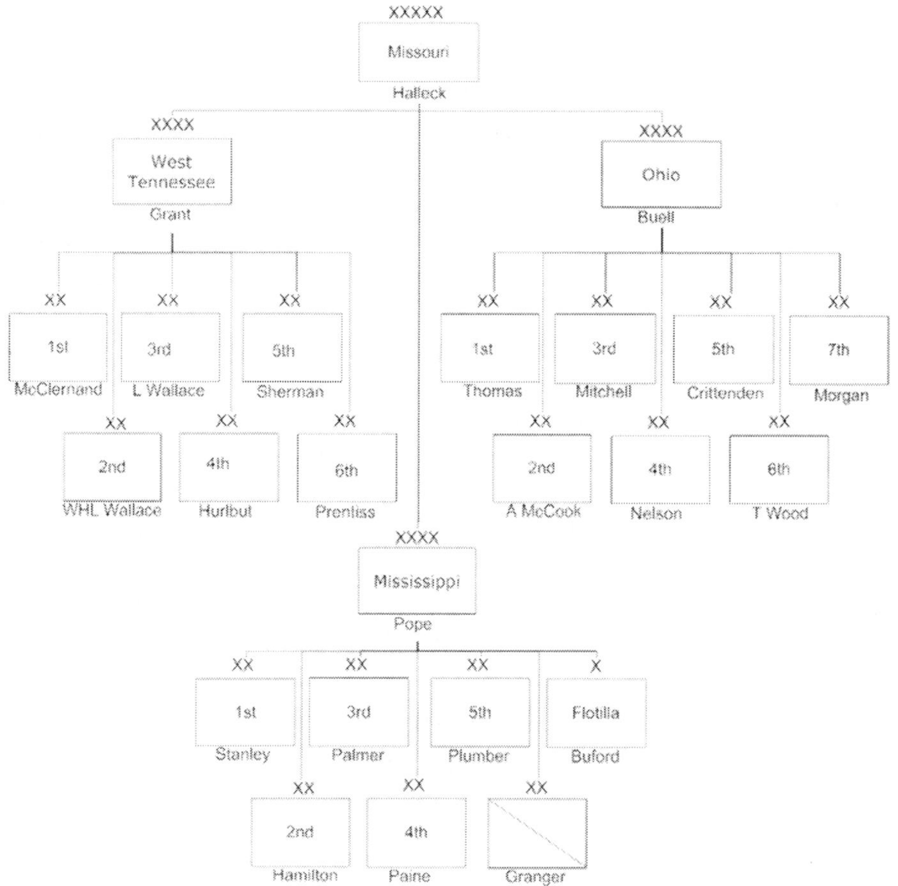

Figure 2-1, Department of the Missouri

Military Department Number Two, Confederate States of America

This area, about half the land area of the Confederacy, was bounded in the east by the Alleghenies, in the west by the White and Black Rivers in eastern Arkansas, and included all of Tennessee, Kentucky,

---

Company, 1908), 256; Jeffry J. Gudmens, *Staff Ride Handbook for the Battle of Shiloh, 6–7 April 1862* (Ft. Leavenworth, KS: Combat Studies Institute Press, n.d. [Electronic version downloaded 2008]), 8.

Missouri, eastern Arkansas, and those parts of Alabama and Mississippi north of the Tennessee River. By the end of 1861 it was commanded by Albert S. Johnston (USMA 1826), a long-serving Professional who had been born in Kentucky and attended Transylvania University (where he met Jefferson Davis), but had spent much of his adult life in Louisiana and Texas. He was first commissioned in the 2nd Infantry, and was chief of staff to Henry Atkinson in the Black Hawk War (1832). He resigned his commission in April 1834 and took up farming in Texas.[2]

Johnston joined the Texas Army during the Texas War for Independence (1835-1836) and acted as aide-de-camp to Sam Houston. By 1837 he was the senior brigadier in the Texas Army. He became Texas' Secretary of War in 1838, and resigned in 1840. He commanded the 1st Texas Rifles in the Mexican War, and in 1849 he was appointed Major/Paymaster in the U. S. Army. In 1855 he was appointed Colonel of the 2nd Cavalry, and two years later was brevetted for service in Utah. He spent 1860 in a post in Kentucky until December 21, when he sailed for California to take command of the Department of the Pacific. Fort Sumter and Texas' secession saw Johnston in San Francisco, where Halleck was living; they likely had met, both being prominent men, but may not have known each other except by reputation. At that time, many in both the North and the South regarded Johnston as the best soldier on the continent.

Johnston resigned as soon as he heard of the secession of Texas in April 1861, but, ever the proper soldier, he stayed in California until June. Before he resigned he was offered the number two spot to Scott, and was also offered a militia command by California, one that was also offered to Halleck: he turned both down. After he was properly relieved and resigned his Army commission (or defected, depending on

---

2. John H. and David E. Eicher, *Civil War High Commands* (Stanford, CA: Stanford University Press, 2001), 884; Patricia L. (Editor) Faust, "Department No. 2, Confederate," in *Historical Times Illustrated Encyclopedia of the Civil War* (New York: Harper and Row, 1986), 216.

point of view), Johnston led a small band of followers on an odyssey to Richmond that was reported in the Southern press like a cross between a horse race and a Homeric quest.

Johnston reached the Confederate capitol in September 1861 and was appointed a full general with a commission backdated to May 1861 (before he resigned), an appointment that was as expected as it was lauded. Because of his rank, he theoretically commanded everything Confederate everywhere. Great things were expected of him, but much of his experience had been administrative; during most of his command time he had been either ill, on detached service or on leave of absence. His chief asset may have been the myths surrounding him.[3]

---

3. Charles P. Roland, "Albert Sidney Johnston," in *The Confederate General*, vol. 3 (Harrisburg, PA: National Historical Society, 1991), 188–9; Civilwarhome.com, "Johnston, Albert Sidney," http://www.civilwarhome.com/asjohnstonbio.htm (Accessed October 2008); Civilwarhome.com, "Johnston, Albert Sidney."

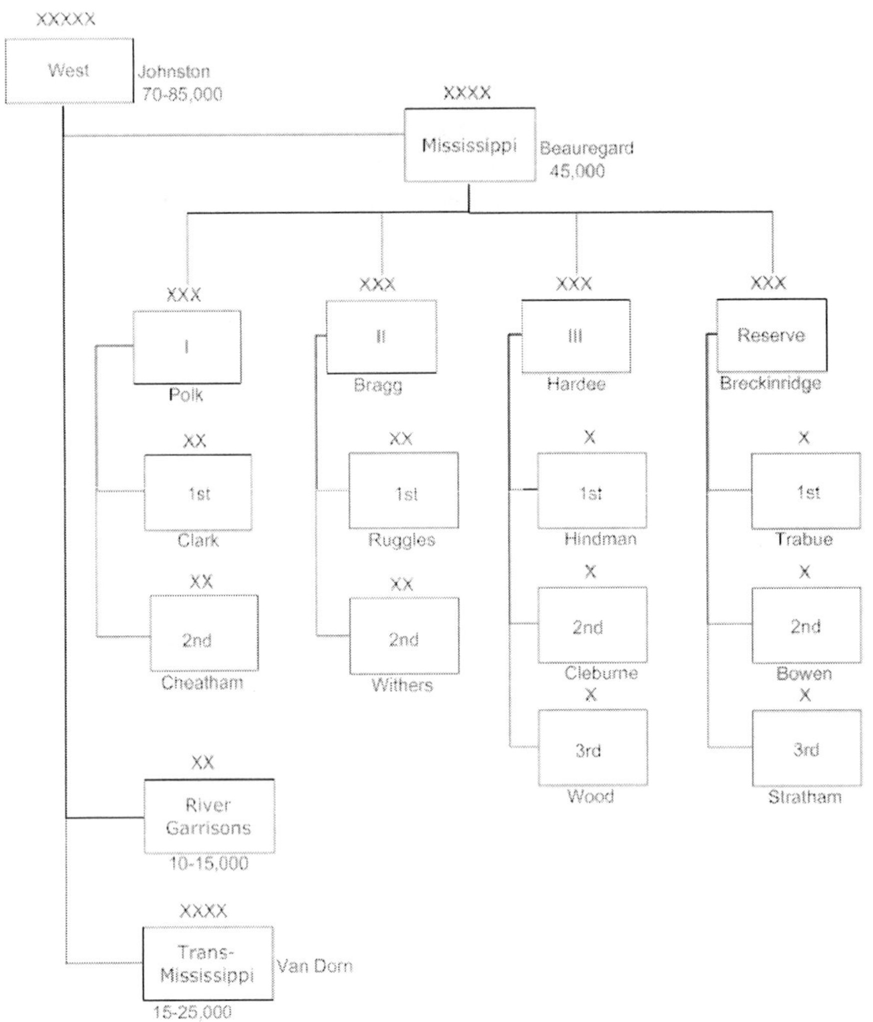

Figure 2-2 Department #2

District and Army of West Tennessee, United States Army

This organization was created in February 1862 with unclear geographic boundaries; the district may never have been officially established. Theoretically the district reported directly to the War

Department, but the troops in it reported to Halleck. Lifelong Professional Charles F. Smith of Pennsylvania (USMA 1825) assumed command of the military forces in the department on 11 March. On 17 March, but Smith was relieved by Former Professional Ulysses S. Grant (USMA 1844) of Ohio.[4]

Grant had gotten into West Point because his father, a successful southern Ohio businessman, had access to a Congressional appointment. He was an indifferent student, excelling only in mathematics and horsemanship. He was commissioned a 2nd Lieutenant in the 4th Infantry, and served as regimental quartermaster during most of the Mexican War. Despite his desk job, he frequently led troops in combat under both Zachary Taylor and Winfield Scott. Grant went to the West coast in 1849 and was promoted to Captain. Considering that the prewar Army had fewer Captains than a WWII infantry regiment that was something. He tried numerous business ventures to raise enough capital to bring his wife to the coast, but he proved spectacularly unsuccessful. In 1854, Grant resigned his commission for reasons traditionally connected to his inability to cordially drink alcohol, but the facts are unclear.

Grant's return to civilian life was less than stellar. He failed at farming his father-in-law's land, failed in a real estate business and at attempts to gain engineer and clerk posts in St. Louis. At one point he was selling firewood and kindling door-to-door to feed his family. He finally became a clerk in a leather goods store in Galena run by his two younger brothers. Offering his services to the War Department when the war broke out, he began organizing and mustering state volunteers without either pay or rank. Elihu B. Washburne, a powerful Illinois congressman, got Grant a commission as Colonel of the 21st Illinois

---

4. Mark M. Boatner, "Smith, Charles Ferguson," in *The Civil War Dictionary* (New York: David McKay & Company, 1988), 769; Patricia L. (Editor) Faust, "Smith, Charles Ferguson," in *The Historical Times Illustrated Encyclopedia of the Civil War* (New York: Harper & Row, 1986), 694–5.

Infantry in June 1861. By July, "Useless" "Sam" (his nicknames) Grant, the habitual failure, was a Brigadier General.

Army officers in blue and gray had mixed opinions of Grant, ranging from absolute loyalty and unabashed respect to open loathing. Among those who disliked him was his boss, Halleck. Halleck knew that Grant's reputation for drink counted heavily against him, and thought him undisciplined and "un-military in bearing." But some of those who had the highest respect for him, even at the beginning of the war, were Confederates.[5]

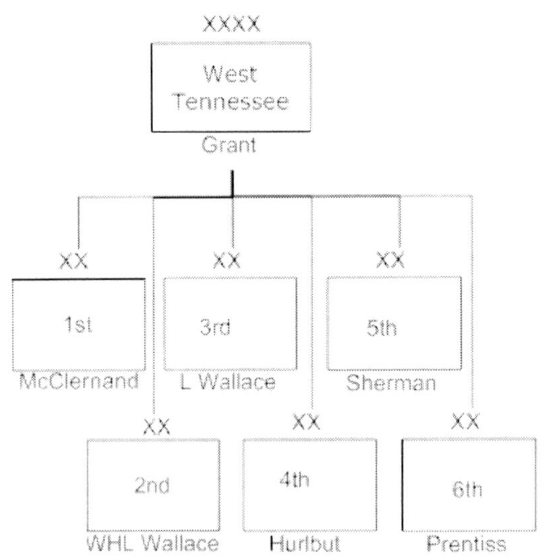

Figure 2-3, Army of West Tennessee

---

5. Bruce Catton, *U.S. Grant and the American Military Tradition* (New York: Grosset & Dunlap, 1954), 74, 77; Eicher, op. cit., 852; William S. McFeely, *Grant: A Biography* (New York: W. W. Norton & Company, 1982), 12, 55; Geoffrey Perret, *Ulysses S. Grant, Soldier and President* (New York: Random House, 1997), 57, 102; Brooks D. Simpson, *Ulysses S. Grant: Triumph Over Adversity, 1822–1865* (New York: Houghton Mifflin Company, College Division, 2000), 13.

John A. McClernand of Illinois' was and Amateur whose sole military experience before 1860 came when he served as a volunteer private in the Blackhawk War (1832). He had served in various posts in the US and the Illinois House of Representatives, including that of Congressman for Abraham Lincoln's district from 1836 to 1860. After his defeat in a bid for the speakership of the House in 1860, he resigned and went home to raise volunteers. For his trouble, and to appease Democratic interests in Southern Illinois, Lincoln had him commissioned Brigadier General in May 1861. By early 1862 McClernand commanded the 1st Division of Grant's army, consisting of nearly 7,000 Iowa and Illinois veterans of the Henry/Donelson campaign.

McClernand's dislike of abolitionism was a plus for his constituents, many of whom once lived in slaveholding states. He had a certain flair for doing just the right thing at just the right time just often enough to keep from getting into too much trouble. He was known for bombastic oratory, was pompous and selfish and distrusted professional soldiers, though he had ambitions to use his war record as a stepping-stone to higher political office. He often claimed credit for the work of others, but was bold, energetic and intelligent enough to look competent.[6]

---

6. Patricia L. (Editor) Faust, "McClernand, John A," in *Historical Times Illustrated Encyclopedia of the Civil War* (New York: Harper & Row, 1986), 456–7; NNDB.com, "McClernand, John Alexander," http://www.nndb.com/people/289/000050139/ (Accessed 1 Nov 08).

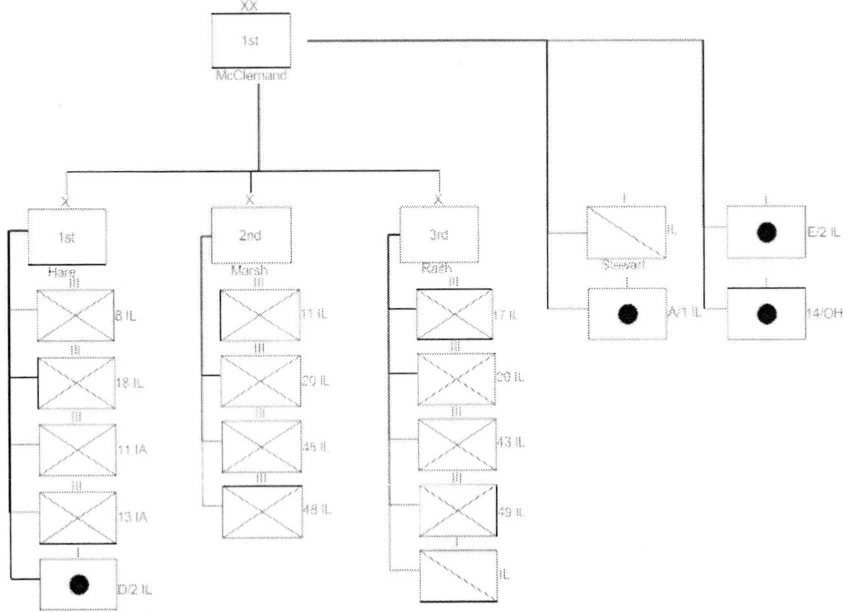

Figure 2-4, 1st Division (McClernand), Army of West Tennessee

William H.L. Wallace was an Amateur too, born in Ohio but who moved to Illinois as a young man. At one time he planned to study law with Abraham Lincoln in Springfield. He was licensed in law in 1846, and then joined the 1st Illinois Infantry for the Mexican War, rising to the rank of lieutenant. Afterwards he became district attorney in Illinois.

After Fort Sumter William Wallace volunteered as a private in a three-month regiment, the 11th Illinois, as it gathered in Springfield, and was mustered in as its colonel in April 1861. In late March 1862 William Wallace took command of Smith's 2nd Division, made up of just over 6,400 men from Iowa, Missouri and Illinois. Fellow division commander Lew Wallace[7] described him as looking like a "farmer coming from a hard day's plowing."[8]

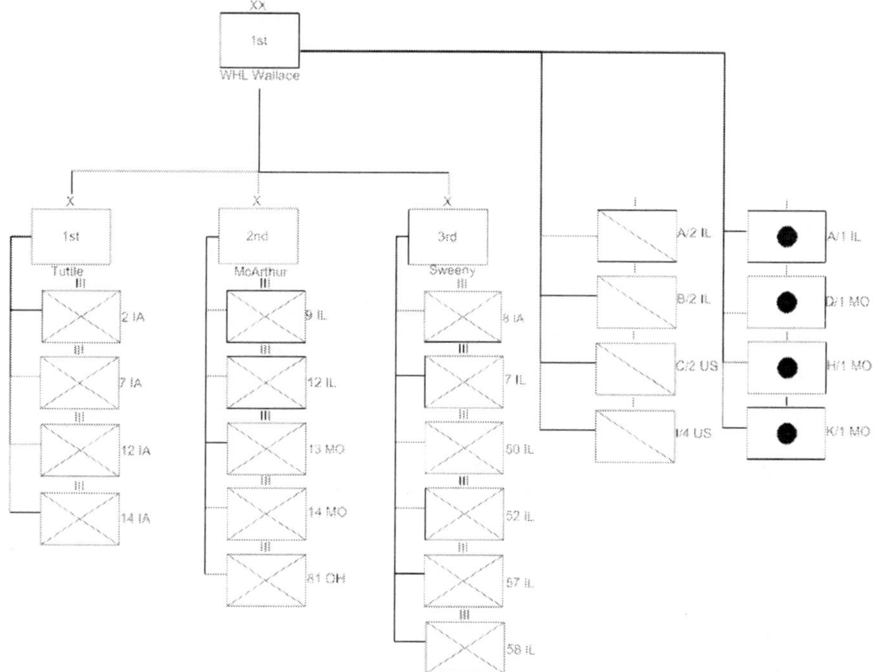

Figure 2-5, 2nd Division (WHL Wallace), Army of West Tennessee

---

7. There were two Wallaces commanding Union divisions at Shiloh; the first is treated as William Wallace; the second as Lew or Lewis Wallace.

8. Mark M. Boatner, "Wallace, William Harvey Lamb," in *The Civil War Dictionary* (New York: David McKay & Company, 1988), 887; Dyer, op. cit., 475; Patricia L. (Editor) Faust, "Wallace, William Harvey Lamb," in *Historical Times Illustrated Encyclopedia of the Civil War* (New York: Harper and Row, 1986), 799–800; Wikipedia.com, "William Harvey Lamb Wallace," http://en.wikipedia.org/wiki/WHL_Wallace (Accessed October 2008).

Lewis (usually Lew) Wallace of Indiana was an enthusiastic Amateur who worked as a clerk and a journalist, and as a young man displayed fascination for Mexico. During the Mexican War he was a lieutenant in the lst Indiana Infantry, but saw only minor action. In 1849, he was admitted to the bar in Indiana and became a crusading lawyer. In 1856, he entered the state senate.

In April 1861 Lew Wallace was named adjutant general of Indiana and Colonel of the 11th Indiana. He was first sent to western Virginia, seeing minor action at Romney and Harper's Ferry under George McClellan, and became Brigadier General of Volunteers that September. He took command of a new 3rd Division in Grant's army made up of just over 7,500 men from Indiana, Ohio and Nebraska while it was marching on Fort Donelson in February 1862. By Shiloh his division was encamped at Crump's Landing, on the western bank of the Tennessee River downstream from Pittsburg Landing. Though Lew Wallace appeared to be nothing more than one more influential civilian in shoulder straps, he must have been doing something right to have performed well enough for Grant to recommend his promotion. But then again, no one expected the war to last quite so long as it did.[9]

---

9. Civilwarhome.com, "Wallace, Lew," http://www.civilwarhome.com/ wallacebio.htm (Accessed October 2008); Patricia L. (Editor) Faust, "Wallace, Lewis," in *Historical Times Illustrated Encyclopedia of the Civil War* (New York: Harper & Row, 1986), 799; Mark M. Boatner, "Wallace, Lewis," in *The Civil War Dictionary* (New York: David McKay & Company, 1988), 887.

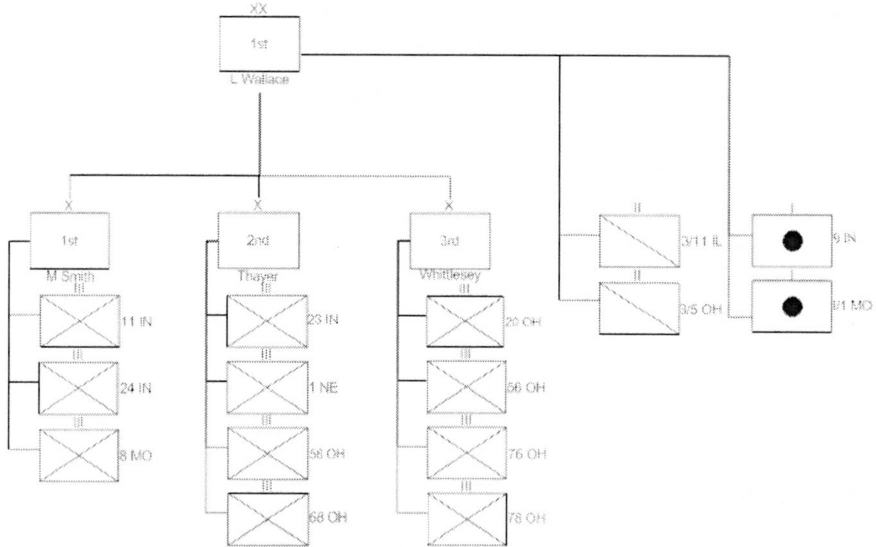

Figure 2-6, 3rd Division (L Wallace), Army of West Tennessee

Stephen A. Hurlbut was a Militiaman born in Charleston, South Carolina. His father was a Unitarian minister from Massachusetts, and his mother was a native of Charleston. As a young man, he took up law and was admitted to the bar in 1837. He practiced law in Charleston until the South Carolina regiment in which he served as adjutant was sent to Florida during the Second Seminole War (1835-43). Hurlbut moved to Illinois in 1845 and was elected to the Illinois House of Representatives in 1859 and 1861. He was appointed Brigadier General in 1861, and by April 1862 he commanded the 4th Division in Grant's army of just over 7,800 Illinois and Indiana men, with a few odd Kentucky, Missouri and Ohio boys thrown in.

Though born in the South, he kept few family ties there. His family condemned slavery as morally wrong, but owned slaves because it was expedient; Hurlbut displayed a highly flexible sense of morality all his life. Hurlbut felt that the political advantages in fighting with the Union in what "everybody knew" was going to be a short war were worth the price of any scorn that his mother's family could heap on him. His family had owned slaves, but so had Grant's. Ambivalence to the

South's "peculiar institution" was not remarkable for Union generals. His name was attached to some real estate scandals and, much to Grant's and his soldiers' annoyance, he drank heavily.[10]

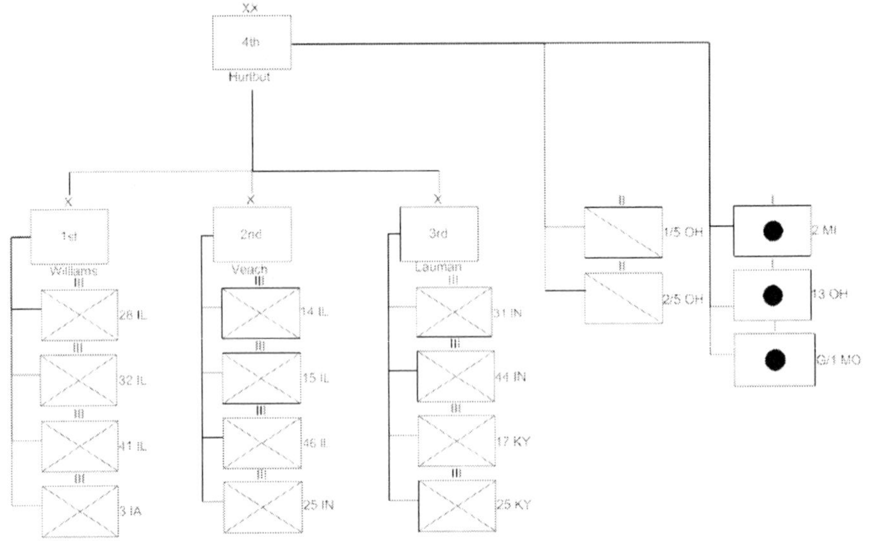

Figure 2-7, 4th Division (Hurlbut), Army of West Tennessee

Former Professional William T. Sherman (USMA 1840) of Ohio, having lost his father at an early age, was raised in the family of Senator Thomas Ewing. Through the influence of this patron he obtained an appointment to West Point and was commissioned in the artillery. He received a brevet for his services in California during the Mexican War but saw very little combat action, having worked mostly

---

10. Larry J. Daniel, *Shiloh: The Battle That Changed the Civil War* (New York: Simon & Schuster, 1997), 109; The Latin Library, "Hurlbut, Stephen," http://www.thelatinlibrary.com/chron/civilwarnotes/hurlbut.html (Accessed October 2008).

in the Commissary Department (the providers of food). He resigned a Captain in 1853.

Like Grant, Sherman's out-of-Army career did not see great success, though not quite Grant's spectacular failure. By 1859 he was superintendent of the military school that later became Louisiana State University. He moved to St. Louis when Louisiana seceded and soon volunteered his services to the Union. Commissioned Colonel of the 13th US Infantry he led a brigade at Bull Run, and was appointed Brigadier General in August 1861. Briefly serving around Washington, he was sent to the Department of Kentucky as deputy to Robert Anderson, the Union's hero of Fort Sumter, and soon succeeded Anderson in command of the department. While there Sherman stated that it might take as many as a half a million men and two years of hard fighting to end the war; the North could not tolerate this in 1861, so the press dubbed him crazy (he did suffer a breakdown of unclear cause shortly after). Senior to Grant in time in service, Sherman waived his seniority so that he could command the green 5th Division in Grant's army, consisting of some 8,500 Ohio and Illinois volunteers.

Sherman was a hypochondriac who suffered from seasonal allergies, and was said to go through a pound of handkerchiefs on some spring days. Persistent insomnia turned him into a workaholic and a worry-wart who, paradoxically, refused to believe anything that didn't fit his vision of the way things were. If Grant had no nerves at all, Sherman was a bundle of them, except when someone was shooting at either of them--when their blood changed into ice water.[11]

---

11. Civilwarhome.com, "Sherman, William T," http://www.civilwarhome.com/ sherbio.htm (Accessed October 2008).

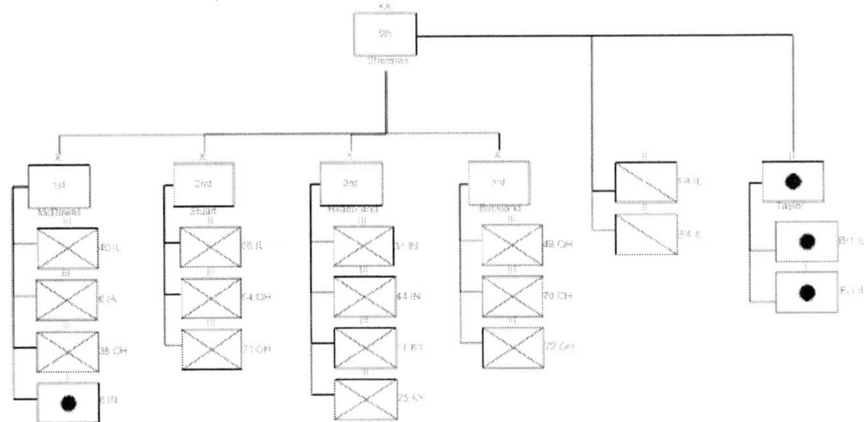

Figure 2-8, 5th Division (Sherman), Army of West Tennessee

Militiaman Benjamin M. Prentiss was born in Virginia and had lived in Missouri before settling in Illinois. As a youth, Prentiss worked in the family rope-making business, and later became an attorney and auctioneer. One source claims that Prentiss got some early military training, though where and when is not known. He got some military experience in Illinois during the Mormon migrations in 1844-5, and in Mexico as a captain with the 1st Illinois Infantry, where William Wallace was a lieutenant. When Lincoln sent out the call for troops in 1861, Prentiss already had a hundred men to offer. In April 1861 when the 10th Illinois was sworn in he was commissioned its Colonel. He was in charge of forces at Cairo for a while, where he feuded with Grant over relative rank and the right to command. Both Prentiss and McClernand had been considered for brigadier general appointments at the same time as Grant, but Washburne managed to send Grant to the head of the list. He was commissioned Brigadier General in August 1861 anyway, backdated to May.

By Shiloh Prentiss commanded the 6th Division of Grant's army, a mixed bag of just over 7,500 Michigan, Missouri, Wisconsin, Iowa and Minnesota volunteers. Though his militia career was typical, he had no patrons in power. His squabbling with Grant over seniority and precedence wasn't unusual for the time.[12]

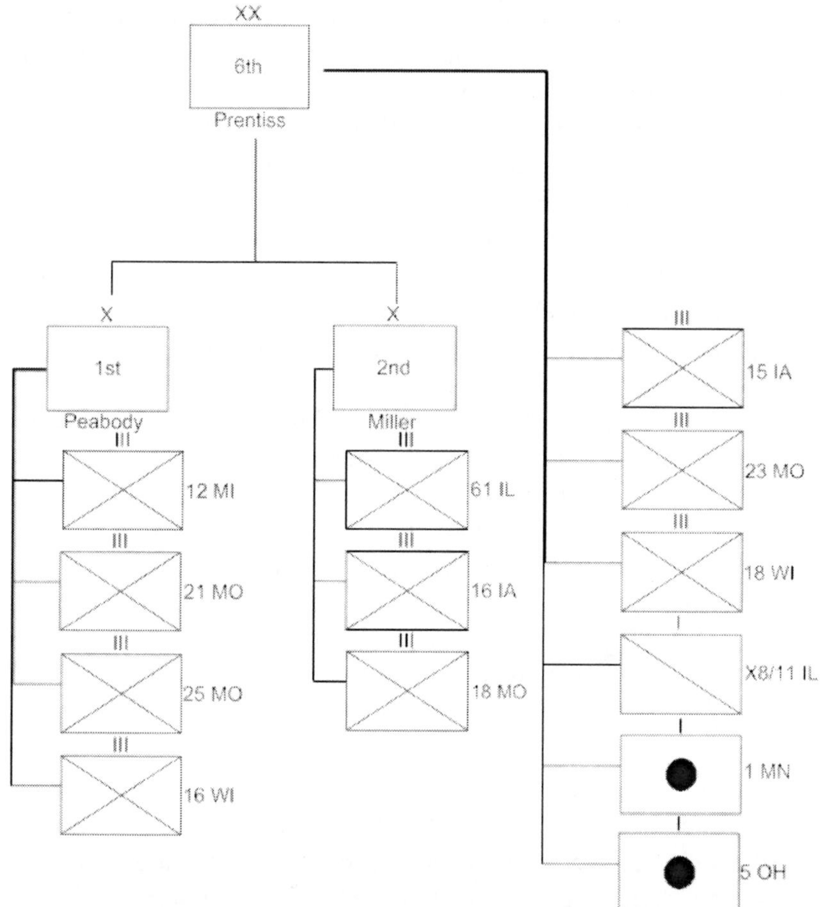

Figure 2-9, 6th Division (Prentiss), Army of West Tennessee

---

12. Rex A. Gootch, "Prentiss, Benjamin," http://members.aol.com/rexagooch/ prentissbiography.html (Accessed October 2008); Patricia L. (Editor) Faust, "Prentiss, Benjamin Mayberry," in *Historical Times Illustrated Encyclopedia of the Civil War* (New York: Harper and Row, 1986), 600–1.

Army of Mississippi, Provisional Army of the Confederate States of America

This command was created on 5 March 1862 at Corinth, Mississippi, and was to consist of every Confederate military unit that Johnston could reach. As Department commander Johnston could command the troops himself, but chose instead to name his highest ranking officer, lifelong Professional Pierre G. T. Beauregard of Louisiana (USMA 1838), to command the Army. Nicknamed "the Little Napoleon," Beauregard was first posted to the artillery, but soon transferred to the engineers, where he worked with Robert E. Lee in clearing and stabilizing the Mississippi River.[13]

Beauregard served on Scott's staff in Mexico, was wounded and won two brevets there. In 1861 he was superintendent of West Point for five days--a record for that institution. He resigned from the Army in February and offered his services to the South. Placed in charge of South Carolina troops at Charleston, he was in command for the victory over Fort Sumter in the heady days in April 1861. The "Little Creole" (another of his nicknames), hailed throughout the South as a military genius, was ordered to Virginia. There he commanded the forces opposite Washington and created the Confederate Army of the Potomac. Reinforced by Joseph E. Johnston and his Army of the Shenandoah, Beauregard was reduced to corps command under Johnston the day before Manassas. Beauregard was made a full general to date from July 1861.

Despite his successes, Beauregard was a lightning rod for self-promotion and controversy, in constant friction with Confederate officialdom. Though an able administrator he made plans beyond his resources. He was also a nag who held just enough cachet and reputation in the salons to garner attention for his more crack brained ideas that just wasted time in their debunking. He was also something of a hypochondriac who was ill primarily between battles. This propensity for illnesses was thought to affect his mind, though some of his maladies were quite real. Beauregard thought that Napoleon was the

---

13. Eicher, op. cit., 887–8.

sine qua non of soldiering, as did many of his contemporaries: anything the French thought about making war was good enough for the antebellum US Army.[14]

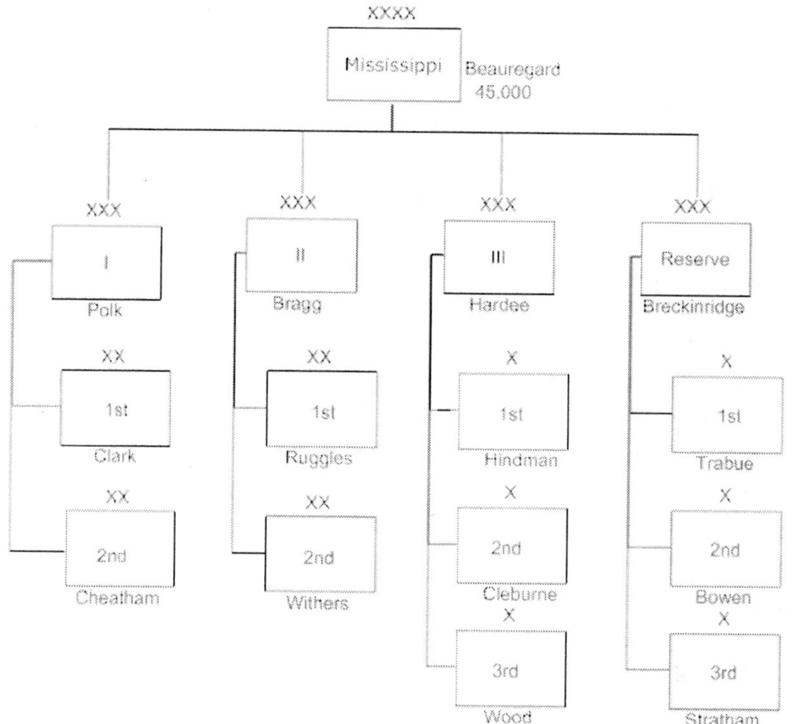

Figure 2-10, Army of Mississippi (Beauregard), Department # 2

---

14. Civilwarhome.com, "Pierre Gustave Toutant Beauregard," http://www.civilwarhome.com/ beaubio.htm (Accessed October 2008); David G. Martin, *The Shiloh Campaign: March - April 1862*, Great Campaigns (Pennsylvania: Combined Books, 1996), 66; Wiley Sword, *Shiloh: Bloody April* (New York: Morrow, 1974), 108; T. Harry Williams, "Beauregard at Shiloh," *Civil War History* 1, no. 1 (March 1955): 17–18.

Leonidas Polk was a West Point-trained Amateur (USMA 1827) born in North Carolina. He resigned his commission soon after graduation, joined the Episcopal Church, was ordained a minister in 1831 and became bishop of the Diocese of Louisiana in 1841. Polk was the driving force behind the University of the South at Suwannee, Tennessee, which opened its doors in 1857 as a keystone for Southern nationalism. Polk's friend from West Point, Jefferson Davis, convinced Polk to join the Confederate Army in 1861, where he was commissioned Major General and became known as the "Fighting Bishop." Polk was in command of Department No. 2 when Johnston arrived.

Polk tended to go his own way, sometimes in opposition to orders or even common sense. Polk had influence at the very pinnacle of the Confederacy and felt that he should command Johnston's department; he could not accept that not everyone could be in charge. At Shiloh Polk commanded I Corps of Johnston's army of some 9,400 men from all over the South.[15]

Charles Clark was an Amateur with a little experience who was born in Ohio but moved to Mississippi at 21. In the late 1830s and early 1840s Clark was a prominent planter and attorney who served in the Mississippi legislature as both a Democrat and a Whig, and who commanded the 2nd Mississippi Infantry by the end of the Mexican War. After Mississippi seceded in 1861, Clark was appointed Brigadier General in the Mississippi militia's I Corps in May. At Shiloh he commanded the 4,400 man 1st Division of Polk's corps, consisting primarily of men from Tennessee and Arkansas. Clark's reputation suffers a common malady: although he was well known locally, beyond scant mentions in dusty references no one has ever said that much about this officer, who lacked significant influence.[16]

---

15. Answers.com, "Polk, Leonidas," http://www.answers.com/topic/leonidas-polk (Accessed 22 October 2008).

16. Wikipedia.com, "Charles Clark," http://en.wikipedia.org/wiki/Charles_Clark_ (governor) (Accessed

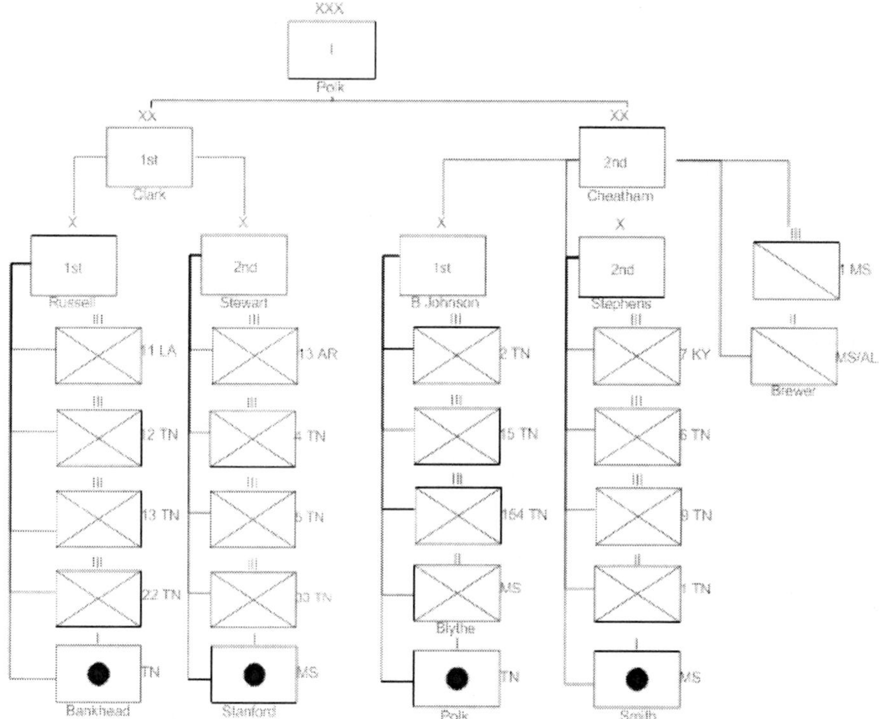

Figure 2-11, I Corps (Polk), Army of Mississippi

Benjamin F. Cheatham of Tennessee had been a prominent Militiaman, a Captain in the lst Tennessee Infantry and Colonel of the 3rd Tennessee in Mexico. Active in the state militia, Cheatham was appointed Major General in the Provisional Army of Tennessee in May 1861, in no small part due to his friendship with Tennessee governor Isham Harris. In July, he became Brigadier General in the Provisional

December 2008); Mark M. Boatner, "Clark, Charles," in *The Civil War Dictionary* (New York: David McKay & Company, 1988), 156; Patricia L. (Editor) Faust, "Clark, Charles," in *Historical Times Illustrated Encyclopedia of the Civil War* (New York: Harper and Row, 1986), 142; Ray Skates, "Clark, Charles," in *Encyclopedia of the Confederacy Volume 1* (New York: Simon & Shuster, 1993), 340–1.

Army of the Confederate States and became a Major General in March 1862. At Shiloh, Cheatham commanded the 3,800 man 2nd Division of Polk's I Corps.

Cheatham had an understanding of the art of managing men. Like Lew Wallace, he had military aspirations all of his life. He was a most fortunate find for a militia officer, with qualities that even some professionals lacked: a developed talent for fighting and a knack for leading. Like Grant, he looked after the men's comfort and safety, but, when duty required it, he was ready to expend them.[17]

Braxton Bragg of North Carolina (USMA 1837) was a Former Professional in 1861. He was originally commissioned in field artillery, saw action in the Second Seminole War and won three brevets in Mexico. His flying battery revolutionized the use of field guns in North America. His methods were copied in Europe and improved on by Louis Napoleon Bonaparte (who would become Napoleon III, Emperor of the French, in 1852). Bragg resigned his commission in the 3rd Artillery in 1856 and became a Louisiana planter. Offering his services to the Confederacy soon after Fort Sumter, Bragg commanded troops in Louisiana and against Fort Pickens in Pensacola Harbor. In March 1862 Bragg served as Johnston's Chief of Staff while he commanded II Corps of over 16,000 men from Louisiana, Arkansas, Florida, Alabama and Texas.

Bragg had earned a reputation in the prewar Army for strict discipline and literal adherence to regulations that went beyond the pale of sanity. One story goes that he had a written dispute with himself while serving as both a company commander and the post quartermaster--proof that it is possible for an Army officer to be both right and wrong simultaneously. For someone of Bragg's nature any

---

17. Civilwarhome.com, "Cheatham, Benjamin Franklin," http://www.civilwarhome.com/ CMHcheathambio.htm (Accessed December 2008); Herman Hattaway, "Cheatham, Benjamin Franklin," in *Historical Times Illustrated Encyclopedia of the Civil War* (New York: Harper and Row, 1986), 135.

staff job would have been a trial, but he was good at it. Bragg was also one of Davis' best friends.[18]

Professional Daniel Ruggles of Massachusetts (USMA 1833) was first commissioned into the 5th Infantry, and married into a wealthy Virginia family. He saw action during the Second Seminole War and won brevets in Mexico. Ruggles avidly served his adoptive region, and was one of many who actively worked for its nascent independence struggle before his resignation in May 1861: while on sick leave in 1859 and 1860 he encouraged the organization of Virginia militia companies.

Ruggles was commissioned a Brigadier General in the Confederate Army in August 1861, and was soon sent to the Western theater. By March 1862 he was in command of the 1st Division of Bragg's II Corps of about 6,500 men. He was a stern and gruff New Englander which, combined with long years of service in isolated outposts on the frontier, made for a generally bad disposition. He was not well thought of: even his secretary didn't like him.[19]

Jones M. Withers of Alabama (USMA 1835) was first brevetted a Lieutenant in the 1st Dragoons. He fought in the Creek Indian War in 1836, resigned his commission and began a law practice in Alabama, where he entered the state's militia forces and became a cotton broker. In March 1847 he was appointed Lieutenant Colonel of the 13th Infantry in Mexico. He was promoted to Colonel of the 9th Infantry in

---

18. Wikipedia.com, "Braxton Bragg," http://en.wikipedia.org/wiki/Braxton_Bragg (Accessed January 2009); Civilwarhome.com, "Bragg, Braxton," http://www.civilwarhome.com/braggbio.htm (Accessed January 2009).

19. Wikipedia.com, "Daniel Ruggles," http://en.wikipedia.org/wiki/Daniel_Ruggles (Accessed December 2008); James I. Robertson, "Ruggles, Daniel," in *Encyclopedia of the Confederacy Volume 3* (New York: Simon & Shuster, 1993), 1351–2; Patricia L. (Editor) Faust, "Ruggles, Daniel," in *Historical Times Illustrated Encyclopedia of the Civil War* (New York: Harper & Row, 1986), 647.

September 1847 and resigned in May 1848 to become a merchant and Alabama state legislator who was elected to the U.S. House of Representatives in 1855. From 1858 to 1861 Withers was the mayor of Mobile, Alabama. He was appointed Colonel of the 3rd Alabama in April 1861, and served briefly as commander of the Department of Norfolk, Virginia. He was promoted to Brigadier General and commander of all Alabama forces in July.

Former Professional Withers returned west and commanded the District of Alabama from September 1861 to January 1862, when his 6,500 man command was re-designated the Army of Mobile, which became the 2nd Division of Bragg's II Corps in March 1862. Like Clark, outside of official records not a lot is known about this Former Professional who was unknown to the halls of national power.[20]

---

20. Wikipedia.com, "Jones Mitchell Withers," http://en.wikipedia.org/wiki/ Jones_M_Withers (Accessed December 2008); Patricia L. (Editor) Faust, "Withers, Jones Mitchell," in *Historical Times Illustrated Encyclopedia of the Civil War* (New York: Harper and Row, 1986), 837.

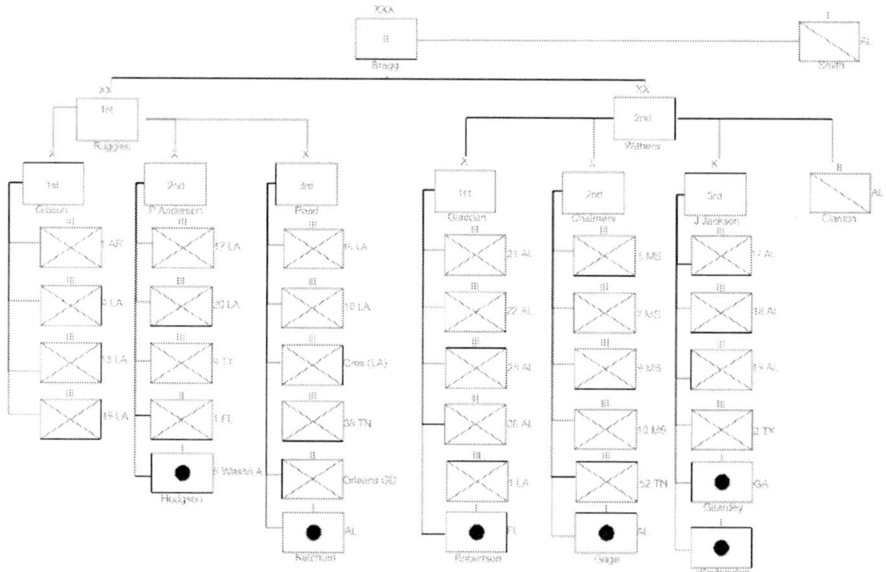

Figure 2-12, II Corps (Bragg), Army of Mississippi

William J. Hardee of Georgia (USMA 1838) spent all his adult life in the Army, and was first commissioned in the cavalry. He served in the Second Seminole and Mexican Wars, won two brevets and was wounded. He briefly studied at the French cavalry school at Samur before the Mexican War, and saw the Piedmont War as an observer on the French side. By 1855 he had translated and modified a French light infantry manual and renamed it *Rifle and Light Infantry Tactics*-- or more familiarly Hardee's *Tactics*-- which was in widespread use on both sides. He returned to West Point as a tactics instructor and was commandant of cadets for a time. By the time he resigned as Lieutenant Colonel of the lst Cavalry in January 1861, he was one of the best known officers in the Army. In the Union's Army of the Potomac five regiments of Midwesterners adopted a distinctive tall black dress hat that bore Hardee's name; the unit was known as the Black Hat Brigade until they were dubbed the Iron Brigade of the West in 1862.

Hardee commanded III Corps in Johnston's army, consisting of about 6,700 men, mostly from Arkansas and Tennessee. Hardee was the kind of officer both sides lacked in sufficient numbers: reliable, widely experienced, respected and well known, combining intellectual ability with leadership skills. Yet, he lacked powerful friends that might have got him a higher command.[21]

21. Civilwarhome.com, "Hardee, William," http://www.civilwarhome.com/ hardeebio.htm (Accessed October 2008); Les D. Jensen, "Hardee, William Joseph," in *Historical Times Illustrated Encyclopedia of the Civil War* (New York: Harper & Row, 1986), 338; Brent Nosworthy, *Bloody Crucible of Courage: Fighting Methods and Combat Experience of the Civil War* (New York: Carroll and Graf Publishers, 2003), 79.

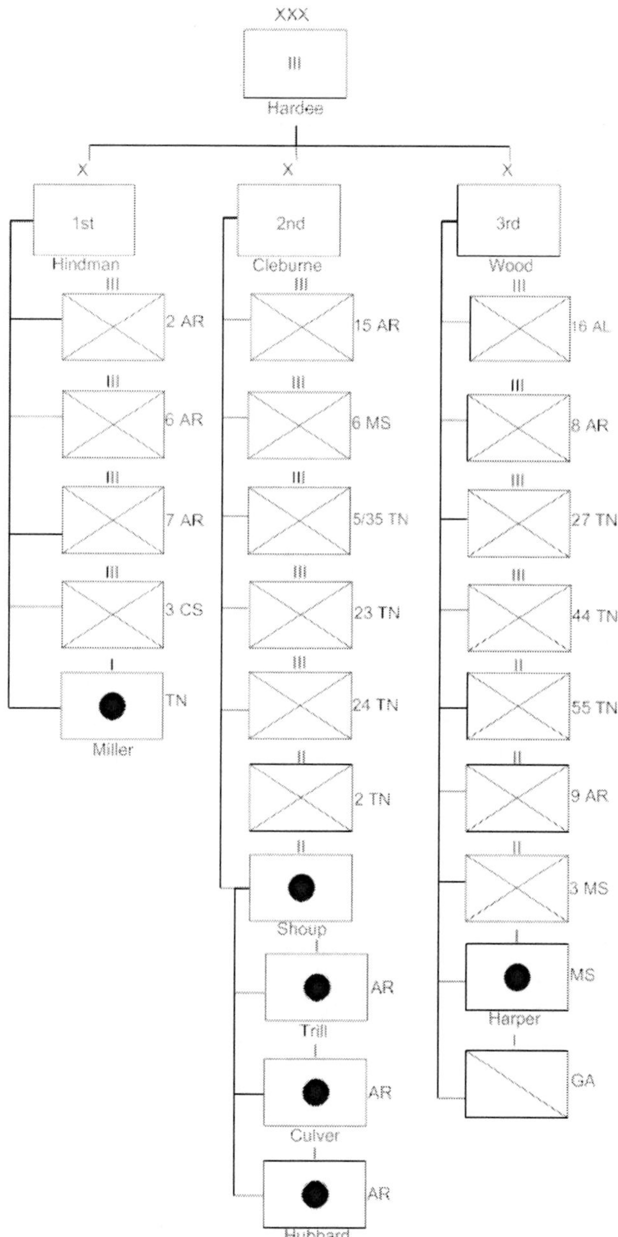

Figure 2-13, III Corps (Hardee), Army of Mississippi

John C. Breckinridge of Kentucky graduated from Centre College in 1839, attended what is now Princeton University, studied law at Transylvania University, and was admitted to the Kentucky bar in 1840. He was a major in the 3rd Kentucky in the Mexican War.

Breckinridge was a member of the Kentucky House of Representatives in 1849, and was elected to two terms in the U.S. Congress from 1851 to 1855. He was elected Vice President of the United States in 1856; at 35, he was the youngest Vice President in American history. In the presidential elections of 1860, Breckinridge was nominated for the top slot on the ticket by the Southern faction of the split Democratic Party. Despite his ticket's loss to Lincoln, the Kentucky legislature elected him to the U.S. Senate in 1860, where he served from March to December 1861. Unlike other Confederate leaders who followed their states, Breckinridge broke with Kentucky after the legislature voted not to secede.

By April 1862 Amateur Breckinridge commanded the Reserve Corps of the Army of Mississippi, consisting of three brigades of just over 7,200 men, mostly from Kentucky and Tennessee. Though he had some military experience he had no formal military training, and his commission was viewed as a sop to Kentucky interests. At this stage of the war, men who showed the leadership ability needed to lead a horse to water were given commissions.[22]

---

22. Answers.com, "Breckinridge, John Cabell," http://www.answers.com/topic/john-c-breckinridge (Accessed October 2008).

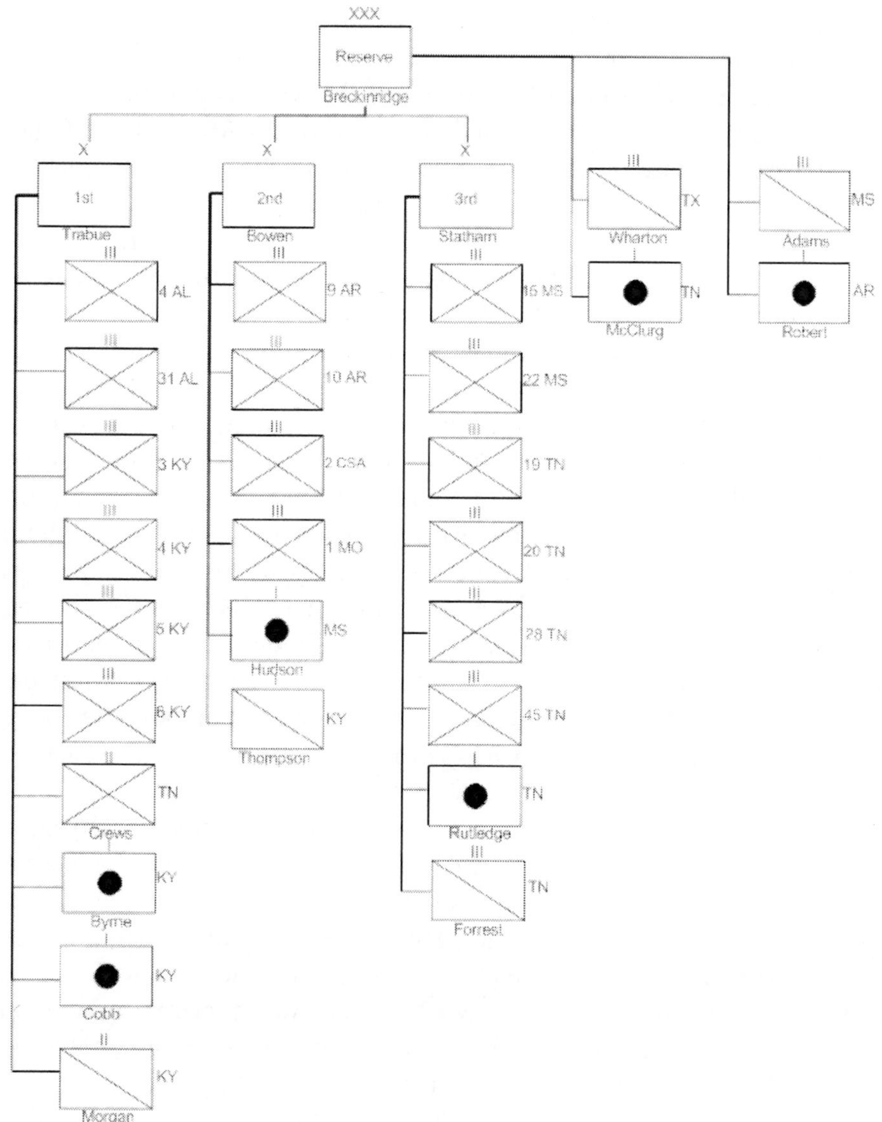

Figure 2-14, Reserve/IV Corps (Breckinridge), Army of Mississippi

Department and Army of the Ohio, U.S. Army

This command went through several evolutions by the time it was consolidated into Halleck's Department of the Mississippi, but its field forces retained its original title and organization as Army of the Ohio. This department embraced Ohio, Michigan, Indiana, Kentucky east of the Cumberland River, and much of the state of Tennessee.[23]

On 15 November 1861, Professional Don C. Buell of Ohio (USMA 1841) replaced Sherman in command of the department, and was coequal to Halleck before the two departments were consolidated in March 1862. Buell's West Point years were trying, and he was nearly expelled several times for excessive demerits, even if his academic work was good. He was commissioned in the infantry at graduation, and during his service at the end of the Second Seminole War he demonstrated remarkable administrative abilities and enthusiasm for enforcing discipline. During the Mexican War he fought under both Taylor and Scott, and was brevetted three times. After Mexico he was in the Adjutant General's office, and was in the Department of the Pacific under Johnston when the war began. Buell was commissioned Brigadier General in May 1861, and helped McClellan to organize the Army of the Potomac after Bull Run. He was given command the Army of the Ohio as a reward and was brevetted a Major General in March 1862 after Fort Donelson.

Buell was stern in expression, formal in manner, stocky in physique and possessed of great physical strength. He is said to have been cold and aloof, lacking the common touch needed to motivate volunteer soldiers. The fact that he was a former slave owner himself (like Grant, through marriage) left him open to charges that he was a Southern sympathizer. Buell is said to have believed in maneuver more than fighting, and in "soft war," to allow the enemy time to contemplate the errors of his ways. By Shiloh, Buell had developed a knack for never being in quite the right place at quite the right time. Buell hated Grant,

---

23. Dyer, op. cit., 425.

even though Buell knew him only by reputation, and Grant knew Buell not at all.[24]

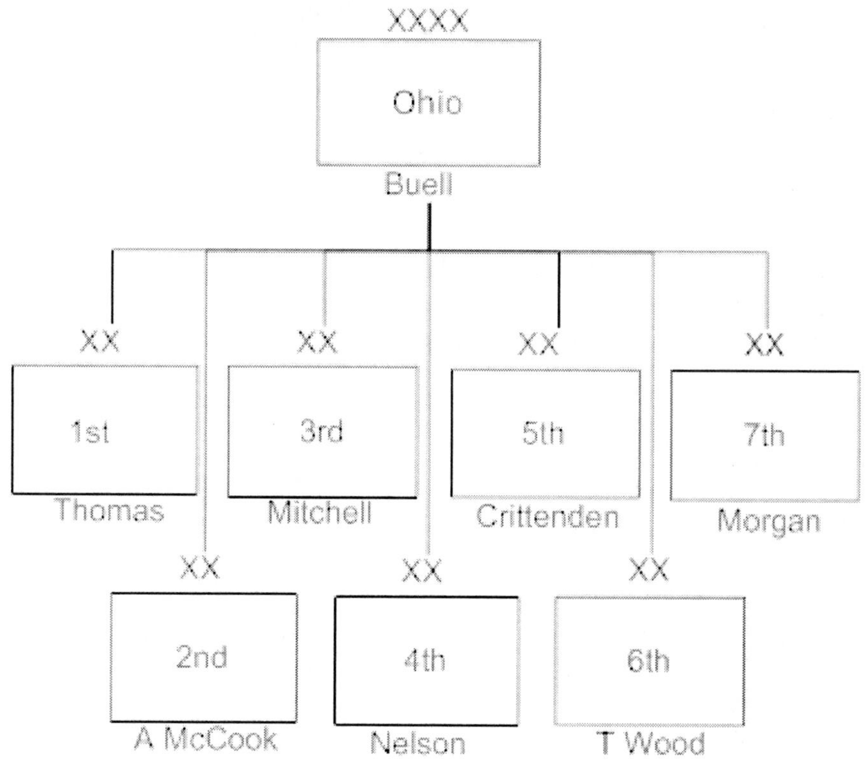

Figure 2-15, Army and Department of the Ohio (Buell)

Alexander M. McCook (USMA 1842) was the third son in the Tribe of Dan of the Fighting McCooks from Ohio, a legendary clan of seventeen brothers and cousins who served the Union armed forces. First commissioned in the infantry, Professional McCook was one of the few Regulars left behind during the Mexican War. He fought Indians in the West from the summer of 1854 until 1858 when he was

---

24. Civilwarhome.com, "Buell, Don C," http://www.civilwarhome.com/buellbio.htm (Accessed October 2008).

appointed an instructor of infantry tactics at West Point, a position he held until April 1861, when he was sent to Ohio as a mustering officer. McCook was commissioned Colonel of the 1st Ohio in May 1861, and was sent to the forces outside Washington, and was at Bull Run with his regiment. McCook had been a lieutenant in the Regular Army for nineteen years, and six months after Fort Sumter he was appointed a Brigadier General of Volunteers.

McCook was sent west in late 1861 where he commanded the 2nd Division of Buell's army, made up of 7,500 men in regiments from Kentucky, Ohio, Indiana, Illinois, and Pennsylvania. His command also included the largest single block of Regulars at Shiloh, who had barely as much time in uniform as their volunteer neighbors. Few remember men like McCook, in part because he lacked influence in high places.

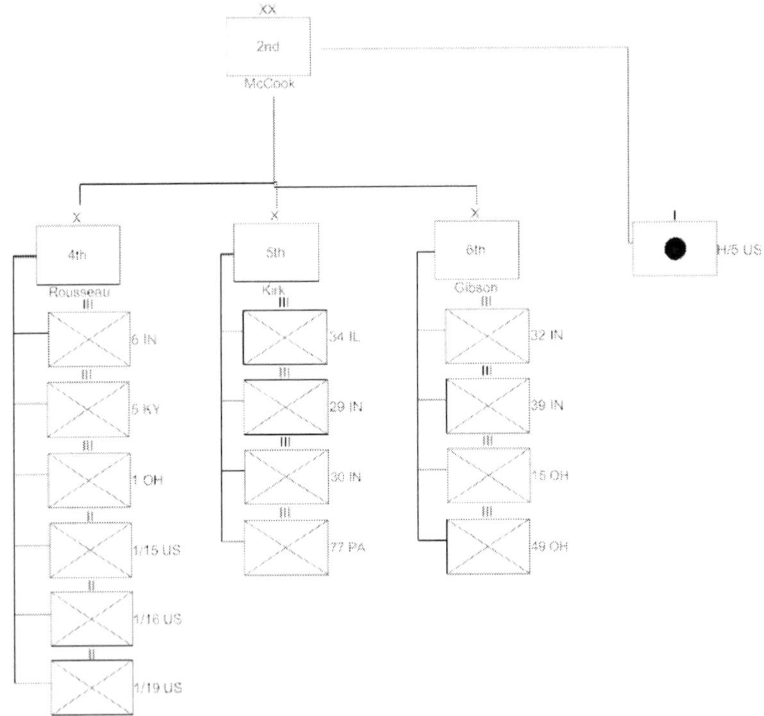

Figure 2-16, 2nd Division (McCook), Army of the Ohio

William A. Nelson of Kentucky had spent all his live and a portion of his youth in uniform: he was thirteen when he joined the U.S. Navy as a midshipman in 1840. He commanded a gun position in Mexico in 1847, and was a lieutenant by 1855. He later served in the Mediterranean and South Pacific stations. In 1858, commanded brig *Niagara* that returned Africans rescued from slaver *Echo*.

After his brother was appointed ambassador to Chile by his old friend Lincoln, Nelson was sent to take the temperature of political sentiment in Kentucky and report his findings directly to the President. By April 1861, Nelson was recruiting in Kentucky and established Camp Dick Robinson, which became a rallying place for Unionist Kentuckians. He was either "detailed" or "detached" by the Navy (sources differ) for duty in the Army in September 1861, and was commissioned a Brigadier General. By December he commanded the 4th Division of Buell's army. His division at Shiloh consisted of just over 4,500 men from Ohio, Indiana and Kentucky.

"Bull" Nelson was physically huge man (about 6'4" and 300 pounds) who was said to roar like his namesake. Up to the spring of 1862, nothing in his long career indicated anything other than his steady duty. Nelson was long accustomed to leadership, the difference between his experience and his Army counterparts being a matter of scale and longevity. Of all the officers at Shiloh, his rise to division command was not just by influence (which had a lot to do with it), but by a demonstrated capacity for leadership developed at an early age.[25]

---

25. Wikipedia.com, "William 'Bull' Nelson," http://en.wikipedia.org/wiki/Bull_Nelson (Accessed October 2008); Martin, op. cit., 161.

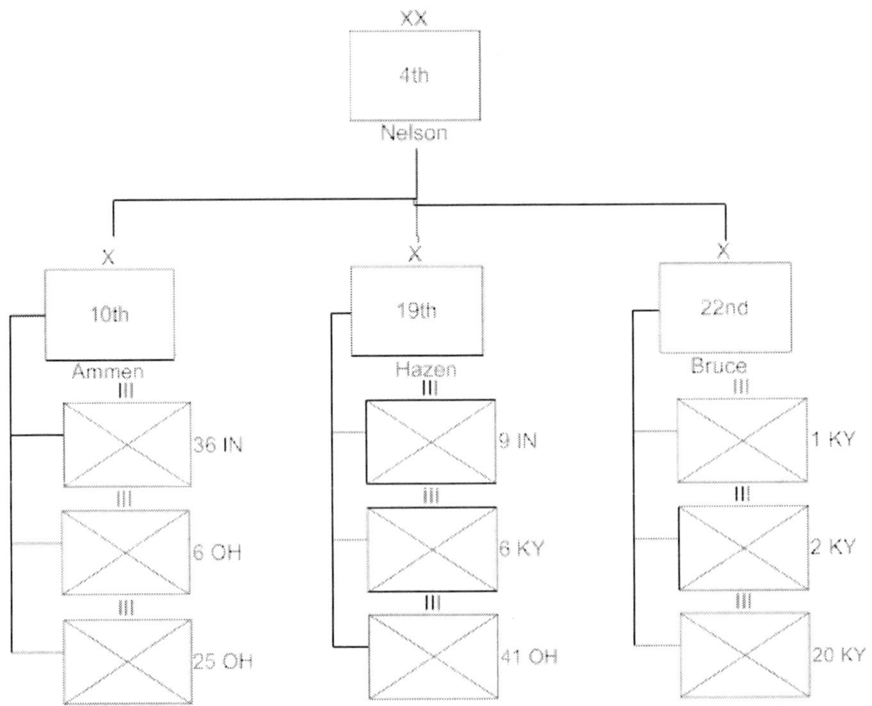

Figure 2-17. 4th Division (Nelson), Army of the Ohio

Thomas L. Crittenden of Kentucky was a prewar lawyer, politician, and a Major General in the Kentucky militia. He was a volunteer aide to Zachary Taylor in Mexico, and was appointed Lieutenant Colonel of the 3rd Kentucky (and was often in the rear with the gear on administrative duties). He was appointed Brigadier General and placed in command of the 5th Division of nearly 4,000 men from Kentucky and Ohio in Buell's army in September 1861. Crittenden was--like fellow Kentuckians Nelson and Breckinridge--a political appointee with lofty family connections to power. Amateur more than Militiaman, he had little leadership experience and no military training. Since he was loyal to the Union and from Kentucky his appointment, like Breckinridge's, was as much to appease Kentucky political interests as it was a recruiting tool. His command was likely thought at the time to have been for show, a Militiaman surrounded by Professionals, since "everyone knew" that the war would soon be over. Crittenden and his father, U.S. Senator John J. Crittenden, had remained loyal to the Union but George B. Crittenden, Thomas' brother, joined the Confederate Army. George resigned his Confederate commission just before Shiloh rather than have to fight Thomas just a few miles away.[26]

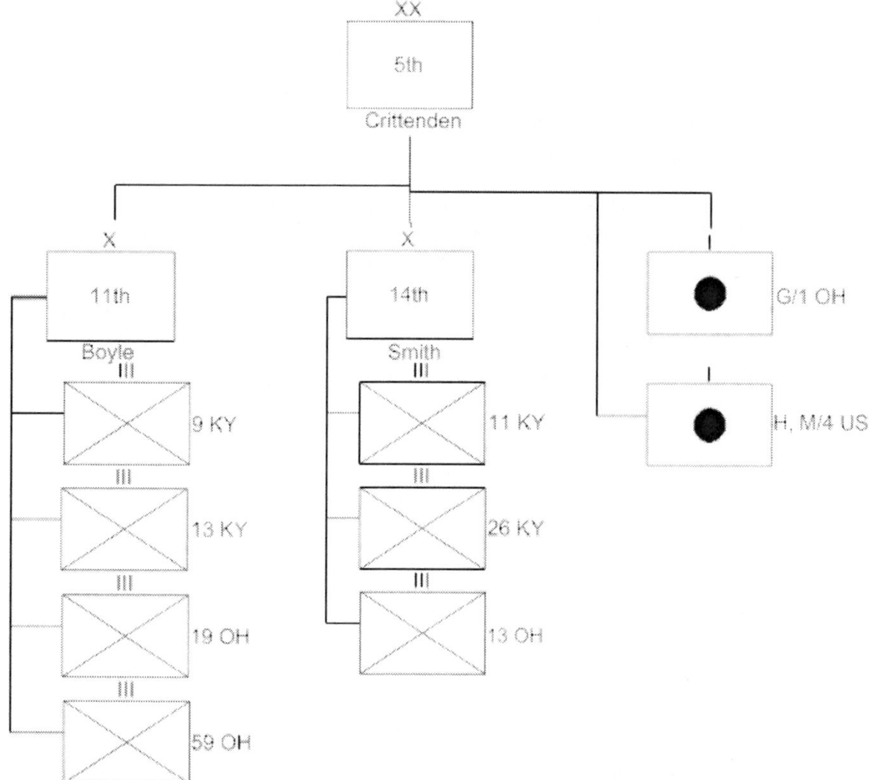

Figure 2-18, 5th Division (Crittenden), Army of the Ohio

---

26. Wikipedia.com, "Thomas Leonidas Crittenden," http://en.wikipedia.org/wiki/ Thomas_Leonidas_Crittenden (Accessed October 2008); Wikipedia.com, "George B. Crittenden, http://en.wikipedia.org/wiki/George_B._Crittenden (Accessed October 2008).

Thomas J. Wood of Kentucky (USMA 1845) was a Professional, a career Army officer who was first commissioned in the Engineers, joined Zachary Taylor's staff for a few months as the Mexican War erupted, and was cited for valor there. He soon transferred to the 2nd Dragoons, where he must have served with Hardee since his succession of cavalry postings in the West, including Utah in 1858 and Kansas in 1859 were practically a mirror to Hardee's. Wood traveled in Europe from 1859 until early 1861, almost certainly with Hardee, while observing the Piedmont War. By March 1861 Wood was Major of the 1st Cavalry. When Hardee resigned Wood assumed Hardee's Lieutenant-Colonel position.

When the war broke out Wood helped organize regiments in Indiana. In October 1861, he was appointed Brigadier General in the Volunteers, and given command of the 6th Division in Buell's army. Since Wood's antebellum career matched that of Hardee, they probably knew each other well. Their story of two long-serving Professionals who shared duty in the antebellum Army--and who ended up facing each other in battle--was not unique.[27]

---

27. Mark M. Boatner, "Wood, Thomas John," in *The Civil War Dictionary* (New York: David McKay & Company, 1988), 946; Patricia L. (Editor) Faust, "Wood, Thomas John," in *Historical Times Illustrated Encyclopedia of the Civil War* (New York: Harper & Row, 1986), 841; Wikipedia.com, "Wood, Thomas J," http://en.wikipedia.org/wiki/Thomas_J._Wood (Accessed October 2008).

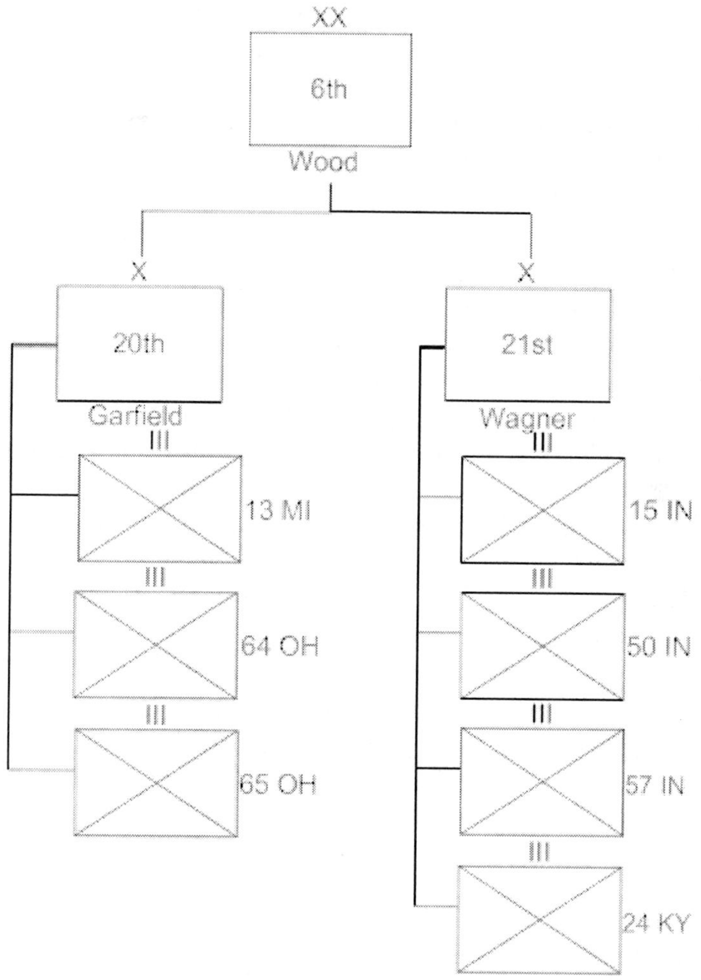

Figure 2-19, 6th Division (Wood), Army of the Ohio

Western Flotilla, US Army/Mississippi River Squadron, US Navy

The antebellum U.S. Navy was even smaller than the Army, with less than a hundred vessels to its name and less than fifty in floating condition. The Army realized early that if they wanted to float a raft across a mill pond they couldn't wait for the Navy to get around to helping. Thus, in the spring of 1862, warships on the Western rivers from converted ferry boats to the mighty *Carondelet* class gunboats, were bought by the Army and were under nominal US Army Quartermaster Corps control (unless the Navy claimed them). They also bought, built and contracted their own transports, supply ships, hospital ships and mortar vessels, using Navy personnel when they were available.

The first gunboats on the Western rivers weren't built for the purpose. *Lexington* and *Tyler* were two of the first three steamboats bought by naval constructor Samuel Pook, who was sent to Cincinnati by Secretary of the Navy Gideon Wells. Pook was to inspect them and *Conestoga* with an eye towards protecting the "city of stinks," Cairo, Illinois, from menaces just across the river in Kentucky. Thus was the handle "stinkpots" attached to wood-armored "timberclad" gunboats on the rivers throughout the war.[28]

Gunboat *Tyler* started life as *A. O. Tyler*, a sidewheeler launched in Cincinnati in 1857 for the Cincinnati-New Orleans trade. She sank in January 1860 but was back in service by 11 January 1861, when she was shot at by secessionists on the Mississippi. After the Army finished converting her she was 180 feet long on her main deck, could cruise at about eight knots, and displaced about 575 tons. John Rodgers, the Navy officer responsible for her conversion, asked that she be renamed *Taylor* after former President James Tyler declared for the Confederacy. Her name was officially changed to *Taylor* but few sources refer to her by that name, causing some confusion for later researchers.[29]

---

28. Ivan Musicant, *Divided Waters: The Naval History of the Civil War* (Edison, New Jersey: Castle Books, 1995), 185.

29. Charles Dana Gibson, *Dictionary of Transports and Combatant Vessels, Steam and Sail, Employed by the Union Army, 1861–66*, The Army's Navy Series (Camden, Maine: Ensign Press, 1995), 4; Paul H. Silverstone, *Civil War Navies, 1855–1883* (Annapolis, MD: Naval Institute Press, 2001), 119; Fredrick Way, *Way's Packet Directory, 1848–1994* (Athens, OH: Ohio University Press, 1983), 2–3.

Gunboat *Lexington* was one of several vessels by that name plying the rivers, and was one of two *Lexingtons* in Army service in the spring of 1862. Gunboat *Lexington* was a sidewheeler launched at Belle Vernon, Pennsylvania, for the Pittsburgh-to-New Orleans route that was sold to the Army practically brand new at the same time as *Tyler*. After conversion she was 177 feet long on her main deck, displaced about 450 tons, and could probably make about seven knots in calm water. At Shiloh, *Tyler* had six 8-inch naval shell guns that threw a 53-pound projectile with a two pound bursting charge, and a 32-pounder rifle. *Lexington* carried four 8-inch guns and two 32-pounder guns. *Tyler* had a crew of 67 officers and men; *Lexington* would have had slightly fewer.[30]

Gunboat crews typically consisted of a Navy officer as captain (and an extra watch-stander if he was lucky), a warrant officer or senior petty officer to oversee the big guns, a contractor-pilot who was paid more than the captain and half the crew put together, and a mixed bag of civilians and soldiers. The Navy was stretched thin and, in terms of trained personnel, the inland river gunboats didn't catch up for a long time.[31]

Commanding the Army's Western Flotilla by April 1862 (known as the Mississippi River Squadron by the Navy) was Andrew H. Foote of Connecticut, a personal friend of Wells and a career sailor who had spent a few months at West Point before signing on with the Navy in 1822. The senior naval officer at Shiloh was William Gwin of Indiana, another lifelong Professional who joined the U.S. Navy as a midshipman in 1847 at thirteen. Gwin's service took him to every major American station afloat in the early 19th Century, under sail and steam, paddlewheel and screw, ship-rig and schooner. He must have shown some talents for leadership since he was commissioned

---

30. Gibson, op. cit., 199; Silverstone, op. cit., 119; Way, op. cit., 284–5.

31. Silverstone, op. cit., 119; Spencer Tucker, *Arming the Fleet: US Navy Ordnance in the Muzzle-Loading Era* (Annapolis, MD: Naval Institute Press, 1989), 247.

Lieutenant at the minimum age (21) in September 1855. Gwin was one of Foote's more energetic officers, displaying initiative and dash. As the senior naval officer at Shiloh, Gwin's responsibility was easily equal to that of a division artillery officer. His two gunboats could throw more metal at once than all the army batteries at Shiloh combined.[32]

When Shiloh was over one of these men would be dead, another dying, one a prisoner, others wounded, and the survivors weary beyond words. One of the survivors would see that there could be no half measures in ending the war, and that the time for soft war had passed.

The campaign that came to this was put into motion from Illinois and Mississippi, Missouri, Virginia and Louisiana, far away from the fighting. Much depended on controlling Tennessee, but no one was sure what that would require.

---

32. Wikipedia.com, "William Gwin," http://en.wikipedia.org/wiki/ William_Gwin_ (naval_officer) (Accessed December 2008); U.S. Navy Historical Institute, "Gwin, William," http://www.history.navy.mil/ books/callahan/reg-usn-g.htm (Accessed December 2008).

CHAPTER 3
FROM CAIRO AND CORINTH TO SHILOH: FALL 1861/SPRING 1862 IN THE WEST

The Western theater had been relatively quiet early in the war compared to the noise along the Atlantic coast. Despite the huge army being built up by George B. McClellan on the Confederate capital's very doorstep, the Western theater was a matter of grave importance. Most people regarded the fighting in the West as "affairs of outposts," and battles such as Pea Ridge and Fishing Creek were simply names of places far away. The Richmond government knew the importance of the country west of the Alleghenies, and of the resources there. Despite this knowledge, as soon as Albert S. Johnston arrived at his command in January 1862, it started to lose both troops and territory.

Planners in both the North and the South realized that the Western rivers and railways were the keys to much of the country, and were the most important objects of military operations in the West. Shiloh was part of a two-year campaign for control of the Mississippi River, the main stream of a web of waterways that fed the commerce of half the country and encompassed at least a third of America's population in 1860. Lincoln had spent most of his life--and Davis had spent his youth--within a day's walk of some of these streams, and both were committed to their control.

The region bounded by the Cumberland River to the east, the Mississippi to the west, the Ohio River to the north and the Gulf of Mexico to the south was predominantly wooded wilderness with scattered farms and plantations, small towns and cities connected by railroad tracks, rivers or both. Most of the rail lines were of lighter capacity than their Northern counterparts, and the area boasted few major roads. When regions needed to connect with markets they built a boat landing if near enough to a river, built a railroad if they could afford it, and cut a road by default if no other routes were possible. Because of this, bridges were few and indifferently maintained, except railroad bridges. Though the Cumberland was easily bridged and ferries were common, the frequently-flooded Tennessee was harder to cross; the latter stream had only one bridge across its northernmost 120 miles in the spring of 1862, and there were few regular ferries. In severe flood years the land between the Tennessee and the Cumberland were one body of swampy water near the border of Tennessee and Kentucky. At one point the two main streams were only ten miles apart in 1862. Both the Union and the Confederacy relied on the rivers as transportation arteries, but only the Union had the steamboats and gunboats to exploit the rivers effectively.

Kentucky and Missouri--slave-holding states that never left the Union but whose sons fought on both sides--were vital to this region. Kentucky's northern border was the Ohio and Cumberland Rivers, and he who controlled them had access to western Virginia, Ohio, Indiana, Illinois and Pennsylvania. He who controlled both Kentucky and Illinois also held the gateway to Missouri, which comprised most of the western flank of Illinois, the southern border of Iowa, and a large proportion of the banks of the Mississippi. And Missouri was the gatekeeper of the entire western half of the country.

Lincoln persuaded Kentucky to try neutrality, but neutrality was fraught with danger: neutrality disputes had precipitated the War of 1812. The Bluegrass State discovered early that neutrality has to be enforced to have any meaning, and Kentucky lacked both the political will and the military forces to keep either the Union's or the Confederacy's armies out. When Leonidas Polk turned Kentucky's neutrality into a legal fiction, it opened the state up for occupation by both sides, and turned the Ohio River into an invasion route that only the Union could control. The sporadic early fighting there was small in scale simply because neither side had the resources in the area to do much more than turn Kentucky's neutrality into a polite joke without a punch line.[1]

Federal planners looked up the Tennessee River to the railroad junctions of northern Alabama and Mississippi. Capturing them would effectively isolate the Trans-Mississippi Theater, but getting there would be no simple task. The most important rail junctions in the area were at Corinth, Mississippi, and at Clarksville, Paris, and Nashville, Tennessee. Corinth was where the Mobile & Ohio Railroad connected the Gulf of Mexico with Columbus, Kentucky. Also passing through Corinth, the east/west Memphis & Charleston Railroad connected Memphis to Chattanooga, Richmond and the Atlantic coast. Nashville was the hub for the Tennessee & Alabama Railroad from Decatur, Alabama; the Nashville & Chattanooga from Stevenson, Alabama; and the Louisville & Nashville Railroad to Bowling Green and the Ohio River. Though it was nowhere near as busy, the Memphis, Clarksville & Louisville Railroad line between Clarksville and Paris, Tennessee was a vital link in the Confederate lifeline that crossed the only major bridge across the Tennessee River above the head of navigation. Until these junctions could be captured, Federal supplies would have to be carried by steamboat, which had never been done on such a large scale with a large volunteer force that had such diverse needs. Together, Corinth, Clarksville, Paris and Nashville were absolutely irreplaceable links for both water and land communications. This was where the Union Army began to split the South and secure its own lifeline.[2]

---

1. Force, M.F. *From Fort Henry to Corinth.* Campaigns of the Civil War, 24. New York: Charles Scribner's Sons [Guild Press of Indiana], 1881 [electronic edition 1999]; Nicolay, John G. *Outbreak of the Rebellion.* Campaigns of the Civil War, 135. New York: Charles Scribner's Sons [Guild Press of Indiana], 1861 [electronic edition 1999].

2. Black, Robert C. *The Railroads of the Confederacy*, xxiii-xxiv, 1–11, 140–1. Chapel Hill, NC: University of North Carolina, 1998; Cunningham, O. Edward, (Gary D. Joiner and Timothy B. Smith, Eds.). *Shiloh and the Western Campaign of 1862*, 31–2. New York:

Skirmishing on the Borders

Davis had charged Albert S. Johnston with holding the upper Mississippi Valley as well as Tennessee and Kentucky. To perform that mission Johnston had about fifty thousand men, most of whom had never heard a shot fired in anger, spread out over the better part of five states east of the Mississippi, and a few thousand between the Mississippi and the White River in Arkansas. The many garrisons, camps and outposts were too far apart to support each other as a true line of resistance, the army was too green to stand in one place for long, and equipment was too sparse to be able to do more than drill and withdraw.

Both Jomini and Carl von Clausewitz, the most formidable European theorists of the time, would have decried his deployment as insufficient concentration. While they may have been right for Europe, they couldn't have been more wrong for the Americas and the economic and political challenges of the Confederacy. More than just communications and invasion routes, central and western Tennessee contained important resource centers: the area produced half the grain, mules and hogs for the western Confederacy, 80% of the gunpowder and two-thirds of the iron. Confederate Secretary of War Judah Benjamin once wrote that his government was willing to abandon the Atlantic coast if it would help hold Tennessee. All the most vulnerable positions were within a few hours' steaming time, or at most a few days' march, of strong Federal forces.[3]

Savas Beatie, 2008; Diamond, Jared. *Guns, Germs and Steel: The Fates of Human Societies*. New York: W.W. Norton & Company, 1999; Simpson, Brooks D. *Ulysses S. Grant: Triumph Over Adversity, 1822–1865*, 110. New York: Houghton Mifflin Company, College Division, 2000; Sword, Wiley. *Shiloh: Bloody April*, 1–6. New York: Morrow, 1974.

3. Johnston, William P. "Albert Sidney Johnston at Shiloh," in *Battles and Leaders of the Civil War Volume 1*, 547. New York: Thomas Yoseloff, 1956 (Electronic Edition 1997 by H-Bar Enterprises); Jones, Archer. *Confederate Strategy from Shiloh to*

From the moment he assumed command Johnston was saddled with poorly sited outposts. Fort Henry was on the Tennessee River, fifty miles south of Paducah and 71 miles from Cairo by water. Fort Donelson was ten miles east of Fort Henry on the Cumberland River. It protected Nashville to the southeast, the rail bridges across the Cumberland, most of the communications with central Kentucky, and some of the largest supply depots in the entire Confederacy.

In far western Kentucky, where Illinois, Kentucky, Missouri and Tennessee were all within a few hour's steaming or a week's march of each other, there was real concern. Southeastern Missouri was a hotbed of rebellion, and Unionists there found themselves outnumbered early. As early as June 1861 there were reports of Confederate buildups in western Tennessee, and there were recommendations from Union authorities that the Ohio River should be secured by occupying the towns on the Kentucky side. Boldly ignoring instructions not to violate Kentucky's neutrality, Leonidas Polk marched to Columbus with 6,000 men, arriving there on 3 September 1861, where he emplaced as many as a hundred heavy guns and threw up an impressive earth work around the town.

The next day, Ulysses Grant loaded fifteen hundred men and four field guns on steamboats that included *Belle Memphis*, a 645 ton sidewheeler (also known simply as *Memphis*), and with gunboats *Tyler, Conestoga* and *Lexington* as escorts, went up the Ohio River 21 miles and occupied Paducah. A 3,800 man Confederate force started for Paducah when Grant landed, but turned back when Lloyd Tilghman, the town's commander, left with all the rolling stock he could move (yet leaving behind two tons of leather and some sensitive dispatches). With Charles Smith in command at Paducah, the Federals were soon digging in for a stay.[4]

Vicksburg, 51–2. Baton Rouge, LA: University of Louisiana Press, 1991; Martin, David G. *The Shiloh Campaign: March - April 1862*. Great Campaigns, 19. Pennsylvania: Combined Books, 1996.

4. Navy Department. "West Gulf Blockading Squadron from January 1, 1865 to January 31 1866; Naval Forces on Western Waters

Polk's force at Columbus was the closest Confederate outpost to the junction of the Ohio and Mississippi Rivers in the fall of 1861. It boasted the strongest physical position with the largest garrison in that part of the state, and was a day's march from the Federal base at Cairo. Johnston had his headquarters to the east at Bowling Green, Kentucky, a recruiting post and depot commanded by William Hardee that also guarded the route from Cincinnati into central Kentucky, and was a tempting, isolated target for the Federals. To round off Johnston's line, weak brigades and recruiting depots at Hopkinsville, Paris and Clarksville guarded the vital east-west rail line between Bowling Green and Memphis. All these outposts could be overwhelmed by bold marches; losing any of them could split Johnston's department in half.[5]

Over the next few weeks, Grant noticed a pattern in Confederate behavior. Repeatedly, Federals forces had attacked Confederate irregular cavalry and militia camps that had been causing trouble in southeastern Missouri, including a "three-shack hamlet" called Belmont just across the Mississippi from Columbus. From time to time

---

from May 8, 1861 to April 11, 1862; Series 1 Volume 22." In *Official Records of the Union and Confederate Navies in the War of the Rebellion*. 1987, 302, 317. Washington, D.C. (reprint Harrisburg, PA): Government Printing Office (reprint National Historical Society), 1908; Perret, Geoffrey. *Ulysses S. Grant, Soldier and President*, 137–9. New York: Random House, 1997; War Department. "Shiloh, Corinth: Series I, Volume X, Part 1." In *War of the Rebellion: Official Records of the Union and Confederate Armies*, 678. Washington, D.C.: U.S. Government Printing Office, 1911 (Electronic version 1999 by Guild Press, Indianapolis, IN); Way, Fredrick. *Way's Packet Directory, 1848–1994*, 319. Athens, OH: Ohio University Press, 1983.

5. Arnold, James R. *The Armies of U.S. Grant*, 38. New York: Arms and Armor Press, 1995; Beringer, Richard E., Herman Hattaway. *Why the South Lost the Civil War*, 181, 200. Athens, GA: University of Georgia Press, 1986; Cunningham, op. cit., 91; Johnston, op. cit., 541; Jones, Archer. *Civil War Command and Strategy: The Process of Victory and Defeat*, 51, 54. New York: The Free Press, 1992.

the Federals had occupied the place. Whenever Bowling Green or the Cumberland Gap were threatened, the Confederates stripped resources from the Mississippi Valley, including Columbus, to reinforce their communications with the rest of Kentucky. This led Grant to think that, despite its formidable position and earth works, the Confederates were using the 11,000 men at Columbus as little more than cannon fodder, making the place a depot and training center only. Since Grant had nothing but contempt for Polk and his second-in-command Gideon Pillow, Grant felt that he had to act on this surmise. The information his scouts were bringing him almost certainly confirmed in his mind the correctness of what he had already wanted to do, which was to advance. He had a tendency to be restless, and inactivity made him nervous.[6]

Grant's military information came from sources that ranged in quality and reliability that ranged from excellent to fraudulent. In Grant's time, the term "military intelligence" meant the scattered data that senior officers obtained themselves, often interrogating sources personally. John C. Fremont, Halleck's predecessor in St. Louis, had organized a small strategic reconnaissance unit called the Jesse Scouts that provided a great deal of information. Halleck kept the outfit when he took over from Fremont, and often shared its product with Grant, who also had his own small scouting group that provided some splendid information. All generals in command of troops had discretionary funds that they used to pay "spies" and other intelligence assets; in late 1861 Johnston requested a "secret service" fund from Richmond of $5,000.[7]

---

6. Feis, William B. *Grant's Secret Service: The Intelligence War from Belmont to Appomattox*, 33. Lincoln, NE: University of Nebraska Press, 2002; Nevin, David. *Road to Shiloh: Early Battles in the West*. Time-Life's The Civil War, 46. Alexandria, VA: Time-Life Books, 1983.

7. Dillahunty, Albert. *Shiloh: National Military Park, Tennessee*. (Reprint 1961), 2. Washington, D.C.: United States Park

On 7 November 1861, Grant took 3,000 men on steamboats to Belmont with gunboats *Tyler* and *Lexington* as escorts. Grant went there as a "demonstration" to keep pressure on a band of guerrillas in the area and to distract from another Federal column in the area. The small Confederate Belmont force was scattered by the first Federal volley. Polk, certain that this was a weak feint aimed at covering a bigger attack on Columbus, sent Pillow and about 3,000 reinforcements across the river. The Federals became vulnerable when they stopped to plunder the Confederate camps, and Pillow's arriving troops tipped the scales.[8]

Belmont ended badly for Grant, but proved part of his earlier theory: getting Polk to strip Columbus was easy It proved that his intelligence network was working and that his assessment of its information was valid, a gratifying moment for any leader: if intelligence does nothing else it can dispel uncertainty. Belmont showed Lincoln that Grant was a general who was willing to fight without complaining about the weaknesses of his resources, and was calm in a crisis and knew how to get his raw volunteers back under command when they strayed.. Halleck, reinforcing success and bold movement despite the poor ending of the Belmont affair, began to send Grant even more men.[9]

On 19 January 1862 George H. Thomas and 4,000 Union troops defeated 4,000 Confederate troops under George Crittenden that had been guarding a ferry at Mill Springs, Kentucky, on the Cumberland River (an action also known as Logan's Crossroads or Fishing Creek). This fight opened a route into Tennessee for the Union; only a few thousand Confederate troops and the unfinished Fort Donelson blocked the Cumberland Gap and the routes to Nashville and beyond. It also

---

Service, Department of the Interior, 1955; Feis, op. cit., 15–16; Navy Department, op. cit., 802.

8. Feis, op. cit., 41; Simpson, op. cit., 97, 100–3.

9. Nevin, op. cit., 46–9; Simpson, op. cit., 102.

made Richmond understand the size and perils of Johnston's department.[10]

So Davis sent Pierre G. T. Beauregard to Johnston. Beauregard, more than capable of taking some of the administrative load off of Johnston's shoulders, was ill by the time he got to Johnston's headquarters on 2 February. After looking around a bit he decided that the condition of the forces in the theater were beyond rescue, and asked permission to go back to Virginia. It was all Johnston could do to get him to stay, sending him to Columbus to help Polk.[11]

Johnston might have made Beauregard an army commander while Johnston himself administered the department. This would have allowed Johnston to concentrate on the administrative minutia that he loved, while Beauregard got to push the troops into shape, an occupation he was greatly enamored of. But once Beauregard said he wanted to go back east Johnston probably thought better of it. Giving Beauregard a substantial ground force might have made Johnston's bad situation even worse if he took part of it to Virginia, which might happen before Johnston knew it. Beauregard's transfer did get him out of official Richmond's hair: absent from Richmond he could be (politely) ignored, but there were many follies he could commit if he had too much authority.[12]

Beauregard was also a ready replacement for Johnston if the need should arise, even if Davis didn't trust him. Of all the senior officers in the Western theater, there were few available that everyone else would cooperate with, or that Davis knew and had confidence in. Most of the senior Union and Confederate leaders were in their positions because

---

10. Gudmens, Jeffry J. *Staff Ride Handbook for the Battle of Shiloh, 6–7 April 1862*, 44. Ft. Leavenworth, KS: Combat Studies Institute Press, n.d. [Electronic version downloaded 2008].

11. Jones, *Confederate Strategy from Shiloh to Vicksburg*, 53; Sword, op. cit., 64.

12. Jones, *Confederate Strategy from Shiloh to Vicksburg*, 53, 61; Williams, T. Harry. "Beauregard at Shiloh." *Civil War History* 1, no. 1 (March 1955): 17–18.

they had influence in the right places to get assignments. Braxton Bragg's efficiency at Fort Pickens in Florida was highly praised, and many thought highly of him, but Bragg was disliked by the other senior officers and, given his prewar reputation for pugnacity, he would not elicit cooperation quickly. Polk, another Davis intimate, lacked practical experience, and lifelong friendship with the Commander-in-Chief would not help an Episcopal bishop command the army tasked with defending half the country. None of the others had significant influence in Richmond. In the lofty world of Civil War senior command in 1862, influence was more important than competence, especially since the war was so new. There was no pool of experienced command talent to draw on at will, and there was no one else that Richmond would approve of. This was a common challenge of the time: the honor of command was a duty for willing gentlemen of influence who were known to the powerful; mere names on lists cleaned stables.[13]

The Confederacy was hoping the Union wouldn't take advantage of their perilous situation, or that they wouldn't notice. But the Union not only noticed the Confederacy's strategic problems, they took advantage of them. In 1862 they were in a position to exploit their industrial capacity and river mobility. The Confederacy could only hope to hold onto what they had.

The Drive South

Grant and Halleck knew that the rivers were indispensable not only for logistics, but also for morale and for regional politics. The Union especially needed to control the Mississippi so that the farms and factories of the Midwestern states could get their products to market.

---

13. Dickison, J.J., Clement A. Evans, (Editor). *Confederate Military History Volume XI (Florida)*. Confederate Military History, 21–41. New York: Thomas Yoseloff, 1962; Nevin, op. cit., 106; Wood, W. J. *Civil War Generalship: The Art of Command*, 126. New York: Da Capo Press, 1997.

Controlling it and its tributaries meant the Union could advance and, just as important, get home.[14]

In early 1862, Federal offensive plans in Kentucky and Tennessee had to be sanctioned by mutually-antagonistic generals: Halleck; Don C. Buell, then commanding the Department of the Cumberland just to the east; David Hunter, who commanded the western half of Fremont's old command when it split in November 1861, and who was losing men to Grant; and George B. McClellan, who became General in Chief after Winfield Scott retired in November. All four generals had their own ideas as to what was important, but two of them (Buell and McClellan) were good friends commanding their own armies in the field. McClellan was planning what would become the 1862 Peninsula campaign to capture Richmond and end the war; he felt than any resources that were not personally managed by him were wasted. In February Lincoln and Stanton relieved McClellan of the General in Chief's job, taking it on themselves for the moment.[15]

Grant began reconnoitering the lower Tennessee River in October 1861, using the timberclad *Conestoga* to look in on Fort Henry. After securing permission from Halleck to move, on 2 February Grant put a force of thirty regiments of infantry, a dozen light batteries and the equivalent of five regiments of cavalry (about 17,000 men altogether) on steamboats and took them to Fort Henry. Andrew Foote commanded the gunboat flotilla that included ironclads *Essex, Carondelet, Benton* and *St. Louis*--none of which had fired a shot in anger--and the three timberclads. After a two-hour duel between the gunboats and the flooded fort on 6 February, the Navy compelled the place to surrender before the Army's transports got there. While Grant was grateful of

---

14. Beringer, op. cit., 154, 237; Hunter, Louis. *Steamboats on the Western Rivers: An Economic and Technological History*, 20. New York: Dover Publications, Inc., 1993.

15. Dyer, Fredrick H. *Dyer's Compendium*. (Electronic Version 1996 by Guild Press), 255–6. Des Moines, IA.: The Dyer Publishing Company, 1908; Jones, *Confederate Strategy from Shiloh to Vicksburg*, 5–6; Sword, op. cit., 20–22.

victory, most of the Confederate garrison, including Pillow, escaped to Fort Donelson. A rather hollow victory for the Army, but one for the Union that no one could begrudge the Western River Flotilla.[16]

Grant barely paused before he had his men and a batch of reinforcements marching cross-country towards Fort Donelson due east, which the industrious *Conestoga* had been scouting since January. During a week on the march Grant organized 25,000 men into three divisions under John A. McClernand, Lew Wallace and Charles F. Smith, and was knocking on Fort Donelson's door by 12 February; hungry, footsore, cold and short on horses and ammunition. Fort Donelson was no pushover like Fort Henry had been: its 16,000 man garrison and batteries were formidable enough to give Foote a good fight that the gunboats ultimately lost. But the place had been neglected by higher command, and contained mostly sick and green troops. The Confederates tried to break out during a bitter cold snowstorm, and succeeded in piercing the Federal lines when McClernand had all but given up the fight. Smith and Grant kept the troops working together and held on until Pillow perceived disaster and called his advancing and nearly successful Confederates back. Grant used Lew Wallace's division to close the hole and, with that, slammed the door on the Cumberland for the Confederacy.[17]

---

16. Arnold, op. cit., 37–8; Dillahunty, op. cit., 5; Lanier, Robert S., (Editor). *The Opening Battles*. Photographic History of the Civil War, 186. New York: The Review of Reviews Company, 1911 (Electronic version 1998 by H-Bar Enterprises); Musicant, Ivan. *Divided Waters: The Naval History of the Civil War*, 191. Edison, New Jersey: Castle Books, 1995; Navy Department, op. cit., 372, 427, 534–5.

17. Cooling, B. Franklin. "Henry and Donelson Campaign." In *Encyclopedia of the Confederacy, Volume 2*, 766. New York: Simon and Shuster, 1993; Porter, James D., Clement A. Evans, (Editor). *Confederate Military History Volume VIII (Tennessee)*. Confederate Military History, 19–20. New York: Thomas Yoseloff, 1962; Wallace, Lew. "The Capture of Fort Donelson." In *Battles and Leaders of the*

With no chance of relief and little chance for another breakout, the Confederate commanders at Fort Donelson tried to negotiate their way out of their predicament. Grant's "ungenerous" reply to his old friend Buckner earned him the nickname "Unconditional Surrender" Grant--and brought him national attention. It wasn't the first time "unconditional surrender" was used in the war (the first was months before Fort Sumter), but it did have a certain harmonic with Grant's initials.[18]

In the ten days of his offensive from Cairo, Illinois, to that snowy day outside Fort Donelson, Grant never flinched, never took a step back and never hesitated in an emergency. He used surprise, economy of force, and units made up of the same green troops that McClellan chronically complained about in Virginia. He maintained communications with his superiors and yet, most gratefully for Lincoln, made no pleas for more resources or time. Grant was renowned in the prewar Army for his capacity for hard work, and was legendary for his loyalty to friends--Buckner had been one of very few intimates. When asked for routine surrender terms Grant replied promptly, clearly and forcefully that there would be no terms except unquestioning and unmistakable submission, and if that was not forthcoming, destruction would follow: Grant had the resources and the will to make either one happen.

The capture of Forts Henry and Donelson electrified the Union and shocked the Confederacy. The twin Confederate losses bagged thousands of prisoners, got Polk out of Columbus and Hardee out of Bowling Green without firing a shot at either of them, forced the abandonment of Nashville, and secured most of Tennessee for the

---

Civil War Volume 1, 406. New York: Thomas Yoseloff, 1956 (Electronic Edition 1997 by H-Bar Enterprises); War Department. "Shiloh, Corinth Series I, Volume VII." In *War of the Rebellion: Official Records of the Union and Confederate Armies*, 637. Washington, D.C.: U.S. Government Printing Office, 1911 (Electronic version 1999 by Guild Press, Indianapolis, IN).

18. Nevin, op. cit., 93–4.

Union. The ensuing Confederate evacuations cleared the Mississippi Valley as far south as Island Number 10. Grant and the Western armies were delighting the Northern press just as much as they were causing Southern anguish, and the successes were invoking Confederate demands for resources from all over the South and exhortations of heroism in official dispatches. In London, the price of United States securities rose with the news of Fort Donelson. A *Times* of London editorial suggested that the war could not last long.[19]

While Beauregard and Johnston were complaining about the loss of Forts Henry and Donelson, they were forming a plan to collect every Confederate soldier they could and smash Grant at the earliest opportunity. We can say many things about the Confederate senior leadership at this time, but Beauregard, especially, was not lacking in aggressive thinking.

---

19. Catton, Bruce. *U.S. Grant and the American Military Tradition*, 78. New York: Grosset & Dunlap, 1954; Cooling, op. cit., 767; Jones, *Confederate Strategy from Shiloh to Vicksburg*, 34; Lewin, J. G., and P. J. Huff, Compilers. *Witness to the Civil War: First-Hand Accounts from Frank Leslie's Illustrated Newspaper*, 45. New York: HarperCollins, 2006; Wallace, op. cit., 399ff; Williams, Kenneth P. *Lincoln Finds a General: A Military Study of the Civil War. Volume Three: Grant's First Year in the West*, 343. New York: The McMillan Company, 1952.

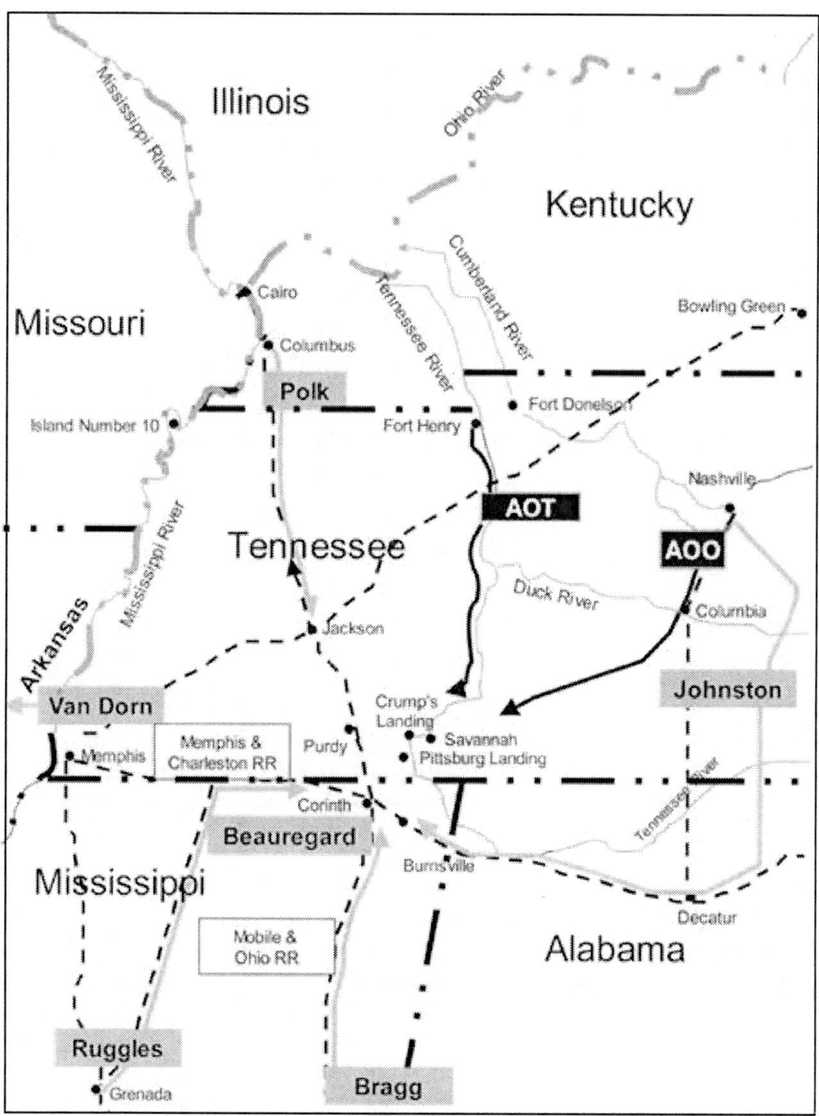

Figure 3-1, The Invasion of Tennessee

The Flight South

Matters in Johnston's area turned very ugly, very quickly, but it appears as if he and his senior officers knew exactly what Grant was up to and acted accordingly. As soon as Fort Henry was attacked and it was clear that Grant was going there, Polk and Beauregard prepared to evacuate Columbus, which would have been outflanked and isolated. Johnston got ready to pull back from the Bowling Green/ Clarksville/Hopkinsville line as soon as Fort Henry fell and Grant turned towards Fort Donelson, where Johnston had sent as many men as he dared. Between the fall of Fort Henry and Buckner's surrender of Fort Donelson, Federal gunboats destroyed the rail bridge over the Cumberland between Bowling Green and Nashville. While Grant was marching on Fort Donelson, Hardee fell back to Nashville.[20]

Johnston knew what Davis expected, and defended as much as he thought possible with a meager army. Johnston's overextension was required by Davis' "hold it all" policy, which led to the calamitous loss of most of Tennessee in a matter of months. At the time, Southern opinion held that Johnston and his incompetent subordinates lost Forts Henry and Donelson to the "drunkard" Grant, and he was cited for poor judgment and inadequate supervision by an angry press and an even angrier Confederate Congress that didn't question Davis' strategy. Federal command of the rivers was crippling, so what little Johnston could do to stop Grant was of questionable merit, given the strategic direction he had to work with. As long as Federal naval control of the rivers went unchallenged, the Union had an unbreakable supply line afloat. The Confederacy's naval assets on the Cumberland River were nonexistent; on the Tennessee, negligible, and on the upper Mississippi were little more than a few armed tugs.[21]

---

20. Jones, *Confederate Strategy from Shiloh to Vicksburg*, 54; Musicant, op. cit., 196–7.

21. Cooling, op. cit., 764; Johnson, Robert U., Buell, Editors. "The Opposing Forces at New Madrid, Fort Pillow and Memphis." In *Battles and Leaders of the Civil War Volume 1*, 463. New York: Thomas Yoseloff, 1956 (Electronic Edition 1997 by H-Bar

Johnston led the evacuation from Nashville himself, while Beauregard commanded the pullback from Columbus. Johnston first moved towards Murfreesboro and Chattanooga, and then cut west towards the Mississippi. Johnston saw his army not as one command but as at least two, and that he would personally command only part of it. He became a very senior traffic cop of necessity just so he could make forward progress himself. His inability to step away from the day-to-day demands on his time compromised his effectiveness, and was made worse by Beauregard's earlier expressed desire to leave.[22]

The department's logistical situation had gone from bad to worse. Men marching constantly without bathing, and sleeping in the same clothes day after week after month destroyed 19th Century cotton and wool fabrics quickly in any season. Foot gear, regardless of composition, could not withstand the brutal beating that the typical infantryman could give it for much more than three or four months. Nashville not only had two gunpowder mills but also a number of clothing factories and shoemakers. Losing Nashville meant the loss of manufacturing capability for uniforms and shoes that couldn't be replaced. Despite being generally better clothed than their eastern counterparts, Confederate forces in the west didn't have supply trains somewhere to the rear. Confederate quartermasters went to local businesses and either bought or contracted for the manufacture of what they needed, from gunpowder and muskets to shoes, packs and cartridge belts. But the Union's industrial organization and

---

Enterprises); McPherson, James M. *Battle Cry of Freedom : The Civil War Era*, 405. New York: Oxford University Press, 1988; Musicant, op. cit., 196–7; Walke, Henry. "The Gun-Boats at Belmont and Fort Henry." In *Battles and Leaders of the Civil War Volume 1*, 367. New York: Thomas Yoseloff, 1956 (Electronic Edition 1997 by H-Bar Enterprises); Wallace, op. cit., 399, 400.

22. Daniel, Larry J. *Shiloh: The Battle That Changed the Civil War*, 46–7. New York: Simon & Schuster, 1997; Johnston, op. cit., 550; Jones, *Confederate Strategy from Shiloh to Vicksburg*, 54; Porter, James D., Clement A. Evans, op. cit., 29–30.

transportation network enabled factories in Illinois to assemble powder from Connecticut, lead bullets from Wisconsin, and linen from Massachusetts to produce a million musket cartridges every month. The Confederacy had to find all of these in adjacent counties to produce perhaps a hundred thousand rounds.[23]

Johnston had shown great promise, but he was also a human being who saw responsibility and took it, even if there was little chance of success. Though he was a "friend" to Davis they were really just acquaintances; Bragg and Polk were closer to the Confederate president. He was lionized in the Confederate press very early, but they turned on him fast enough. His military record was admirable, but not marked with bold leadership.[24]

Although the prisoners from Forts Henry and Donelson were paroled without exchange, their equipment and supplies were lost forever. For the Confederacy, supplying Johnston's army was like making bricks with neither straw nor water; after losing Nashville, Johnston was even running out of clay. His senior officers pled for time, his army begged for food and clothing, and his superiors demanded action. He was under a great deal of pressure to do something to stop the Federals. As he watched Grant and Pope advancing towards him, he had an idea.

Cleaning Up After Donelson

William Sherman was at Paducah during the Fort Henry/Donelson campaign, forwarding reinforcements to Grant. He was restored to field command after Fort Donelson by his friend Halleck, who was probably influenced by Sherman's foster father, Senator Thomas Ewing and by his brother, Senator John Sherman. Grant and Sherman didn't know each other well in early 1862, but had formed a good working

---

23. Dillahunty, op. cit., 2, 4; Gudmens, op. cit., 31; Porter, James D., Clement A. Evans, op. cit., 29; Wilson, Harold S. *Confederate Industry: Manufactures and Quartermasters in the Civil War*. Jackson, MS: University Press of Mississippi, 2002.

24. Johnston, op. cit., 550.

relationship. Sherman respected Grant's cool head, and waived his seniority rights to take the field under the victor of Fort Donelson.

On 14 March 1862, Grant was promoted to Major General as a reward for his Fort Donelson triumph. At the same time Buell, Charles Smith, McClernand and Lew Wallace were also awarded two stars, though it took longer to confirm McClernand and Wallace. Grant took it on himself to venture to Nashville to meet with Buell, where they disagreed on where Johnston had gone and on nearly everything else. Buell was convinced that Johnston had gone south, and then cut west again to cover the Mississippi Valley. Grant chose to believe that Johnston had gone south and kept going, which would have uncovered the Mississippi Valley and left him a clear path to Corinth, Vicksburg, and beyond.[25]

Buell may have been a martinet but he was also a good military thinker with good information. He didn't think uncovering the Mississippi was in Confederate strategic plans, and didn't regard Johnston's two-step as a feint as much as it was an effect of either the shortcomings of the Confederate rail system or of Johnston's indecision. The layout of the Confederate rail network required non-direct movement, which pulled Johnston's army away from what intelligence sources Grant had left, but Buell probably had eyes on Johnston from elsewhere. Buell's information had a bulk of Johnston's forces using the Central Alabama Railroad which led to Decatur, Alabama, while only a brigade used the Nashville & Chattanooga Railroad that went to Murfreesboro to Chattanooga: Grant's information-gatherers didn't see the Central Alabama line used at all.

Buell's information was right, and while the movement confused and scattered Johnston's forces, it had the effect of a feint, and Grant bought it. After abandoning Nashville, Johnston pulled south towards Murfreesboro and Chattanooga, and then cut southwest towards Tupelo and Corinth. In the chaotic retreat, units boarded trains in Nashville

---

25. Feis, op. cit., 80–1; Porter, David D. *Naval History of the Civil War*, 152. Secaucus, NJ: Castle Books, 1984; War Department, "OR I/VII," 614.

haphazardly. While this route lengthened the movement a great deal, it made Grant think that the main Confederate force was gathering in Middle Tennessee instead of northern Mississippi.[26]

Grant's and Halleck's intelligence networks had gone blind. The Jesse Scouts were disbanded and the leaders sent to St. Louis under arrest just after Fort Donelson. The nature of a scout's activities was such that banditry was easy and tempting, and the Jesse Scouts' looting got to be too much to keep passing off. Johnston's movements were beyond the reach of Grant's other sources. Grant was also running short on funds to pay for intelligence activities.[27]

While Grant was in Nashville he sent regular reports to Halleck, but he didn't see them, and apparently didn't want his two principal subordinates conferring. Halleck relieved Grant of his command, putting Smith in charge of the army while leaving Grant in command of the district, a powerless post. There has been a great deal of ink spilled about this event, and scholars great and small have expounded on it, but it comes down to two facts: Halleck didn't like Grant's style and buried him with demands for more and more minutiae, and a Southern sympathizing telegraph operator at Cairo stopped Grant's communications until he was transferred elsewhere.[28]

Halleck was a dyed-in-the-wool professionalist who regarded Grant's "git'er'done" attitude as heretical, regardless of how effective it was. Halleck viewed the volunteerist traditions of Andrew Jackson as old-fashioned. Grant knew he couldn't build a European-class army while treating the volunteers like serfs, as Halleck expected. Grant was just not Halleck's kind of soldier.[29]

---

26. Turner, George Edgar. *Victory Rode the Rails: The Strategic Place of the Railroads in the Civil War*, 118–22. Lincoln, NE: University of Nebraska Press, 1992.

27. Feis, op. cit., 81, 87.

28. Gudmens, op. cit., 36.

29. Catton, op. cit., 80–2; Perret, op. cit., 177–82; Simpson, op. cit., 121–4; Weigley, Russell F. *Towards and American Army:*

Grant was deeply hurt by the charges Halleck brought, which amounted to insubordination. He demanded a full inquiry, using what influence he had in Washington to make his case. Lincoln, too, wanted to know just what was going on with his favorite general. Halleck found that he couldn't prove anything against Grant--indeed, he found just the opposite of what he had charged. As soon as he learned that Secretary of War Stanton was asking about Grant's situation, Halleck became conciliatory, even meek. Grant discussed this in less than a modern page of his memoirs. Grant wasn't in much of a mood to hold a grudge then; he had other things to do, but the whole affair almost certainly affected his later performance.[30]

The Theater of Battle

While Grant and Halleck were having their donnybrook, William Smith began the army's move down to Pittsburg Landing on the western side of the Tennessee northeast of Corinth. The area had a relatively recent history of settlement, though the Indians had been there since at least the 14th Century. A Mississippian culture built a palisade high up on the bluffs south of Snake Creek a century and a half or so before Columbus set sail, where some thirty burial mounds were found when Joseph Hardin surveyed the area that would become Hardin County in 1815. The Cherokee and Muskogee had been there for a time, and it appears that Tecumseh's armed neutrality movement from before the War of 1812 reached that far south from central Indiana. The Red Stick War of 1813 missed the area by a scant few miles; Andrew Jackson used the Tennessee as a supply route during that short conflict. It wasn't until 1816 that anything like a permanent white colony was established in the area, primarily on the eastern bank of the Tennessee, but time and population pressure pushed settlers across the river. A general store and a saloon were erected on the

---

American Military Thought from Washington to Marshall, 58, 80. New York: Columbia University Press, 1962.

30. Grant, Ulysses S. *Memoirs*, 167–8. New York: Da Capo Press, 1982; Simpson, op. cit., 124–5.

western shore and operated by a man named Pitts Tucker. Pitts Tucker's Landing became a popular stopping point on the river for the flatboats and keelboats that were common on the Tennessee, and it eventually became Pittsburg Landing when more families moved in and Pitts himself was forgotten. Hardin County's 11,000 souls were prosperous enough by 1853 for the Southern Methodists among them to build a log church atop a ridge some two miles south and west of the Landing that they dubbed Shiloh--the Place of Peace.[31]

Federal gunboats patrolled up and down the Tennessee and occasionally lobbed shells at Confederate cavalry patrols. They skirmished briefly with Confederate patrols at Pittsburg Landing in early March 1862, and destroyed a battery position there with landing parties. Halleck sent Smith and his division cross-country from Nashville to Savannah, which was about thirty miles downriver from the head of the Tennessee's navigation at Florence, Alabama. Smith finally arrived at Pittsburg Landing, nine miles downstream, with a division on 13 March. Lew Wallace and his division were sent a little further down the river to Crump's Landing.

Pittsburg Landing had more clear space for encampments and better water supplies than the busier river port of Savannah downriver, and that's where the army encamped. In the tangled wilderness around Savannah there was neither time nor equipment to perform the necessary ground clearing for 40,000 men. Grant was moving south;

---

31. Axelrod, Alan. *Chronicle of the Indian Wars: From Colonial Times to Wounded Knee*, 131–2. New York: Prentice-Hall, 1993; Haites, Erik F., James Mak and Gary M Walton. *Western River Transportation: The Era of Internal Development, 1810–1860*, 50–51. Baltimore: Johns Hopkins University Press, 1975; Hollister, John J. *Shiloh on Your Own*, 16, 30. Battlefield Guide Publishers, 1973; King, Duane H. "Cherokee." In *Encyclopedia of North American Indians*, 105. New York: Houghton Mifflin Company, 1996; McIntosh, Kenneth W. "Creek (Muskogee)." In *Encyclopedia of North American Indians*, 142. New York: Houghton Mifflin Company, 1996; Sword, Wiley. *Shiloh: Bloody April*, 115–16. New York: Morrow, 1974.

Pittsburg Landing was always intended to be temporary. In later years Halleck would criticize Grant's Pittsburg Landing choice, but both Smith and Sherman had recommended it.[32]

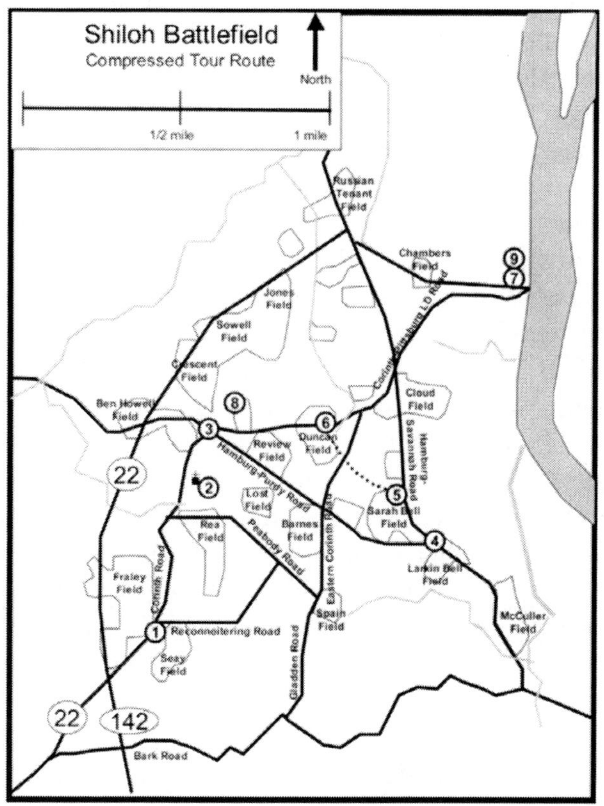

Figure 3-2 Shiloh Battlefield (Today)

---

32. Buell, Don C. "Shiloh Reviewed." In *Battles and Leaders of the Civil War Volume 1*, 490. New York: Thomas Yoseloff, 1956 (Electronic Edition 1997 by Guild Press); Grant, Ulysses S. "The Battle of Shiloh." In *Battles and Leaders of the Civil War Volume 1*, 466. New York: Thomas Yoseloff, 1956 (Electronic Edition 1997 by Guild Press); Nevin, op. cit., 104.

William Gwin commanded the flotilla of *Tyler* and *Lexington* which took Sherman's division on steamboats up the Tennessee to Eastport, Alabama in early March. Sherman was to march overland to cut the Confederate rail line at Burnsville, Mississippi. Heavy rains turned the roads into morasses, and there were no suitable landing spots for the troops. Frustrated, Sherman returned to Pittsburg Landing. Stephen Hurlbut's embryonic division was already there, still on steamboats. It took two days to disembark Sherman's outfit and march it to its campsite on the Shiloh Branch Creek, some two and a half miles west of the Tennessee River, by 16 March.[33]

Though deep in the Confederacy the eastern part of Hardin County, on the fertile eastern bank of the Tennessee, was staunchly Unionist and had voted against secession. The poorer-soil western bank was not as friendly to the Union, and local farmers were intelligence resources for Johnston. In Savannah, a prominent Unionist slave owner named William Cherry had a large mansion and a grudge against the Confederacy. He offered his estate for Grant's use, going so far as to send his slaves into Confederate territory to scout for Grant. All the able-bodied males the Confederate draft could grab had been taken away by early March, but further drafts were blocked by the presence of the Federal gunboats and the 46th Ohio at Savannah, which had no trouble recruiting about forty locals into its ranks, while Gwin recruited hands for *Tyler*. Both armies had Hardin County men in their ranks during the battle.[34]

When Halleck was rewarded with the supreme command in the West he had wanted, Washington combined his old Department with

---

33. Gibson, Charles Dana. *Assault and Logistics: Union Army in Coastal and River Operations 1861–6*. The Army's Navy Series, 78–9. Camden, ME: Ensign Press, 1995; Reed, David W. *The Battle of Shiloh and the Organizations Engaged*, 8. Knoxville, TN: University of Tennessee Press, 2008; Simpson, op. cit., 128–9; Sherman, William T. *Memoirs of General William T. Sherman*, 247–8. New York: Literary Classics of the United States, Inc., 1990; Sword, op. cit., 23.

34. Sword, op. cit., 115–16.

Buell's and gave the lot to Halleck. While Grant was not asking for any particular assistance or reinforcements, Halleck ordered Buell to march his army overland from Nashville to join Grant for a combined operation into northern Alabama. Grant wanted to move towards Florence and Corinth and the rail lines. Buell wanted to go up the Tennessee beyond Muscle Shoals--the rapids that stopped most steamboat traffic on the river--to Bridgeport. The two plans were not opposed; they had adequate forces to do either one or both, but their instructions had been to join and act in concert.

Grant's expedition competed for steamboats and gunboats with John Pope on the Mississippi, who was campaigning towards Island Number 10, New Madrid and beyond. But just being afloat wears out wooden boats, and *Conestoga* had to leave the three-vessel Tennessee River squadron for repairs in mid-March. That left only *Lexington* and *Tyler* on the Tennessee to provide protection to the fleet of steamboats working with Grant. There were probably over a hundred steamboats in the area from time to time, but the numbers are fuzzy (see Appendix, "Steamboats of Shiloh").[35]

The dominant terrain along the Tennessee River was mixed wood forest. The Pittsburg Landing area was relatively flat and marked by small hillocks and promontories only a few yards higher than the surrounding area. The region was overgrown with trees and brush, split by streams creeks and ravines, and patched with farmer's fields and the occasional orchard, cotton field and temporary swamp. Roads of variable quality criss-crossed the area: trails became tributary streams whenever it rained for more than a few minutes. A tree-covered rocky promontory locally known as Pea Ridge (where the Ridge Road on the western side of the battlefield derives its name) is about ten miles west-southwest of Pittsburg Landing, but it provided little in the way of advantage and was not a major part of either Federal or Confederate planning. Crump's Landing, downriver from Pittsburg, was isolated and small though it was the closest to the nearest known Confederate concentration at Purdy.

---

35. Musicant, op. cit., 210.

The landings were important to the local economy, for without them the small farms nearby would have been only for subsistence. Cotton fields, apple and peach orchards were closest to the best north-south road, the Hamburg-Savannah. This turnpike effectively split the future battlefield into two uneven parts, with the smaller part closer to the river and bordered by swamps. The major east-west artery was the Hamburg-Purdy Road that divided the battlefield into the surprised (south of the road) and the alerted (to the north).[36]

We know this now because the maps tell us. Before 1862 this kind of a description was a matter of lore and legend and a handful of sketches made from simple observations. Though people had been living there for a long time and the roads were well-traveled, there had been no good reason to map it formally. The kind of maps that armies needed to plan movement, especially to haul artillery, weren't needed until the 17th Century. Military map making was an art that all the cadets were taught at West Point, but there were a *lot* of maps needed in America, and southwestern Tennessee just hadn't been gotten to yet. The Army's Topographical Engineer branch was the *crème de la crème* of American military society, the original plum posting. Theirs was a combination of skill, talent and artistry, their work tedious and almost cabalistic. There were self-taught cartographer/surveyors, among them Joseph Hardin and Abraham Lincoln, but their work at this was crude in comparison to the precise topographical information that was needed to move armies that the legendary Jedidiah Hotchkiss (Thomas J. "Stonewall" Jackson's map maker) and others began to produce during the war. Both armies had better maps of the Moon than they did of the area around Pittsburg Landing.[37]

---

36. Daniel, op. cit., 107; Dillahunty, op. cit., 6–7; Miller, William J. *Great Maps of the Civil War*, 11 (map). Nashville, TN: Rutledge Hill Press, 2004; Reed, op. cit., 9–10.

37. Black, Jeremy. "A Revolution in Military Cartography? Europe 1650–1815." *The Journal of Military History* 73, no. 1 (January 2009): 52–4; Gudmens, op. cit., 33; Miller, op. cit., 4–6.

Nothing in the layout of Grant's camps betrayed any sign of organization, almost as if he had intended the camps to be indefensible. There was little thought given to connecting unit flanks, erecting field works, or clearing fields of fire. The regimental camps were scattered; from the outlying boundaries of the army's camps and pickets to the river was no more than four miles in any direction. The stream-split area restricted any movement as well as any entanglements could; the streams, woods, farmer's fields, trails provided alternate fields of fire and concealment. The road network in the area made it a good jumping-off point for future operations, but the terrain and camp layouts made organized defense in the event of a surprise attack problematic. The generals could not have made Grant's army less prepared for a surprise attack unless they stripped the men of ammunition and shot their horses.[38]

It has been said that both Grant and Sherman thought that a lack of entrenchments would serve to bait the enemy, that trenches could not be built in the area that would enclose the encampment, and that digging ditches would dull the men's fighting edge (even if more than half their army hadn't heard a shot fired in anger--ever). The position Grant would take in his memoirs was somewhat different: there he stated that he had ordered James McPherson, his engineer, to prepare entrenchments, but that the ground was poorly suited for it. Regardless, it must also be admitted that any entrenchment construction below ground in those conditions would have yielded nothing but mud holes that the troops likely wouldn't have used, and above ground works would have required more saws and axes than the army probably had on hand. Since "everyone knew" (including Europe) that the whole thing would be over in a few more weeks at most, no one was going to admit to being "eskeered" enough to resort to the spade.[39]

There was one exception: Tom Worthington, the colonel of the 46th Ohio, began to loudly complain about the entrenchment situation as

---

38. Williams, Kenneth P., op. cit., 333; McPherson, op. cit., 408; Reed, op. cit., 9.

39. Grant, *Memoirs*, 171; McPherson, op. cit., 408.

soon as he landed, even before he found out where he was supposed to go. Worthington stomped about the Landing demanding axes, picks and shovels so that he could dig his men in, and loudly directed other colonels, including some he didn't know, to do the same, pronouncing a continual string of alarms. Though he may have had a point, he showed little in the way of people skills. Worthington was West Point trained, graduating in 1827 and resigning a year later. He had served briefly in Mexico and his men liked him: since he had been governor of Ohio once, many had probably voted for him. Sherman thought Worthington an insufferable ass, and his peers thought him an eccentric, rude boor. His quest for trench-building equipment and a hundred rounds for each of his men at Pittsburg Landing went unfulfilled.[40]

Grant's camp was laid out in a somewhat rough triangle of about five miles to a side around Pittsburg Landing. One apex pointed north, and the southwest side (where the Confederates were) was scattered rather haphazardly with regimental camps. Sherman's division was one of two to the west of the Eastern Corinth Road that divided the encampment area nearly in half north-to-south. West of the road was John A. McClernand's division, encamped somewhat east and north of Sherman. Benjamin Prentiss's division, deployed to the east of the Eastern Corinth Road and south of the Hamburg-Purdy Road, sprawled to the east and south of McClernand. When Smith barked his shin getting into a boat in February 1862, few thought anything of it at the time. But tetanus and sepsis set in: after thirty five years of Army service, Smith had seen better days. Even though he was sick with a fever, William Wallace took command of Smith's division on 2 April. His command was the closest to the Landing, two miles north and a bit east of Prentiss. Stephen A. Hurlbut's division was encamped slightly south of William Wallace's and a little closer to the river, to the north and slightly east of McClernand.[41]

---

40. Daniel, op. cit., 136; Sword, op. cit., 126–7.
41. Dyer, op. cit., 480.

Sherman's and Prentiss's divisions formed the southern side of the triangle, and between them they didn't have a single veteran unit; some of Prentiss' men had seen action, but not as a unit. The only veteran divisions in the army were in Lew Wallace's and McClernand's, and they had been in but one campaign. All of Grant's divisions and brigades were in the process of being reorganized as they waited for Buell. Many regiments were not a part of any brigade, and thus had no higher commands from which to receive instructions--their orders came direct from their division commanders. Some units had only been assigned to their respective brigades and divisions days or hours before 6 April.

Grant's camp was ideally suited to resist a surprise attack by mostly green Confederate forces--it was hard to imagine and army bivouac could be laid out so haphazardly. Detractors of Grant and Sherman claim that the camp layout and the lack of preparedness was somewhere between incompetence and negligence; their supporters call their lack of defensive preparations a matter of convenience. Grant's deployments appear to have required liberal doses of hubris and arrogance, innocence and self-confidence, with a sprinkling of obedience to instructions. New York newspapers, working on their own information, were reporting that a Confederate offensive in the west was imminent. Neither Grant nor Halleck knew this, but they would hear of about it later.[42]

Grant was convinced that Johnston was cowering in Corinth. He also believed that any major Confederate attack would fall on Savannah or Crump's Landing first, but he also stated that the Confederates would not attack until 8 April at earliest. Exactly where these ideas came from is quite clear: his intelligence network before Fort Donelson told him as much, and his own desires confirmed this opinion in the absence of evidence to the contrary. An attack on Crump's would have been a very Napoleonic *maneuver suer de la derriere* that book-

---

42. Arnold, op. cit., 62–3; Horn, Stanley. *The Army of Tennessee*, 126–7. Norman, OK: University of Oklahoma Press, 1941 (Reprint 1993).

soldiers Buell, Beauregard or Johnston might have planned or even tried. But not so much Grant: he once stated that he had only ever read one book on strategy and that he had forgotten most of it. But the record is clear that Grant expected just that.[43]

Buell and his army left Nashville on 16 March, and by 19 March was at the Duck River, about 80 miles east of Savannah. The Confederates had destroyed all the bridges over the river, so for a week Buell's troops bridged it until William Nelson convinced Buell to try to ford it. By 29 March, Buell was again marching to join Grant.[44]

Before Sunday, 6 April Grant had reports of skirmishing with Confederate cavalry patrols and the occasional infantry formation, but he was unperturbed. At the same time he received reports of low Confederate morale, so as late as 5 April he reported no anxiety or inkling of an imminent attack to Halleck. In fact, Grant didn't much care what the enemy might do. This was unusual among Civil War generals who often saw threats where there were none, and was somewhat dangerous when deep in hostile territory. While he was not indifferent to or insensible of that which was going on around him, and he was very aware of Confederate activity around him, Grant had several priorities, and none of them was to prepare for a Confederate attack that no one expected in a war that all anticipated would be over any day. Halleck had ordered that a general engagement not be brought about, and nearby Confederate forces were not attacked because Grant was under orders not to. Grant didn't feel as if he had the latitude to be alarmed because men under clouds can't look for problems that they know are there. Still smarting after his brief removal from command, Grant probably felt that initiative had been stolen from him by having to wait for Buell to come cross-country before he did anything at all.[45]

Grant had a Confederate deserter in hand who spoke of a force of about 40,000 men in some 75 regiments under Johnston at Corinth. There were other reports that put Johnston's army at 80,000 and even

43. Grant, *Memoirs*, 171–2; McPherson, op. cit., 408.
44. Gudmens, op. cit., 50.
45. Nevin, op. cit., 105; Williams, Kenneth P., op. cit., 348–54.

150,000; all Federal intelligence sources concurred that the Confederates were starving and burning cotton for fuel. As early as 3 April Federal pickets and patrols had taken rebel prisoners who claimed large forces were coming up from Corinth. Grant's sources were giving him as good a picture as his raw intelligence could provide and it should have made him uneasy, but there is no indication that it did, maybe because he was new to intelligence interpretation. Still smarting from Halleck's earlier rebukes, and after days of torrential rains and a fall from his horse on 4 April, Grant was in no mood to violate his boss's orders forbidding any engagement before Buell arrived.[46]

Sherman showed an uncanny ability to look in the wrong place at the right time. He told his wife and his father-in-law in letters that he too was reluctant to react to any alarms, and was frightened of being accused of being unbalanced again and losing command for good. For that reason he remained adamant that no attack was pending, despite growing evidence to the contrary. On 4 April one of Sherman's regiments fought with over two hundred Confederate cavalry for more than two hours, and found large infantry forces supported by artillery to the west. Though Sherman heard the fighting and alerted part of his division, he rebuked the officers involved for forcing a battle that both Grant and Halleck forbade. On the same day another of Sherman's regiments reported seeing a large force of enemy infantry a quarter mile from his picket lines. When it was reported to Sherman, the division commander ordered the men making the report arrested for reporting falsely. When Jesse Hildebrand, his 3rd Brigade commander, confirmed the report after riding out himself, Sherman dismissed it as nothing more than a reconnoitering party or some cavalry with artillery. Some of Sherman's troops had been in picket actions on the 4th and 5th, losing three officers and fifteen men on the 5th. Sherman was more concerned for his detached and remote 2nd Brigade, encamped between Prentiss and the Tennessee and commanded by David Stuart. The Lick Creek that protected Stuart's south flank south had dropped three feet in the days before the battle. A quick reconnaissance on 5 April found

46. Simpson, op. cit., 128; Williams, Kenneth P., op. cit., 337.

no signs of Confederate activity in Stuart's area, satisfying Sherman for the moment.[47]

Grant inspected the camps every day and commuted back to Cherry Mansion every night. On 5 April he welcomed the arrival of Jacob Amman and his brigade of Buell's army at Savannah. Amman had been Grant's friend since childhood, and Buell's arrival meant that the weeks of waiting were over, and the offensive against Corinth could begin. If Shiloh had been scripted for the Marx Brothers it might have made for a good comedy with no blood spilled. But it turned into a tragedy of epic proportions when the green Confederate troops attacked a Federal position accidentally tailored, by their haphazard layout, to aid in the Confederate defeat.[48]

A Plan to Attack

Time was not the Confederacy's friend, and nowhere was this clearer than at Corinth in early March 1862. Beauregard was given the tactical command of the Army of Mississippi on 2 March, but there was very little of it to command. Hardee's 6,000 survivors of the Henry/Donelson campaign scattered around Mississippi, Alabama and south Tennessee were the closest. John C. Breckinridge had about 7,000 in northern Mississippi. Polk had about 9,000 refugees from Columbia in Mississippi. On 6 March Johnston sent word to all his major commands--from Florida to Missouri, and Tennessee to Texas--to come to Corinth.[49]

Earl Van Dorn of Mississippi commanded the Trans-Mississippi Department, a polyglot of competing districts and interests containing

---

47. McFeely, William S. *Grant: A Biography*, 111–12. New York: W. W. Norton & Company, 1982; Sherman, William T., (Brooks D. Simpson and Jean V. Berlin, Editors). *Sherman's Civil War: Selected Correspondence of William T. Sherman, 1860–65*, 196–201. Chapel Hill, NC: University of North Carolina Press, 1999.

48. Grant, *Memoirs*, 172; Williams, T. Harry. *Lincoln and His Generals*, 85. New York: Alfred A. Knopf, Inc., 1952.

49. Williams, T. Harry, "Beauregard at Shiloh," 18.

some 40,000 men in garrisons and outposts spread throughout Missouri, Texas, Arkansas and Louisiana. He was supposed to answer to Johnston but rarely did. As Grant was moving south in Tennessee, Van Dorn put together 16,000 men to invade Missouri. Halleck detected the move and sent Samuel Curtis and an 11,000 man Federal force to meet him. On 7 March they met at a place called Pea Ridge on the Missouri/Arkansas border, and the Confederates were routed by the next day. Van Dorn's army, short on everything but troubles, broke up. Johnston ordered Van Dorn to marshal what troops and supplies he could and come to Corinth. Van Dorn collected 15,000 in a couple of weeks and started east, but northwestern Arkansas had no rails or rivers to use, and there was little hope he could reach Johnston before Buell joined Grant.[50]

The Confederate posts on the Mississippi, had been under daily naval and land bombardment for weeks. There was nothing Johnston could do for Island Number 10, though he and Beauregard knew as early as mid-February what fate would befall that battery and the Confederate forces nearby. Johnston's response to their plight was to order them join the main force at Corinth. Since he didn't have rations or transportation for them by the time New Madrid was taken by Pope, this was a mere formality.[51]

While Pope drove south the Confederates around Corinth watched the Federal forces collect at Pittsburg Landing just a few hours ride away. No one there had a good idea of how the Federal camps around Pittsburg Landing were laid out, or what the terrain in the area was like. Johnston was especially anxious to discover if there were any

---

50. Connelly, Thomas L. *Army of the Heartland: The Army of the Tennessee, 1861–62*. 1995 Edition, 174. Baton Rouge: Louisiana State University Press, 1967.

51. Beauregard, Pierre G. T. "The Campaign of Shiloh." In *Battles and Leaders of the Civil War Volume 1*, 574–5. New York: Thomas Yoseloff, 1956 (Electronic Edition 1997 by H-Bar Enterprises); Beringer, op. cit., 130; McPherson, op. cit., 404–5; Nevin, op. cit., 101; Porter, David D., op. cit., 161.

breastworks in the Federal lines, and received conflicting information from the field. Prisoners reported that the Federals were not expecting an attack of any kind, but the Confederates could not be certain that this was true at the highest levels of command.[52]

To prepare, Beauregard and Johnston collected all the arms and ammunition they could find, all the artillery they could move, and built up a ration surplus for three day's marching rations and another to five day's in wagons. After Braxton Bragg arrived at Corinth with his 16,000 man command from western Florida on 1 April, Johnston was told that Buell had crossed the Duck River and was just hours away from joining Grant. There was yet another piece of information that suggested that Wallace was about to march on the forces at Purdy. At 10:00 on the night of 2 April Beauregard sent Johnston a note insisting that the attack on Grant come sooner than later and later would be too late. To do anything at all, Johnston had do it immediately.[53]

Next question was: attack with what? If Van Dorn could reach Johnston soon enough, the Confederates would have an overwhelming numerical advantage over both Grant *and* Buell. Collected together, the Confederate Army of Mississippi would have 48,000 or more men without Van Dorn, and more than 60,000 with him, a mighty host for that time in the war, in that part of the world. But waiting for Van Dorn wasted time, and everyone likely knew it. As long as the two Federal armies were separated, they thought the plan might succeed without Van Dorn, but there was no chance if the two Federal armies combined before they had Van Dorn with them.[54]

Johnston made a fairly simple tactical attack plan that was easy on green troops and new officers. The plan required a side-by-side corps movement with Bragg in the center, Hardee on the left, Polk on the

---

52. Daniel, op. cit., 125, 128; Davis, William C. *The Orphan Brigade: The Kentucky Confederates Who Couldn't Go Home*, 78–9. Garden City, NY: Doubleday & Company, 1980.

53. Beauregard, op. cit., 579; Gudmens, op. cit., 51; Williams, Kenneth P., op. cit., 354.

54. Johnston, op. cit., 550, 568.

right, and Breckinridge somewhere behind Polk and Bragg. Each corps would move in a compact column that was easily controlled by green officers with green troops. The key was to sweep the right flank hard along the Tennessee River to keep Grant from retreating across it, separating him from his river advantage.

Beauregard made a more complex plan. After moving into position south of Grant's camps, Beauregard required each corps to be spread out along a three-mile wide front, stacked one behind the other. Hardee's brigades, which Beauregard thought were the best trained, would move to contact at 3:00 in the morning on 4 April. Hardee would be followed by Bragg, and behind Bragg would come Polk; Breckinridge would bring up the rear with his reserve. Each corps commander in Beauregard's plan would be responsible for the entire front until his command was either destroyed or retired. Bragg, writing after the war, thought Beauregard's basic offensive idea to be sound, but his tactical plan was "simply execrable."[55]

Beauregard's plans were based on a map made by his engineer, Leon Faceaux, and based on the same information as those made by Johnston's engineer, Jeremy Gilmer. Both plans were made in an information vacuum: though the maps used were fairly accurate in gross features, they had as much topographical information in them as a gas station road map. Though they were generally accurate about general shape and layout of the roads and waterways, other terrain features were completely absent. There was no topographical information to give any impressions about elevations, none whatsoever about woods or clearings. The road network was completely distorted, and Grant's camp placements were completely wrong. Johnston's map had the entirety of the future battlefield in less space than a modern post card. While giving Gilmer credit for making quick work and

---

55. Beauregard, op. cit., 581; Ibid., 553; McFeely, op. cit., 113; Horn, op. cit., 129–30; Miller, op. cit., 11; Williams, T. Harry, "Beauregard at Shiloh," 20; Wood, W. J., op. cit., 126.

preparing at least something, it really didn't help Johnston and Beauregard in their planning.[56]

The army was to be ready to march by 6:00 in the morning on 3 April, moving over forty thousand men in 16 brigades (containing 71 regiments, eight separate battalions and 23 batteries in all, led by two full Generals, four Major Generals and 16 Brigadiers) twenty miles on the two main roads from Corinth, neither of which ran straight to Pittsburg Landing. A polluted water source at Corinth compelled the Confederates to leave some 7,600 sick behind (more than the strength of the average Union division, and more than Breckinridge commanded). Johnston also left a garrison of about 1,500 men and two batteries.[57]

On 3 April, just as the Confederate Army of Mississippi was moving out of Corinth, Johnston telegraphed a message to Jefferson Davis:

> General Buell is in motion, 30,000 strong, rapidly from Columbia by Clifton to Savannah; Mitchel behind him with 10,000. Confederate forces, 40,000, ordered forward to offer battle near Pittsburg. Division from Bethel, main body from Corinth, reserve from Burnsville converge to-morrow near Monterey. On Pittsburg, Beauregard second in command; Polk, left; Hardee, center; Bragg, right wing; Breckinridge, reserve. Hope engagement before Buell can form junction.[58]

---

56. Miller, op. cit., 11, Gilmer map.

57. Arnold, op. cit., 24; Daniel, op. cit., 121; Nevin, op. cit., 108; Sword, op. cit., 98; Williams, Kenneth P., op. cit., 338.

58. War Department. "Shiloh, Corinth: Series I, Volume X, Part 2." In *War of the Rebellion: Official Records of the Union and Confederate Armies*, 387. Washington, D.C.: U.S. Government Printing Office, 1911 (Electronic version 1999 by Guild Press, Indianapolis, IN).

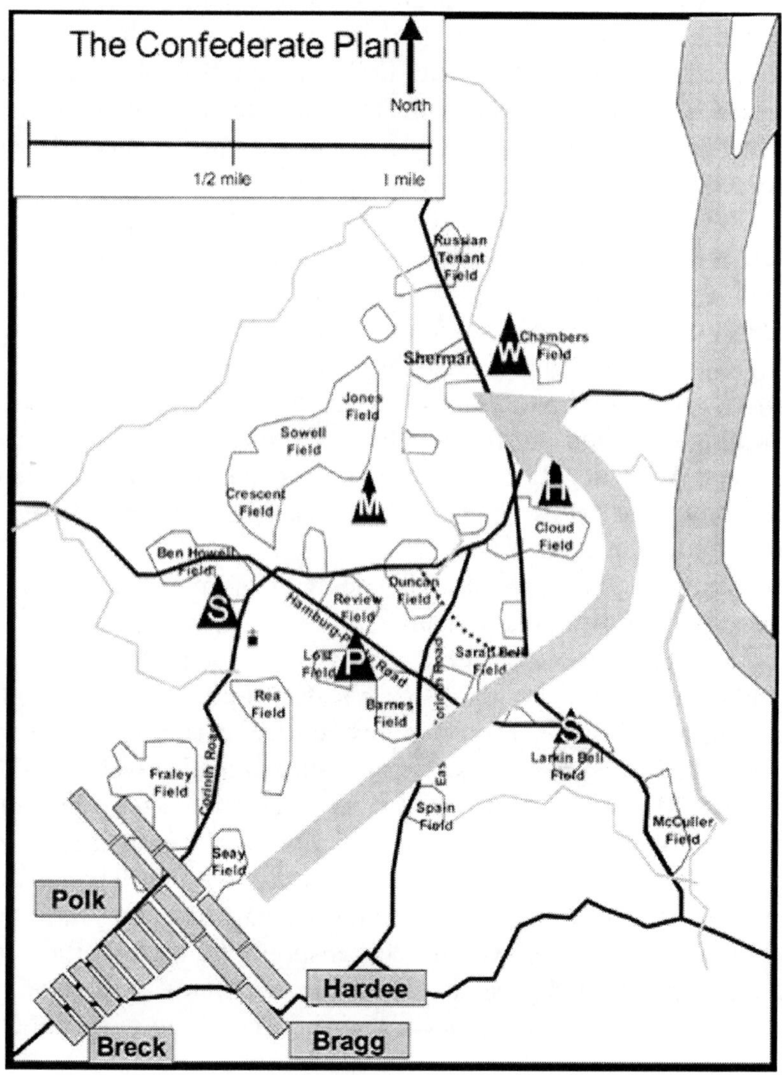

Figure 3-3, One Plan of Attack

"Mitchel" was a reference to Ormsby Mitchell, commanding Buell's 3rd Division of about 9,000 men; the "division from Bethel" was Benjamin Cheatham's; "reserve from Burnsville" was

Breckinridge's force. This message shows the mindset of the Confederate command before the attack, and describes Johnston's relatively simple tactical plan with Polk on the left flank, Hardee in the center and Bragg on the right, with Breckinridge bringing up the rear. It also removes Beauregard as army commander upon contact; Johnston, as department commander, would command his forces himself.[59]

The movement plan went wrong as soon as it was supposed to start; as soon as it was to start it began to rain. Some of Johnston's units had to march nearly forty miles just to get to their movement start points. The Bark, or Ridge Road, that ran north then east from Corinth carried a bulk of the Confederate forces north towards Pittsburg Landing. The other road, the Farmington/Monterey Road, ran from Corinth due east to Farmington, then north to Monterey and beyond, joining the Bark/Ridge road at Mickey's Farm (alternately known as Michie's Farm), some four miles from Pittsburg Landing, and less than a mile from the Federal pickets.[60]

Despite what Johnston told Richmond of his plans, the movement was based on implementing Beauregard's attack plan. Hardee was to march his four brigades on the Ridge Road as far as Mickey's, where he would bivouac for the night, but his start time shifted from 6:00 to noon. Polk's six brigades would follow Hardee, even though Bragg was to be next in line in the attack. Bragg's nine brigades were to take the Farmington/Monterey Road as far as Monterey itself, but in the confusion some of Bragg's command didn't get instructions to do anything at all until moments before they were to move. Though details are unclear, it is known that Hardee didn't start marching until nearly 3:00 in the afternoon, delayed by Polk's supply train moving up on the same road and jamming the streets of Corinth. Some of Hardee's men were on their feet just after dawn and didn't start moving until mid-

---

59. Beauregard, op. cit., 576.

60. Connelly, op. cit., 152–3; Daniel, op. cit., 103, 126; McDonough, James L. *Shiloh--in Hell Before Night*, 77. Knoxville: University of Tennessee Press, 1977; Williams, T. Harry, "Beauregard at Shiloh," 19.

afternoon. One of Hardee's regiments was delayed starting for two days.[61]

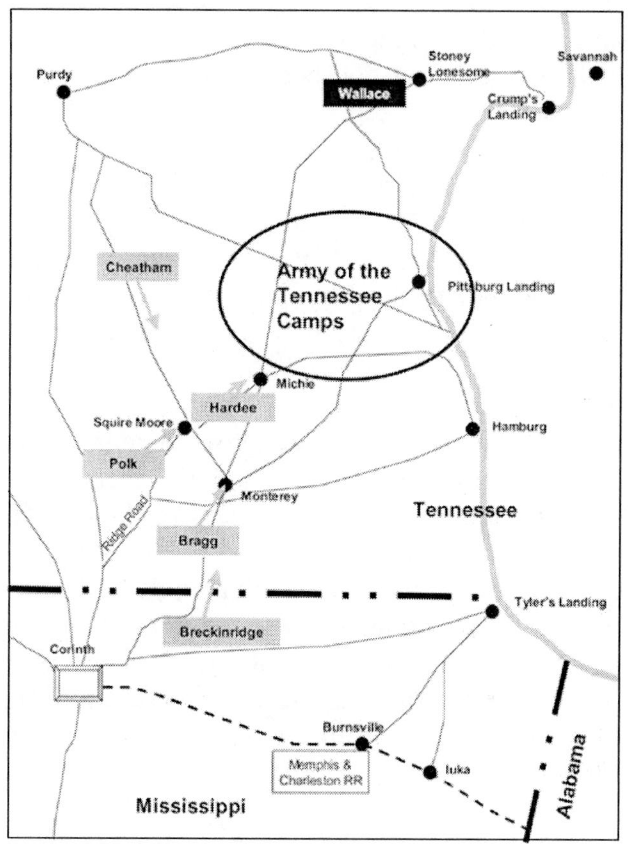

Figure 3-4, Confederate Movement Plan

Despite the difficulties, by the afternoon of 3 April Beauregard and Johnston were confident that the attacks could start on schedule the next morning. Some wagons and artillery batteries had already been on

61. Arnold, op. cit., 21; Daniel, op. cit., 122; Sword, op. cit., 100.

the move all night and were nowhere near their start positions for an attack that was to start in less than twelve hours.[62]

Delay followed delay. There were no guides in the area that could find their way around the rain-swollen creeks. As the rain continued, roads that had been rivers of goo became streams of mud where men drowned and animals broke legs trying to get free. Batteries needed entire regiments of men on ropes to pull the guns free of the sucking mire. The area around Mickey's became a shallow lake where wags dropped mock fishing lines. Scholars in the 21st Century would call this material Type I mud: a potentially bottomless non-surface that cannot support vehicular traffic. No force or cause on Earth could coax, cajole or demand that army to be into position on Beauregard's schedule.[63]

And the rain kept pelting down.

By the time Johnston arrived at Monterey, sometime around noon on 4 April, Beauregard's timetable was a shambles. Parts of the army were at least 24 hours behind schedule. Hardee was mostly in place, but some of his guns and a full regiment were still stuck in traffic and muck. Bragg's corps was hopelessly commingled with Polk's around Mickey's. Part of Polk's command was camping along the Pittsburg-Corinth Road on the night of 4 April after moving only about six miles. Breckinridge's brigades were in the sea of mud behind Bragg, reaching Monterey at about 5:30 in the afternoon of 4 April. Despite all this, Beauregard was reasonably certain that everyone was where they were supposed to be.[64]

At midnight on 4 April the steady rain became a torrential downpour. Even with at least half the army out of place, it was decided to attack at 3:00 that morning. When Hardee's and some of Bragg's

---

62. Sword, op. cit., 103–4; Williams, T. Harry, "Beauregard at Shiloh," 22.

63. Daniel, op. cit., 124; McDonough, op. cit., 79; Sword, op. cit., 86; Wood, C. E. *Mud: A Military History*, 5. Washington, D. C.: Potomac Books, 2006.

64. Arnold, op. cit., 20, 21; Sword, op. cit., 99, 101–2.

men were to start, the moonless, pitch darkness prohibited any movement in the unfamiliar area until at least dawn. At sunrise Hardee and Bragg pushed forward with what they could get into line. By 10:00 that morning they were within two miles of Sherman's camps and dueled with Federal patrols; the large skirmish that Sherman all but ignored. Since most of their artillery and their ammunition wagons were still back on the Ridge Road, an attack was deemed impractical and was delayed until the morning of 6 April. To maintain secrecy and surprise fires were forbidden, an order heartily ignored by soldier and officer alike. Some of Hardee's men built fires within 500 yards of Grant's pickets.[65]

Historians have called these delays both meaningless and crucial ever since. They were meaningless in a strategic sense since there was so little real success by the Confederates that one day would not have mattered much. But they were crucial in that the Confederate soldiers got very little rest in the three days before the attack, and more important got practically no food. The "three days rations" they carried were Spartan at best, likely amounting to no more than 2,500-3,000 calories altogether that would have been mostly starch and carbohydrates. Since the men had been on short rations for months it is far too much to expect them to have hoarded their meager food in three days of hard marching and working in rain, cold and mud. Additional rations in the wagons far to the rear required more men to pull with the horses, further straining resources.[66]

On the night of 5 April, the Confederate high command was in a quandary as to whether they should attack all. At a council of war

---

65. Connelly, op. cit., 155; Daniel, op. cit., 128; Davis, op. cit., 79; Martin, op. cit., 75; Sword, op. cit., 103–4; Williams, T. Harry, "Beauregard at Shiloh," 22–3.

66. Beauregard, op. cit., 587ff; Connelly, op. cit., 156; Daniel, op. cit., 129; Martin, op. cit., 90; McDonough, op. cit., 80; Nosworthy, Brent. *Bloody Crucible of Courage: Fighting Methods and Combat Experience of the Civil War*, 290. New York: Carroll and Graf Publishers, 2003; Sword, op. cit., 109–10.

Beauregard and Bragg both argued against attacking at all. The other corps commanders probably had some input, but we don't know for certain what it was. Hardee, the old Regular, likely would have backed the boss, but Polk and Breckinridge could have gone either way. Beauregard later denied that other views were either solicited or given, but since other sources speak of this session as animated it seems unlikely that all the others would have remained silent.[67]

Beauregard and Bragg argued that surprise was impossible. Some of Hardee's men had camped in the rain and mud within cannon shot of the Federal picket lines for two days. The Federals would not only have entrenched, they claimed, but would also have been reinforced. But the interrogation of a captured Federal officer on the night of the 5th indicated otherwise. Johnston, frustrated by delays and the startling lack of conviction shown by his senior subordinates, remained adamant. Turning back or not fighting by then was unthinkable. To retreat without attacking would have been disastrous to morale in the whole South, and an admission that the darling boy from Texas wasn't so darling. He may have had some misgivings about the attack, but he had already expended all his emotional and persuasive capital just getting this far. To dig in and wait would expose the largest Confederate force in the theater outnumbered, miles from its base and supplied by a miserable mud track. Johnston had tremendous confidence in the ability of his green troops and officers to shock-and-awe the also-green Federals to destruction, and regardless of how they were to do it the fact of the offensive itself was his main strategy. "I would fight them if they were a million," he traditionally told his corps

---

67. Beauregard, op. cit., 583–4; Lockett, S. H. "Surprise and Withdrawal at Shiloh." In *Battles and Leaders of the Civil War Volume 1*, 604. New York: Thomas Yoseloff, 1956 (Electronic Edition 1997 by H-Bar Enterprises); Johnston, op. cit., 556; Jordan, Thomas. "Notes of a Confederate Staff-Officer at Shiloh." In *Battles and Leaders of the Civil War Volume 1*, 598. New York: Thomas Yoseloff, 1956 (Electronic Edition 1997 by H-Bar Enterprises); Williams, T. Harry, "Beauregard at Shiloh," 25.

commanders: he was going to attack regardless of the odds, ignorance of the enemy, weather, hell or high water. "We must conquer or perish," Johnston is also to have said. He may have added, "Tonight we water our horses in the Tennessee River." Johnston's men were wet, tired, hungry and cold, and had been defeated time and again for months by a general "everyone knew" was a notorious drunkard. He would not let them down by just not fighting.[68]

A manifesto/order/declaration was to be read to the troops before the battle, inspiring them to fight well and succeed. It invoked the imagery of the "sun of Austerlitz," and as the sun broke on that Sunday morning and dispelled the fog some of the more erudite Confederates were said to have made a similar observation. On that Austrian battlefield on 2 December 1805, the sun shone brightly as the French veterans made mincemeat of the Russian and Austrian armies one at a time, and in so doing suddenly ended the War of the Third Coalition. Austerlitz is called Napoleon's greatest tactical achievement. But Napoleon's army had already won two other Coalition wars and was at the peak of its powers, whereas Johnston's army had never functioned together for so much as a dress parade.[69]

Johnston had decided that he was going to lead from the front, as any heroic commander would. One account has it that he ordered Beauregard to handle matters in the rear, moving supplies and reinforcements forward and the wounded and prisoners to the rear. Beauregard, who had been sick off and on for weeks before, said this after the war, but it doesn't fit given their working relationship. Another version simply has Johnston riding off to the front leaving Beauregard in the rear essentially without orders. A combination of the

---

68. Connelly, op. cit., 157; Johnston, op. cit., 553; Jordan, op. cit., 598; Sword, op. cit., 108–9.

69. Pope, Stephen, Editor. "Austerlitz, Battle Of." In *Dictionary of the Napoleonic Wars*, 76–80. New York: Facts on File, 1999.

two--where Johnston merely told Beauregard to assume vaguely-defined duties--is likely.[70]

Combined Union Army strength at the end of March was just over 637,000 men. Halleck had over 85,000 men under his command; just over 10% of the whole Union Army; Grant's 44,000 was little less than half of that. At the same time Confederate army strength was in the neighborhood of 400,000, making Johnston's army of around 44,000 at Shiloh somewhat more than 10% of all Confederate forces. Commanding such a large proportion of the Confederacy's military assets was a tremendous responsibility that Johnston did not take lightly. This was the first major offensive the Confederacy undertook in the Western theater, and was the first strategic offensive of the Confederate States of America. Because his army was so big, what he did in the first week in April 1862 would have an influence on everything Confederate between the Alleghenies and the Ozarks, whether he or Beauregard or his army or Richmond or Washington or St. Louis knew it or not.[71][72]

Any victory had to be total and decisive; it is unlikely that the Confederacy would have seen wisdom in a Southern army retreating from a hurt or withdrawing Northern one; further employment for

---

70. Connelly, op. cit., 158; Cunningham, op. cit., 150; Force, op. cit., 122; Johnston, op. cit., 559; Jordan, op. cit., 599; Sword, op. cit., 108.

71. Beauregard, op. cit., 583; Beringer, op. cit., 25; Cunningham, op. cit., 137–8; Jordan, op. cit., 596; Perret, op. cit., 187; Sword, op. cit., 107; War Department, "OR I/X/1," 385.

72. Dillahunty, op. cit., 9; Grant, *Memoirs*, 187; Gudmens, op. cit., 45; Luragi, Raimondo. *A History of the Confederate Navy*, 103–4. London: Chatham Publishing, 1996; McDonough, op. cit., 84; Musicant, op. cit., 122; Parker, William H., Clement A. Evans, (Editor). *Confederate Military History Volume XII (Confederate States Navy)*. Confederate Military History, 56. New York: Thomas Yoseloff, 1962; Porter, David D., op. cit., 176–8; Williams, Kenneth P., op. cit., 344.

Confederate generals who did so was not to be expected, especially those who had lost so much already. Johnston had gotten an unofficial letter from Davis, who was concerned about Johnston's situation and Davis' ability to keep him in place after the loss of Kentucky and Tennessee; and he wasn't sure if he could keep Beauregard in command, either. No matter what Johnston did, his career was doomed if he did not destroy Grant's army or Buell's, preferably both.[73]

The 600-man 47th Tennessee slogged through the mud up the Ridge Road on the morning of 5 April, arriving at Bethel Station from their camp of instruction at Trenton, Tennessee. They ate two crackers each (the same rations they had had since the 2nd), and bedded down at about 1:00 Sunday morning, without tents in the mud and the rain. Between them they had no more than half a dozen bayonets and less than a dozen military arms, the rest being sporting arms and fowling pieces. They were roused at 5:00 Sunday morning, ate two more crackers, and marched some more.[74]

For both North and South, Shiloh played out as an epic, unplanned-for tragedy, because this was a fight that both commanders and their armies simply had to win. No matter what else they did, when it was over one of them would be dead upon his shield, and the other would be carrying his in triumph.

---

73. Beringer, op. cit., 474.
74. Daniel, op. cit., 264.

CHAPTER 4
CRY HAVOC! PREDAWN TO MID-MORNING, 6 APRIL

Early in the afternoon of 5 April, James E. Powell of the 25th Missouri Infantry saw a dozen or so Confederates peering through the underbrush, watching the Saturday review of Everett Peabody's brigade of Benjamin Prentiss's division at the Spain field.[1] Powell had been an NCO in the Mexican War and had been in the Regular Army since. His unit was among the few veterans in Prentiss' division; they had been organized in 1861 as the 1st Missouri, and had fought in the Confederate tactical victory at Wilson's Creek, their one battle together. The 25th Missouri had joined Grant's army only two weeks before.[2]

Powell reported what he saw to William H. Graves of the 12th Michigan Infantry, the Officer of the Day (roughly the same as a Staff Duty Officer) for the division. Graves had been at Bull Run with the 1st Michigan and was disinclined to take any chances, so he went with Powell to see Prentiss. Though unconcerned, Prentiss sent Powell and two companies of the 25th Missouri out to have a look around. For

---

1. This narrative uses the currently common names for the fields around Pittsburg Landing where possible.

2. Kenneth P. Williams, *Lincoln Finds a General: A Military Study of the Civil War. Volume Three: Grant's First Year in the West* (New York: The McMillian Company, 1952), 357; William M. Wherry, "Wilson's Creek, and the Death of Lyon," in *Battles and Leaders of the Civil War Volume 1* (New York: Thomas Yoseloff, 1956 (Electronic Edition 1997 by H-Bar Enterprises)), 289–97.

insurance, Prentiss also dispatched David Moore and three companies of the 21st Missouri, placing Moore in command of the foray.[3]

At about 4:00 that afternoon, Moore and his patrol ventured into the heavy woods to the south. One account had this patrol getting as far as the cotton field maybe a half mile due south of Peabody's camp. Slaves working there reported a large Confederate patrol just hours before--likely one of Hardee's. Moore said that he went out about three miles and returned with the patrol sometime after 7:00, perhaps an hour after dusk, and reported no enemy activity. Powell was junior to Moore and thus was not expected to have an opinion, and is not known to have shared his thoughts. Prentiss went to bed believing there was nothing to worry about.

What Powell saw during the review that afternoon may have been elements of the 44th Tennessee from Sterling A.M. Wood's brigade, which was far forward of the main Confederate line for part of the afternoon of the 5th. A three mile straight-line penetration due south would have encountered either parts of Braxton Bragg's corps or the wayward 44th Tennessee. Moore may have gone south, then west, or southwest, but it's just as likely he got lost in the heavy brush, timber and deep ravines, marching around in disoriented circles that may have felt like three miles.[4]

Prentiss, like Sherman and Grant, convinced himself that the Confederates were miles away, cowering from the oncoming Federal

---

3. War Department, *Michigan--Ohio*, Official Army Register of the Volunteer Force of the United States Army (Washington, D.C. (Gaithersburg, MD): Adjutant General's Office, United States Army (Ron R. Van Sickle Military Books), 1865 (Reprint 1987)), 291; Wherry, op. cit., 289–97.

4. Larry J. Daniel, *Shiloh: The Battle That Changed the Civil War* (New York: Simon & Schuster, 1997), 141; M.F. Force, *From Fort Henry to Corinth*, Campaigns of the Civil War (New York: Charles Scribner's Sons [Guild Press of Indiana], 1881 [electronic edition 1999]), 119; Wiley Sword, *Shiloh: Bloody April* (New York: Morrow, 1974), 137.

forces. After days of patrol contacts with Confederate units large and small, Peabody wasn't so sure of that assessment, and earlier in the day told Prentiss that he wanted artillery to protect his exposed brigade. Despite the fact that Peabody's men were the farthest south of any Federals and out of supporting distance of nearly everyone, Prentiss said no; since he only had two batteries in his division, perhaps this is understandable.

On the evening of 5 April William Hardee's three Confederate brigades camped about two miles due south of Sherman's camps, deployed in a line roughly a mile and a quarter long generally northwest to southeast from the Howell field to about the Fraley field, facing northeast. On the way to the start line Hardee formed a two-brigade division of Wood's and Thomas Hindman's brigades, placing Hindman in command of it and putting R.G. Shaver in command of Hindman's brigade. Wood's 2,500-man brigade edged the Pittsburg-Corinth Road behind the Wood field; Shaver's 2,300-man brigade was on Wood's right with his right flank nearly on the Ridge Road Patrick R. Cleburne's 2,800-man brigade was on the left of this line at the Howell field, with a 149-man artillery battalion of three batteries under Francis A. Shoup attached to him. Hardee didn't have enough men to cover his assigned zone, so he had to borrow Adley Gladden's brigade from Jones Withers' division of Bragg's corps. Gladden's right flank rested on Lick Creek on Shaver's right. The 3rd Mississippi Battalion under Aaron Hardcastle was put about a quarter mile in front of Wood's brigade sometime after dusk.[5]

It can be inferred from his organization that Hardee expected either Hindman's division or Cleburne's brigade to make contact first, holding the enemy in place while the other swung around a flank: a

---

5. David W. Reed, *The Battle of Shiloh and the Organizations Engaged* (Knoxville, TN: University of Tennessee Press, 2008), 67–8; War Department, "Shiloh, Corinth: Series I, Volume X, Part 1," in *War of the Rebellion: Official Records of the Union and Confederate Armies* (Washington, D.C.: U.S. Government Printing Office, 1911 (Electronic version 1999 by Guild Press, Indianapolis, IN)), 607.

simple, straightforward holding attack that any lieutenant or corporal can understand, and was the bedrock of tactical theory for American armies in WWII.

At about 8:30 Gilbert Johnson, who had taken a company of the 12th Michigan--a completely green outfit that had not yet drawn ammunition--out to reinforce the picket lines, returned to camp to report hearing bugles and drums to the south and west. He and Graves went to Prentiss. Prentiss had orders not to provoke a fight, like everyone did, and told Johnson to withdraw his company. Johnson's force got back to the camp at about 10:00.[6]

Johnson, Powell and probably by then Graves were convinced that there was a large Confederate force in the area, and that the army should be alerted. If anyone could have saved Grant's army in the next few hours it was Everett Peabody, the former railway builder commanding Prentiss' 1st Brigade, a veteran of the siege at Lexington, Missouri and an impressive bull of a man. Peabody was simultaneously convinced of his imminent death *and* of an imminent attack on the Federal camps around Pittsburg Landing. The junior officers explained the dire danger they saw to him.[7]

Around midnight, Peabody ordered Powell and Johnson to find out what was going on to the south and west. It took until 3:00 in the morning of 6 April before Powell led about 400 men from two companies each from the 25th Missouri and the practically disarmed 12th Michigan out of the camp. As they disappeared south down the Seay field road, with dawn three hours away, Peabody bade them good-bye, convinced he would be killed that day.[8]

The pieces we have of this story form a fair picture of colonels who thought the generals were out of touch with reality. Peabody had no authority to send Powell out, but it didn't seem to matter. What Johnson was seeing and hearing was more than pickets and patrols: pickets don't have drums and bugles, and nearly everyone knew it. The

---

6. Sword, op. cit., 137.
7. Daniel, op. cit., 142–5; Ibid., 138–9.
8. Daniel, op. cit., 142.

colonels had seen heavy enemy activity, the generals had not. But colonels must remain silent when their views do not support what generals are told to believe.

Powell's patrol, moving southwest from their camps, encountered a picket force from one of Sherman's regiments somewhere near the Pittsburg-Corinth Road and received scattered fire. Picket skirmishing wasn't unusual; armed units on the edges of any army at war expect to get into a scrap about something, or about nothing at all, with desultory and inaccurate firing as a result. As the patrol moved just beyond the road they took more scattered fire from some scouts who moved off before they could be identified. Taking no chances, Powell formed his force into a line and moved south into the Fraley field, forty acres of cotton ground bisected by the west branch of the Shiloh Branch Creek. Powell's men kept moving south until about 4:45, over an hour before sunup, when they found Hardcastle's pickets.[9]

Powell's men heard three muskets fire, then silence. They returned a ragged volley into the darkness about ninety yards from the Confederates; the Confederates later claimed it went too high. Confederate riders dashed down the Pittsburg-Corinth Road to alert Hardcastle and Hardee. Powell's men kept moving until they encountered seven more pickets, who fired once and rolled back while the Federals returned with a volley and kept moving southwest. When the Confederate skirmish squads reached Hardcastle's main body, Powell's patrol was about two hundred yards away. Hardcastle's two hundred muskets erupted in the dank darkness, and were joined by as many as four hundred more from four companies of the 8th and 9th Arkansas that were moving forward by 5:00. Powell had to have known that so much firepower that early on a Sabbath morning meant trouble was on the way.[10]

---

9. Ibid., 143, 149; Reed, op. cit., 12; War Department, "OR I/X/1," 602.

10. O. Edward Cunningham, (Gary D. Joiner and Timothy B. Smith, Eds.), *Shiloh and the Western Campaign of 1862* (New York: Savas Beatie, 2008), 146, 148–9; John J. Hollister, *Shiloh on Your Own*

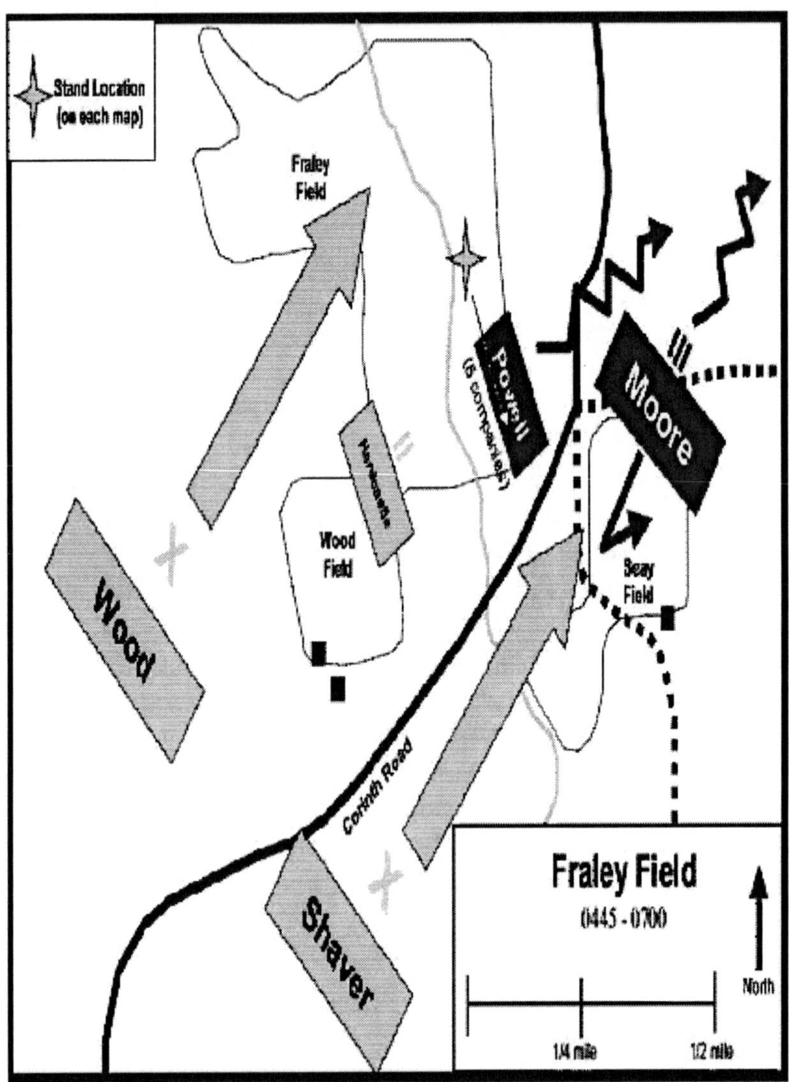

Figure 4-1, Powell's Patrol

(Battlefield Guide Publishers, 1973), 18; War Department, "OR I/X/1," 577, 591, 603.

Hardee's main force was in action within minutes of Hardcastle's first contact because his corps was in starting position and more or less ready to advance. When the shooting started before 5:00 it was as unexpected, and as unwelcome, for the Confederates as it was for the Federals. Since the Confederate attack wasn't to start until after 6:00 Hardee, with concern for his men, wanted to wait until the last possible moment to rouse his wet, tired, hungry corps. Beauregard later claimed that the action commenced as planned.[11]

Having the initiative also means knowing what's going on. The Confederates had a goal, and the Federals were still trying to figure out what all the fuss was about. Thus, back in Federal camps the situation was unclear. Peabody could hear the firing, but likely wanted to think it was only a picket action. Prentiss rode into the 21st Missouri's camp, probably no later than 5:30 when it was just getting light and angrily demanded to know what the shooting was about. When Peabody said he had sent out a patrol, Prentiss stormed at his subordinate for precipitating an attack, but sent Moore and five companies of the 21st Missouri out to support Powell. While shamelessly shifting blame, Prentiss was no fool.[12]

By 6:00, a full hour into the battle, Powell could see the rest of Hardee's corps, and sent word back to Peabody that he was engaging a force of some 3,000. Sunrise at 6:16 lifted some fog, revealing even more Confederates moving towards the Federal camps. Powell spotted some mounted men working their way around his left flank; these may have been mounted scouts looking for an artillery route, or Bragg's chief engineer scouting the terrain. Doubtless sensing he was in too

---

11. Pierre G. T. Beauregard, "The Campaign of Shiloh," in *Battles and Leaders of the Civil War Volume 1* (New York: Thomas Yoseloff, 1956 (Electronic Edition 1997 by H-Bar Enterprises)), 586; Force, op. cit., 124; Sword, op. cit., 142–44.

12. James R. Arnold, *The Armies of U.S. Grant* (New York: Arms and Armor Press, 1995), 61; James R. Arnold, *Shiloh 1862: The Death of Innocence* (Oxford, England: Osprey Publishing, LTD., 1998), 32; Cunningham, op. cit., 153–4.

deep already, Powell had the bugler sound retreat. Marshall Woodyard, commanding another part of the 21st Missouri, was left alone in the Seay cotton field, but was soon joined by five companies of the 16th Wisconsin that had been on picket duty.[13]

At about 6:30 Powell found Moore. Enraged, Moore relieved Powell and ordered the able-bodied of his command to join him in "licking" the Confederate "skirmishers." They were joined by Woodyard's force at the northwest corner of the Seay field. By this time the Federal patrol was nearly two regiments strong, and included nearly all of the 21st Missouri. Near 7:00 Moore ordered the men to dismantle a rail fence to facilitate a charge against an enemy he could not see through fog and dense brush. As the Federals went into line heavy fire erupted from the southern edge of the field and a ball shattered Moore's right leg below the knee. Powell took command again and ordered the men back northeast.[14]

By this time Prentiss' picket force was hotly engaged with a force three times their size. When Peabody heard the firing he may have thought his prophecy of doom was coming true, and ordered the drummers to sound the long roll--the infantry's signal to form up--shortly after 7:00. Both the 12th Michigan and the remainder of the 21st Missouri responded, but the other half of the 16th Wisconsin, some distance away, did not. Prentiss, shaking out the rest of his division, sent word to the other division commanders that he seemed to be under attack. By the time Powell's survivors reached the division camps, Peabody's brigade was formed up about a hundred yards southwest of their company streets.[15]

---

13. Daniel, op. cit., 144, 149, 150; Hollister, op. cit., 20; S. H. Lockett, "Surprise and Withdrawal at Shiloh," in *Battles and Leaders of the Civil War Volume 1* (New York: Thomas Yoseloff, 1956 (Electronic Edition 1997 by H-Bar Enterprises)), 604.

14. Cunningham, op. cit., 151–3; Daniel, op. cit., 147–8; Williams, op. cit., 357.

15. Daniel, op. cit., 145, 147; Sword, op. cit., 151; Williams, op. cit., 368.

Prentiss, the career militiaman, had two organized brigades, two artillery batteries, two battalions of cavalry, and another infantry regiment submitting morning reports to him. With no command staff to speak of, he had to personally direct all seven of them. Any order he gave had to be either written out or dictated and sent to seven different places, provided he could find someone to go. With green troops this made for a real control issue. Traditionally, another four infantry regiments and another four artillery batteries were also "assigned," to his division, but were not with him early Sunday morning. Three of the infantry outfits landed from steamboats as the battle was beginning (and two never made it to him), the extra artillery was sent elsewhere, and the one infantry regiment that did arrive didn't have all its equipment. All in all, Ben Prentiss started his battle against a quarter of Johnston's army with less than half his assigned units under his direct command.[16]

Some authorities have dismissed the early surprise caused by Powell's patrol as irrelevant; some have claimed it was crucial. The truth, as always, is somewhere in between, since neither side was really ready for the day's events.

But the battle had begun.

Prentiss' First Battle

On Sunday morning Peabody's brigade was encamped four hundred yards south of the Barnes field on the west side of the Eastern Corinth Road. Madison Miller's 2nd Brigade of three regiments pitched their tents on the east side of the Eastern Corinth Road, east-northeast of Peabody. This slight gap saved much of Miller's command for the next few hours. The cavalry and the artillery, as per tradition, were encamped behind (to the north of) the infantry camps.[17]

By 7:30, Peabody formed a line about 400 yards wide southeast of the Rea (also Rhea) field. The 25th Missouri--at least half the Federal

---

16. Reed, op. cit., 58–9; War Department, "OR I/X/1," 280, 282, 283, 284, 285.

17. Daniel, op. cit., 146 (map), 320; Reed, op. cit., 58–9.

line--was made up of recently-organized former Regulars, veterans of "bleeding Kansas" and Indian campaigns who had been discharged before 1860, and volunteered in Kansas City and St. Joseph as the national crisis deepened. As Woodyard's survivors came in on their left flank to extended Peabody's line, the 55th Tennessee and 3rd Mississippi Battalion of Wood's brigade broke out of the tree line in front of them. The Tennessee regiment had been organized less than three months before; the Mississippi battalion was only four months old, and Hardcastle had become separated from it. Robert T. Van Horn of the 25th Missouri gave the order to his men to open fire, and the Federal line exploded in a cloud of lead and smoke that filled the 125 yards of wet morning air between the two forces.[18]

The Federals likely delivered a very dense blast of balls that arrived at their two hundred-yard wide target in the space between an arm's length over the target's heads and about their knees. The Federal line was twice the width of the Confederate, which would have made the Federal volley very dense. Any low-flying balls would have bounced obliquely off the ground and made secondary projectiles out of almost anything: at 125 yards a clod of mud thrown up by an errant bullet would cause a painful abrasion at minimum. Henry Stanley, then a private in the 6th Arkansas in Shaver's brigade, and who would later presume to find Dr. Livingstone in Africa, later described being on the receiving end of a volley like this as "a mountain had been upheaved, with huge rocks tumbling down the slope."[19]

The Confederates *at that instant* had to make a very human, biology-based choice that everyone who has ever fought in open battle *must* make; a choice that has nothing to do with causes or comrades, hearths or homes or speeches: the choice to fight or to flee. The Mississippians and Tennesseans streamed for the rear, stampeding

---

18. Daniel, op. cit., 151; Sword, op. cit., 152; Williams, op. cit., 368.

19. Arnold, *Shiloh*, 32; Daniel, op. cit., 151; Paddy Griffith, *Battle Tactics of the Civil War* (Mansfield, England: Fieldbooks, 1986), 36–39; Sword, op. cit., 154.

Shaver's right wing outfit, the 7th Arkansas. Hardee's tactical alignment vanished; with Wood out of the line there was practically no connection between Hardee's flanks. Shaver's officers managed to get their people moving forward again while others, including Wood and Albert Johnston himself, tried to get the panicked men back into line. The rest of Hindman's division of about 2,200 men marched to within 75 yards of Peabody's position before they opened fire. The effect was as devastating as it could have been, dropping Peabody's people in windrows as they had to make that same fight-or-flee decision: with their comfortable camps behind them, for the most part the Federals fought.

Charles Swett's Mississippi Light Artillery (also called the Warren Light Artillery), a battery containing four 6-pounder smoothbore cannon and two 12-pounder howitzers, deployed on Shaver's right and opened fire. Swett's guns could deliver 48 pounds of screaming iron with a battery volley, blasting through troops, tents and trees alike, and tearing up the ground in great clouds of dust and flying fragments. If they were brave and had the resources, the gunners could stuff the tubes almost to the muzzle with whatever they could find that would draw blood. A well-drilled gun crew could fire about every 45 seconds under combat conditions; even this small battery could shred an infantry company every half minute. Because of this destructive power, Swett's gunners became the main targets for every Federal who could see them. The battery had 13 men killed and wounded and lost 11 horses before Hardee and Hindman got them to pull back. Despite Swett's withdrawal, Peabody's brigade was gradually being outflanked by Shaver's regrouped brigade, and began to creep northeast towards the brigade camps under terrific pressure to their front.[20]

---

20. Daniel, op. cit., 151, 152; David G. Martin, *The Shiloh Campaign: March - April 1862*, Great Campaigns (Pennsylvania: Combined Books, 1996), 54; Sword, op. cit., 151, 153, 154; George F. Witham, *Shiloh, Shells and Artillery Units* (Memphis, TN: Riverside Press, 1980), 70.

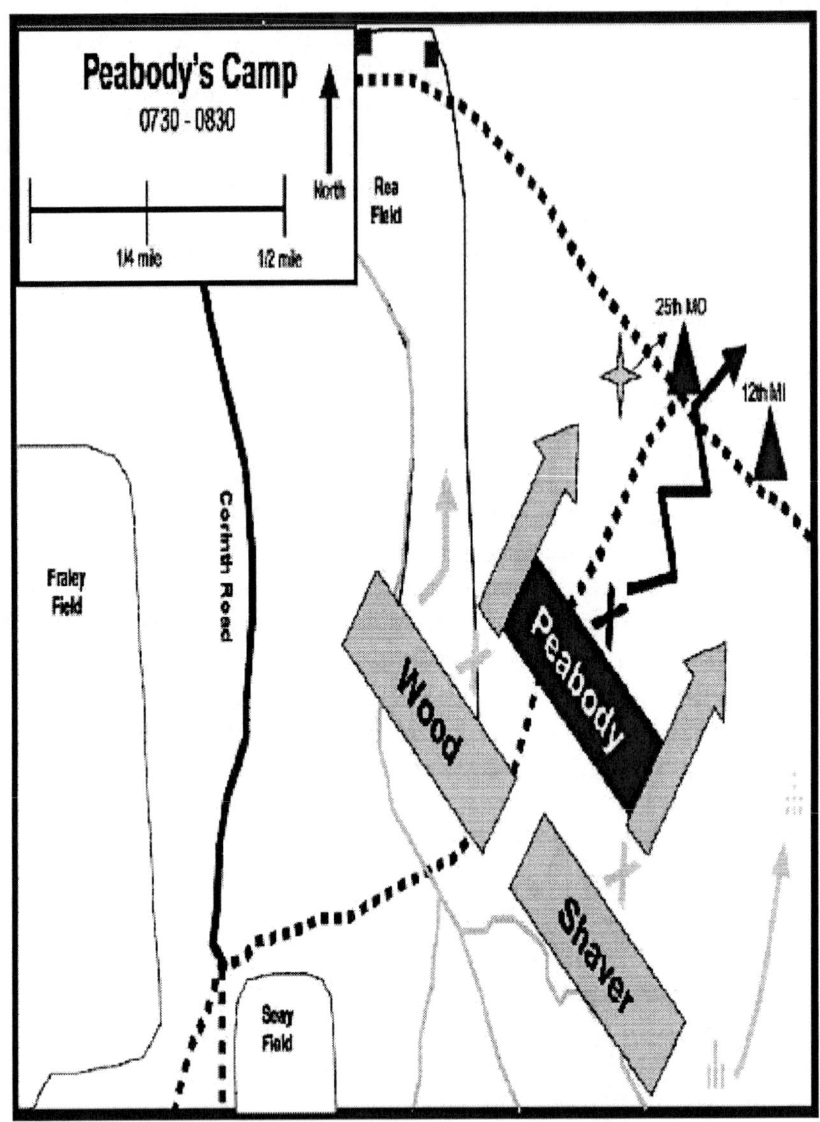

Figure 4-2, Prentiss' First Line

Prentiss ordered men forward to buy some time. As the long roll sounded in more camps, the 18th Missouri and 61st Illinois Infantry had fallen in on the 16th Wisconsin's left flank at the Spain field, with Andrew Hickenlooper's 5th Ohio Battery and Emil Munch's 1st Minnesota Battery filling the gap between the brigade lines. The 16th Wisconsin had only arrived in camp the day before, hadn't eaten since Friday and was short on ammunition. Also falling in, somewhat to the rear, was the rest of the 12th Michigan that had reported for duty only minutes before. Since each regiment was responsible for its own ammunition, the Michiganders may not have had any interchangeability with their fellows, and would have to wait for casualties to collect usable arms. With one of the four regiments essentially unarmed, and another short on everything but fear and hunger, half of Prentiss's division front consisted of one fully armed and equipped infantry regiment, two 6-pounder smoothbore cannon, two 12-pounder howitzers, eight 14-pounder James rifles, and bits and pieces of whoever else was stopping to fight--about 1,700 fully armed men--that would have to stop Gladden's brigade of about 2,200.[21][22]

21. One of the most challenging aspects of the Shiloh battle is that most of the Confederate units larger than regiment were so hastily organized that their real strength was never known; Gladden's total strength was never officially reported; they reported 829 casualties.

22. Daniel, op. cit., 152–3; Martin, op. cit., 53; Sword, op. cit., 156–7.

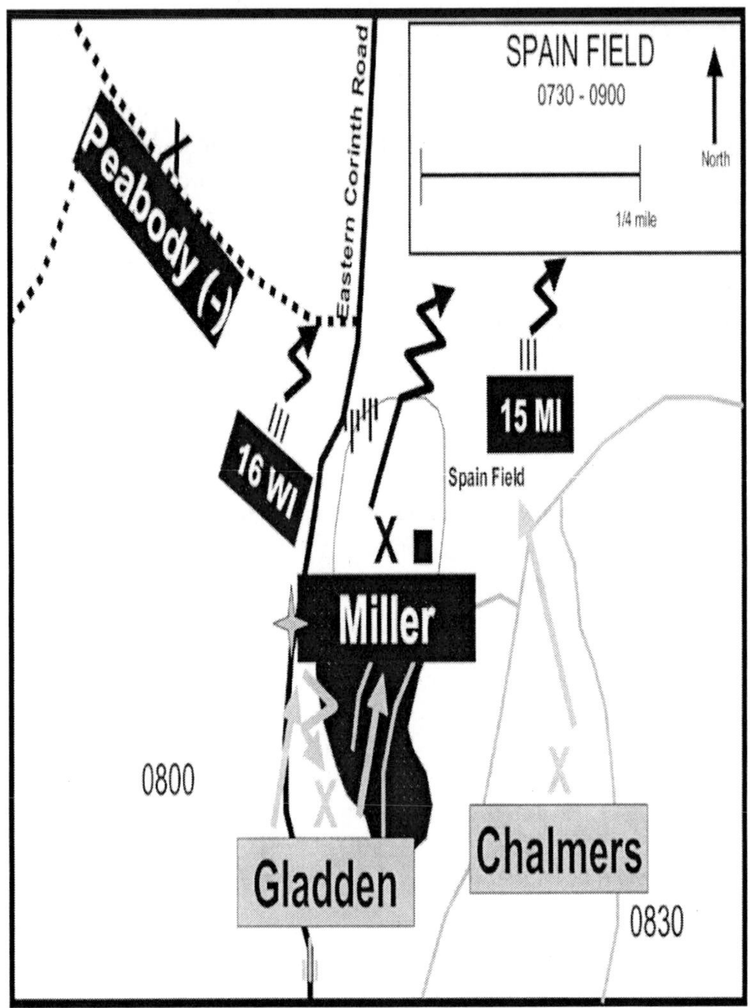

Figure 4-3, Prentiss Disintegrates

Just after 8:00 the Federals saw Shaver's brigade struggling through the brush and swamp coming at them from the south. Prentiss adjusted the line to help Peabody meet Shaver's onslaught, and in so doing caught Gladden's flank just as Gladden was aiming at Miller. As the 1st Louisiana crossed a branch of the Locust Grove Creek ahead of the

26th Alabama, they marched up a slight rise to within 200 yards of Miller's line on the edge of the Spain field and came under a galling fire from Peabody on their left. Soon Hickenlooper's howitzers were firing double canister--about 24 pounds of musket balls at a time from the two 12-pounders--which they could do for about one and half minutes, because that was all the canister they had with them. The James rifles had no canister ammunition and had better range than the Confederate guns, but the fuses for their shells had to be cut quite short, and in those changing range conditions it was nearly impossible for green gunners to get right. Gladden's left arm was nearly ripped off by one of these guns, and he fell mortally wounded. The Federal line held while Gladden's brigade fell apart.

Peabody's brigade came apart gradually--death by a thousand cuts. Some of Peabody's men had been on their feet for five hours and had expended their ammunition twice over. At first the refugees heading for the rear were few--wounded men, non-combatants in the camps and a few skulkers. As Peabody's companies stepped back for ammunition, more and more men would simply dash for the rear, exercising the prerogative of combat troops to run away to find another place to fight, joining the column of refugees that began to choke the roads.[23]

Without steady supply of water no Civil War battle line could function for more than a few minutes. Black powder cartridges were paper or linen tubes containing ball and powder that were bitten off at the base so the powder could be poured into the barrel. Each cartridge fired meant that some of the charcoal/sulfur/saltpeter mix got swallowed. Each cartridge bitten was like taking a pinch of salt directly into the mouth. Under extreme battle conditions--two or three rounds a minute and more for ten minutes or longer-- was as dehydrating as getting a dash from a shaker in the mouth every minute, not to mention the effects of the smoke. Also, artillery pieces had to be swabbed out after each shot so that embers from the last cartridge wouldn't pre-

---

23. Earl J. Hess, *The Union Soldier in Battle: Enduring the Ordeal of Combat* (Lawrence, KS: University of Kansas Press, 1997), 87.

ignite the new charge and maul the loader. Dehydration and pre-ignition were alleviated only by great gouts of water. Those fetching water for the line were often carried along with the other refugees.

Everett Peabody, true to his premonition, was killed by a ball through the head, his fifth wound, before 8:00 in the morning, while trying to rally his shaky troops. Powell took command of the survivors; no longer a brigade, just a bunch of grim men fighting to survive.[24]

At 8:15 James Chalmers' brigade from Bragg's corps began a bayonet charge that shattered what cohesion remained on Prentiss' left. Then it fell on Miller's left flank and the 12th Michigan. When the 12th Michigan broke, Prentiss' left flank was in air (with nothing to protect it and not covered by other units), and the advancing enemy was behind him. At about 8:30 Felix H. Robinson's Florida battery made an appearance. Their four 12-pounder Napoleon guns started spraying nearly a hundred pounds of canister at Hickenlooper's battery every minute until they, too, had to switch to other ammunition. Munch was wounded; Hickenlooper dismounted and stunned; horses were killed in their harnesses; gun trails broke; guns got stuck between trees and the battery area turned to a bedlam with refugees as wounded and dying men and horses screamed in pain and panic while gunners withdrew their pieces from the oncoming Confederates as well they could. Hickenlooper saved his four James rifles while giving up his brass howitzers to onrushing Confederates. Munch got his James rifles away while Powell and Miller pulled their survivors back through their camps.

Prentiss' seven regiments had defended their camps against four brigades and three batteries. Three hours after the long roll sounded for the 6th Division of the Army of West Tennessee it had been defeated, one of its brigade commanders killed, its camps and supplies taken by

---

24. Griffith, op. cit., 20, 38–9; Brent Nosworthy, *Bloody Crucible of Courage: Fighting Methods and Combat Experience of the Civil War* (New York: Carroll and Graf Publishers, 2003), 426; Bell Irvin Wiley, *The Life of Johnny Reb* (Baton Rouge: Louisiana State University Press, 1978), 69.

the enemy, and its hospitals captured. Johnston was on his way to a reprise of Sam Houston's glorious victory over Santa Anna at San Janctio.[25]

Surprise at Shiloh Church: Sherman is Attacked

At most of the camps of the 5th Division of the Army of West Tennessee the morning was relatively calm. Before dawn there had been some picket firing, and as reveille sounded around 5:30 there was some rumbling somewhere off to the south, but no one at headquarters seemed perturbed by it. William Sherman was up early and had breakfasted by 6:30. The division's camps were getting ready for inspection, but had not yet eaten.

But at Jesse J. Appler's 53rd Ohio Infantry camp near the Rea field, there had been confusion and mild panic since about 6:00. Former naval officer Appler had been hearing gunfire for two hours before dawn. The prospect of battle so early didn't trouble him quite as much as the idea that he might overreact to another skirmish. Sherman had already belittled him for his concern over the scuffle of two days before. If he reacted as he thought he should, and this was just another picket action, he would be humiliated yet again. If he did not do what he thought he should do and it really was an attack ... Appler chose not to think of that. In his situation not many men would.[26]

If Sherman had been paying attention to Appler's camp layout he would have found much more to be unhappy about, but Jesse Hildebrand, commander of the 3rd Brigade, hadn't paid attention either. Appler had ignored all common sense in choosing his camp site near the Rea field, and had ignored orders about the facing and spacing of regimental camps. He laid out his regiment's company streets some four hundred yards from the main body of the division, with a spring

---

25. Daniel, op. cit., 145, 151–4, 155; Philip Katcher, *American Civil War Artillery 1861–65* (Oxford, UK: Osprey Publishing, 2001), 18; Sword, op. cit., 162, 166–70.

26. Cunningham, op. cit., 165; William S. McFeely, *Grant: A Biography* (New York: W. W. Norton & Company, 1982), 112.

between him and the next camp west. About 650 yards separated Appler and Prentiss. Most Federal officers treated the Pittsburg Landing site as a resting place on a healthful hike in the wilderness while toting artillery.

While Appler was trying to decide what he should do, the picket force he had sent out the night before ran back in to the camp. They had seen Confederates (possibly part of Wood's brigade) moving north and east. There was no time for weighing options, for hesitating, or for thinking too hard, but that's what Appler seems to have done. He started to send his adjutant to Hildebrand and to fall the regiment into line, but he waffled again. Then, one of Powell's survivors stumbled into camp clutching a bloody arm and yelling something on the order of "the Rebels are coming!"

Appler finally evolved a spine and called for the long roll, shouting orders to Robert A. Fulton to ride to Hildebrand's headquarters, and to Warner Fulton to go to Sherman's. He then sent two companies out to reinforce the brigade pickets--to either buy a few minutes or to quell the problem altogether--while his regiment marched a few yards north of their camp and set up a hasty bastion of hay and logs.[27]

Just to the north of Appler was Allan C. Waterhouse's Battery E of the 1st Illinois Light Artillery, a Chicago outfit that could not have been any greener. They had been together for about three months, had arrived at Pittsburg Landing only a week before, had only received their horses--still unused to artillery harness--just ten days before, drilling them only three times before that morning. The battery had not fired a single round from their guns before 6 April.[28]

But Waterhouse was a conscientious young officer who had his battery up and limbered before Appler was falling into line. Sherman's chief of artillery, Ezra Taylor, heard the shooting early and decided to have a look for himself. Taylor ordered Waterhouse to move his six James rifles of two different calibers to a small prominence just north

---

27. Cunningham, op. cit., 165–6; Daniel, op. cit., 156–7; Sword, op. cit., 171–2.

28. Arnold, *Armies*, 61.

of the Rea spring just to the west of the 53rd Ohio, where most of the ground to the south could be easily seen. Waterhouse sent a section of two guns immediately, to follow with the rest of the battery as soon as he could.[29]

While Appler was forming his outfit and Waterhouse was getting into place, the rest of Hildebrand's brigade was falling into line near the Rea field. Though Hildebrand was quite ill (possibly malaria, but the man *was* 62), he got up and formed his brigade. The 77th Ohio was camped almost due south of the Shiloh Church and marched perhaps fifty yards to the northern edge of the Rea field. Hildebrand's third regiment, the 57th Ohio, camped north of the Rea field, moved south toward the Shiloh Branch Creek and the northeast corner of the field.[30]

Ralph Buckland was a state senator from Ohio who had enough influence to have obtained command of Sherman's 4th Brigade of three Ohio regiments camped near the Shiloh Branch Creek northwest of the meeting house. Buckland had been restless all night and was at breakfast when he got the word that pickets were engaged with a Confederate force, sometime between 6:00 and 7:00. Wasting no time, Buckland ordered his regiments to fall into line near their camps at the southern edge of the Howell field by about 7:00 with his left flank at the meeting house and his right on the Pittsburg-Corinth Road. Sherman, alerted but still unalarmed, ordered Buckland to send a regiment forward to reinforce the pickets.[31]

John A. McDowell's 1st Brigade camped north of Buckland on the Hamburg-Purdy Road near the Owl Creek on the far left flank of Sherman's encampment, fell in on the Howell field by 7:00. McDowell's officers had been hearing the same firing as everyone else, and had seen Buckland's movement forward that left a quarter-mile gap between them. He sent two companies of the 6th Iowa and a two-gun

---

29. Daniel, op. cit., 157; Sword, op. cit., 173, 174.

30. Cunningham, op. cit., 166; Daniel, op. cit., 157; Reed, op. cit., 57; Sword, op. cit., 175.

31. Daniel, op. cit., 161; Reed, op. cit., 58; Sword, op. cit., 180–1.

section of Frederick Behr's 6th Battery of the Indiana Light Artillery (probably two of his four 6-pounder smoothbores; Behr also had two 12-pounder howitzers) to guard the Purdy Road/Owl Creek bridge; a bridge that led to the Shunpike connecting Sherman with Lew Wallace's brigades at Adamsville and Stoney Lonesome to the north.[32]

Sometime between 7:00 and 8:00, Sherman rode into the Rea field with part of his staff, still convinced that this was nothing more than noisy skirmishing. Looking south and seeing knots of Confederates move through the woods, he remained unperturbed. When a Confederate regimental battle line broke into the field just a pistol shot to Sherman's right, he shouted "My God, we are attacked!" Within moments he was wounded in the hand by a ball and his orderly/bodyguard was decapitated by a cannon shot.[33]

Sherman galloped back to his headquarters near the Shiloh Church, shouting at Appler to hold on. He sent messages off to fellow division commanders John McClernand, William Wallace and Stephen Hurlbut asking for support in the wide gap between his left flank and Prentiss' right; that he was able to think of this at that time, with enemy soldiers so close, is somewhat remarkable, though we're not sure if he had heard from Prentiss yet. Sherman was likely as "skeered" as he imagined Appler to have been only hours before, yet he still did not believe that this was a general attack on Pittsburg Landing yet, and would later admit as much.[34]

---

32. Daniel, op. cit., 172; Reed, op. cit., 56; Sword, op. cit., 187.

33. There are at least two versions of what Sherman said, and several versions of when he said it. The words "God" and "we are attacked" are contained in all versions, and he certainly said whatever it was between 7:00 and 8:00. Without a time machine that's the best we'll get.

34. Cunningham, op. cit., 167; Daniel, op. cit., 158; Force, op. cit., 127; Martin, op. cit., 108–10; James L. McDonough, *Shiloh--in Hell Before Night* (Knoxville: University of Tennessee Press, 1977), 92; Sword, op. cit., 175–6, 188–9.

Patrick R. Cleburne, an Irish-born former enlisted man who may have campaigned in Afghanistan with the British Army's 41st Foot, was attacking Sherman alone. Hardee was with Wood's brigade and busy keeping Hindman's division together, either forgetting his earlier plan or too distracted by events; Bragg would later write about a "want of officers" that might have gotten Cleburne to ignore Sherman and wheel on Prentiss' open right flank. Cleburne's brigade had little trouble moving up until they reached the southern end of the Rea field, where they encountered boggy mud, swamps, and rocky wastes. In the middle of the Rea field Cleburne elected to break up his brigade, sending about a thousand men of the 6th Mississippi and the 23rd Tennessee toward the 53rd Ohio on the eastern side of the Rea field and the Pittsburg-Corinth Road, while his other four regiments marched straight up the west side of the road towards the church.[35]

The 53rd Ohio's line ran northwest to southeast just south of the Shiloh Branch Creek, near the northeast corner of the Rea field. A quarter hour before Sherman's position was hit by the 15th Arkansas, the 6th Mississippi and the 23rd Tennessee were slogging through boggy fields and through Appler's camp towards the 53rd Ohio. About 50 yards from their targets, the 53rd Ohio fired their first volleys of their war.[36]

The 23rd Tennessee and 6th Mississippi broke after the first or perhaps the second blast of lead and smoke from the 53rd Ohio. Using an expression that Iranians would use during the Gulf Wars, the Confederates later said they ran from an "iron storm" that mercilessly cut down all that stood in its way. John T. Trigg's Arkansas battery of two 6-pounder smoothbores and two 12-pounder howitzers, positioned nearby, began shelling the 53rd Ohio's position ineffectively, unable to

---

35. Arnold, *Shiloh*, 21; Cunningham, op. cit., 173; Daniel, op. cit., 158–9; John E. Stanchak, "Cleburne, Patrick Ronyane," in *Historical Times Illustrated Encyclopedia of the Civil War* (New York: Harper and Row, 1986), 145; Sword, op. cit., 176–7.

36. Cunningham, op. cit., 159; Daniel, op. cit., 159; Sword, op. cit., 177–8.

see well enough to correct the fire but causing grievous injury to at least one tree. Soon Trigg shifted his battery away from the Rea field.[37]

While Appler's men were butchering the advancing Confederates, Waterhouse's battery joined in the carnage. Each of his James rifles could throw a fused antipersonnel round of about 12 or 14 pounds weight; the bursting charge and fuses together were about three quarters of a pound, the rest was frangible metal. The battery's throw weight was something on the order of 84 pounds to the volley. Unlike their fellows in Prentiss' line, the range in front of Sherman was longer and didn't change as fast, which simplified fuse cutting and drastically improved the battery's effectiveness. Waterhouse eventually shifted targets, firing over the Rea field to a part of Wood's brigade that was attacking Peabody to the battery's far left. The 27th Tennessee took shell fire that killed six men while the 16th Alabama changed its front to attack Waterhouse. But the 16th shifted away again, so Waterhouse returned to his bombardment of the Rea field, shifting targets again to take on Trigg and his gunners. Soon Waterhouse was joined by Samuel Barrett's Battery B of the 1st Illinois Light Artillery, who brought his two 12-pounder howitzers and four 6-pounder smoothbore guns to bear on Trigg. No one flinched when a Confederate shell blew up a caisson.[38]

Though the 6th Mississippi managed to rally about three hundred men to charge again, it was once again slammed by a hail of lead from both the 53rd and the 77th Ohio. The 6th Mississippi's colonel was among the fifty-odd dead in the 53rd's camps; they had brought over 400 men to Tennessee and the regiment would have only 60 in ranks after the battle--70% dead, wounded and missing in less than half an

---

37. Christopher Miskimon, "The Multiple Launch Rocket System," *Military Heritage Magazine*, December 2008, 10; Williams, op. cit., 366.

38. Cunningham, op. cit., 168–9; Griffith, op. cit., 26–7; Sword, op. cit., 174; Harold L. Peterson, *Notes on Ordnance of the American Civil War: 1861–1865* (Washington, D. C.: American Ordnance Association, 1959), 10.

hour. Its battle mate, the 23rd Tennessee, was also destroyed as a unit by the 53rd and 77th Ohio.[39]

The 53rd Ohio had nothing to be ashamed of; they had helped destroy two Confederate regiments in 30 minutes, but Appler himself was unsteady and grew worse with each volley. The 53rd's position had always been untenable in the long-term, but was acquitting itself better than well and the Confederates were nowhere near getting by them where they were until their commander became unglued. Without warning, Appler marched the 53rd about until at one point they were facing north while the Confederates were coming at them from the south. Finally getting them pointed in the right direction again, Appler at last shouted "retreat and save yourselves!" and ran away north. Most of the 53rd Ohio broke and ran, leaving behind their two right flank companies that hadn't heard the "order." Jesse Appler was not meant to command 19th Century infantry in combat, but would still fight as a private soldier for the rest of the battle. Sherman, aware of all of this after the battle, was later amused to read accounts of how his division folded in the first assault.[40]

The 77th Ohio, which Hildebrand had ordered to a position just behind Waterhouse, moved forward after one Confederate repulse to collect souvenirs. The advisability of such an action was not the point, but soon they were surprised by their pickets rushing in because the Confederates were coming again, and because Trigg began firing on them. They decided to run back to where the last two companies of the 53rd were still in formation, if barely, covered by Waterhouse's guns. Between them, the 53rd and the 77th Ohio had lost 11 men.

While Appler was preparing himself to be defeated and his men fought on, Buckland sent the 48th Ohio south to "reinforce the pickets" as Sherman instructed. Led by an Irish veteran of the Mexican War named Sullivan, they marched in line some five or six hundred yards south until they saw enough Confederate troops to know that this was

---

39. Force, op. cit., 129.

40. Cunningham, op. cit., 169; Daniel, op. cit., 159; Sword, op. cit., 179; Williams, op. cit., 366.

more than a picket action. The 48th "countermarched at the double quickstep"--in theory a controlled run at shoulder arms not unlike double-time, but under those circumstances it was probably a more like a dead run--back north again, falling in between the 72nd and the 70th Ohio at about 7:45, just as their two sister regiments were moving forward some 200 yards.[41]

Not a moment too soon. Cleburne, who had in the neighborhood of 1,500 men with him, didn't know that over 2,200 Federals awaited him around the Shiloh Church. At a hundred yards the 2nd Tennessee fired a volley at the 48th Ohio that dropped many and unnerved the 48th's color-sergeant, but Buckland's regiments opened on them with devastating effects. The 2nd Tennessee lost a hundred men in a few minutes; the 5th/35th Tennessee[42] lost three color bearers in as many minutes, and regimental command briefly fell to the senior captain. Buckland was supported by Barrett's well-sited battery firing in enfilade, and George Nispel's Battery E of the 2nd Illinois Light Artillery from John McClernand's division, adding the power of two more 6-pounder smoothbores and two more 12-pounder howitzers to Buckland's line. In perfect enfilade, Buckland's men cut loose at their attackers at ranges as short as thirty yards, reducing one Confederate regiment by a third in a few moments.

For a few minutes Cleburne was checked by three regiments and two batteries, but not without cost to the Federals. One of McDowell's regiments, the 40th Illinois, had moved up to protect Buckland's right flank, but would not move into line to relieve the 70th when it ran out of ammunition. The 72nd Ohio became effectively leaderless before 7:45 with all three field-grade officers down; the 70th Ohio was under attack from two Confederate regiments, and though they kept up a

---

41. Daniel, op. cit., 161; Reed, op. cit., 58; Sword, op. cit., 180–1.

42. There were two 5th Tennessee Infantry Regiments in the Confederate Army at this time. The one that survived Shiloh was later known as the 35th. Some histories refer to this unit as the 35th, and some use both.

galling fire it was only a matter of time until the Confederates had to back off; no mounted officers survived to 9:00 unhurt on either side of this fight. The Confederate dead and wounded were said to have been stacked knee-high in some places; some of those still fighting used the bodies for cover from the whirring balls and shrieking shells. By 8:00, Shoup had reorganized the Arkansas batteries that had started concentrating on Nispel's guns. They were joined by the two 6-pounders smoothbores and two 12-pounder howitzers of Irving Hodgson's 5th Battery of the Washington (Louisiana) Artillery from Ruggles' division of Bragg's corps.[43]

By 8:00 about 6,000 Federals were facing nearly 10,000 Confederates on the Federal right flank. Sherman was finally convinced that the Confederates were making a determined attack on his positions, but was also satisfied that he was in good shape for the moment. Hildebrand's brigade, the lynchpin of Federal line, appeared to be holding.[44]

Johnston and Bragg both appeared on the Confederate left sometime between 8:00 and 9:00, and realized that Cleburne's brigade had been practically destroyed. The 6th Mississippi's colonel and major were both hit in a failed assault on the 53rd Ohio's camps. Johnston ordered Charles Clark--who was just then hearing his first shots in anger--to organize the seizure of Waterhouse's and Barrett's gun positions to relieve the logjam. More Southern junior officer *beau sabeurs*, wanting to show their courage by leading from the front, were getting killed every minute in futile frontal attacks without result. Johnston, critically short of officers, must have simply looked around and saw an officer, not much caring if he could do actually the job or not. Desperation is the midwife of delegation.[45]

---

43. Arnold, *Shiloh*, 21; Cunningham, op. cit., 168–9; Daniel, op. cit., 167; Martin, op. cit., 54; Sword, op. cit., 182–3.

44. Cunningham, op. cit., 174–5; Daniel, op. cit., 177; Reed, op. cit., 47; Sword, op. cit., 199–200.

45. Arnold, *Shiloh*, 36; Cunningham, op. cit., 177; Daniel, op. cit., 167; Sword, op. cit., 186.

Robert Russell's Tennessee/Louisiana brigade from Polk's corps had spent the night astride the Pittsburg/Corinth Road behind Alexander Stewart's brigade. Patton Anderson's brigade from Bragg's corps was crowded to the right of the same road all night, and had spent much of the morning trying to find enough room to deploy into line. The thousand-yard interval between corps that Beauregard required was impractical given the ground: one of Anderson's officers said he passed through a thicket so dense he couldn't see an arm's length ahead. Anderson's and Russell's brigades had never worked together, had not yet been fired on, and had taken no casualties. Yet, between 8:00 and 8:30 on Sunday morning, in their first attack of the war, they were marching just minutes apart, apparently without benefit of prior planning other than some vague "go over there and fight" instructions. The two simply marched to the Napoleonic sound of the guns. It seemed as if they were being ordered to attack stationary infantry and artillery, fully alert and formed, holding Sherman's left flank. In truth, they were about to attack a mob of nervous Ohioans who by then were probably thinking that they would just as soon have stayed home.[46]

Confounded in the brush and torn by lead and iron, only a fraction of Russell's men got into attacking position, but did little more than run away after a ragged volley. Russell was assisted by parts of Bushrod Johnston's brigade of Cheatham's division from Polk's corps that included Marshall Polk's Tennessee Battery of two- 12-pounder howitzers and four 6-pounder smoothbores, a Mississippi battalion led by A. K. Blythe, and the 154th Tennessee Infantry (Senior).[47] Numbers and initiative were breaking Sherman's position, but at a cost to the attackers in precious time and resources.[48]

---

46. Cunningham, op. cit., 177; Daniel, op. cit., 165–7; McDonough, op. cit., 116, 122; Reed, op. cit., 71, 77, 80; Sword, op. cit., 175, 184–5, 187.

47. An old militia number. Some Confederate units were allowed to retain their militia designations.

48. Cunningham, op. cit., 179; Daniel, op. cit., 168; Martin, op. cit., 54; Sword, op. cit., 195.

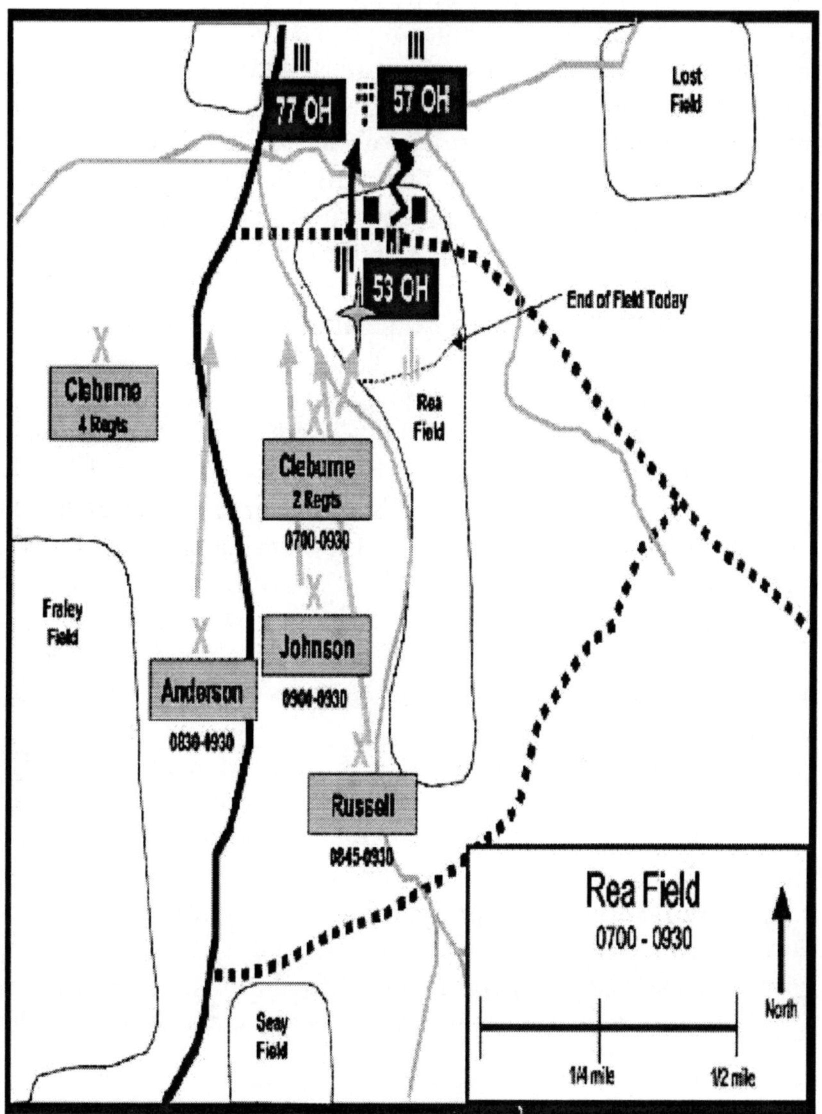

Figure 4-4, Attack on Sherman's Right

Not So Surprised: McClernand Joins the Fight

John A. McClernand, commanding the 1st Division, had been suspicious of Confederate activity for days, and was the only division commander at Pittsburg Landing who suspected a major attack early on Sunday. When he heard gunfire at about 7:10, his fears were confirmed. Encamped to the east and north of Sherman's division, his camp layouts suggest a half-thought of a defending against attack from the west (Purdy), but he was poorly deployed to even react to that. McClernand seems to have sent a rider off to find out what was happening from Sherman. Shortly thereafter a runner from Sherman may have arrived at McClernand's headquarters with news that he needed support. McClernand wasted no time.

Abraham Hare commanded McClernand's 1st Brigade of two Illinois and two Iowa regiments encamped at the Jones field just west of the Tilghman Branch Creek. The 13th Iowa of Hare's brigade was at the Water Oaks Pond somewhat east of the camps, supported by Battery D, 2nd Illinois Light Artillery of six James rifles commanded by James P. Timony.[49] Hare was in position just north of the review field--a twenty-acre patch of smooth and level ground that had been used for dress parades--about a hundred yards south of the Hamburg-Purdy Road by 9:00.[50]

The four Illinois regiments of C. Carroll Marsh's 2nd Brigade pitched their tents half a mile north of the Woolf field. On Sunday morning Marsh had no artillery he could count on. Nonetheless, his brigade fell in on their parade grounds and were marching south by 8:00, then shifted west to form up along the western edge of the Review field.[51]

Leonard Ross's 3rd Brigade included four Illinois regiments and a cavalry company that had spent the night along the Hamburg-Purdy

---

49. Most accounts call this "Dresser's battery" for unclear reasons.

50. Cunningham, op. cit., 222–3; Daniel, op. cit., 176, 178; Reed, op. cit., 46–7; Sword, op. cit., 314.

51. Cunningham, op. cit., 222; Reed, op. cit., 46.

Road. Ross was burying his wife back home, which left James Reardon in charge. But Reardon was sick, so command fell to Julius Raith (McClernand's report of the battle renders it "Wraith"). Raith, a veteran of the Mexican War and former flour mill owner, learned that he was in command about ten seconds before he was ordered to march to the sound of guns. At first, Raith's regimental commanders thought it was all a bad joke, but the 49th Illinois in the brigade had heard gunfire before dawn, and on their own initiative fired off their wet powder to get ready for an engagement.[52]

All three of McClernand's brigades were formed on their color lines no later than 8:00. As bewildered as Raith may have been, his new command was marching within minutes of hearing the long roll. They moved to the 77th Ohio's camps on the north edge of the Rea field about 350 yards north and east of Waterhouse's battery and edging Oak Creek on their right, filling the gap between Sherman's left and Prentiss' right, and started receiving fire by 8:00. Raith had the best of intentions, but the brigade was badly placed to do anything but have a grandstand seat to the disintegration of Sherman's left flank, and to trade potshots at whatever Confederates were in range. Raith seemed to have known this and had sent back to Marsh for some help. Sherman's position was coming apart, Raith's uneasy men were returning desultory fire, and the fields and woods were filled with refugees.[53]

At about 9:00 McClernand ordered Raith back to the Water Oaks Pond, but the order was confused and Raith stayed put for the moment. Some of Hildebrand's men from broken outfits ran into and then past Raith's hardworking infantry, while his stalwarts joined Raith's steadier, fresher men. At about the same time a mixed force of Confederates, having overrun the last of Hildebrand's camps, hit Raith's men in their front and left flank hard enough to rattle many into submitting to their fears and heading for the rear. Because his left was protected by a ravine that prevented his line from being rolled up, the

---

52. Daniel, op. cit., 177–8; Reed, op. cit., 47; Sword, op. cit., 308–9; War Department, "OR I/X/1," 115.

53. Cunningham, op. cit., 186; Sword, op. cit., 310.

brigade didn't break but became a slightly ordered mob. A year later, Raith's men might have just changed facing to blaze away like Regulars. Later...but not yet.

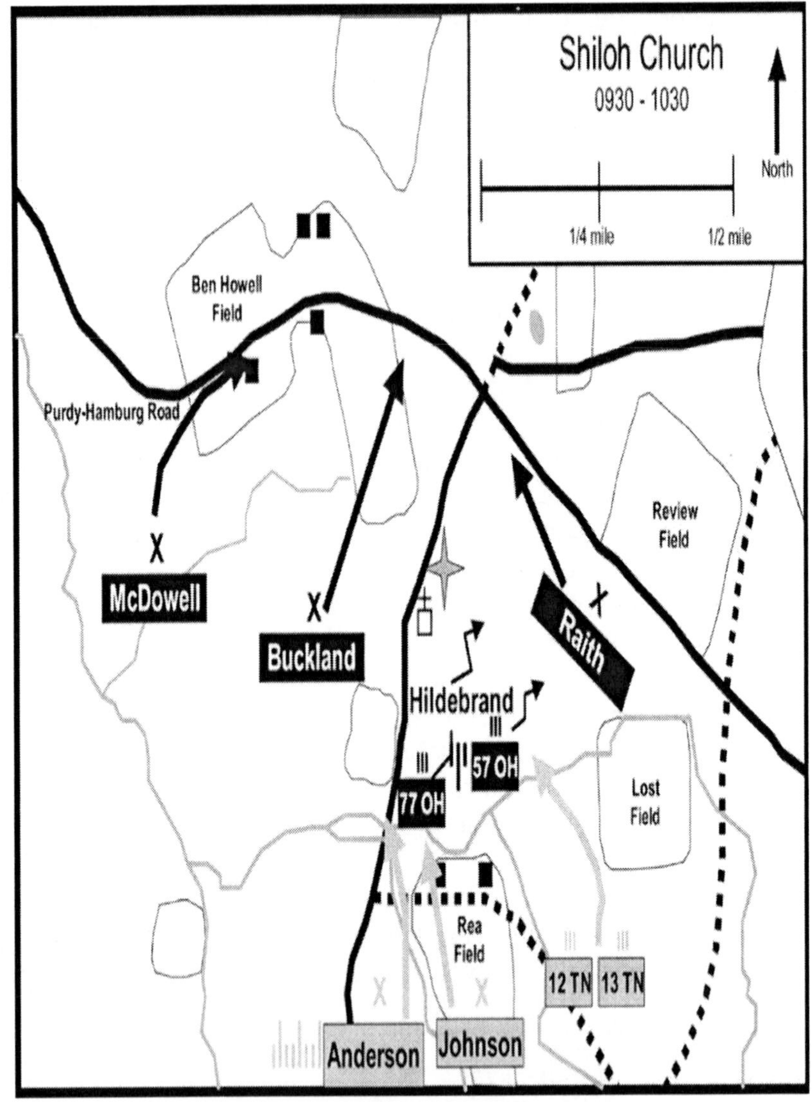

Figure 4-5, Raith Joins Sherman

This Confederate attack was notable. Bits and pieces of five brigades (Anderson's, Johnson's, Russell's, Stewart's and Wood's) from three different corps (Bragg's, Hardee's and Polk's) hit Raith's men from two directions nearly simultaneously. These units hadn't filed their first-ever morning reports and here they were attacking formed infantry on two sides. Wood's survivors had been in action for better than five hours, and the rest had been on their feet for at least four hours and fighting for nearly three. That they were still working at all by 19th Century militia standards was almost unheard of. Southern officer ranks had been shredded, but these unschooled backwoodsmen certainly acted as if they knew what they were doing without them. A year later, this Confederate host might have been able to halt, dress ranks and blast Raith and his boys to atoms. Later, but not yet.[54]

Down by the River: Stuart Fights for Life

Far detached from the rest of Sherman's division, David Stuart's three-regiment 2nd Brigade was encamped around the Larkin Bell field along the Lick Creek, watching the Federal far left and the important junction of the Hamburg-Purdy and the Hamburg-Savannah Roads near the Tennessee River. Stuart's brigade had been stripped of its battery the day before as a result of Sherman's ongoing reorganization, and Stuart himself was under a cloud. A former Michigan Congressman and well-to-do Chicago lawyer, he had been named in an Illinois divorce scandal so notorious in the public mind that Illinois governor Richard Yates had to deny him permission to raise a company before Bull Run. Whatever the public stink was, the Union was hard up for those who could lead. He somehow got a lower-profile commission, and by the end of October 1861 had become Colonel of the 55th Illinois.[55]

Like most of Grant's army, Stuart's men had no thought of fighting on Sunday morning. Some had been clearing their muskets of damp powder when the rattle of small arms from Prentiss' camps reached

---

54. Cunningham, op. cit., 175, 225; Daniel, op. cit., 160, 178; Sword, op. cit., 178, 199–201.

55. Daniel, op. cit., 197–8; Reed, op. cit., 56–7.

them, but this passed unremarked. The booming of artillery was harder to ignore. Stuart received a message from Prentiss that he was under attack at about 7:30. Stuart's three regiments fell in on their color line shortly after 8:00 as their pickets came streaming back in a panic, but still most of the militiamen failed to grasp the gravity of the situation.[56]

Stuart reorganized his panicky pickets and sent four companies back south. Three were to watch the junction and the Hamburg-Savannah Road ford across the Lick Creek, and one would keep an eye on a ravine east of Locust Grove Branch Creek. The ford on the Lick was a vital piece of real estate about three feet deep but 80 to 100 yards wide Sunday morning. The Lick had probably overrun its banks and may have been running fairly swiftly with little bottom, making it more like a pond and difficult for heavy traffic to cross.[57]

Stuart looked west towards Prentiss' camps and saw the distinctive pelican flag of the 1st Louisiana flying over it sometime around 8:00. He sent a message to Stephen Hurlbut to the north that Prentiss was being overrun, and that his own command was going to need help soon.[58]

John Jackson's brigade from Withers' division of Bragg's corps spent the night south of Gladden's brigade on the Confederate right flank. Their day started just after sunrise, advancing behind Gladden towards Prentiss' camps on Chalmers' left. Jackson's brigade consisted of three Alabama regiments, one more from Texas, and an attached Georgia battery of four 6-pounder smoothbores and two 12-pounder howitzers under Isadore Girardey.[59]

---

56. War Department, "OR I/X/1," 258.

57. Cunningham, op. cit., 214; Daniel, op. cit., 198; Martin, op. cit., 54; Reed, op. cit., 57.

58. Cunningham, op. cit., 207–9; War Department, "OR I/X/1," 203, 257.

59. Daniel, op. cit., 196; Martin, op. cit., 54; Reed, op. cit., 75; Sword, op. cit., 223–4; War Department, "OR I/X/1," 553.

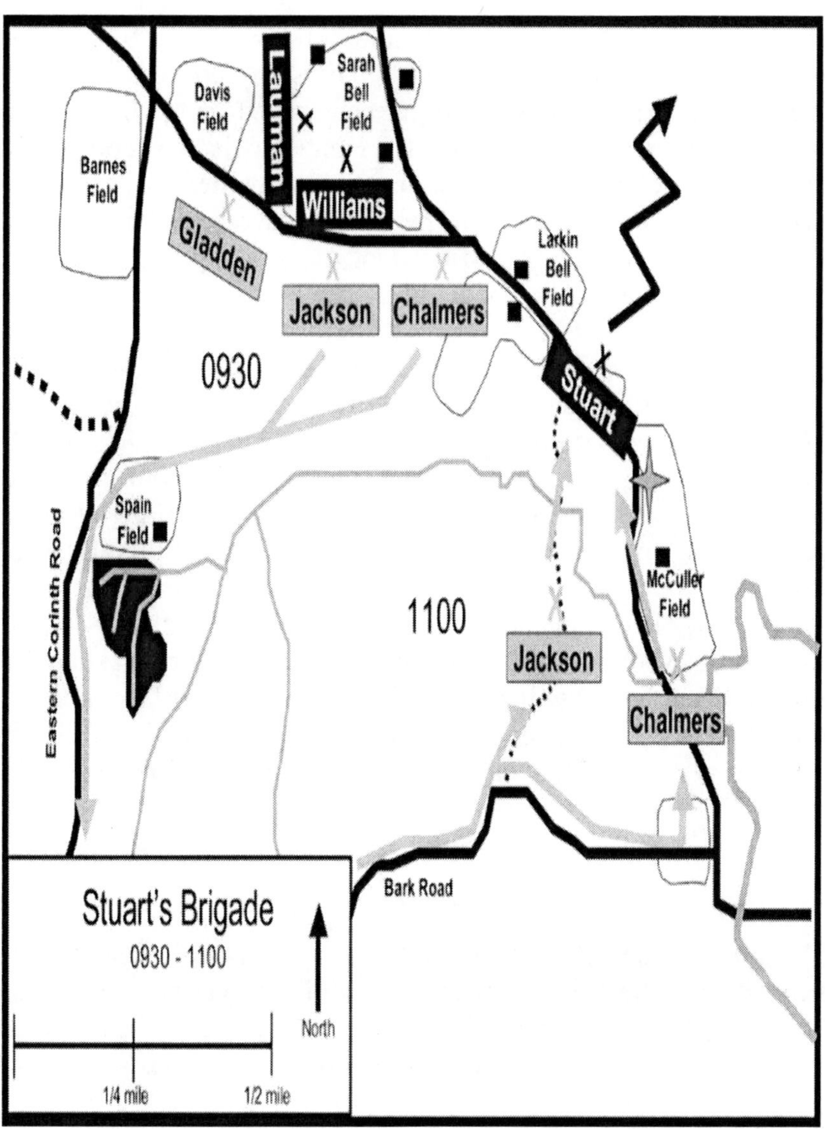

Figure 4-6, Stuart's Stand

Sometime after 9:00, Charles Mann's Battery C of the 1st Missouri Light Artillery of two 6-pounder smoothbores and two 12-pounder howitzers from Stephen Hurlbut's division arrived in Stuart's battlespace. Mann was absent and the command of the battery fell to Edward Brotzmann. Stuart later wrote that he tried to reposition this battery for a better crossfire but it moved out before he got there. Brotzmann wrote that they were near a "Zouave regiment" camp (the 54th Ohio was a Zouave outfit). Brotzmann's report stated that he discharged several solid shot and shells at an enemy battery (Girardey's) about 1,100 yards south before he was ordered to shift west. Girardey claimed to have driven the Federals out.[6061]

At about this time Jackson was ordered to help Wood and Shaver on the Confederate left against Sherman, taking Girardey's guns with him. This order was countermanded and Jackson was told to go with Chalmers to the Confederate right. Samuel Lockett, Bragg's energetic engineer scout, thought there was an entire division on Prentiss' far left by the river.[62]

Stuart's whole command was nearly isolated and probably forgotten. Stuart didn't even know what unit Brotzmann's battery was days after the battle when he wrote his report (and he may never have known for sure). Stuart and his unsupported little brigade of some 1,200, far from the main action, were neglected by both sides for most of the morning.[63]

---

60. Girardey says "silenced," which could mean either destroyed or simply packed up and moved; in this case the latter. An official report assumed that "silencing" a battery was the same as destroying it, especially since they were often used as press releases for the hometown papers.

61. Cunningham, op. cit., 208; War Department, "OR I/X/1," 246, 258.

62. Arnold, *Armies*, 63; Cunningham, op. cit., 202; Martin, op. cit., 52; McFeely, op. cit., 113.

63. McDonough, op. cit., 126.

Sometime after 9:00 John McArthur's 2nd Brigade from William Wallace's division would anchor Prentiss' left along the road just east of a twenty acre peach orchard just off the right flank of the 71st Ohio and their camps. The 71st would need help soon.

Sherman's Line Breaks

By 9:00 Sherman knew Prentiss was falling back by the sounds of battle, and that his left was going to be open for about a quarter mile. Sherman's left was held by one barely intact regiment (Hildebrand's own 57th Ohio), clots of refugees trading fire with advancing Confederates, and three green artillery batteries that would have been running low on ammunition--with the lot of them commanded by an unwell sixty-two year old former stage coach driver (Hildebrand).[64]

About 9:10 Beauregard ordered Polk to release a brigade to attack Sherman. Clark sent the 11th Louisiana from Russell's brigade into the fray, but their numbers were too few, they were enfiladed by Barrett's guns, and they became disorganized in the brush around Shiloh Branch Creek. While Russell got them back under control, he lined up the 22nd Tennessee to assist in another try for Waterhouse while Clark led the 12th and 13th Tennessee against Hildebrand and the 57th Ohio. Hildebrand's already shaky remnants broke when hit in the flank, pushing the 57th back five hundred yards. Hildebrand's rear was in chaos as the sick, non-combatants, hurt and ne'er-do-wells bolted. Clark was hit in the shoulder, taking him out of the fight.

By 9:30, facing six separate Confederate brigades, what was left of Sherman's line was running short of the many different calibers of ammunition they needed, and water was running out. Buckland's position was becoming shakier by the minute, even though the ground in front of him was later called "a pavement of dead men." Once more Anderson launched the 9th Texas, the 19th Louisiana and the Confederate Guards Response Battalion at Buckland. Blythe was killed, his second in command mortally wounded, and Bushrod Johnston was struck by a shell fragment and put out of the fighting.

---

64. Daniel, op. cit., 160; Sword, op. cit., 178, 200–1.

Federal batteries had been double-shotting their guns for hours while slaying hundreds of Confederates; Barrett's and Nispel's gunners destroyed Polk's battery. This made them very tempting counterbattery targets, a task for which the Confederate guns were neither well-positioned nor suited, but they tried anyway. A barely-credible chain of events in the Confederate waves led to Tennesseans shooting Arkansans and even other Tennesseans; regiments in attacking columns being detached for unclear purposes by senior officers; senior officers being killed and wounded, unhorsed and stunned by both enemy and friendly fire. Wood's brigade arriving from the other side of the battlefield must have made the Confederate rear resemble the confusion in the Federal. Only the front-line Confederate units that were actually engaging Federals were under command control; the rest were being tossed around like straw in a cyclone.[65]

The Federal line was thinning in small numbers, gradually falling away until there was nothing left. Nispel, under heavy fire on two sides, withdrew three of his four guns. So many horses were down that pulling Waterhouse's battery back was becoming problematic. Between 9:30 and 10:00 he was hit in the thigh by a volley and carried away, leaving Abial Abbot in charge. Five of the guns were finally withdrawn, leaving Barrett's flank somewhat exposed while Abbot fell back north a hundred yards before unlimbering to blast away to both front and rear. Bragg personally ordered the 13th Tennessee to attack Abbot's guns. Battery horses were falling fast, then Abbot was wounded and command fell to John A. Fitch. When the 13th Tennessee was fifty yards away Fitch ordered a retreat: soon it was no longer a battery. Three of their six guns and all the battery equipment were abandoned for want of horses, and the gunners made for the rear having lost one man killed and 17 wounded. They abandoned a fourth gun

65. Cunningham, op. cit., 180; Martin, op. cit., 119; Sword, op. cit., 201–8, 210; Witham, op. cit., 58–9.

later. The surviving guns and gunners served other batteries for the rest of the day.[66]

Between 9:00 and 10:00 Johnston had some 8,000 men against about 4,000 of Sherman's. The right flank of Grant's army was open. Johnston had an opportunity to be watering his horses in the Tennessee River by noon. But it appears as if he didn't know of his opportunity; even if he had known of it he barely controlled the mob his army had become. With another season's campaigning under their belts the Confederacy's premier army in the west might have crushed Sherman, pushed McClernand aside, and marched past Prentiss, William Wallace and Hurlbut to the Landing. But not this army; not yet.[67]

The 40th Illinois was returning to McDowell's line from Sherman's collapsing position when the Louisiana Crescent Regiment hit them in the flank and scattered it, then followed McDowell's brigade as it moved northeast. Behr's gunners began firing while the two remaining regiments changed fronts and some of Hildebrand's refugees streamed through the line. Neither Behr nor his gunners spoke much English, but Behr knew gunnery, and was able to silence some sniping Confederates before he was killed and his men abandoned their pieces. McDowell knew that with Buckland's retreat there was nothing for him to do but pull back and try to connect with the rest of the division. He moved towards McClernand's forming line with what Sherman could gather around the Crescent Field and the Hamburg-Purdy Road. Of all of Grant's army on the front lines, only McDowell's brigade retreated in good order, if without their gunners (they did haul the guns away). Johnston's men, as they did while overrunning Prentiss' camps, stopped to scrounge[68] from the abundance of Sherman's stores for nearly an hour.[69]

---

66. Cunningham, op. cit., 180–1, 182–4; Daniel, op. cit., 169–70; Sword, op. cit., 195, 196; Williams, op. cit., 367; Witham, op. cit., 24–26.

67. McDonough, op. cit., 106–7.

68. Soldiers draw a fine line between looting (stealing anything from civilians), and scrounging (acquiring for immediate use that

At about 9:30, McClernand, who had positioned himself with the 13th Iowa by the Water Oaks Pond, started to move Hare and Marsh south to support Sherman's left. In the rapidly deteriorating situation McClernand thought better of it, and instead took up a line on a ridge north of the east-west Corinth Road overlooking the Review field that was about a half mile northeast of Sherman's headquarters near the Shiloh meeting house. Raith's runner found Marsh marching south just before McClernand gave the countermarch orders, and was given a bad set of instructions to join a divisional position that was never going to exist. McClernand, acting with remarkable speed and decisiveness while using equal measures of common sense and timidity, likely saved Sherman's forces and the whole of the Federal right by providing an anchor for Sherman when his first line gave way.[70]

It was about 10:00 when Sherman ordered Barrett to pull back to the Hamburg-Purdy Road position, where Buckland's remnants, centered around the 70th Ohio, was forming the nucleus of a line with McDowell's brigade and the other battered survivors of Sherman's command. Sherman had held up parts of three of Johnston's attacking corps for three hours. The fight for the control of the Rea and Howell fields had seen seven Confederate attacks from a dozen brigades, ranging in size from companies to two brigades, most repulsed with great loss. Through it all, Sherman had remained cool and collected, had lost two horses and was twice wounded. In the heat of the fighting he seemed imperturbable. Critics say that he was simply baffled by the reality of the attack itself. While there may be a nugget of truth to this, it is equally true that if he couldn't believe it was happening and was

---

which is of military necessity, like food and drink, weapons, ammunition and medical supplies). There was a little of both at Shiloh, but mostly the Confederates were after grub, bandages and bullets.

69. Cunningham, op. cit., 184–5; Daniel, op. cit., 172, 173; Force, op. cit., 131; Martin, op. cit., 115; Sword, op. cit., 187, 208.

70. Sword, op. cit., 308–9.

angry at his own mule-headedness, he gave better than he got in a desperate fight.[71]

Surprise at Savannah: Grant, Nelson, Lew Wallace and Buell

Sam Grant could have been at peace with the world Sunday morning. One of his oldest friends was at hand; he commanded one of the most successful land forces in the country and was near the pinnacle of the only profession he was ever any good at. As far as he knew for certain the enemy was far away, cowering and in poor morale. The campaign that he and many others believed would end the rebellion was about to begin and he could soon go home to show his family that, for the first time in a long time, he could succeed on his own.[72]

He could have been sanguine, but he was not. An accident with his horse the week before had cost him sleep. A painful ankle obliged him to hobble on a crude Army crutch that pained the lymph glands in his armpits that became swollen and inflamed in wet weather, a long-term effect of his "ague." Aggravating his discomfort, the steamboat masters hauling his army up the Tennessee always wanted more money for delivering ammunition and gun batteries, alleging that their decks were damaged by the extra weight: in fact cannon weighed less per square inch of horizontal surface (with the wheels off) than an average cotton bale, which the boat skippers gleefully carried whenever they could find them on the run downriver. Doubtless the move upriver to new headquarters at Pittsburg Landing, scheduled for that day, would cost his dwindling cash box more money. Though the Army Quartermasters contracted the boats, they did not operate them and neither did the

---

71. Ibid., 204–5.

72. Bruce Catton, *U.S. Grant and the American Military Tradition* (New York: Grosset & Dunlap, 1954), 81–85; McFeely, op. cit., 112; Geoffrey Perret, *Ulysses S. Grant, Soldier and President* (New York: Random House, 1997), 186–88; Brooks D. Simpson, *Ulysses S. Grant: Triumph Over Adversity, 1822–1865* (New York: Houghton Mifflin Company, College Division, 2000), 129–31.

Navy. Besides, a contract sitting in St. Louis did not prevent the skippers from locally demanding more money for "overages." To make matters worse, the fractious quartermaster captain overseeing the steamboats and their contracts in St. Louis had managed to anger even the most mild-mannered of the rivermen.

Grant's headquarters was moving not because of enemy or command pressure, but military need. Two days before Grant had received word that McClernand and Lew Wallace were confirmed as Major Generals. The orders made McClernand--who Grant distrusted with command of anything more than a corporal's guard--the senior officer at Pittsburg Landing. That made him dangerous, and required that Grant be present at the Landing to keep his army from marching off the nearest cliff or committing some other folly or mayhem. Grant was expecting no attacks, and only grudgingly planned to leave Cherry house after meeting with Buell.[73]

Great scorn has been heaped on Grant for sleeping away from the army. While sleeping in a bed in a frame house may have rankled those sleeping on the ground in tents as much then as ever, there's no correlation between Grant's comfort and the lack of preparation for an unexpected attack. Grant went to the Landing every day, and if he didn't notice the state of his encampments during those visits, it's not likely that sleeping with the troops would have changed anything.[74]

A lieutenant on William Nelson's staff named Horace N. Fisher on a picket inspection heard gunfire at about 5:20 in the morning. He first thought it was artillery practice, but the noise continued. When Fisher returned to camp, he saw others listening intently. This was the earliest that Buell's army knew of the battle and, as the sun rose, the rest of

---

73. Daniel, op. cit., 173–4; Ulysses S. Grant, "The Battle of Shiloh," in *Battles and Leaders of the Civil War Volume 1* (New York: Thomas Yoseloff, 1956 (Electronic Edition 1997 by Guild Press)), 467; Jeffry J. Gudmens, *Staff Ride Handbook for the Battle of Shiloh, 6–7 April 1862* (Ft. Leavenworth, KS: Combat Studies Institute Press, n.d. [Electronic version downloaded 2008]), 8.

74. Martin, op. cit., 62.

Buell's army could hear it--seemingly before the generals did--and knew that there was trouble at Pittsburg Landing. Buell himself, hearing the firing while at his breakfast, dismissed it.[75]

There are two major versions of how news of the fighting got to Grant. One version has Grant and some of his staff eating breakfast at about 7:00 when they heard a distinct BOOM, possibly Peabody's brigade and their first murderous volley. When James Webster, Grant's Chief of Staff, wondered where it was from, Crump's or Pittsburg, Grant is said to have declared the latter. The other version has a headquarters orderly named Edward N. Trembly delivering a report of firing, after which Grant went outside to listen for himself. Charles Smith, dying in an upstairs bedroom of the Cherry house, also heard the firing but insisted it was nothing more than a picket skirmish.[76]

The truth is probably a combination of the two, but regardless, the headquarters was immediately in motion, breakfast forgotten. While Grant waited on the boiler deck for his 321- ton headquarters boat *Tigress* to raise steam, he dictated several messages to Buell and Nelson. Grant apologized to Buell for not meeting with him, but he feared his army was heavily engaged. Nelson was instructed to take his division to the riverbank opposite Pittsburg Landing and take steamboats across. Grant also wrote an order to Thomas J. Wood, his old West Point roommate who was commanding Buell's 5th Division, to march to Savannah with all possible haste, not realizing that Thomas

---

75. Don C. Buell, "Shiloh Reviewed," in *Battles and Leaders of the Civil War Volume 1* (New York: Thomas Yoseloff, 1956 (Electronic Edition 1997 by Guild Press)), 492; Daniel, op. cit., 242; Ulysses S. Grant, *Memoirs* (New York: Da Capo Press, 1982), 172–3; Gerald J. Prokopowitz, *All For the Regiment: The Army of the Ohio, 1861–1862* (Chapel Hill: University of North Carolina Press, 2001), 99; Sword, op. cit., 212–13.

76. Cunningham, op. cit., 156; Daniel, op. cit., 173–4, 242; Sword, op. cit., 213.

L. Crittenden's 1st Division was closer to Savannah than Wood's was. By the time Nelson got to the Cherry house, Grant was gone.[77]

The Tennessee was better known for flatboat traffic, and few steamboats were native the stream (see Appendix, "Steamboats of Shiloh"). Savannah, the southernmost river port in Union hands, was so jammed with Grant's supplies that there was no space for Buell's divisions to camp within a mile of the town: marching through Savannah would have been impossible for Buell's men. Grant had been told local guides could be obtained who knew a spot across the river from Pittsburg, and he passed this on to Nelson and Buell.

Lew Wallace had been hearing the sounds of battle to the south since sunup, and had his men up since about 6:30. Because he and the 1st Brigade of his division were sitting on an enormous volume of supplies he didn't dare move. It is unknown if he alerted his other two brigades strung out at Stoney Lonesome and Adamsville on the road to Purdy before Grant came to call. *Tigress* has been described as "a small fast vessel" that needed under an hour to make the eight mile trip upstream between Savannah and Crump's Landing. Between 8:00 and 8:30 *Tigress* pulled alongside Lew Wallace' headquarters boat *Jesse K. Bell*, a sternwheeler of about 325 tons. Though Wallace was convinced that the noise was a general attack at Pittsburg Landing, Grant, who believed the nearest threat was at Purdy, believed it was a diversion for an attack on Crump's Landing. He told Wallace to hold his division in readiness, and that more definitive orders would be forthcoming. At about 8:30 *Tigress* pulled away from *Jesse K. Bell.* Wallace then sent staff officers off to alert the brigades and prepare them for movement

---

77. Cunningham, op. cit., 157; Daniel, op. cit., 174; Charles Dana Gibson, *Dictionary of Transports and Combatant Vessels, Steam and Sail, Employed by the Union Army, 1861–66*, The Army's Navy Series (Camden, Maine: Ensign Press, 1995), 316; McDonough, op. cit., 95; Sword, op. cit., 213–14; Fredrick Way, *Way's Packet Directory, 1848–1994* (Athens, OH: Ohio University Press, 1983), 455; Williams, op. cit., 359–60.

orders ... as soon as he got some. Patrols that morning sent as far west as Purdy found no Confederates.[78]

Whitelaw Reid was aboard *Jesse K. Bell.* Reid was a newspaper reporter who filed his stories under the pen name "Agate," and had been sick with diarrhea for two weeks, like much of the army. Some accounts suggest that Reid got aboard *Tigress,* but others state that the two vessels were only in hailing distance and didn't come together. It is not clear if Reid was on the battlefield Sunday morning.[79]

On the way upstream, *Tigress* was hailed by *John Warner,* a steamer sent to Savannah by militia officer William Wallace to alert Grant that there was a fight going on. This was the first definitive news that Grant had that there really was a battle. *John Warner* came about in midstream and followed *Tigress* back to Pittsburg Landing. *Tigress* got to Pittsburg Landing at about 9:00, and Grant rode his horse up the bluffs.[80] He issued orders to the 23rd Missouri, just then disembarked, to draw ammunition and join their assigned command, Prentiss' 6th Division. He instructed the 15th and 16th Iowa Infantry regiments, more recent arrivals, to load their cartridge boxes and form a line along the top of the bluffs to keep the Landing clear so that Buell's army could unload. Edward Bouton's Battery I of the 2nd Illinois Light

---

78. Cunningham, op. cit., 158; Gibson, *Army's Navy I*, 176; Sword, op. cit., 216–17; Way, op. cit., 246.

79. Bruce Catton, *Grant Moves South* (New York: Little, Brown and Company, 1960), 255; Cunningham, op. cit., 158–9; Daniel, op. cit., 174; McDonough, op. cit., 96; Perret, op. cit., 188; Simpson, op. cit., 131; Sword, op. cit., 215–16.

80. Grant's morning timeline in his memoirs and his *Century Magazine* article is consistently off by an hour; it comes into synchronization with other accounts in the afternoon. The cause of this is unknown.

Artillery joined the Iowans, facing their six James rifles roughly southwestward.[81]

On most 19th Century battlefields, those fleeing the battle were scattered behind the fighting lines, but Shiloh was no ordinary battlefield. The rain-swollen creeks on the flanks and the road layout tended to funnel Shiloh's refugees until they gathered along the river like sheep in a pen. They included the laundresses and seamstresses, other camp followers and visiting families: there would have been scores--if not hundreds--of women, children and non-soldier men mixed in with the soldiers. New refugees joined the mob with wild stories and fear, bewilderment and confusion in their eyes. By some accounts, there were about 3,000 of them there by the time Grant arrived; Grant would later write that there were four or five thousand at about 1:00 in the afternoon. How many had been fighting men is anyone's guess.[82]

Pittsburg Landing Sunday morning was still just a guarded supply dump, fairly calm and quiet. Grant's staff fanned out and began to organize the camp guards and fatigue details. Like many supply dumps of the time, this one was just disorganized piles of stores, some of which might be useful now, and some maybe later. Sorting the ammunition from the uniforms, medical supplies, stacks of forms, rations, horseshoes and other supplies was a key task that needed doing whether under attack or not. Grant likely instructed his people to simply get on with their jobs as if the headquarters was moving as planned, albeit without a leisurely Sunday breakfast. He wasn't going to have a repeat of the Fort Donelson supply debacle.[83]

---

81. Cunningham, op. cit., 159; Daniel, op. cit., 175; Grant, *Memoirs*, 173; Grant, "Shiloh," 468; Hollister, op. cit., 34; Martin, op. cit., 53; Sword, op. cit., 217–8.

82. Catton, *Grant Moves South*, 225–6; Grant, *Memoirs*, 178–9; Grant, "Shiloh," 474; McDonough, op. cit., 122; Simpson, op. cit., 131.

83. Catton, *Grant Moves South*, 226; Cunningham, op. cit., 159; Daniel, op. cit., 175; Williams, op. cit., 361.

Grant started riding from the Landing to the sound of guns no later than 9:30. Grant soon met William Wallace, who assured him that there was a major fight going on, but Grant needed very little persuading. Most accounts agree that Grant found Wallace was a half mile south of the Landing and no more than a mile north of where he and Prentiss were forming a line. Since some authorities claim that at this stage of the war most of the muskets in the West were smoothbores, Grant had to have got into visual range of the battle because his staff could hear bullets in the canopy overhead falling like rain. They could also hear that the isolated river flank was becoming engaged by then, and also knew that Sherman was holding to the west, if barely. The woods and fields must have been dotted with refugees, the roads and trails clogged with the fearful and the trapped.[84]

Grant ordered John A. Rawlins, his close friend and most trusted aide, back to the Landing to instruct the district quartermaster, A. S. Baxter, to use *Tigress* to get a message to Lew Wallace. The timing of this decision, different in several sources, including Grant's own accounts, is important given the confusion that followed. Because of the controversy that followed, Grant may have been better off if had sent Rawlins with a message himself.[85]

Grant also sent a message to Buell's army (he may not have known where Buell was exactly, but had the foresight to address his message to whoever was in charge):

> COMMANDING OFFICER ADVANCE FORCES (BUELL'S ARMY),
> Near Pittsburg:
> The attack on my forces has been very spirited from early this morning. The appearance of fresh troops on the field now would

---

84. Edward Hagerman, *The American Civil War and the Origins of Modern Warfare* (Indianapolis: University of Indiana Press, 1992), 183.

85. Catton, *Grant Moves South*, 230; Cunningham, op. cit., 160; Daniel, op. cit., 175; Grant, "Shiloh," 468; Sword, op. cit., 218.

> have a powerful effect, both by inspiring our men and disheartening the enemy. If you will get upon the field, leaving all your baggage on the east bank of the river, it will be a move to our advantage, and possibly save the day to us. The rebel forces are estimated at over 100,000 men. My headquarters will be in the log building on the top of the hill, where you will be furnished a staff officer to guide you to your place on the field.
> U.S. GRANT,
> Major-General, Commanding.

This was an appeal for help, not a desperate quest for rescue. Grant could not have thought about the 100,000 figure much. As an old quartermaster Grant knew that an army of that size couldn't be provided for without control of the river or a railhead nearby, and he knew the Confederates had neither. A hundred thousand men meant a million rations every three and a half days, plus twenty or thirty pounds of fodder every day for every horse, which was logistically unlikely by wagon in southwest Tennessee in 1862, regardless of who had to do it. It had some of the bravado reminiscent of Pershing in the Meuse-Argonne, and some of the confusion of Dutch Cota in the Huertgen Forest, but none of the pleading that later accounts suggest.[86]

According to most accounts Buell waited impatiently for boats to arrive at Savannah. It is peculiar that a major general with his years of experience in the Regular Army would have waited for another general (one he didn't like) who was fighting off a surprise attack to send him transportation--so peculiar that it is unlikely. He probably spent much of his morning getting a route through town cleared, a herculean chore that took most of the day to perform and would have taken several hours to merely organize. Buell later wrote that he heard the battle at

---

86. Buell, op. cit., 492; Catton, *Grant Moves South*, 229–30; Charles Dana Gibson, *Assault and Logistics: Union Army in Coastal and River Operations 1861–6*, The Army's Navy Series (Camden, ME: Ensign Press, 1995), 601–2; McDonough, op. cit., 124; Williams, op. cit., 352.

least as early as Grant did (7:00), but he couldn't have left Savannah before noon if he and a small staff arrived at Pittsburg Landing at about 1:00 in the afternoon. There was no reason, military or otherwise, for him to be there any earlier.

Steamer *Fort Wayne* of 321 tons brought pontoon boats to bridge the river sometime before the battle, but we know very little else about them. The only engineer units in the Western theater were on the Mississippi with John Pope: Buell's small engineer detachment had just been disbanded. Though Buell had built a bridge across the Duck River on the way to Shiloh, the Duck wasn't half as wide as the Tennessee and could be forded. 19th Century pontoon bridging with little rudderless wooden or canvas boats was hard work that required skill and lots of manpower and equipment. There were no ready-made stringers or any other specialized parts that we know of, so they would have to have been made on-site. Though later Western armies would bridge rivers easily and quickly with a minimum of training or equipment, there simply wasn't the time just then. At nearly a mile across in some places, walled by steep bluffs and mudflat beaches, and with a strong current because of heavy rain, bridging the Tennessee was not something anyone was thinking of at that moment.[87]

The bend in the main road from the east of the river that should have led to a commercial landing opposite Pittsburg Landing led up to Savannah. The river bottom there was shallow most of the year, making that spot commercially useless and thus would invite few roads. Several cavalry horses were killed in the mire along the river while looking for a route to the river from the road south. The rains had washed out most of the trails to the shore. Finally a local physician led Nelson's scouts to a bluff opposite Pittsburg around noon. The trail through the wilderness brush was suitable only for single horsemen and foot traffic.

---

87. Bruce Catton, *Reflections on the Civil War* (Norwalk, CT: Easton Press, 1987), 182–84, 190–91; Buell, op. cit., 491; Francis Alfred Lord, *They Fought for the Union* (Harrisburg, Pa.: Stackpole Co., 1960), 82–3; Gibson, *Army's Navy II*, 76; Gibson, *Army's Navy I*, 118; Prokopowitz, op. cit., 96; Way, op. cit., 170.

The bluff was steep there, the beach nonexistent, and the mudflat under water for the moment.[88]

Help for Grant was on the way, but it might take a while, and would only be infantry with whatever they could carry on foot. It would have to be enough.[89]

Breaking Through: Stuart Disintegrates

Chalmers' brigade had been regrouping after the collapse of Prentiss' division and was on the move forward again. At about 9:30 Johnston ordered Chalmers to fall back and shift east towards the Tennessee. According to one account, Chalmers halted his command while waiting for a guide, which fits the tenor of the whole, confused day.[90]

From their position and all that is known about other dispositions at that time, the 71st Ohio was isolated, without any cover whatsoever and near their brigade camps, in plain view of both enemy infantry and artillery. Stuart's other two regiments were together along the road. Rodney Mason, the commander of the 71st Ohio, told Stuart that his men had never heard a shot fired in anger, had never seen a single enemy soldier, and would not endure artillery. Mason's lament apparently made no impression on Stuart. Stuart might have been a bit more sympathetic since he knew what it was like to have a bad reputation, but he simply did not have the time.[91]

Stuart's second group of skirmishers saw Jackson's brigade as the Confederates topped a small rise sometime between 9:00 and 10:00.

---

88. Structures that appear opposite Pittsburg Landing in post-battle imagery were built after the battle.

89. ---, *Navigation Charts for the Tennessee River* (Washington, D.C.: U.S. Government Printing Office, 2003), Charts 28, 29; Buell, op. cit., 492; Catton, *Grant Moves South*, 289; Daniel, op. cit., 242–3; Prokopowitz, op. cit., 99–100.

90. Reed, op. cit., 75; Sword, op. cit., 225; War Department, "OR I/X/1," 564.

91. Cunningham, op. cit., 208; Daniel, op. cit., 199.

They watched the pageantry of the evolution of infantry briefly, but soon withdrew to cover and began sniping at the Confederates as they moved up. These Federals were displaced from their hide by Girardey at 9:40, a time precisely noted by one of the gunners. Mason, in his report to Stuart dated 10 April, states that his 510 men were in line and fell back to a ridge about a hundred and fifty yards north of Shake-A Rag Church when Girardey opened fire. The four guns on the prominence near Shake-A-Rag Church then turned their attentions to the 71st Ohio.[92]

Two companies of the 71st under Thomas Bowen were positioned at a log cabin, a part of the 55th Illinois' camps. This position was taken at the run by the 2nd Texas Infantry, a hard-marching, bedraggled and footsore outfit that had been on their feet for nearly a month, route-stepping from Houston to Corinth and on to Shiloh. The 71st Ohio loosed one or perhaps two volleys at Jackson's oncoming force and, according to most accounts, at least part of it fled when Mason bolted for the rear. Another part of the 71st under Barton Kyle, their well-liked lieutenant colonel who had raised and organized the regiment, stuck around for another few minutes blazing away at Jackson's 1,500 men as they marched towards them and Girardey's guns shelled them. Somewhere in this hopeless fight Kyle was mortally wounded, which unnerved the forward parts of the 71st and they broke. Mason organized those men with him on the ridge to the north, while Kyle's remnants eventually clumped in with the 55th Illinois.[93]

Under these circumstances it is easy to understand why the 71st Ohio Volunteer Infantry broke and ran. They had been organized in Ohio and at Paducah from September 1861 to_January 1862. Mason had been imposed on them and was not popular; he had been the adjutant-general of Ohio and was seen as a tool of Ohio Governor William Dennison. According to Mason the 71st was sent to the Pittsburg Landing unarmed, and had had less than ten hours of battalion drill, all of which is credible given what we know of other units.

---

92. War Department, "OR I/X/1," 261.
93. Daniel, op. cit., 199; Sword, op. cit., 229–30.

Mason's account has the 71st falling back a hundred and fifty yards then reforming, but this does not agree with other reports, which may not mean much. He admits that "the regiment did not bear themselves with ... steadiness." Shiloh is not among the 71st Ohio's battle honors. Their losses at Shiloh were about 20%, which shows that they were courageous enough fighting for the short time that they did stay together, and as knots of individuals, but the 71st could not have been better set up to fail at Shiloh.[94]

At about 10:00 Chalmers' guide arrived and the brigade began marching around the Locust Grove Branch Creek. They marched for half an hour until they halted to wait for a cavalry reconnaissance of the area south of McCullers's field and astride the Hamburg-Purdy Road . They had at least an hour and a half of standing around idle with a golden opportunity hanging before them: the largest Confederate army west of Richmond was hammering away at Grant's army; the vulnerable river flank was under attack by a lone and weary brigade, and Chalmers' 2,000 heavy infantry waited for guides and scouts.[95]

Jackson was enough for Stuart's fragmented command to contend with, but eventually Chalmers got back into the fighting. Chalmers' brigade engaged skirmishers from the 55th Illinois' between 10:30 and 11:00, but in a confusion of orders the 52nd Tennessee fell apart while clearing a path for Charles P. Gage's Alabama battery of two 12-pounder howitzers and two 3-inch rifles. Gage and Girardey had been shelling Stuart for an hour when Chalmers came up and masked Gage's guns[96]

The 54th Ohio, a Zouave regiment and the only intact part of Stuart's brigade left on the field, may have worn the costumes of fierce mountain fighters of North Africa, but the 54th was not peopled by

---

94. Cunningham, op. cit., 209; Daniel, op. cit., 199; Martin, op. cit., 53; Sword, op. cit., 229–30; War Department, *OAR VI*, 163; War Department, "OR I/X/1," 261.

95. Sword, op. cit., 225–7; War Department, "OR I/X/1," 548–9.

96. Daniel, op. cit., 95, 200; Martin, op. cit., 54.

half-wild tribesmen inured to hardship and danger. These were mostly townsmen, militiamen of middling income who could afford the fancy dress and the free time to learn the elaborate drill. They had somewhat less than 400 men in line, watching as a host that their commander later thought was ten thousand marched relentlessly towards them. The 9th Mississippi's skirmishers encountered the 54th for the first time at about 40 yards somewhere near 11:00, and suffered for it severely. Gage's guns shifted targets to pound the 54th until they finally pulled back in bare order. The 55th Illinois, or what was left of it, had been ordered to perform a complex parade-ground maneuver by Oscar Malmborg, their lieutenant colonel and a former Swedish Army engineer. Impossibly confused and under fire, the 55th disintegrated as Stuart watched. Bellowing with rage he was struck by a bullet in the left shoulder, and his brigade was no more. Grant's river flank was open as far back as his hastily-placed Iowans and the stragglers under the bluffs.[97]

Then, at about 11:00, Chalmers was out of ammunition. There was practically nothing to stop Chalmers from marching to the Landing, but, after having stood around waiting for guides for at least an hour, no one thought to check the men's ammunition pouches. A few more experienced and attentive officers and a file of cavalry might well have changed things enough to have taken the fight out of Grant's army and ended the battle before Sunday lunch. The threat to Grant's river flank ended as Chalmers turned his attention to the bullet magnet that would come to be called the Hornet's Nest.

As the last of Sherman's command was falling back at about 10:00, Johnston's men had managed to offset Grant's numbers and tactical defensive posture (Sherman and Prentiss between them had about 12,000; Anderson, Chalmers, Russell, and Withers had about 8,000 or so, Hardee had 6,700).[98]

---

97. Daniel, op. cit., 200; Sword, op. cit., 228.

98. Thomas L. Connelly, *Army of the Heartland: The Army of the Tennessee, 1861–62*, reprint, 1995 Edition (Baton Rouge: Louisiana State University Press, 1967), 165; War Department, "OR I/X/1," 549.

It appeared that Johnston and Beauregard had caught Grant just flat-footed enough to destroy him before Buell arrived. In Johnston's mind, triumph was near. Grant's army had been split in two, with both flanks in air. Two of Grant's divisions had been smashed, and Johnston still had substantial numbers that had not been committed. He may have got revenge for Forts Donelson and Henry by dark, providing he avoided a Confederate Borodino, Napoleon's Pyrrhic victory over the Russians in 1812 that cleared the road to Moscow...and doomed his army.[99]

The green solders performed better than the professionals expected. Federals were surprised at their Sunday breakfast: none but the sick were in their tents as some press reports had it. Confederates were astonished at the storm of metal that struck them time and again, and frustrated by the terrain. Units on both sides broke and never reformed, even firing on senior officers. Many men still had something of a militia mentality, with many refugees simply deciding that they had had enough fighting for one day, or for a lifetime. But most men on both sides fell into formation when a threat became clear, mostly obeying orders regardless of who gave them. They sought cover and joined firepower, and when they fell back under pressure they did so in many cases in tolerable order with little panic.

Even when they broke, the men didn't simply become mobs of individuals running away from the fighting; many formed ad-hoc units that lasted just long enough to achieve something. On the Confederate side, some of these units may have stayed together long enough to rush a battery. On the Union side they may have held a corner of a field long enough for a battery to get clear. We don't know a lot about these organized stragglers, but we know they were there.[100]

It's been said that green troops will either run away all at once or not at all. The experience of Shiloh showed that some green American troops may run only so far before they turn and fight again. Irwin Rommel would say it best in North Africa in 1943; when some

---

99. Arnold, *Shiloh*, 20–21; Daniel, op. cit., 164; Martin, op. cit., 122–3; McDonough, op. cit., 96, 98.

100. Arnold, *Shiloh*, 40; Wiley, op. cit., 84.

Americans ran for a while then turned to fight he declared they were "the first to run and the first to rally." The Americans repeated this pattern in 1944 during the Battle of the Bulge, and again in 1950 in Korea.

But in 1862, this was a new thing.

CHAPTER 5
OPPORTUNITIES LOST AND FOUND: MID-MORNING TO NOON

By mid-morning some of Prentiss' men had been on their feet for nine hours and fighting on and off for five. They were joined by two other divisions and an assortment of hastily-arriving new regiments ready to staunch the Confederate onslaught. Reinforcements that arrived at the fighting front were dispatched not according to any discernable plan but because earnest men in high positions thought it best to send them someplace that appeared to need them. Frontier militia leaders like Stephen Hurlbut and William Wallace couldn't wait for a situation to clarify like professionals could; they had to respond to pleas for help quickly and decisively before urgent situations became *real* problems.

Casualties on both sides by mid-morning were not insubstantial but neither were they devastating by the standards of the time. By professionalist standards it was remarkable that these frightened and hard-worn militia-minded neighborhood regiments still possessed weapons and self-control, could still defend themselves, and could even contemplate finding a place to fight from.

Hurlbut's Sunday started not when he heard the sounds of firing, but with a message from Sherman at about 7:30 saying he needed help. Minutes later, he got a similar message from Prentiss. James C. Veatch's 3,000-man all-Illinois 2nd Brigade whose artillery had been "reorganized" away was encamped across the Hamburg-Savannah Road just north of the Corinth Road. Veatch got orders to march to Sherman's aid at about 8:00, was moving about ten minutes later, and was in position behind Marsh between 9:00 and 10:00. That was the last Hurlbut saw of Veatch for the rest of the day. Hurlbut took his two remaining brigades, three batteries and two battalions of cavalry and marched south towards the increasing sounds of battle, and from where alarming numbers of refugees were coming. His two-brigade division was the largest intact Union unit on the Federal left.[1]

They marched to a position between a small stream just east of the Hamburg-Savannah Road, across the Eastern Corinth Road to the northern edge of the Duncan field just west of the Corinth Road to the northwest. To the west there was an old worn-down and sunken southeast-northwest wagon trail (much later referred to as the sunken road). This vital piece of real estate was an almost perfect infantry trench, complete with firing steps, protected in part by a rail fence and partly hidden by several stands of trees only then budding out. The Duncan field provided a perfect glacis for grazing fire to the south and southwest. On the eastern end of this line were a blossoming peach orchard and a cotton field in full bloom. To provide much-needed water and protection for the position's rear and right flank there was a small pond (called the Bloody Pond in many postbattle accounts) where many regimental aid stations set up. Anyone in this area looking south looked down slightly at everything around it for three hundred yards and more. Eventually eight batteries and men from at least fifteen regiments of five divisions would occupy these woods, thickets, fields and roads.[2]

---

1. O. Edward Cunningham, (Gary D. Joiner and Timothy B. Smith, Eds.), *Shiloh and the Western Campaign of 1862* (New York: Savas Beatie, 2008), 201, 230; Larry J. Daniel, *Shiloh: The Battle That Changed the Civil War* (New York: Simon & Schuster, 1997), 178, 192; David W. Reed, *The Battle of Shiloh and the Organizations Engaged* (Knoxville, TN: University of Tennessee Press, 2008), 53–4; Wiley Sword, *Shiloh: Bloody April* (New York: Morrow, 1974), 235, 315; War Department, "Shiloh, Corinth: Series I, Volume X, Part 1," in *War of the Rebellion: Official Records of the Union and Confederate Armies* (Washington, D.C.: U.S. Government Printing Office, 1911 (Electronic version 1999 by Guild Press, Indianapolis, IN)), 203.

2. James R. Arnold, *Shiloh 1862: The Death of Innocence* (Oxford, England: Osprey Publishing, LTD., 1998), 55; Bruce Catton,

Nelson G. Williams' 1st Brigade had been camped across the Corinth Road about a mile and a half from the river. On Hurlbut's order his regiments (three from Illinois and one from Indiana) marched down the wheatfield road and fell into line with Prentiss' survivors at the southern edge of Sarah Bell's cotton field, anchored on the left by the Hamburg-Savannah Road. Jacob G. Lauman's 3rd Brigade of four regiments (two Kentucky and two Indiana) pitched their tents on the south side of the Dill Branch Creek near the Hamburg-Savannah Road. Lauman had been in command of the brigade--which had been a part of Buell's Army of the Ohio until Fort Donelson--for less than a day. At about 8:00 they moved out, and by 9:00 they has rolled in at an angle to the 1st Brigade's right flank with the cotton field between them, forming a front that extended to the treeline. Two companies of the 22nd Alabama sent to draw fire was shooting at them almost as soon as they got in place. Brotzmann's battery came to rest between Williams and Lauman.[3]

Williams' brigade shot at a Confederate formation far out of range at around 9:00; probably Chalmers one of his halts. Williams, a West Point classmate of Grant's who was intensely disliked by his men, ordered his brigade to lie down in a ravine when the Confederates opened fire. As artillery shells passed harmlessly over their heads they began to see wisdom in this martinet, but it was the last they saw of him. A shell burst from one of Felix Robertson's 12-pounder Napoleons killed Williams' horse and he was paralyzed when it fell. White-haired Mexican War veteran Isaac Pugh of the 41st Illinois took command of the brigade. William Ross' Battery B, 2nd Michigan Light

---

Grant Moves South (New York: Little, Brown and Company, 1960), 226–7; Daniel, op. cit., 205, 220; John J. Hollister, *Shiloh on Your Own* (Battlefield Guide Publishers, 1973), 27, 28; David G. Martin, *The Shiloh Campaign: March - April 1862*, Great Campaigns (Pennsylvania: Combined Books, 1996), 124; James L. McDonough, *Shiloh--in Hell Before Night* (Knoxville: University of Tennessee Press, 1977), 134; Sword, op. cit., 237.

3. Reed, op. cit., 54–5.

Artillery planted their two 10-pounder and two 20-pounder Parrot rifles and a lone 6-pounder smoothbore behind Pugh.[4]

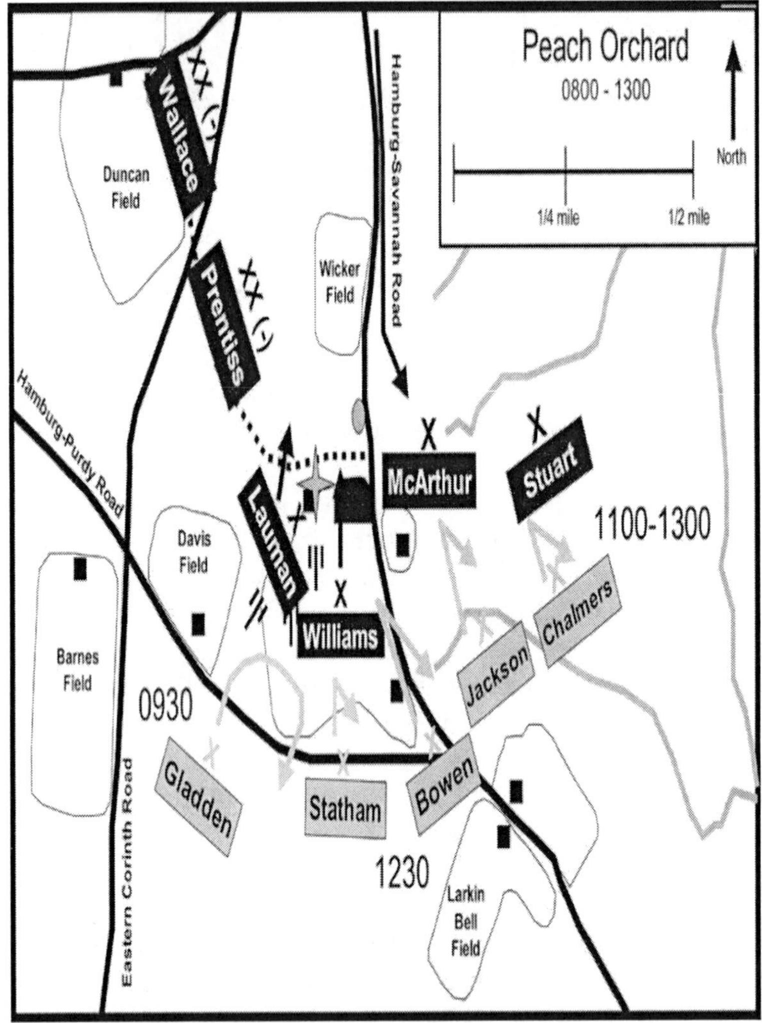

Figure 5-1, The Peach Orchard, Morning

4. Daniel, op. cit., 193–4; Martin, op. cit., 54; Sword, op. cit., 236.

William Wallace had been at breakfast when the first sounds of battle reached him as he was preparing to meet his wife, who he thought had just landed. He shook out his division of 8,500 men and formed them into a line between Lick Creek and the Corinth Road within sight of the Landing by 8:00. The ongoing army reorganization had left Wallace' three brigades with four, five and six regiments respectively, four artillery batteries and four companies of cavalry (including two of Regulars from two different regiments). Despite this, there was sufficient confidence in this outfit to use it to plug holes in the Federal line.[5]

James M. Tuttle's 1st Brigade of William Wallace's division consisted of four Iowa regiments that had encamped north of the Corinth Road by the river. Tuttle's orderly got him up to the sounds of gunfire and he rode to the division commander's headquarters for orders. He was told to lead the division's march to the fighting as the right flank unit of the division, and like the others joining the fight they met a stream of refugees, stragglers and wounded men heading for the rear. Tuttle was in position in the sunken road overlooking the southwest corner of the Duncan field and was soon under fire from Randall Gibson's brigade of Ruggles' division. His brigade followed the six 6-pounder smoothbores of John W. Powell's Battery F of the 2nd Illinois Light Artillery, which had spent the night in a reserve artillery park by the river. Powell's outfit had been shuffled to three different divisions during the "reorganization," and on Sunday morning was "unassigned," as if by then there was a distinction. Disorganization seems more usual at Shiloh than anything else.[6]

John McArthur's five-regiment 2nd Brigade was a self-styled Highland outfit in tall hats that made camp on the Hamburg-Savannah Road near Snake Creek. McArthur's 13th Missouri was sent to help Sherman; the 14th and 81st Ohio was dispatched to guard the Snake

---

5. Arnold, op. cit., 21; Daniel, op. cit., 204.

6. Daniel, op. cit., 203–4; Martin, op. cit., 52; George F. Witham, *Shiloh, Shells and Artillery Units* (Memphis, TN: Riverside Press, 1980), 35.

Creek Bridge. The brawny Scot took command of the two remaining Illinois regiments, marching to the sounds of a regimental band (no doubt with pipers) as they skirted east of Wicker Field, then to the pond along the east side of the Hamburg-Savannah Road. They picked up at least 50 stragglers along the way. They formed their first line in a ravine a half mile south of the Wicker field, joining with the 50th Illinois of Thomas W. Sweeny's 3rd Brigade. Bringing up McArthur's rear was Battery A of the Chicago (or 1st Illinois) Light Artillery under the command of Peter P. Wood.[7] The four 6-pounder smoothbores and two 12-pounder howitzers of the battery had been commanded by Ezra Taylor for a time, but Taylor moved to Sherman's division before the battle.[8]

Thomas W. Sweeny's 3rd Brigade of William Wallace's division boasted six regiments (five Illinois and an Iowa) on Sunday morning. Just after hearing faint gunshots in the 52nd Illinois' camp an unknown officer galloped in shouting that they were under attack. Soon after Sweeny, a one-armed veteran of Mexico, put his men on the road behind Tuttle and moved into a reserve position on the Eastern Corinth Road. Sweeny's brigade, like McArthur's, would not fight as a unit but as individual regiments, fed into the fight where they were needed. The 7th and 58th Illinois moved to the Duncan field to hopefully connect with McClernand on Tuttle's right, taking up positions by 9:30. The 15th Illinois was marched east soon after, joining McArthur's outfits to the left of Prentiss and Hurlbut.[9]

---

7. Sources also call it Willard's battery, Chicago battery, and Board of Trade battery.

8. Daniel, op. cit., 203, 221–2; Martin, op. cit., 52; Reed, op. cit., 49–50; Sword, op. cit., 242; Witham, op. cit., 6–7; War Department, "Reports, Union Correspondence, Etc. Series I, Volume LII, Part 1," in *War of the Rebellion: Official Records of the Union and Confederate Armies* (Washington, D.C.: U.S. Government Printing Office, 1911 (Electronic version 1999 by Guild Press, Indianapolis, IN)), 24.

9. Daniel, op. cit., 203–6; Reed, op. cit., 50.

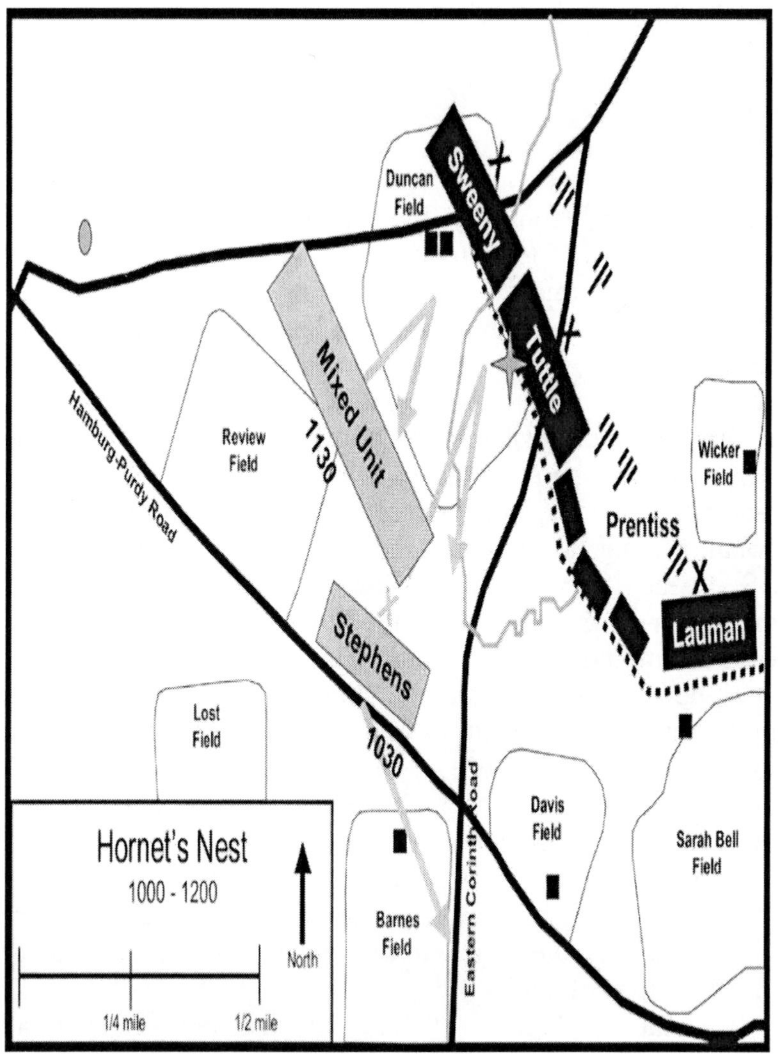

Figure 5-2, The Sunken Road, Morning

At about 9:30 a dispute as to where to put the four James rifles and two 6-pounder smoothbores of John Myers' 13th Ohio Battery resulted in the guns being placed far in front of the line, on a knoll at the western edge of the cotton field in front of Lauman and Pugh. After waiting for an hour for orders and the worst imaginable positioning, Myers battery was mauled by Robertson's, Harper's, Swett's and Girardey's (and possibly Melanchthon Smith's) guns. Soon one piece was destroyed, a caisson blew up, and a number of horses were slaughtered. The guns and all equipment were abandoned in musket range of both sides before they fired a shot. Gunners from Brotzmann's and Ross' batteries had to rush out later to spike the pieces.[10]

As Prentiss re-formed those still willing and able to fight, Grant's left flank began to take shape. He still at least 1,200 effectives (possibly as many as 1,500) forming ragged ranks between Hurlbut's and William Wallace's fresh units. Prentiss himself was somewhat dazed by the fury and speed of the Rebel attacks. He wanted his remnants to fight their way back to their camps, which by then were being pillaged. As Wallace and Hurlbut arrived Prentiss recovered his reason somewhat, putting his refugees shoulder-to-shoulder with the fresher men. Sixty men from the fought-out 21st Missouri joined the fresh (having gotten off the boats at 7:00) 600-strong 23rd Missouri; knots of survivors from the battered 18th Wisconsin fell in with the 18th Missouri; bewildered parts of the 12th Michigan met the 15th Michigan that presumably got ammunition from somewhere. They all fell in with the survivors of the well-tried 25th Missouri, scattered between the cotton field, peach orchard and sunken road. Hickenlooper's and Munch's surviving guns unlimbered among them. Though his was a division in name only, Hurlbut would later claim that Prentiss had brought together a "considerable portion of his command," but he was being generous. The whole length of this part of the front was no more than three quarters of a mile.

By 10:00 those of Prentiss' division who had survived the first hours of this battle and were still able and willing to fight had fallen in, but brigade organization was only a dim memory. Lauman and Pugh had moved back to link with McArthur just north of the peach orchard and

---

10. Cunningham, op. cit., 203; Daniel, op. cit., 193–5; Martin, op. cit., 54; Sword, op. cit., 236–8; Witham, op. cit., 17, 59.

with Prentiss in the sunken road by then. They were all tired, hungry, thirsty and more than a bit skittish, but they were in willing to be in line and armed, and that was what mattered.[11]

A battalion of Parrot rifles was positioned at the end of the line, on the east edge of the Duncan field. This was three batteries of the 1st Missouri Light Artillery; Henry Richardson's Battery D, (four 20-pounders), Fredrick Welker's Battery H (two 10-pounder and two 20-pounders), and George H. Stone's Battery K (four 10-pounders), the lot commanded by George S. Cavender, William Wallace's chief of artillery. In aggregate these 12 guns could launch about 160 pounds of metal at a time, and had the range to fire all the way to the Hamburg-Purdy Road, enfilading the entire western flank of the Federal position. Grant's left was a ready as it was going to get by about 10:00.[12]

Grant met with Prentiss sometime before 10:00 and is said to have given him a legendary "hold at all hazards" order. Grant also praised Prentiss' efforts of the morning, apparently satisfied that he had done all that could have been expected. Grant's attitude towards Prentiss and all the others, including Sherman, is characteristic of his ideas. Grant knew that these green troops were not the equal of professionals, but he also felt that that they could become just as seasoned and capable... someday, learning on the job. But in April of 1862 he could not have believed that they were there yet. Militia officers Benjamin Prentiss, William Wallace and Stephen Hurlbut were being asked to perform a delaying action against great odds with farmers, clerks and mechanics in blue uniforms who just hours before imagined that they were on a picnic in the woods while hauling cannons.[13]

---

11. Daniel, op. cit., 218; Albert Dillahunty, *Shiloh: National Military Park, Tennessee*, reprint, (Reprint 1961) (Washington, D.C.: United States Park Service, Department of the Interior, 1955), 10–11; Sword, op. cit., 241–2; War Department, "OR I/X/1," 203–4, 211, 234.

12. Cunningham, op. cit., 308; Martin, op. cit., 52; War Department, "OR I/X/1," 167–8; Witham, op. cit., 9–11.

13. Catton, op. cit., 229; Daniel, op. cit., 202–3; Dillahunty, op. cit., 11; McDonough, op. cit., 124–5; Kenneth P. Williams, *Lincoln*

While meeting with William Wallace the second time that morning, Grant apparently decided that this was the main attack by Johnston's main force from Corinth, not a feint for an all-out assault on Lew Wallace at Crump's. Certain of his strategic judgment, he sent word off to Lew Wallace to march his division south to join the main army. Somewhere in here Grant sent Rawlins off to get Buell moving to the battle. Grant knew that if his army was to survive, Pittsburg Landing had to remain under his control. William Wallace, Prentiss and Hurlbut blocked the most direct route to Landing, and their men were going to have to fight like veterans to hold on until Lew Wallace arrived.[14]

Or until the Regulars came up....

The Confederate Plan at Mid-Morning

Exactly how much the Confederate command knew of the situation for certain after Sherman's position broke is unanswerable. The Confederate command had a poor image of what the overall battlefield looked like and how precarious Grant's situation was, so there was little perceived need for urgency. The Confederate command, especially Bragg, seems to have thought that their battle was won, and that just one more good push would topple Grant's remnants.[15]

The lost Confederate opportunity was the thin spot between the Federal flanks on Sunday, barely held by Sherman's remnants and McClernand's survivors and a mob or two of scattered regiments between the Water Oaks Pond and the sunken road. The undefended parts of this vulnerable area varied in size from a few hundred smoky

---

Finds a General: A Military Study of the Civil War. Volume Three: Grant's First Year in the West (New York: The McMillian Company, 1952), 369.

14. Edward H. Bonekemper, *A Victor, not a Butcher: Ulysses S. Grant's Overlooked Military Genius* (Washington D.C.: Regenry Publishing, 2004), 46–7; Catton, op. cit., 229; Cunningham, op. cit., 189; Daniel, op. cit., 177–78, 204–7; Sword, op. cit., 310; War Department, "OR I/X/1," 204.

15. McDonough, op. cit., 136.

yards to a couple of miles as the day wore on. But this was unknown to the Confederates, who lacked the resources for tactical information gathering and analysis that might have shown them the weakness. However, even if they had known of it, they lacked the forces and organization needed to exploit it. There is enough evidence to support Samuel Lockett's contention that Johnston believed Prentiss to be Grant's left flank unit that his maps and understanding of the area was so poor other conclusions were, to him, unlikely.

There was enough command confusion without shifting weight. While Bragg and Hardee were working over Prentiss' two brigades, Johnston had to decide what to do with John Breckinridge's three brigades. Breckinridge's corps had spent the night near Mickey's without tents or new rations, had been roused at 3:00 and had been marching since sunup. Breckinridge's 1st Brigade, that included Robert Trabue's Kentucky "orphans," had been sent to attack Sherman at about 8:00. An order at about 7:30 sent Breckinridge towards Sherman, but this was countermanded by Beauregard who, an hour later, placed John Bowen's 2nd Brigade and Winfred Statham's 3rd Brigade under Trabue and sent the ad hoc division towards the Confederate right. With most of his infantry strength detached, former Vice President Breckinridge still commanded some two or three thousand souls to follow the last orders given, to march north behind Polk. He did not realize that where he was pointed was the gap in Grant's line that might have ended him up at the Landing. But other orders and the Hornet's Nest trap would divert him. Between 8:00 and 1:00 Trabue's men marched east by north through defeated Federal camps and the carnage of battle, and along the way had two regiments, an infantry battalion and a battery sent elsewhere.[16]

As the Confederates moved towards the sunken road, cotton field and peach orchard they surveyed a forbidding 300 yards or so of open ground between the treelines and the Federals. This was a good spot to

---

16. Daniel, op. cit., 196; William C. Davis, *The Orphan Brigade: The Kentucky Confederates Who Couldn't Go Home* (Garden City, NY: Doubleday & Company, 1980), 83.

defend but lousy to attack with infantry. As soon as anything Confederate broke cover, the Federals could see the difference between a well-dressed officer and a private in rags, could see a musket go up to a shoulder, and could tell if the gunners were loading the cannons with ball or canister. This was a zone where courage and tactics, leadership and devotion to cause would not count as much as sharpshooters and good gunnery, masses of men and raw energy, cover and firepower. It was nearly a mile of killing zone well covered by some 11,000 men and 38 guns--the Western Front of 1914-18 without the machine guns or the gas.[17]

If a Confederate San Janctio was out of the question by mid-morning so was their Austerlitz. This fight was stacking up to be a Borodino unless they could crack the Federal left; otherwise it was to be Grant's New Orleans.

Gwin and the Gunboats Sunday Morning

Out on the Tennessee River, William Gwin in *Tyler* and James Shirk in *Lexington* spent the early morning in routine duties; routine, that is, for gunboats on western rivers. Shipboard routine on river gunboats was different from their open-water cousins in that they did not see the dawn with decks cleared and guns run out. There were only a handful of men on the little vessels who would have known what real naval routine was like.

Part of their routine may have been a daily count of rat carcasses, for *Tyler* was said to have been a rat-infested scow. The pest problem was rampant on all wooden ships with food on board, but was more manageable at sea. Where the river gunboats never left sight of land vermin like rats, fleas and mosquitoes simply could not be got rid of. Another job was to feed the bear (with what is not known), kept on

---

17. Paddy Griffith, *Battle Tactics of the Civil War* (Mansfield, England: Fieldbooks, 1986), 36–37; Brent Nosworthy, *Bloody Crucible of Courage: Fighting Methods and Combat Experience of the Civil War* (New York: Carroll and Graf Publishers, 2003), 214; Sword, op. cit., 239, 243.

Tyler as a mascot that frequently swiped at the dogs the men kept to control rats. A duty familiar to all coal-burning vessels was filling the coal bunkers, a grueling and filthy half-day chore that had to be done about once every two weeks or less. Filling *Lexington*'s bunkers once required 2,375 sacks of coal (each sack was about a bushel of around a hundred pounds) and only the captain, the surgeon and the ill-near-death were exempt from working it.[18]

Tyler had spent Saturday night patrolling the river south of Pittsburg Landing. By 9:25 Sunday Gwin realized that something was going on ashore and had positioned his vessel a mile south of Pittsburg Landing.[19] *Lexington* had spent the night in the vicinity of Crump's Landing, and heard firing from Pittsburg. It wasn't until 10:15 that she joined *Tyler* off Pittsburg Landing. Since it took Grant's headquarters boat an hour to make the same trip we may surmise that either *Lexington* heard the firing at least an hour after Lew Wallace and Grant did; that *Lexington* was a slow boat; or that 321 ton, 178 foot unarmed *Tigress* was a very fast one.[20]

---

18. Dennis J. Ringle, *Life in Mr. Lincoln's Navy* (Annapolis, MD: Naval Institute Press, 1998), 39, 51, 85.

19. The attentive logbook entries were needed for precise navigation on open water, and it was that need that provides us with the exact times. If the US Navy contributed nothing else to the Army's gunboats it brought them leadership, discipline and the need for careful record keeping.

20. Charles Dana Gibson, *Dictionary of Transports and Combatant Vessels, Steam and Sail, Employed by the Union Army, 1861–66*, The Army's Navy Series (Camden, Maine: Ensign Press, 1995), 316; Navy Department, "West Gulf Blockading Squadron from January 1, 1865 to January 31 1866; Naval Forces on Western Waters from May 8, 1861 to April 11, 1862; Series 1 Volume 22," in *Official Records of the Union and Confederate Navies in the War of the Rebellion*, reprint, 1987 (Washington, D.C. (reprint Harrisburg, PA): Government Printing Office (reprint National Historical Society),

When the gunboats came under some fire by late Sunday morning the situation was so confused that they did not shoot back for fear of hitting Federal troops. Lacking instructions to the contrary, Shirk took *Lexington* back north again to support Lew Wallace as the Federal prebattle plan apparently dictated. By the time he got there Wallace was gone. Lew Wallace got the order to join Grant at about 11:30 and was on the move within a few minutes, so it may have been afternoon before Shirk arrived off Crump's. It was 4:00 in the afternoon before *Lexington* rejoined *Tyler* south of Pittsburg Landing.

For the moment we need to remember that it took a steamboat with no known speed trials but rated at seven knots two hours to cover the distance between Crump's Landing (upstream from Savannah) and Pittsburg Landing, and an unknown time (probably an hour) to get back down again.[21] *Tigress*, unarmed and not carrying many passengers, needed about an hour to go upstream from Crump's Landing to Pittsburg Landing.[22]

No-Man's Land

As much as shifting the mass of attack around towards the river would cost them in time, confusion and exposure, Johnston and Beauregard nonetheless tried it at about 9:30 with poor results. Beauregard issued the orders first to Breckinridge, then Johnston issued orders through Jacob Thompson, a volunteer aide on Beauregard's staff

---

1908), 762; Fredrick Way, *Way's Packet Directory, 1848–1994* (Athens, OH: Ohio University Press, 1983), 455.

21. Since the Army bought *Lexington* practically new her builders hadn't tried her yet, and the Army would have had no particular reason to find out just how fast she really was. At the time the only way to know was to take an average of runs between points, which made sense when setting freight rates but was somewhat frivolous for a gunboat.

22. Navy Department, op. cit., 765; War Department, "OR I/X/1," 169.

and an antebellum friend of Prentiss, that Beauregard should shift Breckinridge to the right about half an hour later. With this instruction Johnston told Beauregard that he should act on his own information. This effectively ceded tactical command to Beauregard, making Johnston a supernumerary of a very senior kind.[23]

One of the relatively unblooded Confederate brigades by midmorning was under William Stephens, a part of Cheatham's division. Stephens was bringing up the rear of Polk's corps, and had spent the night across the Pittsburg-Corinth Road. Beauregard ordered Stephens to move his two regiments and two infantry battalions to the east. Cheatham joined Stephens at the south end of the Duncan field at about 10:00, just as William Wallace was getting into position. Cheatham saw the foolhardiness of such a small unit committing to an assault on such a strong position. Waiting for more units to join him, Beauregard brought up Melanchthon Smith's Mississippi battery of two 6-pounder smoothbores and four 12-pounder Napoleons. Munch's battery killed several of Smith's battery horses before they could unlimber. Continuing to deploy, Smith's gunners came under heavy fire from the Missouri Parrots. Smith's gunners, very exposed in their Duncan field position, lasted for an hour before they withdrew.[24]

By 10:30 Bragg's attention and much of his command was involved with the Federal left flank, and had given the position the "Hornet's Nest" moniker. Swett's battery, separated from Hardee by miles by then, blasted some sharpshooters from Sweeny's brigade out of a hide near the Duncan farm buildings. Bragg found Randall Gibson's brigade standing around waiting for something to do, and Bragg had to get them going. A small fire broke out just west of the cotton field, contributing more smoke to the confusion. Men were being struck down by hot metal and other deadly missiles almost at random, with

---

23. Cunningham, op. cit., 336; Daniel, op. cit., 197; Reed, op. cit., 44.

24. Cunningham, op. cit., 245; Martin, op. cit., 54; Reed, op. cit., 84; Sword, op. cit., 244; War Department, "OR I/X/1," 168, 437; Witham, op. cit., 9–12, 59–60.

Federal artillery shelling anything outside their lines that even looked Confederate. The Confederate battlespace was only barely managed at the edge of chaos.[25]

George Maney commanded a scratch Confederate brigade that had been guarding Greer's Ford on Lick Creek, waiting for Buell's possible arrival from Hamburg. They departed this position at about 11:00. One version of why they abandoned their post says there was an order from Beauregard calling them up; another has Nathan B. Forrest's cavalry threatening to desert and join the battle.[26]

The position occupied by William Wallace, Prentiss, Hurlbut and scatterings from other units quickly became a bullet magnet. This appellation has been given to high-value targets by wargamers and other military thinkers to describe the mystical power of battleships, aircraft carriers, heavy bombers, bunker complexes, tanks and crew-served weapons have to draw attention and combat strength. This kind of distraction is also used by magicians who use pretty girls to draw the audience's eyes, even if ever-so-briefly, so rabbits can pop neatly out of hats. The trick works because the audience doesn't know to look elsewhere, and often wants to be fooled. While magicians are harmless and games are amusing the Hornet's Nest was neither, and the Confederates were suckered into attacking it because they didn't know *not* to.

James Powell was killed at about 11:00, somewhere near the sunken road. A color bearer of his beloved 25th Missouri died next to him. One of the only Union officers who saw danger in the woods early Sunday died knowing he should have been heeded earlier, but the attitudes of the time did not give themselves to recriminations in that way. Powell died having seen to it that his neighbors and friends had prepared themselves for the fight of their lives.[27]

---

25. Cunningham, op. cit., 245; Daniel, op. cit., 209.
26. McDonough, op. cit., 133.
27. Sword, op. cit., 255.

The Federal Right Holds

Sherman's refugees were drawing up ragged bunches and uniform ranks on McClernand's right. Hare formed McClernand's left flank some hundred yards south of the Hamburg-Corinth Road edging the Review field and was soon under fire at about 200 yards, losing the two senior officers of the 18th Illinois. Marsh's brigade made up the right of the division line, containing some 1,500 men and three batteries on the Corinth Road. Between Hare and Marsh, at the northeast corner of the Review field with a clear field of fire, was Edward McAllister's Battery D of the 1st Illinois Light Artillery, consisting of four 24-pounder howitzers. "Light" here had nothing to do with these guns, because artillery pieces of this caliber were meant to smash seasoned oak ship hulls. The guns were unwieldy because they were so heavy and their ammunition was so bulky, but one of McAllister's guns could spew a regiment's volume of musket balls with a single discharge.

Jerome Burrows' 14th Ohio Battery took up positions behind Marsh. Burrows was equipped with four 6-pounder Wiard rifles and two 12-pounder Wiard howitzer cast from low-carbon cast iron (a low-grade steel), some of the most technologically advanced guns in the area. Norman Wiard, the Army Superintendent of Ordnance Stores before the war, had introduced the gun system in 1860, and only 11 batteries of Wiard guns were ever made. How this battery and the one in Buell's army got to Shiloh in the hands of volunteers is anyone's guess.[28]

Raith's worn and flighty brigade finally found the rest of its division and fell in to the right of McClernand's line by 9:30, with Sherman forming on his right. Nispel's three surviving guns joined the line at about the same time as Raith. Adolph Schwartz, Battery E's

---

28. Cunningham, op. cit., 222–3; Daniel, op. cit., 178–9; Philip Katcher, *American Civil War Artillery 1861–65* (Oxford, UK: Osprey Publishing, 2001), 42–4; Martin, op. cit., 52; Reed, op. cit., 46–7; Warren Ripley, *Artillery and Ammunition of the Civil War* (New York: Promontory Press, 1970), 165–67; Ibid., 310; Witham, op. cit., 2, 4, 6.

commander and St. Louis organizer, took charge of them once again.[29] They took positions at the intersection of the Hamburg-Purdy Road and the Hamburg-Corinth Road southeast of the Water Oaks Pond just to the left of Raith. When Marsh, Raith, and Hare were all in position, and what was left of Hildebrand's brigade, McDowell's more or less intact command and Buckland's ragged outfit joined to the west, they tied in with the sunken road line: Grant had something of a continuous front from the Tennessee River to Owl Creek for the first time all morning. Sherman's and McClernand's line, with Veatch's brigade, contained about 15,000 men and 25 guns, a formidable force. But the men were shaky and many of the units were not in supporting range of each other. The line looked better on paper than it really was on the ground.[30]

By 10:00 Sunday morning the best the Confederates could do was to keep moving roughly north and hope for the best. William Hardee's corps was a decimated fiction, consisting of what was left of Hindman's division--by then no more than a regiment--and Patrick Cleburne's survivors. Braxton Bragg's men were primarily interested in chasing what they thought was Prentiss' refugees; Leonidas Polk's were divided between the two fronts and John Breckinridge's brigades were still marching but were nearly forgotten.[31]

Most of Johnston's combat strength was engaged by 10:00, or was about to be. Ignoring the firepower of the gathering Hornet's Nest, which would have done him no good whatsoever and shifting around to

---

29. Nispel is credited as being the battery commander because Schwartz was busy as chief of staff to McClernand.

30. Cunningham, op. cit., 222; Daniel, op. cit., 178–9; Reed, op. cit., 24, 37, 54; Sword, op. cit., 310, 319–20; War Department, "OR I/X/1," 146.

31. Thomas L. Connelly, *Army of the Heartland: The Army of the Tennessee, 1861–62*, reprint, 1995 Edition (Baton Rouge: Louisiana State University Press, 1967), 165.

another flank meant stretching his already thin center and left flanks. He was stuck with having to attack a nearly impregnable position.[32]

By 10:00, Grant sent for the 15th and 16th Iowa regiments that had been left at the Landing. Unless he did something to shore up his right flank he couldn't hold it. About then, Sherman met Grant on the Jones field, about a mile northeast of where his division was coming off the ridge near the Shiloh Church. By most accounts Sherman told Grant of his wounds (he had two by then) his loss of two horses and his need for ammunition. Sherman's men had been in action for four hours and more, his camps were overrun and his ammunition wagons were God-knew-where. Grant said that the ammunition situation was being addressed, and then left Sherman to do what he was supposed to do. Though Sherman was nervous about his performance, Grant had other things to worry about than a professionally-trained division commander who had held his position against a sudden attack for over two hours; and apparently he was never worried about Sherman's ability to fight his battle on his own. By the time Grant met McClernand by the Water Oaks Pond, both men were weary and likely didn't have much to say to each other; no one recorded what was said. Grant was not one for idle conversation, particularly on *that* morning, so it likely wasn't much.[33]

---

32. S. H. Lockett "Surprise and Withdrawal at Shiloh in *Battles and Leaders of the Civil War Volume 1* (New York: Thomas Yoseloff, 1956 (Electronic Edition 1997 by H-Bar Enterprises)), 608; McDonough, op. cit., 106–7.

33. James S. Brisbin, "The Battle of Shiloh," in *New Annals of the Civil War* (New York: Stackpole Books, 2004), 56; Ulysses S. Grant, "The Battle of Shiloh," in *Battles and Leaders of the Civil War Volume 1* (New York: Thomas Yoseloff, 1956 (Electronic Edition 1997 by Guild Press)), 473; Ulysses S. Grant, *Memoirs* (New York: Da Capo Press, 1982), 178; Geoffrey Perret, *Ulysses S. Grant, Soldier and President* (New York: Random House, 1997), 189–90; McDonough, op. cit., 124–5; Brooks D. Simpson, *Ulysses S. Grant: Triumph Over Adversity, 1822–1865* (New York: Houghton Mifflin Company,

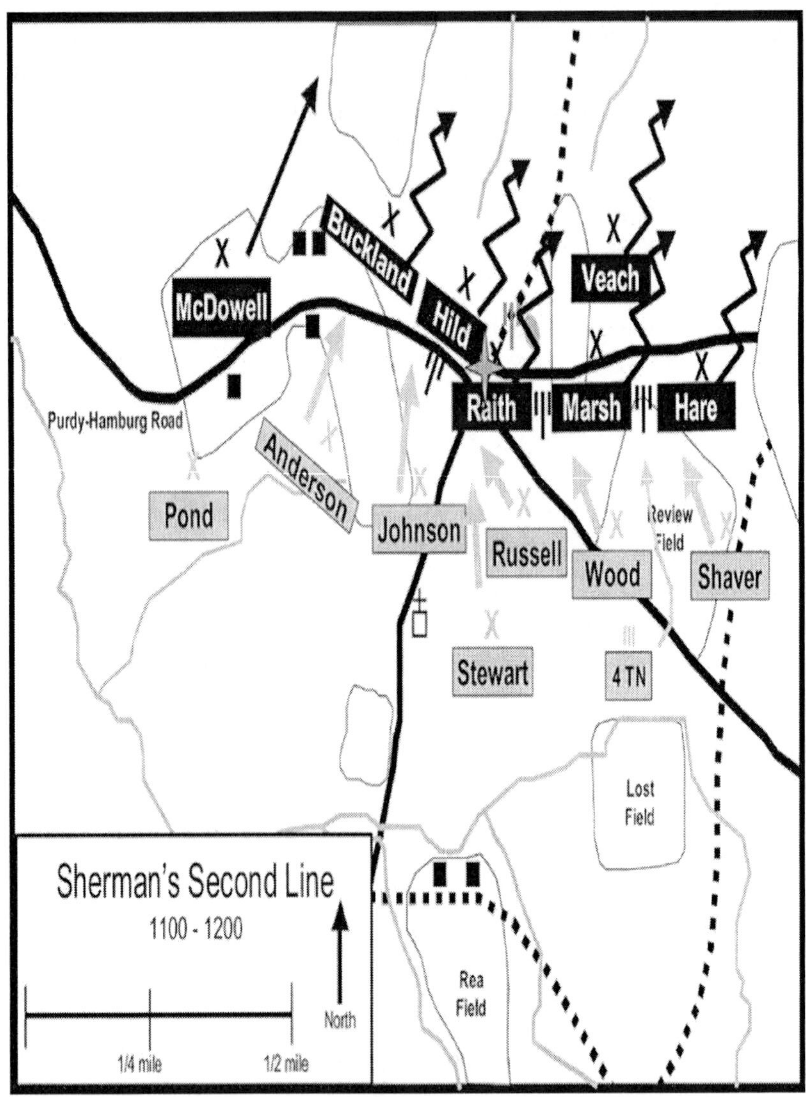

Figure 5-3, Sherman and McClernand, Late Morning

College Division, 2000), 131; Sword, op. cit., 324; War Department, "OR I/X/1," 288; Williams, op. cit., 365.

The Confederate assault on this line started with an attack on Marsh sometime after 10:00. S.A.M. Wood's remnants, on their feet for more than five hours already and without their commander, didn't get very close before they went to ground; without a recognized commander and few officers left they were just a well-intentioned mob. Smith P. Bankhead's Tennessee Battery of four 6-pounders and two 12-pounder howitzers dueled with Burrows' guns to limited effect, being severely outranged. The 4th Tennessee of Stewart's brigade, commanded by Rufus Neely, had become separated but was in Bragg's eye line. At about 10:30, the 4th Tennessee was either ordered to take McAllister's battery, or they volunteered for the job (sources differ). As Hindman went down after his horse was destroyed by one of McAllister's guns, he is said to have cried, "Tennesseans, take that [McAllister's] battery" before he was carried off the field.[34]

The 4th had been watching the battle for about four hours, had already lost their Major and one company commander, and marched forward unsupported with Hindman's plea ringing in their ears, a forlorn hope if ever there was one.[35]

McAllister's guns could wipe out a company in the blink of an eye, but on the Tennesseans came. Crossing in a maelstrom of hot metal for about 800 yards through the Review field to a stand of light timber, they kept moving. The 45th and 48th Illinois mistook the Tennessee flag for a Federal color for a moment, and then cut loose; the 4th Tennessee lost a man down every four steps forward to musketry and McAllister's guns.[36]

Then the 4th Tennessee stopped, dressed ranks, loosed a cloud of lead and charged the Federal line through the smoke and hot metal with fixed bayonets.

---

34. Daniel, op. cit., 179.

35. A forlorn hope was the first group of volunteers that rushed into a breach in a fortress' walls. They usually did not survive the effort.

36. Cunningham, op. cit., 235.

With both their colonel and lieutenant colonel down the 48th Illinois broke, and the 45th Illinois went after them. Then the 4th Tennessee slammed into McAllister's gunners. Wounded four times himself and with barely enough horses and time to get three guns away, McAllister left one of his monsters and two gunners to the Confederates. In their impetuous charge, the 4th Tennessee suffered nearly 200 casualties, but they alone broke a stationary infantry brigade supported by artillery and captured a battery position; by then they were a quarter mile in advance of the rest of their army. They lost 219 total casualties at Shiloh, about half what they brought.[37]

The 4th Tennessee attacked--and McAllister's battery defended--because of motives much older and deeper than states or unions. What drove them is what drives everyone who has ever fought for their lives anywhere. The 4th traced their lineage to the Tennessee militia that fought in the 1781 battle of King's Mountain—a battle fought without a Continental in sight--but they weren't the only unit at Shiloh with ancient roots. For good or ill, all these militiamen were needed for an important job, and they did it simply because it needed doing. That's all any American fighter needs to know: here's this dirty job; it needs doing; there's no one else; if it don't get done we're in it deep; now go do it 'cause you know your sup'osed to.

By 10:30, Raith's brigade, linked with the rest of McClernand's division only visually because of the Water Oaks Pond to its left, wavered and fell apart, streaming to the north and east. More Confederates were moving past Sherman's position and into McClernand. Wood's remnants aimed themselves at Burrows' battery, which had been left without support and were loading whatever they could stuff into the tubes. While men, trees and thickets were being blasted by his screaming metal Burrows, all his officers, his orderly and seventy of the battery's horses were hit during a charge of the 16th

37. Daniel, op. cit., 179–80; William Fox, *Fox's Regimental Losses* (Albany, NY: Randow Printing Company, 1889 [Electronic version 1997 by Guild Press of Indiana]), 561; Sword, op. cit., 312–13; Ibid., 234–5; War Department, "OR I/X/1," 432; Witham, op. cit., 2.

Alabama and 27th Tennessee, which grabbed the battery's guns in a rush. The last of Marsh's regiments, the 11th Illinois, had been fighting for about ten minutes when Burrows battery was overrun, and they bolted for the rear without much hesitation. As Burrows' surviving horses and mules panicked, they dashed through Veatch's 14th Illinois, throwing them into confusion.[38]

The 154th Tennessee regiment and Blythe's Mississippi Battalion marched over Waterhouse's former position and straight into Timony's six James rifles and the hard-firing 11th Iowa. As with Burrows' battery, Timony's horses died in their harnesses as the Confederates came within 50 yards of the battery, endangering the guns as the Confederates surged onwards and surrounded both the battery and the 11th Iowa. As all but three companies of the 11th Iowa scattered, both their commander and their Major were killed, but Timony managed to save two of his guns and a caisson. As Blythe's battalion went after Sherman's remnants their commander, a former US ambassador to Havana, was killed by a canister ball that blew a one-inch hole through his chest. But McClernand's artillery was gone by 11:00, and so was the left of his line.[39]

Crossroads

In about the middle of the Shiloh battlefield is a triangle of joining roads, the Pittsburg-Corinth, Ridge, and the Purdy-Hamburg of a nature to be critical in mot battles. With both armies striking each other with a mixture of panic and resolve, the best positions at Shiloh were those that afforded cover, clear fields of fire, and access to water. In the confused soldier's battle of Shiloh this "crossroads" area was between Grant's two wings; the bullet magnet of the Federal left and the more open Federal right flank, both with access to water that the crossroads between lacked. Since Johnston's stated plan was to overload the

---

38. Cunningham, op. cit., 228–9, 231; Daniel, op. cit., 180–82; Sword, op. cit., 313–5; Witham, op. cit., 6.

39. Cunningham, op. cit., 231–2; Daniel, op. cit., 183; Sword, op. cit., 314, 320; Witham, op. cit., 1.

Confederate right flank along the river, the importance of the crossroads was minimal to the Confederates. Shiloh didn't really have a "center" for more than a few hours, despite Grant's later claim that, except for a few minutes after the Hornet's Nest collapsed; he held a continuous line between the Owl and Lick Creeks all Sunday.[40]

If Johnston had any idea that Grant had no real joining between the flanks, and *if* he had the resources to exploit the gap--very big *ifs*--he *might* have been able to bypass the bullet magnet around the pond and gone straight to the Landing, but he never did. At about 10:30 the senior Confederate officers tried to address the disorganization problem by having the corps commanders take charge of parts of the battlefield. By the end of the day, Hardee was in the western end of the area, with Polk to his east, then Bragg, and finally Breckinridge by the river. But Hardee only fought Sherman and McClernand and would have known of the hole for certain (and that isn't clear), while the other three were all working over the Hornet's Nest.

Though Sherman's survivors and Raith's brigade had stopped running on or near this road junction by 11:00, all they doing was ineffectually sniping at advancing Confederates. Patton Anderson's brigade was to the left of Blythe's battalion advancing on Sherman's position, but was brought to a halt by Schwartz's guns. Irving Hodgson's Louisiana Battery (also known as the 5th Company of the Washington Artillery of New Orleans) of two 6-pounder smoothbores, two 12-pounder howitzers, and two 3.3-inch Parrot rifles rolled up and started working on Schwartz's position. Anderson goaded his men forward while Behr's battery took a position west of the intersection. Then Behr was killed off his horse and, since his gunners could understand no English at all, everything went sour at once and they bolted, leaving all five guns behind (one was still with McDowell) that the Confederates were happy to grab, but 65 of the battery's horses

---

40. Grant, "Shiloh," 473; Grant *Memoirs*, 177.

were already dead, making the guns hard-to-use prizes. Sherman's shaky second line broke.[41]

Schwartz's battery was in trouble and without effective support. He pushed parts of the 17th Illinois forward to obtain a better field of fire and withdrew two guns. The 17th ran out of ammunition and pulled back. Schwartz was hit in the leg and Nispel, resuming command, was compelled to drag the remaining howitzer out by hand since all the gun's horses had already been killed or wounded. Though part of the 43rd Illinois was still fighting in support the ground was too soft to make good time, so Nispel spiked the last piece and left it behind.[42]

At about 11:00, Raith's right thigh was shattered by a ball. Command of McClernand's 3rd Brigade would have come back to Reardon if there was still a brigade to command, but by then there was no cohesion to it. Without the 11th Iowa, Hare's brigade consisted of the 8th and 18th Illinois and 13th Iowa. Hare's men were hit by Hindman's, who was back on his feet and personally leading Shaver's survivors and the 12th Tennessee in a frontal attack. Shaver's men had little left to fight with except bayonets, and as they closed the range their ranks thinned with every step. Uneasy because of Marsh's disintegration, the 8th Illinois on Hare's left crumbled and the other two regiments broke for the rear. As the 46th Illinois tried to reform half the officers and two color bearers were cut down in crossfire. As the 46th came apart again, the 15th Illinois' colonel was badly wounded. He roared at his men to form up before he was shot in the chest and killed. Moments later the 15th's Major was shot in the head. With all the officers but two captains killed or wounded, the 15th Illinois ran off.

As Marsh's and Raith's commands fell apart, Veatch was in for it. Trying to hold his remaining two regiments together, Veatch told the men to lie down. After a volley hummed over their heads they stood up

---

41. Cunningham, op. cit., 223; Daniel, op. cit., 183; Ripley, op. cit., 111–12; Sword, op. cit., 320–21; War Department, "OR I/X/1," 497; Witham, op. cit., 17, 19, 60.

42. Sword, op. cit., 321; Witham, op. cit., 4.

and fired a roll of musketry that was simply not enough to stop the oncoming Confederate tide, and they broke for the rear. Before noon, most of McClernand's division was a gang of refugees, and Southern infantry dominated this part of the world, having captured enough artillery equipment to make up two batteries.[43]

But these were still militiamen, and they didn't run for long. Hare's men only ran for about 100 yards before they turned back around to fight. The 14th Illinois and 25th Indiana stepped back for a bit, and then formed alongside Hare. McAllister's three brutes wheeled in on line with the 14th Illinois. The Confederates were fading fast and, for the moment, paused. That was enough for Grant's right flank to survive.[44]

The Federals on the Hamburg-Purdy Road couldn't stay much past 11:00, and fell back a half mile north to the Jones field in the face of only sporadic fire from the Confederates. By 11:00, the 15th and 16th Iowa had arrived on the battlefield, over 1,500 of them, on the northern edge of the Jones field near the 70th Ohio. They were issued their first ammunition while they were standing in the firing line. The 15th Iowa marched forward in columns of fours and took fire in flank from Russell's brigade, who had advanced as far north as Marsh's camps. The Iowans swarmed into a coherent line and lurched forward with the 16th on their left flank. The 70th Ohio that had been on the 16th's right departed the field. The Iowans took appalling fire, both regiments losing their colonels to dangerous wounds.

By 11:30, Sherman and McClernand were organizing skeletons of fourteen regiments from whatever troops they could reach. These included perhaps a thousand of Buckland's stoics, including most of the 70th Ohio, and about five hundred of Hildebrand's nervous and weary refugees that included Jesse Appler, the 53rd Ohio's former commander who was toting a musket and fighting as a private. Joining them was McDowell's relatively unblooded brigade, the only intact Federal brigade in the area and still dragging one of Behr's guns. Ezra

---

43. Daniel, op. cit., 184–5.

44. Ibid., 185–6; Sword, op. cit., 316–17; War Department, "OR I/X/1," 124.

Taylor took charge of the scatterings of a half dozen batteries, including Waterhouse's two pieces, McAllister's monsters, Timony's survivors and Barrett's lone gun, and positioned them on a ridge at the south of the Jones field. While Raith's remnants were clinging to Sherman because of proximity, McClernand had a handful of Hare's men, two coherent regiments from Marsh's brigade, and whatever Veatch could lay hands on; altogether about 2-3,000 or so, or 2/3rds of his numbers from four hours before. Also by 11:30 the 15th and 16th Iowa pulled out of the Jones field, having suffered 316 casualties for their troubles. In less than an hour Sherman and McClernand had ruined another Confederate attack, silenced another battery, and bought Grant more time.[45]

A Nest of Hornets

Even though there was a Confederate shift to the east and the river, those units that were already by the river and shooting at gunboats insisted on being drawn to the cluster of the Federal left. After the 2nd Texas expended itself flanking the 55th Illinois and putting the 71st Ohio to flight on the river flank, Jackson's brigade moved on to assault McArthur's position east of the peach orchard at about 11:00 with no appreciable results other than to blast the blossoms into what looked like a snowstorm.[46]

This attack was just the first. Somewhere about 11:20, Cheatham personally led Stephens' brigade in an assault on the sunken road, while Smith's battery banged away in support. The four regiments of Iowans on that part of the line were fighting from a reverse slope and had all the advantages. To the Cheatham's northeast the 8th Illinois of Hare's brigade from McClernand's division that had been routed maybe an hour before rallied enough to join the 7th Illinois of Sweeny's brigade on the edge of the Duncan field. The Confederates gamely marched towards the Federal line but didn't get halfway across

---

45. Cunningham, op. cit., 247–8; Daniel, op. cit., 186.

46. Daniel, op. cit., 207–9; Hollister, op. cit., 27; Sword, op. cit., 237; War Department, "OR I/X/1," 479–80.

before the fire of six regiments behind cover drove the Confederates to ground and then back. Stephens was hurt when his horse fell and was out of the fight but so was his scratch command, out of it for hours.[47]

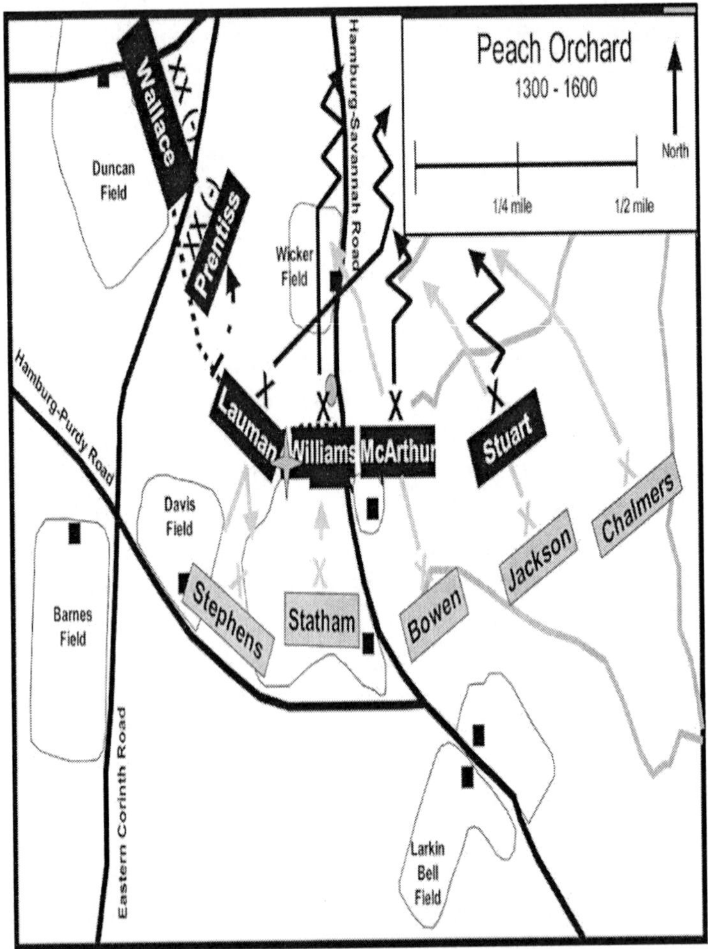

Figure 5-4, Act One of the Magic Show

47. Cunningham, op. cit., 245–6; Sword, op. cit., 246.

Randall Gibson's brigade of three Louisiana and an Arkansas regiment had started with 2,350 men on Sunday morning. They had been following Hindman for a while, and were hit by Federal artillery without a chance of returning fire. Bragg ordered them up from the Barnes' field and across the Davis wheatfield to attack Lauman and Prentiss at about 11:00. Lauman's Indiana/Kentucky brigade was in cover so dense the Federals could barely tell that the Confederates were attacking. Lauman told his men to open fire at about a hundred yards, traditionally when he saw the gleam of Confederate bayonets. Gibson's men got ten yards away from the treeline and no closer. The 4th Louisiana stayed on the field for a volley or two then pulled back; the 19th Louisiana stood in the open for about half an hour before they too pulled out.[48]

Gibson's militiamen did this, or something like it, four times without artillery support or coordination with other attacks. His men were so tried that his report was a bitter indictment of the entire operation. In his request for a board of inquiry about the whole affair he wrote:

> ...the concentration of fire, especially on our flanks, was so great that the command, unaided by artillery, could not carry the position. I had sent [an aide] to [Bragg] after the first assault for artillery; but the request [to stop] was not granted, and in place of it he brought me orders to advance again on the enemy. In the execution of this order we charged repeatedly, as described, and were repulsed on account of his severe artillery fire, advantageous position, superior numbers, and the almost impenetrable thicket through which we had to advance. [The attacks] were repeated until the officers reported many of their men as having exhausted their ammunition....The loss of officers of every grade and of

48. Daniel, op. cit., 212; Sword, op. cit., 246.

> men had been heavy; most of the mounted officers had their horses killed....The... growth [was] so thick as to prevent anyone from seeing, or being seen, but for a short distance. It was clear to all...that we were but making a vain sacrifice of the lives of the troops.[49]

This was not a minority opinion; Cheatham expressed similar sentiments in his report of 30 April. If Gibson and Cheatham knew how bad it was, why did it continue all afternoon? Why would Bragg later write that Gibson was an "arrant coward" while blaming him for his failure to carry the position when others couldn't either? Bragg seems to have thought there was very little else he could do, and lacked command control to do anything but penny-packet assaults through that smoky hell. He had to be doing *something,* even if it was *immediately* as hopeless as Pickett's Charge was, and with about the same casualty rate (20-25%). Johnston, who was with Polk, probably thought the same way.[50]

But too there's another point: The Confederates were *ultimately* successful after an afternoon of bloodletting. One source claims Bragg lacked imagination, but that is impossible to know. If so many lives hadn't been used up we cannot know for certain what the outcome would have been. Fighting a war can be perceptually like looking for lost keys: every battle fought that is not decisive--and everywhere you look without result--is wasted until the battle is won (or the keys are found). One of the best things about history is that historians can pass judgment on things they know about, but one of the worst is that historians often make declarations about things that they cannot show. We cannot, ultimately, *know* that the Confederate charges were

---

49. War Department, "OR I/X/1," 483–4.

50. Daniel, op. cit., 213–4; McDonough, op. cit., 136; Grady McWhiney, and Perry D. Jamieson, *Attack and Die: Civil War Military Tactics and the Southern Heritage* (University, AL: University of Alabama Press, 1982), 163; Ibid., 438–9.

completely wasted. Based on modern standards we can declare that we *think* they were futile, but we cannot prove it.[51]

Sherman and McClernand had at least some ammunition for the men still paying attention to their officers and their little functioning artillery, hammering some 5-7,000 men into a sort-of line north of the Pittsburg-Corinth Road by midday. It wasn't enough to hold onto the road line, and their position was badly sited for artillery support, but it was enough to slow the Confederates down some more, and that's what mattered. But Prentiss, William Wallace and Hurlbut commanded a blue island in a surging sea of butternut that could see, but not get help from, the rest of the army.[52]

Grant would not have made a comparison between his left flank and the Confederate obsession with it and the walled farms on Wellington's flanks at Waterloo that attracted Napoleon's attention for much of his last great battle. The Emperor finally took one of them by late afternoon, but he had lost too much time; night was coming, the Imperial Guard broke on Wellington's thin red line, and Blucher's Prussians were coming up the road.[53]

Beauregard, a much better scholar of war, should have seen this and done something about it. If he and the other senior officers saw the Federal position along the sunken road and into the peach orchard as the very last of Grant's effectives, then surrounding it and destroying it made sense. If Johnston had held control of the battle up until his death that would have made sense, but he had effectively ceded it to Beauregard by early afternoon. Perhaps Johnston's control of the fighting remained even after he had tacitly given it up. Beauregard had decided that Grant was beaten, that this knot of artillery and infantry was the only resistance worth Confederate attention and pulled in everything to defeat it.

---

51. McDonough, op. cit., 138.

52. Daniel, op. cit., 185; Sword, op. cit., 323–4.

53. Geoffrey Wootten, *Waterloo 1815: The Birth of Modern Europe* (Oxford, UK: Osprey Publishing, 1992), 74–81.

If everyone is entitled to one blunder, this would have been Beauregard's. But it was not his first, nor was it his last.

CHAPTER 6
NOT BEATEN YET: SUNDAY AFTERNOON

An hour after breaking the second Federal line the Confederates on the western flank were showing no inclination to fight. Casualties mounted on the Confederate side as quickly as they did on the Federal, but were felt more deeply by the Confederates. Before midday the 27th Tennessee was led by a captain, having lost half its strength and all but three officers. Only half of S.A.M Wood's survivors were still on their feet by noon, but they were out of ammunition for a third time and could not find more for hours.

By 12:00 Shaver's brigade gallantly charged Hare's position but was massacred by McAllister's guns and the 14th Illinois frantically blazing away from their stand of trees just north of the Corinth Road. Shaver then withdrew for ammunition and to "await orders." Hindman's brigade was out of the fighting, exhausted. Hindman himself was dismounted and stunned when another of his mounts was killed. After two days of marching in the rain, many muskets were fouled by wet powder. The 4th Tennessee, no cowards they, couldn't reload any more after their wild charge and had to withdraw just to clean their weapons, and they were probably not the only outfit that had to do the same. Though muskets abandoned by friend and foe alike littered the ground, the diversity of calibers forbade rearming by scrounging. Confederate ordnancemen scoured the battlefield all day matching muskets to ammunition in effective lots. As slow as this process sounds, some Kentucky companies were rearmed as early as mid-morning.[1]

---

1. O. Edward Cunningham, (Gary D. Joiner and Timothy B. Smith, Eds.), *Shiloh and the Western Campaign of 1862* (New York: Savas Beatie, 2008), 236, 249–50; William C. Davis, *The Orphan*

Ammunition was also becoming critical for the Federals. Though Grant had promised Sherman ammunition it wasn't coming up fast enough; there weren't enough horses to move the wagons. All available animals were being grabbed to haul artillery and ambulances. The dead and wounded had to be stripped of cartridges in a hurry, but when the artillery ran out all they could do was run to the Landing. The infantry resorted to loading any cartridge that would fit the bore, resulting in a great number of misfires, stuck bullets, and ineffectual firing. Such was the ammunition exhaustion that some Federal units, including the 40th Illinois, took a cue from the Confederates that simply stopped fighting and found a quiet place to wait it out.[2]

Taylor's guns occupied the Confederates while Sherman and McClernand gathered up more bits and pieces of their commands. The 13th Missouri, fresh from the boats and unblooded, came up to support Taylor. As early as 11:00, Grant met with Sherman again, telling him to hold on as long as he could. It was probably clear by then that the Confederates were stalled. Since a large proportion of the Confederates had stopped to watch the Prentiss-Wallace-Hurlbut Magic Show, the timing was right for a counterattack on the Confederate left. Sherman, rattled but still bloody-minded, was probably thinking about a counterattack to recapture Marsh's and Hare's camps south and west of the Jones field as soon as Taylor's guns and fire from the 13th Missouri took effect, and may have mentioned this to Grant.[3]

Brigade: The Kentucky Confederates Who Couldn't Go Home (Garden City, NY: Doubleday & Company, 1980), 89; Wiley Sword, *Shiloh: Bloody April* (New York: Morrow, 1974), 317–18.

2. Spencer Jones, "The Influence of Horse Supply upon Field Artillery in the American Civil War," *The Journal of Military History* 74, no. 2 (April 2010); Sword, op. cit., 332.

3. Larry J. Daniel, *Shiloh: The Battle That Changed the Civil War* (New York: Simon & Schuster, 1997), 186, 188; Sword, op. cit., 325.

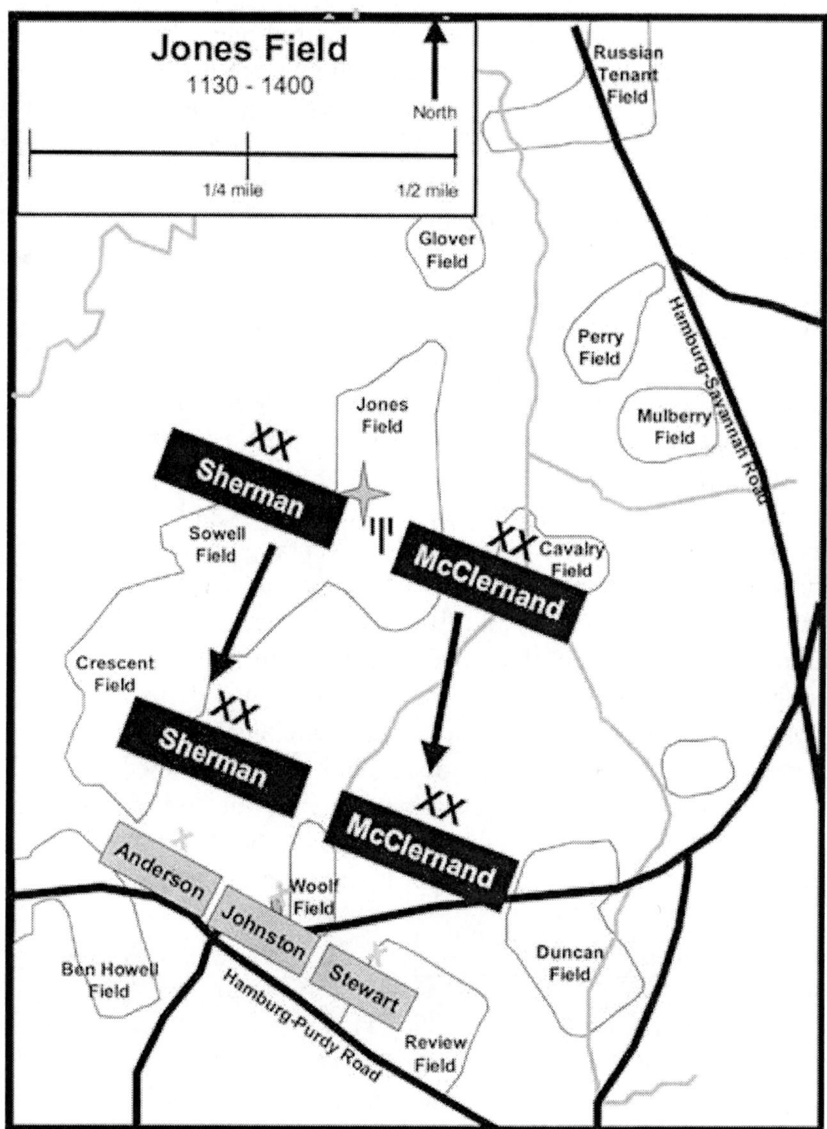

Figure 6-1, Sherman and McClernand Counterattack

As Marsh's and McDowell's brigades stepped forward and reached Taylor's guns on a low ridge, they encountered one of the Confederate miracles of the day: timely reinforcements from Robert Trabue's brigade that arrived just southeast of the Crescent field. With them was Robert Cobb's Kentucky battery of four 6-pounder smoothbores and two 12-pounder howitzers that set up in the 45th Illinois's camps just east of Hodgson's battery, north of the Woolf field and just north of the Corinth Road. Slightly behind Cobb was what was left of Johnson's and Russell's brigades. They weren't much, but they were more than the Federals were expecting. Trabue's were also the last fresh troops that Johnston had.[4]

The Federal counterattack caused the Confederates some confusion and doubtless some consternation. Behr's lone remaining gun, now handled by McDowell's footsoldiers, dehorsed George Johnson, the Confederate Provisional Governor of Kentucky. Cobb lost nearly two score men and 68 horses to Marsh's advancing infantry. Half of the 15th Iowa's remaining officers went down as casualties, and their flagstaff was shot in half by the fire first from the 154th Tennessee. The 2nd and 15th Tennessee of Johnson's brigade took the 15th Iowa under fire when the 154th ran out of ammunition.[5]

Trabue moved up through trees and thickets until he confronted McDowell's brigade moving down. Trabue got in the first volley, which hit Tom Worthington's 46th Ohio in front and in flank. They fired once and ran off and Worthington was unhorsed, but he managed to rally them a few yards back, holding out with the rest of McDowell's

---

4. Cunningham, op. cit., 249, 251; Daniel, op. cit., 188–91; Davis, op. cit., 81–2; Sword, op. cit., 326–7; Kenneth P. Williams, *Lincoln Finds a General: A Military Study of the Civil War. Volume Three: Grant's First Year in the West* (New York: The McMillan Company, 1952), 371.

5. Davis, op. cit., 84; Sword, op. cit., 330; George F. Witham, *Shiloh, Shells and Artillery Units* (Memphis, TN: Riverside Press, 1980), 77.

brigade for about an hour and a half. McDowell's brigade was reduced by a third; McDowell himself hurt in a fall from his horse.[6]

Trabue pressed on while Hardee forced more troops into a hasty attack. The 5th and 33rd Tennessee of Stewart's brigade charged wildly through an open space and into McClernand's organized rabble, which broke for the rear. Gradually the renewed Confederate attack slowed the Federal counterattack. McClernand decided that he couldn't hold where he was and ordered a withdrawal. By 1:00, the spent Federals had returned to their starting positions around the Jones field, and had backed away from their tenuous connection with Sweeny and Tuttle near the sunken road. Only about 500 men of McClernand's 3rd Brigade--Raith's old command--were still paying attention by 2:00 Sunday. This outfit was so confused that Abram Ryan, a lieutenant on Raith's staff, commanded the cohesive parts of the outfit briefly on Sunday, and turned it over to Enos Wood of the 17th Illinois, who was soon stunned after being thrown from his horse. The artillery survivors of the counterattack dueled with Confederate guns for half an hour, withdrawing eight guns when their ammunition was expended; Barrett had to leave a gun behind because of horse losses.[7]

Grant probably knew what Johnston had planned by the time Sherman's counterattack was launched. He appears to have been comfortable amid the storm of shell and smoke, riding imperturbably all over the battlefield, getting his information first hand, watching men die around him. More than once his nervous staff told him to get out of the line of fire for his own safety. He may have had it in his head that, with Lew Wallace and William Nelson on hand he could launch a double envelopment of Johnston and wipe him out, winning the war in the west by dark. But they weren't around, so Grant had to work with the material at hand. Grant and a handful of Confederate officers

---

6. Cunningham, op. cit., 254; Daniel, op. cit., 188–9; Sword, op. cit., 326, 331.

7. Cunningham, op. cit., 254, 256; Daniel, op. cit., 190–1; Davis, op. cit., 86; Sword, op. cit., 330–2.

(Chalmers among them) could read a battle like a book, an art their subordinates and superiors had not yet learned.[8]

At the Landing

By midday the object of all this *sturm und drang*--Pittsburg Landing--must have looked like a five-alarm fire in a schoolyard: boats unloading, officers moving men and crates around, refugees arriving in panic, gunners repairing their pieces and searching for ammunition, and the dull rumbling of furious battle in the near distance. Relly Madison's five 24-pounder siege guns of Battery B, 2nd Illinois "Light" Artillery were landed in this chaos by John Webster's order. These old (cast in 1838) wall-battering behemoths weighed five tons each and needed ten horses to pull. Even with steam winches on their transports (and that was not a given) these pieces would have needed hours of time and scores of men and draft animals to unload.[9]

Grant and some of his staff were on *Tigress* when Buell arrived from Savannah between 1:00 and 3:00. Back at Savannah the impression was one of a sharp skirmish, and that was the impression Buell likely had before he landed. Imagine his shock when he landed in the rear area of a terrible battle between two principle armies with thousands of refugees huddled by the river, many shouting of disaster. Buell railed in vain at those under the bluffs to form up and fight, even

---

8. Bruce Catton, *Grant Moves South* (New York: Little, Brown and Company, 1960), 230–2; Geoffrey Perret, *Ulysses S. Grant, Soldier and President* (New York: Random House, 1997), 192–3.

9. Cunningham, op. cit., 306–8; Daniel, op. cit., 249; Albert Dillahunty, *Shiloh: National Military Park, Tennessee*, reprint, (Reprint 1961) (Washington, D.C.: United States Park Service, Department of the Interior, 1955), 13–14; Philip Katcher, *American Civil War Artillery 1861–65* (Oxford, UK: Osprey Publishing, 2001), 62; James L. McDonough, *Shiloh--in Hell Before Night* (Knoxville: University of Tennessee Press, 1977), 171–3; Brooks D. Simpson, *Ulysses S. Grant: Triumph Over Adversity, 1822–1865* (New York: Houghton Mifflin Company, College Division, 2000), 133; Witham, op. cit., 33.

going so far as threaten them with gunboats. This had no effect other than some snide and nasty comments from the refugees, raising the haughty Buell's ire even more.

Buell later wrote that Grant seemed apprehensive when he met Grant, a claim that others deny. The traditional imagery of Grant midday Sunday has him serenely smoking a cigar, confidently planning for the next day's operations, expecting both Lew Wallace's and Nelson's divisions to arrive at any moment. Grant showed Buell his broken sword scabbard, hit by a piece of metal fired by Smith's Mississippi battery earlier in the day that killed James McPherson's horse. Traditionally, Buell asked what measures were being taken for Grant's retreat back across the river. Grant is said to have replied "I have not yet despaired of whipping them, General," which Buell later denied having heard. It sounds more or less like Grant, but perhaps is more colorful than the truth.[10]

Believing Grant to be worse off than he was, Buell sent word back to Nelson to backtrack to a point across the river and await steamboats, while the rest of his army was ordered to do whatever was needed to clear Savannah for traffic. To execute this movement, Buell is said to have asked Grant for steamboats, but it seems unlikely that Major General Don Carlos Buell would ask an officer he openly hated to provide for simple transportation for his own men. It seems clear that Buell thought Grant was done; it is also clear that Buell wanted Grant to *be* done.[11]

---

10. James S. Brisbin, "The Battle of Shiloh," in *New Annals of the Civil War* (New York: Stackpole Books, 2004), 57–8; Don C. Buell "Shiloh Reviewed," in *Battles and Leaders of the Civil War Volume 1* (New York: Thomas Yoseloff, 1956 (Electronic Edition 1997 by Guild Press)), 493, 493ff; Daniel, op. cit., 243; Simpson, op. cit., 132; Sword, op. cit., 350–1.

11. Brisbin, op. cit., 57; Catton, op. cit., 235; Daniel, op. cit., 243, 244; Ulysses S. Grant, *Memoirs* (New York: Da Capo Press, 1982), 178–9; McDonough, op. cit., 161–2; Perret, op. cit., 195; Sword, op. cit., 350–1.

A Version of Hell

Most accounts of the Hornet's Nest are vague on time and units for the period between 11:00 and 5:30 on Sunday, and for good reason: the place was an inferno that continued without relief, where troops blazed away at less than forty yards on occasion. When not under direct attack, continual bombardment from artillery and sniping from pickets and sharpshooters wore away at both sides. The dead and severely wounded were stripped for ammunition, canteens were shattered for the last drops, and all the water sources in the area turned vivid red even as they were used up. Cotton blooms and peach blossoms carpeted the southern edge with white and pink, interspersed with the blue and brown, gray and black of the dead and wounded that littered the area.[12]

Johnston led his battle from the front, riding to the embattled eastern flank at about noon. He became convinced that cracking the peach orchard would win his battle, and threw some 18,000 men against the combined total of no more than 4,300 Federals for hour after bloody hour. But the Confederates were so lacking in command control that none of their attacking forces ever numbered more than 4,000. Johnston had numbers available, but the cruel mathematics of time, ammunition, energy, and knowledge of the enemy didn't allow his army to mass an overwhelming infantry force for most of the day. All that the Confederate officers could do was push men into attacking lines, holding them together long enough to get within musket shot. Both armies were whipped and ragged by mid-afternoon.[13]

---

12. John J. Hollister, *Shiloh on Your Own* (Battlefield Guide Publishers, 1973), 27; Brent Nosworthy, *Bloody Crucible of Courage: Fighting Methods and Combat Experience of the Civil War* (New York: Carroll and Graf Publishers, 2003), 576.

13. Stanley Horn, *The Army of Tennessee* (Norman, OK: University of Oklahoma Press, 1941 (Reprint 1993)), 135–6; McDonough, op. cit., 143; Sword, op. cit., 250; T. Harry Williams, "Beauregard at Shiloh," *Civil War History* 1, no. 1 (March 1955): 26.

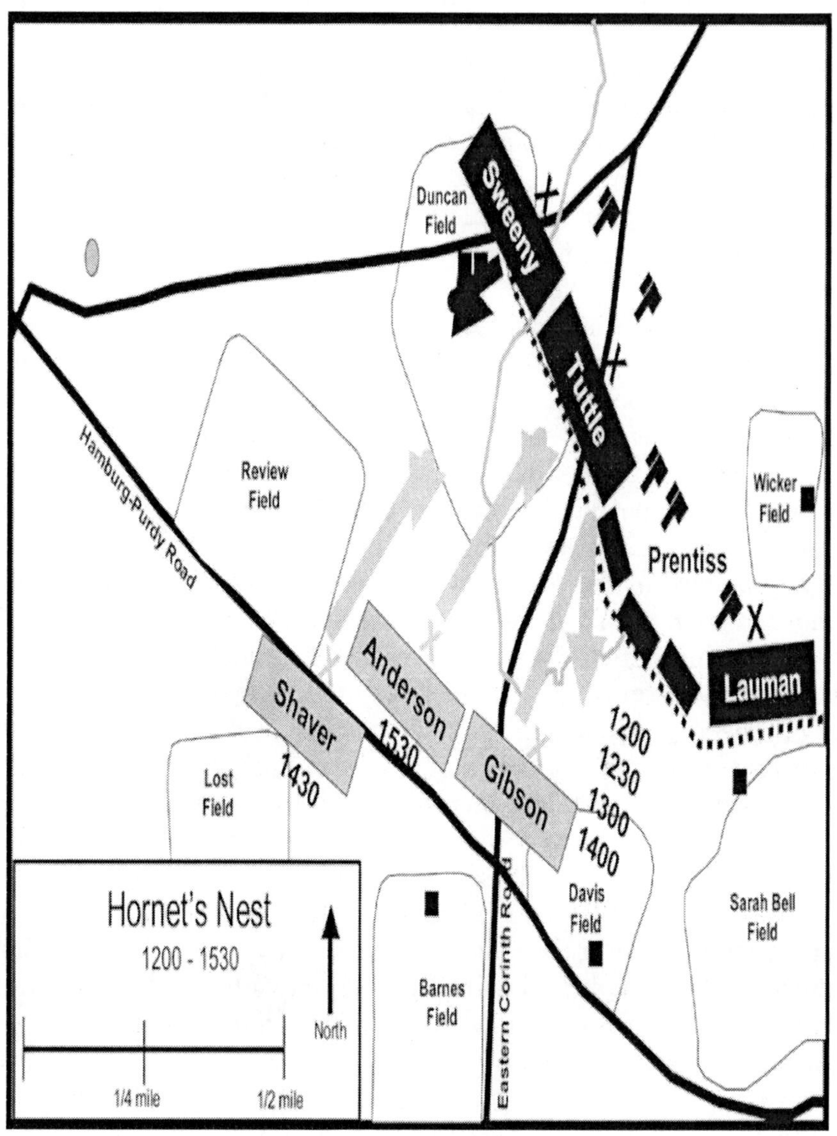

Figure 6-2 The Magic Show, Act Two

Alexander Stewart of Polk's corps built a composite force of one of his regiments, parts of Wood's surviving regiments, and all that Shaver had left, gathering them in the northwest corner of the Duncan field opposite the sunken road. Parts of Cleburne's brigade joined them by noon. There was about 3,600 Confederates in this composite, and the fact that they had never operated together wasn't very important since before that morning few Confederate brigades had. This group attacked the Federals by 1:00 and failed to get within a hundred yards of the Federal line.[14]

The omnipresent, all-consuming presence in the woods and fields, orchards and creek bottoms was noise, smoke, and the coppery smell of blood. Added to this was the earthy stench of fear in the sweat of men reeking of powder and parched till their mouths bled, with the acrid smell of burning bodies in the grass fires, mixed with smells of tree sap, peaches and hay cut by gunfire wafting in the breeze. The booming of the artillery socked eyes and brains and often caused soft palates and lungs to bounce in the overpressure of sound and rushing air, stealing breath and sight briefly from already desperate men. To avoid being hit by the buzzing bullets they stood in files behind trees, their muzzles blasting the deadened ears of their comrades in front as they blazed away at shadows barely seen through the noisy, sulfurous clouds. Every few moments another bullet, ball, shell or fragment would buzz by, striking trees and brush and men like blind stones. Splinters of wood, bark, leaves, metal, parts of human bodies and the occasional ramrod were just as dangerous as bullets themselves. Men and animals would be hit in their bedrolls, saddles, haversacks, halters, hats, blankets and coats, accumulating bruises and abrasions as well as nicks from flying metal and debris. Wounded animals, spattered with blood and foam and hurt beyond their reason, charged madly through the woods and fields.

By 2:00 the Hornet's Nest was completely isolated, far from the nearest Union units; communications in and out had ceased; command control was but a memory. Stuart's remnants, consisting of perhaps 800

---

14. Daniel, op. cit., 209.

men under Malmborg, had joined them by then, and withstood the very best that Chalmers could send at them, which was apparently nothing more than skirmishing. At about 2:15 the 54th Ohio's Kilby Smith on the far left of the Hornet's Nest had had enough. Out of ammunition, the former U.S. marshal's regiment bolted north because they could no longer contribute anything to the defense except the growing body count.[15]

At about 1:30 William Gwin sent an officer ashore see how to get his gunboats into the fight. After the 54th Ohio departed Hurlbut's left flank was in danger and he knew it. When Gwin commenced fire at 2:30 south and east of Hurlbut's lines it was startling to Breckinridge's men, who nonetheless tried to return fire but lacked the range, position and big guns to deter the gunboats and had to fall back. The gunboats were instrumental in saving Hurlbut from being flanked, and thus have been credited by some with saving Grant's army.[16]

The din was so intense that even four-footed Confederates were affected by it. A rabbit dashed out of some scrub brush and huddled next to a Federal soldier, its fear of man overwhelmed by the shrieking frenzy of sight and sound. All that men or beasts wanted was for this terrible trial to be over, but just stopping was impossible: too much

---

15. Ibid., 206, 221–3; War Department, "Shiloh, Corinth: Series I, Volume X, Part 1," in *War of the Rebellion: Official Records of the Union and Confederate Armies* (Washington, D.C.: U.S. Government Printing Office, 1911 (Electronic version 1999 by Guild Press, Indianapolis, IN)), 259.

16. Navy Department, "West Gulf Blockading Squadron from January 1, 1865 to January 31 1866; Naval Forces on Western Waters from May 8, 1861 to April 11, 1862; Series 1 Volume 22," in *Official Records of the Union and Confederate Navies in the War of the Rebellion*, reprint, 1987 (Washington, D.C. (reprint Harrisburg, PA): Government Printing Office (reprint National Historical Society), 1908), 762–3; Sword, op. cit., 283–4; War Department, op. cit., 550.

blood had been spilled, too much emotional capital invested to simply cease what had become a primal fight for life.[17]

Between 1:45 and 2:00 a spent ball hit the back of Sidney Johnston's right knee and severed his popliteal artery. Traditionally this wound was a serious but relatively minor "bleeder" that might have been treated easily with a tourniquet or sutured by a doctor. Johnston either didn't feel it or didn't think it remarkable; an old dueling wound left part of his leg insensible. An aide heard it strike and noticed that either the general or his horse, Fire-eater, was bleeding. Johnston refused to withdraw to cover and was more worried about the progress of the battle than his wound, but someone rode off to find a doctor: Johnston had sent his personal surgeon to treat casualties sometime before 1:00.

According to some accounts, Johnston reeled on Fire-eater soon after Isham Harris returned sometime after 2:00, and was already incoherent. Johnston was laid down, but quick searches found no other wounds immediately. For a "minor wound" to have this effect so quickly is remarkable, as is one account of a six or eight foot stream of blood emanating from Johnston's leg. An unused tourniquet was found in his pocket later.

There have been many claims as to who fired the shot, from small arms to artillery to even friendly fire, but in that storm of flying particulates it hardly matters. Johnston had been hit four other times that day that no one noticed: a spent object struck the middle of his right thigh, another glanced off the back of his right hip, another cut his left boot sole, another grazed around a shoulder blade. Only one of these could have drawn blood, the others merely added to the misery of a 59-year old man who probably hadn't slept more than six hours in four days, who likely hadn't had a square meal in a week or so out of empathy with his men, and who had lived with unrelieved

---

17. Catton, op. cit., 132–3; Earl J. Hess, *The Union Soldier in Battle: Enduring the Ordeal of Combat* (Lawrence, KS: University of Kansas Press, 1997), 25, 46–9; McDonough, op. cit., 131, 139–43; Nosworthy, op. cit., 215–19; Sword, op. cit., 301–2.

disappointment and strain for four months. His life had turned to chaos, his attack plan a failed gamble, his vision of glory dying in a shrieking nightmare of blood and smoke. Further straining his constitution, he was compelled to breathe the acrid smoke of the biggest battle to date in North America. Johnston may have bled to death, had a coronary or a stroke, or simply gave up in disappointment. One might wonder if he thought of the battle fought on Plains of Abraham above Quebec in 1759 as his life slipped away. Perhaps he imagined himself to be like Wolfe, who died there after he was told he had won, or like Montcalm, who died there knowing he had lost. But it doesn't matter: General Albert Sidney Johnston, Commander of Confederate Department Number 2, General Commanding the Western Department of the Army of the Confederate States of America, was dead by 2:30 in the afternoon of Sunday, 6 April 1862, the senior ranking officer killed in a Civil War battle.[18]

The Confederate senior officer's reaction to the news as it spread among the commanders (the troops weren't told about it until after the retreat, though many probably already knew) was an indication of the desperate straits the army was in. Beauregard, hearing the news just after 3:00, merely kept riding all over the battlefield, trying to get a grip on the battle. The corps commanders took the news stoically. Few of them knew Johnston well, and though many on his staff idolized him there's little evidence that his corps commanders even liked him, and all were too busy to mourn one more dead soldier on a field piled with them. By the time Johnston died the Confederate army was so battered

---

18. Edward H. Bonekemper, *A Victor, not a Butcher: Ulysses S. Grant's Overlooked Military Genius* (Washington D.C.: Regenry Publishing, 2004), 46; Thomas L. Connelly, *Army of the Heartland: The Army of the Tennessee, 1861–62*, reprint, 1995 Edition (Baton Rouge: Louisiana State University Press, 1967), 166; Cunningham, op. cit., 273; Daniel, op. cit., 226–7; McDonough, op. cit., 152–4; David G. Martin, *The Shiloh Campaign: March - April 1862*, Great Campaigns (Pennsylvania: Combined Books, 1996), 157; Sword, op. cit., 270–72.

and worn out there was little to do other than fight out the battles to their front and hope that the Federals never got strong enough to counterattack. There was probably nothing else Johnston himself could have done.[19]

As Johnston lay dying parts of Breckinridge's outfit joined with Stevens' survivors, some of Jackson's and the odd bit of some other outfits in a linear mass of about 3,000 that Jomini would have approved of but Napoleon would have derided as obsolete. Their assault on McArthur's 1,500 defenders sometime after 2:00 failed to break the Federal line but did persuade Hurlbut to contract under continual fire. Some fifteen Confederate batteries were firing into the position by early afternoon, rising in intensity during the many fruitless infantry assaults.[20]

Here there was only agony, noise and smoke and a biology-based habit to fight to stay alive. With fields on fire, woods laced with acrid clouds, blossoms blown to bits and trees shot to kindling by flying metal, life had become purgatory. Those hurt or out of ammunition in this ghastliness had reason to repair from the butchery of the battle zone for the quieter miseries of the rear. The nearest creeks and ponds were contaminated by mid-afternoon with blood and other liquid matter as desperate men sought succor and often, having found it, just died.

At the dressing tents and hospitals, both sides did an adequate job with their limited supplies and experience at dealing with the numbers of severe trauma and shock cases. Harried surgeons would probe or amputate or both with a dose of chloroform (or ether if they had it, but that only in daylight), and when they could not anymore their assistants would do the deeds. After scores of teeth and bone splinters were pulled out of wounds it was no longer remarkable. Confederate and

---

19. Cunningham, op. cit., 277–8; Daniel, op. cit., 228; Horn, op. cit., 134–5; T. Harry Williams, op. cit., 27.

20. Daniel, op. cit., 215–16, 223; Davis, op. cit., 79–80, 83–86; Hollister, op. cit., 26; David W. Reed, *The Battle of Shiloh and the Organizations Engaged* (Knoxville, TN: University of Tennessee Press, 2008), 85–7.

Union surgeons cared for their charges without distinction of uniforms, using the supplies at hand, and working side by side in each other's facilities. Many Union medical men stayed with their patients as the armies swarmed and fought around them.[21]

The Last Lines

By 2:00, Sherman and McClernand were forming their fifth battle line of the day. Every backward movement came closer to the mountain of ammunition at the Landing, and to the artillery being repaired, replenished and unloaded there. Grant knew that the Prentiss-Wallace-Hurlbut Magic Show couldn't hold its audience forever, and when it was finally reduced the Confederates would keep moving north as long as there was daylight, because that's what he would have done. To counter the inevitable attack on the Landing, at about 2:30 Grant directed James Webster to form a defensive line from the Landing west for about a mile to the Chambers field. Grant had eleven still-unblooded siege guns with a combined throw weight of 240 pounds, and cannoneer Webster knew how to emplace them.[22]

At about 2:00, Hodgson's battery opened fire on Hare and Veatch at the edge of the Cavalry field with limited effect. When Trabue's brigade reached the Cavalry field they saw the blue uniforms of Alfred Mouton's 18th Louisiana, came to a dead halt and open fire. Mouton was thoroughly confused and angered by the exchange and pulled his slightly rested men out of the area. McAllister still had ammunition enough to rain fire on both Trabue and Pond, and this prompted both Confederate brigades to wait for artillery to come up. Ketchum and Hodgson both shifted from the sunken road line and started in on McAllister, but Hodgson was running short on ammunition.

---

21. Jeffry J. Gudmens, *Staff Ride Handbook for the Battle of Shiloh, 6–7 April 1862* (Ft. Leavenworth, KS: Combat Studies Institute Press, n.d. [Electronic version downloaded 2008]), 40–41; Hollister, op. cit., 28; McDonough, op. cit., 143; Sword, op. cit., 245.

22. Cunningham, op. cit., 305; War Department, op. cit., 117.

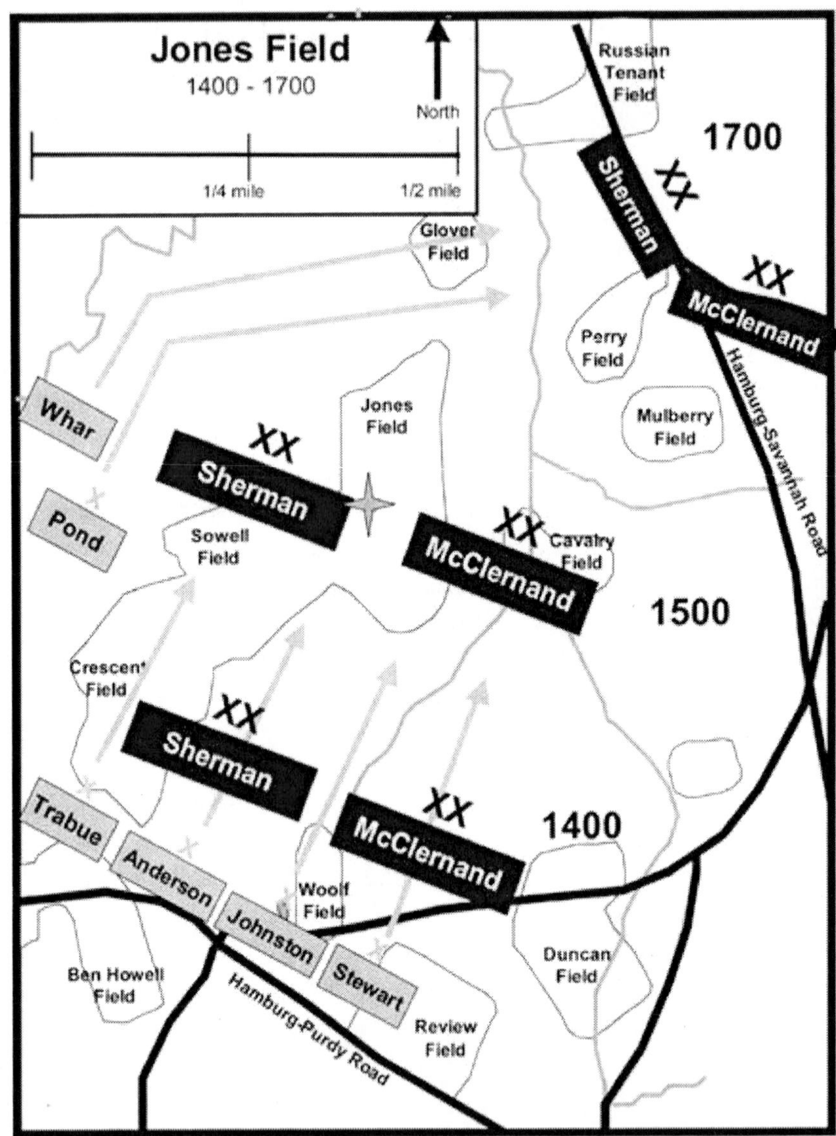

Figure 6-3, Sherman and McClernand Fall Back

Then another tragedy of errors struck. Hardee sent Samuel Ferguson of Beauregard's staff to take charge of a "leaderless" brigade that was still commanded by a hurt but effective Preston Pond. Then it began: Ferguson ordered Ketchum's battery shifted back to the sunken road; Mouton was still furious about the uniform confusion; Pond was senior but Ferguson had (wrongheaded) orders and were fuming at each other. Both tried to command a hapless brigade of tired remnants with little result other than a shouting match. Supported by only two 6-pounders, Pond's brigade went into a frontal attack against McAllister's three 24-pounders, two of Veatch's regiments and three of Marsh's. The result was Balaclava without horses or heroic "half a league, half a league" verse to gain inspiration from the disaster. The 18th Louisiana alone was down by 40% by the time the debacle stopped, and was out of the fighting for the day.[23]

At about 2:30, Wharton's Texas Rangers of Breckinridge's division charged Hurlbut's position nearer the river. The terrain was too broken for cavalry, the men were unfamiliar with their animals (these were not cavalry mounts; most of the beasts had been pulling wagons or caissons just a few minutes before), and the attack fizzled quickly.

George Maney's brigade attacked the northern edge of the Davis wheatfield while Shaver's remnants were thrown at the sunken road at about 2:30. Maney's men were so mauled they were out of the fighting for an hour; Shaver's just added to the body count. At about 3:00 two of Sweeny's Illinois regiments pushed forward during a lull in the fighting. They occupied the Duncan cabins for a few minutes until William H. Ketchum's Alabama battery of four 6-pounder and two 12-pounder howitzers, a section from George T. Hubbard's Arkansas battery and the Louisiana Crescent Regiment evicted them. Patton Anderson hit the sunken road again at about 3:30, with familiar results.

By 3:00, Sherman and McClernand had fallen back again under steady if indifferent pressure until Buckland's survivors reached the Perry field a mile northeast of the Shiloh Church, a mile and a half due

---

23. Cunningham, op. cit., 280–85; Daniel, op. cit., 239–40; Sword, op. cit., 336–8.

west of the Landing. Their mission was to keep the Confederates west of the Tilghman Branch Creek so that Lew Wallace's division, rumored to be arriving any minute, would be able to come down the Hamburg-Savannah Road. Between them they still had 4-5,000 on their feet and under orders and both were constantly collecting loose men coming up from the Landing and elsewhere on the battlefield. Though the number running *from* the fighting was far greater, there was a steady trickle of men who marched to the sound of the guns, fighting on their own in small groups for this stand of trees or that corner of a field, or with whatever units they could find. Hardee was in loose pursuit with perhaps 1,500 men in hand, both too far away to do anything to help the Confederate right or to harm either Federal flank. Like his Union opponents, Hardee also gained the odd Confederate "shirker" who recovered himself enough to fight a little more.[24]

By the time Sherman and McClernand were defending a line around the Perry field, Grant was in the area again. Grant is said to have speculated to Sherman that much of the steam had run out of the Confederate attack, though they both may have also observed that their own army was pretty beat up. Veatch, who still had two regiments in hand along the Corinth Road, was resupplied with ammunition at about 3:00.[25]

Morale was shaky on both sides by mid-afternoon, and in an effort to recover it, one Federal officer resorted to propaganda while galloping around in the Federal rear. "Sidney Johnston is dead," he shouted; "Beauregard is captured! Buell is coming!" Most of the Federals knew about Buell, and had only heard whispers about Johnston. But, in psychological operations, two out of three ain't bad.[26]

---

24. Cunningham, op. cit., 271, 278; Daniel, op. cit., 213–14, 219–20, 238.

25. Cunningham, op. cit., 278; Sword, op. cit., 335–6.

26. Cunningham, op. cit., 279–80.

The End is Nigh

Hurlbut had had enough by 4:00, eleven hours into the battle. His survivors were running desperately short on ammunition and energy. Pugh's and Lauman's tattered remnants pulled back north bringing with them all the guns of Brotzmann's batteries that could still move, Cuthbert W. Laing's lone surviving gun from Ross' battery, and. McArthur withdrew from his position near the river. Having pulled back from the sunken road, one-armed Thomas Sweeny from William Wallace's division led some of his own men and some of Sherman's north to protect a ravine in the area of Snake Creek. The Missouri Parrot battalion, Hickenlooper's battery, William Pfaender's (formerly Munch's) and other batteries that still had horses began to plan their exit.

After Hurlbut pulled back Prentiss and Wallace shifted their lines to turn their left flank back almost due north to south along the western edge of the Wicker field: for them there could be no orderly withdrawal. Neither had coherent organizations left above regiment, and in many cases barely that. It seems unlikely that either officer knew where their units began or others ended. Less than three thousand Federals were still alive in the position (most were Wallace's), and many of them were wounded. Casualties lay everywhere, potable water was completely gone, there were no more medical supplies left and there were more wounded men than there were wagons or ambulances. Neither Prentiss nor Wallace knew for certain that Sherman and McClernand had withdrawn too far to help them, and believed the last news Grant gave Prentiss at about 3:30: Lew Wallace was on his way.[27]

By 4:00, the Landing itself was under artillery fire. *Rocket* and her ammunition-laden barges provided artillery ammunition for most of the day, but pulled into mid-river and out of range. She was ordered back to shore by an angry Webster. *Fort Wayne*, still loaded with pontoons, stayed away from the landing at Rawlins' order; he was afraid that her little boats might be used to escape downriver. As the sun went down

27. McDonough, op. cit., 164; Sword, op. cit., 289, 300.

feelings at the Landing were mixed, but barely-controlled confusion still reigned.[28]

At about 3:50 Gwin stopped shooting along the river and steamed back to the Landing, sending Herman Peters ashore to find out what to do next. Peters found Grant between 4:00 and 4:30, just as Hurlbut was pulling back and leaving Grant's left flank open. Grant is said to have told Peters that the gunboats should "do what you think best." Grant had only a dim understanding of naval gunnery support of infantry at that stage of the war and besides, he had other things on his mind. He may not have been able to tell where his own lines were, and figured anything south of the Landing was fair game.[29]

Confederate communications, battle sense, ammunition and energy were also short. The fighting was so confused, the army so new to war and even to itself, the men so green that they knew no better, and the Confederates simply lacked those who did know to keep them moving and fighting. Whole regiments and brigades were standing around behind the Confederate lines, sometimes for hours. The Federals were hard-pressed all day and were squeezed into an ever-smaller area with few units idle for long. If Pittsburg Landing was crowded with refugees, just imagine how many Confederate stragglers hid in the woods south of the Sara Bell place. It is somewhat remarkable that the Confederates were still attacking at all.[30]

A Finale for the Magic Show

After Johnston died, Bragg took personal command of the right side of the battlefield, with Breckinridge on the river. Bragg put Daniel Ruggles in charge of the sunken road sector and the western side of the cotton field on the edge of the Hornet's Nest.

Ruggles was an infantryman by training and by assignment, and he and every other trained officer at Shiloh knew just what the Federals

---

28. Daniel, op. cit., 245; Sword, op. cit., 351; War Department, op. cit., 247.

29. Navy Department, op. cit., 763.

30. Cunningham, op. cit., 293, 296; Sword, op. cit., 286.

inside the Hornet's Nest were doing: shifting gunfire and positions to meet Confederate assaults one by one. He also knew what had to be done about it: pin Grant's men with iron and fire so they didn't dare break from cover. After the artillery was suppressed or driven out and the infantry pinned, Confederate foot soldiers could crack this salient like an egg. Musketry and bayonets alone weren't going to do it. He needed artillery, and lots of it.[31]

This is the traditionally what happened, but the details are still debated. Ruggles may have claimed credit for the grand battery later, but others disputed this claim almost as soon as it was made. One source suggests that Beauregard had always intended his corps to concentrate their artillery in twelve-gun battalion on single points, and had thought of an artillery concentration on the Federal left as early as 2:00 in the afternoon. Both Francis Shoup from Hardee's corps and James Trudeau, the army's chief of artillery, were claimants to assembling the guns. Regardless of whose idea it was, the Confederate command finally realized that Southern pluck alone was not going to move infantry behind cover and supported by artillery.[32]

Every gun section that still had ammunition, horses and gunners anywhere near the Confederate right were collected into two masses on the west side of the Duncan field and southeast of the Review field. While they were at it the Confederates collected infantry--pieces of Gibson's and Anderson's brigades from Ruggles' division, Shaver's and Wood's from what was left of Hardee's corps, and Stewart's from Clark's division and Stephens' brigade from Cheatham's out of Polk's corps. More from Stratham's and Bowen's, Jackson's, Chalmers' and Trabue's commands were pushed into line. Gladden's brigade had been led by John Adams until he was wounded at about 11:30; Zachariah Deas commanded what was left of them, putting them between Shaver

---

31. Sword, op. cit., 291.

32. Daniel, op. cit., 229; Grady McWhiney, and Perry D. Jamieson, *Attack and Die: Civil War Military Tactics and the Southern Heritage* (University, AL: University of Alabama Press, 1982), 117; War Department, op. cit., 472, 474.

and Stephens. After twelve hours this brigade probably had no more than 200 effective original members, and an unknown number that simply attached themselves.[33]

Since the guns couldn't move while they were shooting, collecting all these resources created a lull in the fighting. By 4:30, half the cannons in the Army of Mississippi were firing no less than eighteen pounds of screaming metal a second into the tangled ruin of woods, fields and sunken road; an area about a half mile long and perhaps fifty yards deep that contained perhaps three thousand Federal effectives. The exact numbers are debated, but there was at least fifty and perhaps as many as 62 guns stretched for yard after smoky yard (as many as 13 batteries and two other gun sections).[34]

A cannonade of a magnitude had never before been seen in North America struck the Federal positions. The surviving Federal artillery fired off their small supplies of ready ammunition as Confederate infantry worked their way around the flanks. As the Union infantry sought refuge from the hurricane of metal, their supporting artillery withdrew to save themselves from an ever-worsening situation. In this barrage Powell lost his arm and his battery withdrew with the rest.[35]

---

33. James R. Arnold, *Shiloh 1862: The Death of Innocence* (Oxford, England: Osprey Publishing, LTD., 1998), 62–3; Connelly, op. cit., 166–67; Daniel, op. cit., 218–21, 234–5; Witham, op. cit., xii.

34. James R. Arnold, *The Armies of U.S. Grant* (New York: Arms and Armor Press, 1995), 66; Hollister, op. cit., 8, 10; McDonough, op. cit., 162; McWhiney, op. cit., 117; Sword, op. cit., 292; War Department, op. cit., 472–79.

35. Grant, *Memoirs*, 177; Simpson, op. cit., 133.

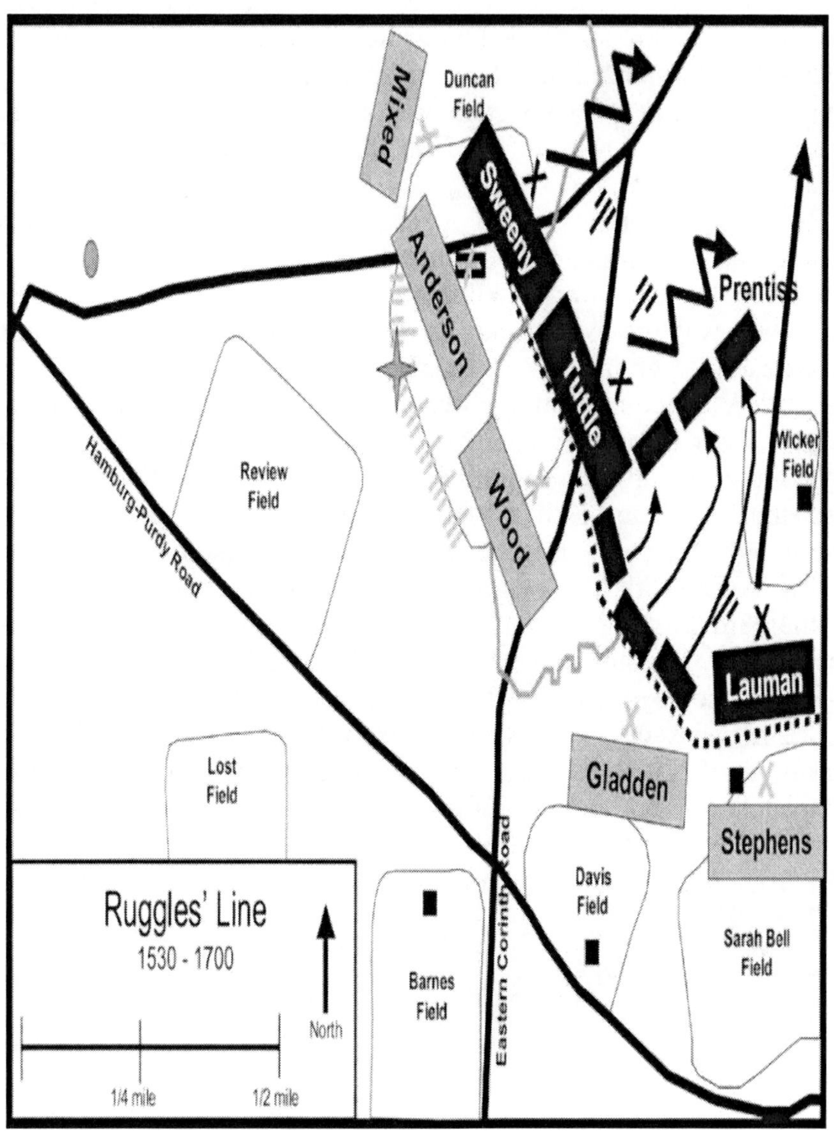

Figure 6-4 Ruggles' Battery

John Morgan's Kentucky mounted squadron, despairing of attacking along the sunken road, clashed with Hickenlooper's recently withdrawn battery in Sherman's line. Here, Morgan is historically credited with having said "thar ain't no *good* way to charge a battery." Blasts of canister and a volley from the 29th Illinois ended Morgan's ill-fated attack.[36]

Remnants of Russell's and Pond's brigades moved in from the north to close the trap, while Polk and the Louisiana Crescent Regiment led the sweep from the west. William Wallace ordered his survivors to make their way out as best they could. Much of Wallace's division got out, if barely, fighting past or running through Trabue's men blocking the road. Wallace himself was wounded and left behind, presumed to be dead. Four Illinois regiments from Sweeny's brigade got out, but his 58th Illinois and 8th Iowa didn't escape. Tuttle's brigade broke out, but McArthur's 12th and 14th Iowa were taken.[37]

Prentiss' surviving brigade commander, Madison Miller, and the 147 men of his18th Missouri that were still on their feet were captured. Of the 23rd Missouri's nearly 500 casualties, over 400 of them were prisoners or missing. Its colonel, Jacob T. Tilghman, was the only officer in the regiment killed; the rest were captured with their men. The 23rd Missouri's combat life had been about eight hours in the sunken road. Other bits and pieces of units were either destroyed completely or got out as individuals. Prentiss himself surrendered between 5:30 and 6:00. The dressing stations held a thousand and more men from five Federal divisions when the Confederates found them.

---

36. Cunningham, op. cit., 310; Daniel, op. cit., 190–1; McDonough, op. cit., 146; Sword, op. cit., 333–34.

37. Cunningham, op. cit., 291; Hollister, op. cit., 8.

The fighting in "Hell's Hollow" behind the pond may have continued sporadically as late as 6:00.[38]

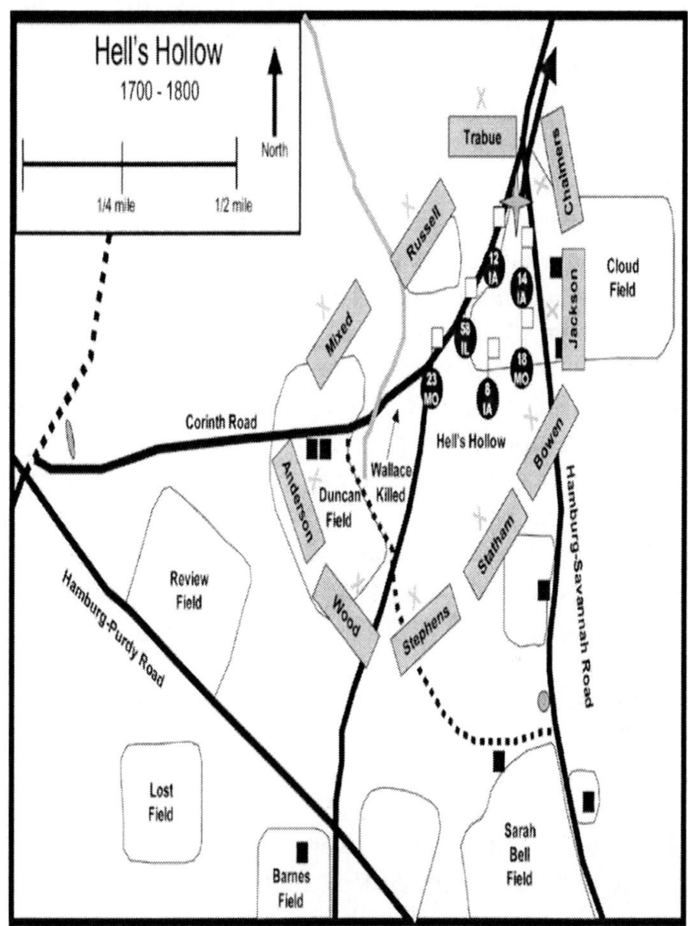

Figure 6-5 The Final Act of the Magic Show

---

38. Connelly, op. cit., 167; Daniel, op. cit., 251; Dillahunty, op. cit., 13; Grant, *Memoirs*, 177; Sword, op. cit., 292, 326; War Department, op. cit., 105, 246, 279; Witham, op. cit., 15–16.

Those of Prentiss' and William Wallace's commands that could escape ran headlong into the Federal lines, breaking the more fragile parts. Using their enemy's rout as a battering ram, Trabue followed them into Veatch's position, which broke under the weight and fell back towards the Landing. But Trabue was out of ammunition and went no further.[39]

The sun was going down and the magic show had ended.

The End of the Day

Polk sent the 1st Mississippi Cavalry to cut off the Federal retreat at the Landing. The Landing was the only means of either retreat or reinforcement for the hard-pressed Federals and all around must have known it. However, this particular order is an indicator of just how clueless Polk was about the topography and the condition of Grant's army. The 1st Mississippi's lieutenant colonel, John H. Miller, led his troopers--some mounted Texans and Forrest's command--into the underbrush and stumbled onto Ross's withdrawing Parrots, capturing all but one gun of the battery, proving that the only good way to charge a battery was when it was limbered. Moving north by east they reached the Tennessee, and could have watered their horses in that stream by just scrambling down the bluffs and wading through the thousands of refugees.[40]

Though the sun had not yet set, the Confederates had reached the Tennessee. It had all the military effect that the leading Germans who caught a glimpse of the sun reflecting off the onion domes of the Kremlin in Moscow in December 1941 had on the Soviet counteroffensive that uncoiled that very day and pushed them back 200 miles, or that the advanced American troops passing water on the frozen Yalu in November 1950 had in Korea, when they already had a quarter million Chinese behind them who, a day later, would push them hundreds of miles south. Bragging rights do not win wars.

---

39. Daniel, op. cit., 241; Sword, op. cit., 338.

40. Cunningham, op. cit., 309; Sword, op. cit., 342.

In the Confederate rear the milling around, scrounging, pillaging and simply waiting for orders continued. Organizing Federal prisoners took Jones Withers about a half an hour, and getting them to the rear with Eli Shorter's 18th Alabama Infantry as escort through the littered battlefield took much longer. When Gwin's gunboats started blazing away about 200 yards south of the Landing at 5:35 and forcing Confederate batteries back from the bluff it came as a surprise. Polk had never heard naval gunfire before, and became anxious about the roaring of the 8-inch guns and 32-pounders. Other professionals were somewhat more sanguine, but they must have known what a tremendous psychological effect those big guns had on their weary men. Facing musketry and even 24-pounders was one thing, but 62-pound solid ball and spherical case (shrapnel) whirring through the air was much different.[41]

Even so, geometry limited the effectiveness of the gunboats. To get above the bluffs the guns had to elevate a great deal, creating a dead zone close to the river. As the Confederates moved towards the river, they were less and less affected by it until the gunboats could see them, when many got a whiff of grapeshot. It makes one wonder, though, why--contrary to the evidence--three Confederate corps commanders and their boss all blamed the Federal gunboats for their failure to destroy Grant on Sunday.[42]

The Army of Mississippi had lost its commander and 20 of 78 regimental commanders; 25% of its brigade commanders were casualties; two of four corps commanders were wounded, and three of five division commanders were hurt. Cleburne had but 800 effectives of 2,700 just twelve hours before. Some regiments were commanded by lieutenants; others had no officers at all. Some of the men had been on their feet for 14 hours; some hadn't eaten in two days. Despite all this, Bragg and Polk rounded up men and ammunition, eager to exploit the collapse of the Federal left and push on into what they were convinced

---

41. Cunningham, op. cit., 313–14; Navy Department, op. cit., 763; Sword, op. cit., 344.

42. McDonough, op. cit., 175; Sword, op. cit., 344.

was nothing but refugees. Chalmers and Jackson were sent forward--Chalmers with ammunition, Jackson without. Two of Trabue's regiments were rearmed with Federal Enfields and joined Chalmers. Deas formed all that was left of Gladden's brigade, all 224 of them, on Jackson's left. Gage's battery collected all the horses they could to move their surviving guns to support this last attack on the Landing.[43]

Confusion at Pittsburg Landing had turned to chaos. Steamboats were cutting their mooring lines to avoid being swamped by panicking men. *Minnehaha,* the big steamer that brought 15th Iowa, was overloaded with refugees trying to get away. One of the passengers still aboard, William Wallace's wife Ann, was terrified by the panic some of the men who managed to get aboard showed. Refugees tried to swim the Tennessee or the Snake Creek, both swollen and running fast. Refugees under the cliffs and wandering around the Landing confused the situation even more, and disgusted those who were still obeying orders. But few had much time for them, except for a few officers whose entreaties and exhortations, it has always been said, had no effect. Grant himself made a last personal appeal to the refugees under the bluffs at about 4:30, even threatening them with cavalry, but he was at least as effective as any others were at the time. Buell raged and fumed at an officer seeking ammunition, exactly why is not clear. Ambulances were cut loose of their teams and abandoned; chaplains and medical men desperately tried to save the sick and injured.[44]

Grant and his staff hustled everything that could draw blood into a line south and west of the Landing. It wasn't a straight line, but one that jutted at multiple angles: from the Dill Branch Creek bluffs northwest for a hundred yards, due west parallel with the Pittsburg-Purdy Road for another thousand yards, then bending back northwest to the Tilghman Branch Creek crevasse another thousand yards. To the north

---

43. Connelly, op. cit., 167–8; Cunningham, op. cit., 304; Davis, op. cit., 89–90; Hollister, op. cit., 31; Sword, op. cit., 341, 344–45; Witham, op. cit., xiii.

44. Cunningham, op. cit., 320; McDonough, op. cit., 155–6, 170–1; Sword, op. cit., 356–7.

and east, Sherman's weary regiments and McClernand's battered veterans faced south and west, parallel to the Pittsburgh-Corinth Road. Sherman's and McClernand's men joined the survivors of William Wallace's division under McArthur and Tuttle, and Prentiss' survivors under no one in particular. Hurlbut's division, closest to the river and remarkably intact, had about 4,000 men or so, even if some of his regiments had only a few score men left in ranks. Joining the infantry was every cannon that Grant's army had left: Louis Margraf's 8th Ohio Battery of two 24-pounder Parrots; Axel Silversparre's four 24-pounder Parrots of Battery H, 1st Illinois; two batteries of the Missouri Parrot battalion; Hickenlooper's and Munch's ragged refugees and Bouton's survivors; three of McAllister's field-clearing 24-pounders; Powell's five 6-pounders under Joseph Mitchell. Joining them on a line just north of the Dill Branch Creek were Nispel's guns, and Brotzmann's and Wood's scrambling to fill their depleted ammunition chests as Behr's lone gun and Ross's surviving 10-pounder Parrot took places in line, possibly served by some of Waterhouse's gunners. Madison's massive siege guns centered the line. With a range of nearly three miles, whatever these behemoths managed to hit wouldn't care that they had never fired a shot in anger. This mass of resistance is traditionally called "Grant's Last Line," and though he was responsible for it, Grant didn't build it himself. As the sun went down it held somewhere between ten and eighteen thousand men and as many as sixty operational guns--nearly half his army and 2/3rds of his artillery strength from the morning.[45]

---

45. Arnold, *Armies*, 66–7; Bonekemper, op. cit., 51; Cunningham, op. cit., 306–8; Daniel, op. cit., 249; Dillahunty, op. cit., 13–14; Katcher, op. cit., 62; Ulysses S. Grant, "The Battle of Shiloh," in *Battles and Leaders of the Civil War Volume 1* (New York: Thomas Yoseloff, 1956 (Electronic Edition 1997 by Guild Press)), 475; Grant, *Memoirs*, 179–80; Hollister, op. cit., 6; McDonough, op. cit., 171–3; Simpson, op. cit., 133; Kenneth P. Williams, op. cit., 374–5; Witham, op. cit., 33, 35.

The line was solid enough to hold the ragged Confederate army that Grant knew was as badly hurt as his was, even if some of the Federals had been on their feet for eighteen hours, and their units were mere shadows of what they had been. The 12th Iowa had lost 98% of its men; all Federal regiments had lost at least 10% of their men and most of their baggage. Some batteries only had horses and harnesses to move two guns. Of five Federal division commanders one was mortally wounded and in Confederate hands, another had been captured and a third hurt several times. Nine of 15 Federal brigade commanders were casualties. Of 81 officers at regiment, brigade or division level Grant had lost 45 killed, wounded or captured. When Grant and his staff realized that the Hornet's Nest had fallen, someone is said to have asked if the Confederates had won. "Oh no," a stoic Grant is said to have answered, "they can't break our lines tonight. It is too late."[46]

Amman's brigade was coming across the river, but the Landing itself would have been extremely crowded with steamboats, refugees, and other activity, and unloading would have been difficult (see Appendix, "Steamboats of Shiloh"). The first to unload was a sutler boat that Nelson flagged down, and the passengers included nine mounted officers and about 200 men. Nelson rode his seventeen-hand horse Ned off a steamboat at about 5:20 and greeted Grant with a hearty "if you're looking for fighting fools, here we are," or something like that. William Grose's 36th Indiana crossed four companies at a time in two boats--about 380 men altogether, making the ten miles from Savannah to the firing line in about four and half hours. Nicholas Anderson's 6th Ohio of 598 men got off the boats at the Landing at about the same time as the 36th Indiana. Fred Jones' 24th Ohio of 550 men disembarked at about 5:30. The "safety of the rear" was an illusion: the 36th Indiana was under fire while they formed up, and took casualties before they joined the line around Stone's battery 150 yards from where they landed. Amman's brigade joined Grant's line in

---

46. Catton, op. cit., 237–8; Perret, op. cit., 196; Reed, op. cit., 20–21; Witham, op. cit., xiii.

pieces, but they carried muskets and had fingers willing to pull them, and that was what was needed. None of Amman's men got to the firing line before 5:30, at the very earliest; the entire brigade was likely not in place before 6:00.

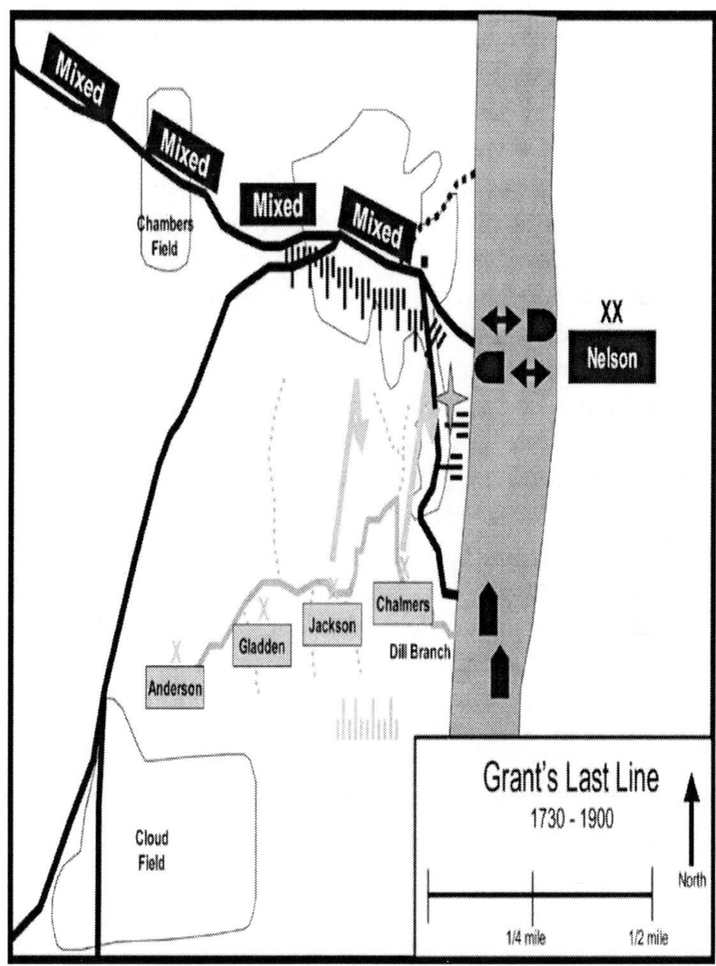

Figure 6-6 The Last Line

As they arrived, the regimental bands played "Hail Columbia," and refugees along the river cheered. Polk's Confederates, close to the river, heard the bands and the cheering and joined in, perhaps believing they had taken the Landing or captured Grant himself.[47]

With Amman's brigade came a detachment from a signals company that was soon wig-wagging to their counterparts on the other side of the river. The detachment's commander, a Lieutenant Hinson, bellowed at a mounted officer who blocked their line of sight. Grant, who knew nothing about tactical signaling, apologized and moved out of the way.[48]

By 5:40 the Confederates were moving north warily, believing Grant had withdrawn north or was trying to cross the river. Beauregard still expected Van Dorn and his army to be marching up the road. The 1st Mississippi Cavalry moved up expecting to find nothing much at all. They encountered a Union line that opened fire briefly, but high the troopers to escape unscathed. The line fell quiet again.

The Confederates had not taken the Landing, and had lost the race to keep Buell from joining Grant. "They have been pressing us all day," Grant traditionally told Rawlins around then. "I think we will stop them here."[49]

As Bragg watched the men move up, Chalmers', Jackson's, Trabue's and Deas' hungry and tired Confederates reached Dill Branch Creek in good if ragged order, with Gage' guns close behind. The sudden BOOM and torrent of fire, smoke and screaming iron from Grant's line blew hats off, concussed some infantrymen so badly their ears and noses bled, denuded what little was left of the tree canopy

---

47. Daniel, op. cit., 248; McDonough, op. cit., 178–9; Perret, op. cit., 189; Reed, op. cit., 100, 102; Sword, op. cit., 358–9; War Department, op. cit., 324, 328, 337, 339, 348; Witham, op. cit., 11.

48. Gudmens, op. cit., 37.

49. Cunningham, op. cit., 319; William B. Hazen, *A Narrative of Military Service* (Boston: Ticknor & Company, 1885), 24–5; Hollister, op. cit., 31; Perret, op. cit., 196; Sword, op. cit., 352–3; War Department, op. cit., 348, 353–4.

overhead, and in at least one case, the shock wave may have broken a man's back.[50]

For at least a half an hour there were three 24-pound or larger rounds hitting the Confederates every few seconds or so. A fused shell from a 24-pound Parrot rifle or a spherical case round from siege gun spewed an infantry brigade's worth of hot metal at once. Under ideal conditions it came out in a cone slightly smaller than a hundred yards around. Similar ammunition from a 62-pounder 8-inch naval gun blasted a division's worth of balls, with a similar pattern that could cover twice a football field; the 32-pounder naval guns scattered about four regiment's worth. Add to this the round ball, shell, canister and scrap metal from every smaller piece of ordnance Grant's survivors could lay hands on and get to work, plus everything the infantry could fire. Nothing living could penetrate that curtain of screaming iron and noxious smoke. 21st-Century Specter gunships can't throw that much hot metal for that long.[51]

Gage's battery tried to return fire--a mouse hissing at an oncoming hawk--until, hammered by a dozen Parrot rifles, they pulled back. As Chalmers valiantly tried to get up a ravine to Hurlbut's position across the Dill Branch Creek, fire from the gunboats stopped them cold. Jackson's brigade, brave lads without ammunition, hugged ground and there was nothing that anyone could do to make them go forward. Bragg must have been stunned by the carnage and by the withdrawal that followed, raging at the men for "one last try." This furious barrage likely caused more psychological than physical damage to the Confederates. After finally crushing a Federal pocket that had held out all day just a cannon shot to the south, it would have been mentally

---

50. Arnold, *Armies*, 67; Catton, op. cit., 240; Daniel, op. cit., 253–4; McDonough, op. cit., 180; Alexander R. Chisholm, "The Shiloh Battle Order and the Withdrawal Sunday Evening," in *Battles and Leaders of the Civil War Volume 1* (New York: Thomas Yoseloff, 1956 (Electronic Edition 1997 by H-Bar Enterprises)), 606; Simpson, op. cit., 133; Sword, op. cit., 360–1.

51. Catton, op. cit., 240; Daniel, op. cit., 249.

devastating to find that their supposedly defeated enemy still could manage that kind of firepower. James Shirk in *Lexington* later claimed that the gunboats were solely responsible for the repulse.[52]

Around sunset at 6:10, Beauregard called it off. The first day of Shiloh was over.

Some writers believe that this line was not invulnerable, and that Beauregard might have prevailed over Grant in the last hours of daylight, but the evidence to support this is unconvincing. Johnston's son--who was not present--wrote that the final Confederate assault was a "reconnaissance" intended to capture Grant that would have succeeded if Beauregard hadn't stopped it. But at the time even Bragg knew it was hopeless. As he watched Polk's retreating brigades in the growing darkness, he was said to have muttered, "My God, my God, it is too late!"[53]

Some of these men had been on their feet for more than eighteen hours. Some must have swallowed the equivalent of three ounces of raw salt in that time with very little water and nothing to breathe but smoke and the stench of death. After fighting from before sunup to nearly sundown many men on both sides of the firing line, especially James Powell's and Aaron Hardcastle's, were so weary they could barely lift their weapons. Some Confederates didn't have shoes, half of both armies were sick, many didn't have ammunition, and others still hadn't eaten in days despite the widespread scrounging. Beauregard's

---

52. Cunningham, op. cit., 322–7; Hollister, op. cit., 32; McDonough, op. cit., 173–5, 180; Navy Department, op. cit., 764; Sword, op. cit., 362–3; Kenneth P. Williams, op. cit., 377.

53. Cunningham, op. cit., 323–7; Daniel, op. cit., 246; William P. Johnston, "Albert Sidney Johnston at Shiloh," in *Battles and Leaders of the Civil War Volume 1* (New York: Thomas Yoseloff, 1956 (Electronic Edition 1997 by H-Bar Enterprises)), 567–8; Grant, *Memoirs*, 180; Horn, op. cit., 134; Thomas Jordan, "Notes of a Confederate Staff-Officer at Shiloh," in *Battles and Leaders of the Civil War Volume 1* (New York: Thomas Yoseloff, 1956 (Electronic Edition 1997 by H-Bar Enterprises)), 602; Martin, op. cit., 142–51.

army had done all that it could have done, and nothing and no one could have made it do more.[54]

Beauregard thought that Grant would either run off or be easy pickings in the morning since, it seemed, no one could save him. He had received a message that afternoon from President Lincoln's brother-in-law, Ben Helm, in Decatur, Alabama, saying that "Buell" was marching to Decatur. This force was just Mitchell's detached division several day's march away around Fayetteville, Tennessee, but no matter. Beauregard, like Grant before, believed what he wanted to believe. Beauregard later wrote that he believed his forces were out of control and not capable of offensive action by sundown. At sunset Beauregard was at the meeting house: how much he knew what was going on at the front is an open question.[55]

Sanders Bruce's 1,589 man 22nd Brigade crossed the river at around 5:30 but probably didn't get on the line until after 6:30. William Hazen's 19th Brigade crossed during the night, arriving sometime after 9:00. Nelson's division was the first of Buell's four unblooded divisions that joined Grant during the night: he wasn't going anywhere.

If McArthur had any pipers left, their skirling might have added to the tableau of roiling smoke and denuded trees peppered with the dead, dying and maimed; the fans of grass scorched and burning in front of hot gun muzzles; the begrimed and weary men covered in filth and

---

54. Connelly, op. cit., 168–69; Daniel, op. cit., 255–6; Horn, op. cit., 136–8; McDonough, op. cit., 168–70, 177–8; William S. McFeely, *Grant: A Biography* (New York: W. W. Norton & Company, 1982), 114; McWhiney, op. cit., 112; Sword, op. cit., 364; Bell Irvin Wiley, *The Life of Johnny Reb* (Baton Rouge: Louisiana State University Press, 1978), 73–74; T. Harry Williams, op. cit., 29–30.

55. Pierre G. T. Beauregard, "The Campaign of Shiloh," in *Battles and Leaders of the Civil War Volume 1* (New York: Thomas Yoseloff, 1956 (Electronic Edition 1997 by H-Bar Enterprises)), 590; Daniel, op. cit., 250–1; Horn, op. cit., 138; Johnston, op. cit., 568; Jordan, op. cit., 602; McDonough, op. cit., 181–2; Sword, op. cit., 364–6.

gore, standing in ragged bunches and serried ranks clutching weapons too hot to touch; horses and mules dashing around in panic and pain; the birds circling and swooping for tender morsels provided by artillery and small arms; the refugees huddled under the bluffs while gunboats thundered and roared from the river.

After the shooting was done and the sun was down, Grant is said to have been staring into the gloom where the Confederates had been, and may have muttered, "Not beaten yet by a damn sight." Ulysses Grant had known failure intimately in his life, but he and those around him had always managed to survive aided by his raw effort, even if it was sometimes clumsy. Neither he nor his army failed at Shiloh.[56]

56. Arnold, *Armies*, 67; Simpson, op. cit., 133; Sword, op. cit., 367–8.

CHAPTER 7
THE ODDESSY OF LEW WALLACE

All his life, Lew Wallace imagined himself as the winner of martial glory, of great victories on the field of honor, a champion of the republic lionized in the press. Even though he had come from an important political family and had been speaker of the Indiana state legislature, only the sound of drums and guns seemed to appeal to him. His performance at Fort Donelson gave Grant enough confidence in his abilities to position his command far from the rest of the army. On 6 April Lew Wallace's lifelong dreams of laurels and accolades were lost in a confusion of misunderstood instructions and plans.[1]

Long before the battle, Wallace fretted that he was more than four miles from the main army. To compensate, he prepared a plan to join the main army in case of an attack. There were two existing routes through the wilderness between Crump's and Pittsburg, both little more than muddy tracks: the River Road close to the Tennessee River that ended at William Wallace's camps along the Pittsburg Landing Road; and the Shunpike Road that twisted through the countryside, crossed the Snake Creek and ended behind Sherman's camps. Wallace decided to repair the Shunpike because he considered it the better of the two roads, and felt it would be easier to repair.[2]

On 24 March Bushrod Johnson, commanding Confederate forces at Purdy, reported that the Snake Creek Bridge had been washed out on

---

1. Geoffrey Perret, *Ulysses S. Grant, Soldier and President* (New York: Random House, 1997), 191.

2. Jeffry J. Gudmens, *Staff Ride Handbook for the Battle of Shiloh, 6–7 April 1862* (Ft. Leavenworth, KS: Combat Studies Institute Press, n.d. [Electronic version downloaded 2008]), 51.

17 March. This would have made the Shunpike impassable, but unknown to Johnson it was back in use by 21 March. On 27 March Beauregard ordered a strong force to watch this road and protect the route from Purdy to Adamsville. On 31 March Preston Smith reported a skirmish between a Confederate patrol from Purdy and Wallace's cavalry pickets while accurately describing Wallace's order of battle, believing it was on the march to Purdy since they thought the bridge was washed out. This was the "movement" that stirred Johnston to attack Grant.[3]

By 8:30 Sunday 6 April Grant ordered Lew Wallace get his division ready, and by all accounts he did just that. Implementing his part of the plan he and Sherman had worked out weeks before, Wallace concentrated his forces at Stoney Lonesome and Adamsville, stretching two and a half miles west of Crump's, ready to descend the Shunpike as soon as he got positive orders. Wallace knew this road joined the Hamburg-Purdy Road behind Sherman's camps some two miles west of the Landing. This movement, if executed as soon as Grant met with Wallace, should have put Wallace behind and to the west of the Federal right flank, about the middle of Johnston's distant left flank, by about noon. But Grant gave no "positive order" to Lew Wallace when they met early in the morning. "Hold yourself in readiness" is not "get your behind moving" in any lexicon.[4]

James Shirk in *Lexington* left for Pittsburg Landing when he heard firing upriver, meeting William Gwin in *Tyler* at about 10:15. If Shirk could hear firing as early as Grant could, it took *Lexington* a little better than three hours to reach Pittsburg Landing from Crump's, steaming

---

3. War Department, "Shiloh, Corinth: Series I, Volume X, Part 2," in *War of the Rebellion: Official Records of the Union and Confederate Armies* (Washington, D.C.: U.S. Government Printing Office, 1911 (Electronic version 1999 by Guild Press, Indianapolis, IN)), 359, 367–8, 374–5.

4. Larry J. Daniel, *Shiloh: The Battle That Changed the Civil War* (New York: Simon & Schuster, 1997), 256; Wiley Sword, *Shiloh: Bloody April* (New York: Morrow, 1974), 347.

against the current. It took *Tigress* two hours to cover the same four and a half miles *and* another five and a half miles.[5]

Grant first had Rawlins send a message to Wallace at about 10:00.[6] A.S. Baxter, the district assistant quartermaster, took *Tigress* to Crump's. Wallace later said that he spoke with Baxter "precisely" at 11:30, when he was handed an unsigned order from Rawlins. If the upstream trip took her two hours from Savannah, the downstream should have taken much less--possibly as little as half an hour. We can guess, therefore, that Rawlins took as much as an hour to find Baxter, write the note, and get *Tigress* moving downstream. All we know for certain about this message is that the text here was reproduced from Rawlins' memory more than a year later, and that the original is not known to survive:

> Major-General WALLACE:
> You will move forward your division from Crump's Landing, leaving a sufficient force to protect the public property at that place, to Pittsburg Landing, on the road nearest to and parallel with the river, and form in line at right angles with the river, immediately in rear of the camp of Maj. Gen. C. F. Smith's division on our right, and there await further orders.[7]

---

5. Navy Department, "West Gulf Blockading Squadron from January 1, 1865 to January 31 1866; Naval Forces on Western Waters from May 8, 1861 to April 11, 1862; Series 1 Volume 22," in *Official Records of the Union and Confederate Navies in the War of the Rebellion*, reprint, 1987 (Washington, D.C. (reprint Harrisburg, PA): Government Printing Office (reprint National Historical Society), 1908), 763, 765.

6. The merging of several texts and reports indicate that Rawlins' watch was an hour slow, or everyone else's was an hour fast. This text uses the time indicated by most sources, and all times are one hour ahead of Rawlins report of 1 July 1863.

7. War Department, "Shiloh, Corinth: Series I, Volume X, Part 1," in *War of the Rebellion: Official Records of the Union and*

Smith's division was commanded by William Wallace by then: odd that Rawlins misrembered it a year later. Baxter also told Lew Wallace that the Confederates had been repulsed, reassuring but quite wrong. By noon Wallace was moving not on the river road to Pittsburg--it would have taken him hours to reroute his brigades the way they were strung out--but on his preplanned route to Sherman, leaving behind two regiments and a gun section to guard the camps.[8]

At about 11:00 Grant sent a captain of the 2nd Illinois Cavalry who was acquainted with the roads to hurry Wallace up. Baxter was back at Pittsburg Landing on *Tigress* by 1:00, and Grant met with Buell aboard her soon after. Baxter reported that Morgan Smith's scouting parties had found no sign of Confederate activity around Purdy that morning: useful, but tardy information. At about 1:00 the anonymous cavalryman reported to Grant:

> ...that when he delivered {Grant's} message to Major-General Wallace {Wallace} inquired if he had not written orders. He replied in the negative, and General Wallace said he would only obey written orders. He further stated that it had been more than one hour since he left General Wallace, and that his division was then all ready to move.[9]

Any request for written orders, even from a militiaman, would have been written carefully and formally to protect him in the event of an inquiry, and just as carefully preserved. No such written request is known, and no one ever mentioned seeing one. Wallace never mentioned this cavalryman.

Confederate Armies (Washington, D.C.: U.S. Government Printing Office, 1911 (Electronic version 1999 by Guild Press, Indianapolis, IN)), 185.

8. O. Edward Cunningham, (Gary D. Joiner and Timothy B. Smith, Eds.), *Shiloh and the Western Campaign of 1862* (New York: Savas Beatie, 2008), 160; Daniel, op. cit., 256.

9. War Department, "OR I/X/1," 185–6.

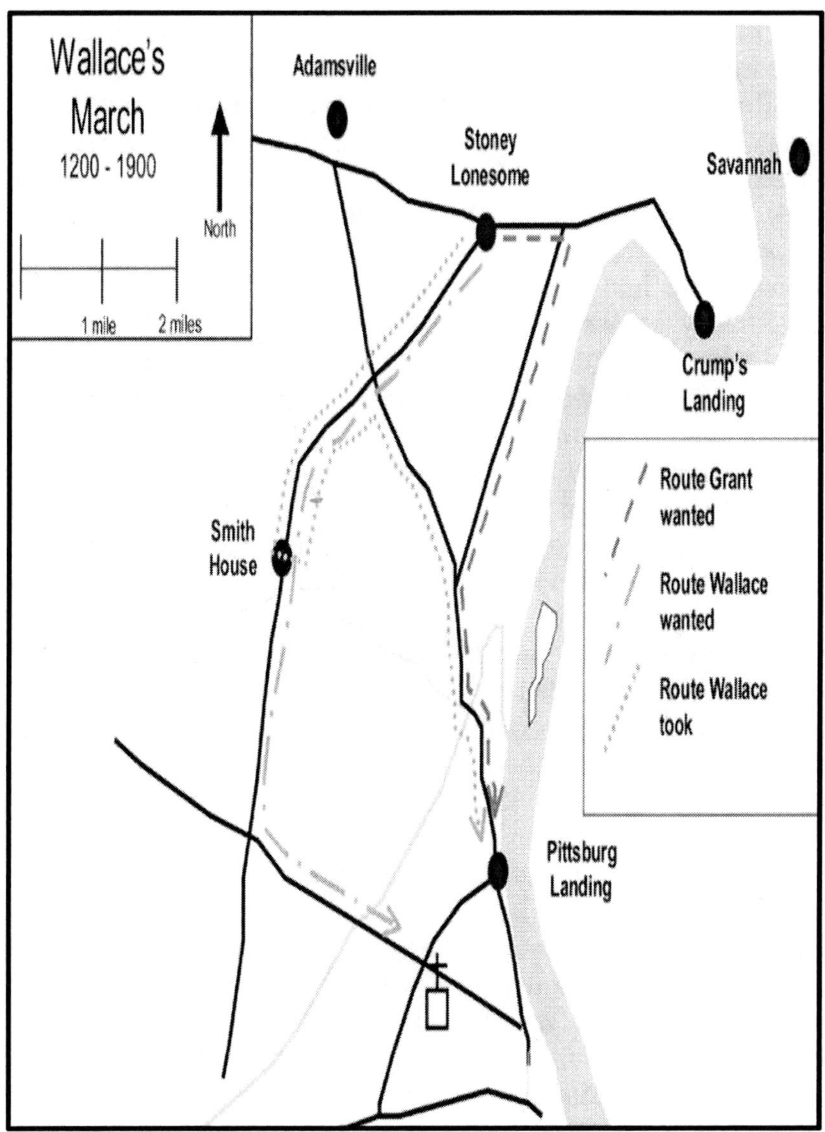

Figure 7-1 The Odyssey of Lew Wallace

Furious with Wallace's apparent inactivity and frustrated in his counterattack plans, Grant sent W. R. Rowley with a small escort and Grant's full authority to do whatever it took to get Wallace moving. En route, Rowley thought it odd that he wasn't seeing any marching columns on the road, and was even more curious when he reached Crump's to learn Wallace had moved off to the west hours before. Rowley headed west, then south on the Shunpike, finally reaching Wallace at about 2:00 in the afternoon.[10]

Rowley laid into Wallace as soon as they clapped eyes on each other. Rowley accused Wallace of refusing to move. Wallace called Rowley a liar since it was obvious his command was on the march to support Sherman. Rowley exploded that Sherman had been driven back and the entire army was in danger of destruction, a revelation that shocked Wallace, especially since Baxter had said that the Confederates had already been defeated. Rowley, who had no idea where he was, no clue about the roads in the area, had never been on that road, and could not have known where it led, nonetheless said it was the wrong road. The only way Rowley could find out where the Shunpike ended just then was to go where Wallace was heading, but his back was too far up for that.[11]

If Rowley was right, continuing south on the Shunpike would cut 5,000 veterans of Fort Donelson off from the rest of Grant's army with unclear results. Taking the River Road south, a route that Wallace knew nothing of, would take time and bring him much closer to the Landing, and was where Rowley thought Grant wanted Wallace to go, but it would require going back north to Adamsville and east to the Overshot Mill--after having already marched six miles closer to the battlefield than he had been two hours before--and at that time was a half hour's quick march from the far left flank of the Confederate army. All was confusion and exhaustion in that murky hell by then, but Wallace had no way of knowing that. Nor did anyone have any idea what to expect

---

10. Daniel, op. cit., 256; Gudmens, op. cit., 37; Sword, op. cit., 345–6; Ibid., 186.

11. Daniel, op. cit., 259; Sword, op. cit., 346.

if they kept marching south, as Wallace said he believed the *spirit* of Grant's order wanted. Mounted scouts riding south on the Shunpike reported that they could hear musketry. Wallace could still affect the battle they heard, but was in a position no one wants to be in: one wrong move and you're toast, but the right move could bring lasting fame and glory. Sherman was trying to hold the Owl Creek bridge right up to about 4:00 Sunday afternoon, when he simply had to pull back. Both he and Grant were expecting Lew Wallace at almost any time before then. Sherman's persistence suggests that Wallace was doing what someone else expected him to, but regrettably that "someone else" was not his boss. In his memoirs, Sherman stated that Grant told Wallace to march south via the river road, but he had no way of knowing that directly.[12]

Wallace decided to turn his lead brigades around. Why the countermarch on narrow roads is something of a mystery to modern audiences--despite the urgency, Nelson had done it too. McClernand and Lew Wallace commanded the 1st and 2nd Divisions of Grant's army because they were perceived to be the most capable, but there was still a great deal of honor of place on the 19th Century battlefield.[13]

At about 2:30 Grant sent James McPherson and John Rawlins to find Wallace and get him to the army's river flank. They found Wallace between 3:30 and 4:00, his division a tangled and strung-out mess on unimproved wilderness roads. The men had been on their feet for eight hours and marching 'twixt pillar and post for as much as four. By the

---

12. William T. Sherman, *Memoirs of General William T. Sherman* (New York: Literary Classics of the United States, Inc., 1990), 266; William T. Sherman, (Brooks D. Simpson and Jean V. Berlin, Editors), *Sherman's Civil War: Selected Correspondence of William T. Sherman, 1860–65* (Chapel Hill, NC: University of North Carolina Press, 1999), 202; Sword, op. cit., 346; War Department, "OR I/X/1," 250.

13. James L. McDonough, *Shiloh--in Hell Before Night* (Knoxville: University of Tennessee Press, 1977), 159; Sword, op. cit., 346–8.

time McPherson and Rawlins started barking at him, Lew Wallace had had four junior officers in five hours tell him, sometimes at the top of their lungs, what *their* impressions were of what was in Grant's mind, and *not once* was he handed a clear and absolute instruction from Grant himself as to what he should do. The staff officers fumed about Wallace's insistence that he wait for his brigades to untangle themselves and get back in order, but Wallace felt that Grant wanted *all* his troops, not just the parts that could make it through the traffic jam or survive a double-quick march for four miles or so. He did agree to push the infantry forward, and the division started crossing the Snake Creek Bridge at about 7:15, having covered fourteen miles in just over seven hours.[14]

Wallace always said that the note from Rawlins instructed him to join Sherman's flank. Wallace's reports to Grant and Halleck both stated that his planned movement was what he believed Grant had wanted all along. Wallace's adjutant, Frederick Knefler, acknowledged seeing the first note some years after the war, but he never said that he ever read it or knew what it said, and later lost it. By the time the order that Wallace said he saw--and that Knefler lost--was written, at least one scholar believes it said something altogether different from what Grant wanted. Worse, there have been at least three different versions of what that inconveniently lost note *did* say.[15]

The exchanges between Lew Wallace, Rowley, McPherson and Rawlins could only have happened in the American Army. Since Lexington Green, American soldiers have followed orders (usually, when it suited them), but their leadership has always been of *them*, not of some higher class. Any private *might* expect to be a general in the

---

14. Bruce Catton, *Grant Moves South* (New York: Little, Brown and Company, 1960), 241; Daniel, op. cit., 260–1; McDonough, op. cit., 156–7, 159; William S. McFeely, *Grant: A Biography* (New York: W. W. Norton & Company, 1982), 113; Sword, op. cit., 348–9.

15. Daniel, op. cit., 257–58; McDonough, op. cit., 156–9; Perret, op. cit., 191; Sword, op. cit., 346; War Department, "OR I/X/1," 170, 174–5, 185.

Civil War, and that conflict saw several men do just that. The egalitarian nature of West Point made all cadets in a class more-or-less equal after commissioning, but the militia officers were elected by their men, and there were more of them. Officers arguing among themselves were like foremen on factory floors, or draymen on the road: equals with a job to do, and if this fellow is in the way...well, we'll just see about that. West Point-trained or not, Wallace, Grant, Rowley, McPherson and Rawlins all shared the grass-roots egalitarian "all men created equal" mindset of American traditions. The fundamental friction between the Professionalists and the Volunteerists in 19th Century American military polity could never get past that simple fact. A corporal could yell at a colonel without fear in the right circumstances, and no general could simply order a private to do anything without either explanation or dire need. Americans have always had to know "the reason why."

Lack of reconnaissance and poor maps could have been the cause of Lew Wallace's odyssey, but the ill-prepared pre-battle army that never told Grant of the contingency plan Wallace and Sherman had worked out was probably the biggest contributor to the mess. Decades of acrimony might have been avoided if Lew Wallace had sent a memo to Grant outlining his reinforcement plan before the battle. That Grant failed to communicate clearly, forcefully and decisively exactly what he wanted his subordinate to do (and made a copy of that instruction) didn't help. The last error, however, would infrequently be repeated as long as the war lasted. Wallace's late arrival at Pittsburg Landing gave Grant an anchor on which to base his defense for the night, and the necessary weight for his counterattack in the morning, but Shiloh was an opportunity for the kind of lasting military fame and martial glory that Lew Wallace wanted all his life, but would never have a chance for again.[16]

---

16. Edward H. Bonekemper, *A Victor, not a Butcher: Ulysses S. Grant's Overlooked Military Genius* (Washington D.C.: Regenry Publishing, 2004), 44; Ulysses S. Grant, "The Battle of Shiloh," in *Battles and Leaders of the Civil War Volume 1* (New York: Thomas

Yoseloff, 1956 (Electronic Edition 1997 by Guild Press)), 468–9 ff; Ulysses S. Grant, *Memoirs* (New York: Da Capo Press, 1982), 173–4.

CHAPTER 8
UNDER THE BLUFFS, IN THE RAIN: LATE SUNDAY TO DAWN MONDAY

The casualties at Shiloh were more numerous than anyone had seen in America: if the oft-cited 23,000-plus casualties for is correct, there must have been about 15,000 on the Confederate side of the line, since they held nearly the entire battlefield at sunset. The casualties on Monday were negligible in comparison, so probably 7,000 were on the Federal side of the line. The ratio of dead to wounded in this tally was about 1:5, meaning there were probably 3,000 and more dead from both armies on the Confederate side of the line by dawn.

One scholar calls Sunday night a "Night of Horrors." Treating the thousands of wounded was a horrible migraine that would not be relieved. Shelter was short but scraps of canvas and muslin kept being found and erected, and small parties kept bringing in the hurt and sick to wait their turns with the surgeons; many would wait for days. Steamers *Continental* and *Minnehaha* were packed with casualties with no one to care for them but a few compassionate civilians. At about 10:00 the rain began again, a cold pelting rain that kept those who were not either dead or dead on their feet from sleeping. The plaintive cries of the hurt and dying would haunt the survivors for the rest of their lives--a ghastly foretaste of what was to come in 1898 and 1917.

There was disorder on both sides of the line. Sutler's stores were ransacked and at least some men got drunk and belligerent. The food problem was addressed by butchering some of the bullocks and other animals around, but some Confederates were so worn out they couldn't even cut up their own food. Regimental bands played concerts off and on, joining on both sides of the line in popular airs like "The Girl I Left Behind Me," or a hymn or two. These were two armies of miserable and weary Americans, not strangers; most of them far from home.

Trading songs would have been as natural to them as trading coffee for tobacco, or canned milk for fatback, as doubtless also happened.[1]

Gwin's gunboats ceased fire at 6:25 Sunday evening, after it was clear the Confederate attack had stopped. Nelson had the idea for Gwin to fire intermittently into Confederate lines just to keep them awake. This harassing fire began with *Tyler* at about 9:00. The great guns lobbed a round into the Confederate rear with a fuse cut to go off from five to fifteen seconds. After a sighing, hissing passage it would go off with a satisfying noise and flash of light. Every once in a while the gunboats fired a blast of canister on the bluff to push back Confederate watchers. *Lexington* looked in on Crump's Landing early in the evening, returning to relieve *Tyler* in the harassing fire at about 1:00 Monday morning. Nearly all survivor accounts mention the all-night naval fire, and it certainly served its purpose. Few Confederates got any sleep, even if physical damage done was slight. One Federal infantryman, wounded and caught behind the lines, was terrified by the all-night flash and bang. One account has several fires burning in the woods behind Confederate lines, and there are other accounts of incinerated bodies the next morning. Grant ordered the shooting to stop at daybreak, but the Navy didn't get the order until 7:00 or so, about an hour after sunrise.[2]

---

1. James R. Arnold, *The Armies of U.S. Grant* (New York: Arms and Armor Press, 1995), 67; Larry J. Daniel, *Shiloh: The Battle That Changed the Civil War* (New York: Simon & Schuster, 1997), 263; James L. McDonough, *Shiloh--in Hell Before Night* (Knoxville: University of Tennessee Press, 1977), 188; Wiley Sword, *Shiloh: Bloody April* (New York: Morrow, 1974), 370–1, 373.

2. James S. Brisbin, "The Battle of Shiloh," in *New Annals of the Civil War* (New York: Stackpole Books, 2004), 57; Daniel, op. cit., 265; McDonough, op. cit., 184–5; Sword, op. cit., 374; Kenneth P. Williams, *Lincoln Finds a General: A Military Study of the Civil War. Volume Three: Grant's First Year in the West* (New York: The McMillan Company, 1952), 382; Navy Department, "West Gulf Blockading Squadron from January 1, 1865 to January 31 1866; Naval

Some of Grant's regiments were less than company strength by dark, and some companies were no more than a file or two. Federal wounded and separated filtered back through the picket lines all night. The Army of West Tennessee had an "organized" strength Monday morning somewhere between fifteen and 24,000; between them Grant and Buell had 26-35,000 men. The largest unit in Grant's army Monday morning was Lew Wallace's division at about 5,800. The survivors under William Sherman, John McClernand, Steven Hurlbut, and John McArthur were "divisions" in name only. Hurlbut's 4,000 were about 2/3rds of what he had Sunday morning. McClernand's 3-4,000 survivors were about half what he had just a sunset before; half of them were positioned around Pittsburg Landing as a security force. Sherman's 2-3,000 was about a third of his former strength. McArthur, commanding what was left of William Wallace's old division, had no more than 2,000 men in the ranks; McArthur had been wounded, leaving field command to James Tuttle. Francis Quinn, commanding the 12th Michigan and Prentiss' senior surviving officer wrote 6th Division's battle report--a division that was no more.[3]

Buell's army spent the night crossing the river, but it was painfully slow. The Army of the Ohio had about 13,000 at most on the western side of the Tennessee River on Monday morning. Buell's first two divisions, Crittenden's and Nelson's of about 8,000 strong between

---

Forces on Western Waters from May 8, 1861 to April 11, 1862; Series 1 Volume 22," in *Official Records of the Union and Confederate Navies in the War of the Rebellion*, reprint, 1987 (Washington, D.C. (reprint Harrisburg, PA): Government Printing Office (reprint National Historical Society), 1908), 763.

3. O. Edward Cunningham, (Gary D. Joiner and Timothy B. Smith, Eds.), *Shiloh and the Western Campaign of 1862* (New York: Savas Beatie, 2008), 224; Daniel, op. cit., 183–4; Sword, op. cit., 322; War Department, "Shiloh, Corinth: Series I, Volume X, Part 1," in *War of the Rebellion: Official Records of the Union and Confederate Armies* (Washington, D.C.: U.S. Government Printing Office, 1911 (Electronic version 1999 by Guild Press, Indianapolis, IN)), 139–40, 142.

them, were in place by 10:30 or 11:00 Sunday night, on a line about 300 yards south of Grant's. It was so Buell's men had to move literally by touch. Alexander McCook's division loaded at Savannah early Sunday evening, but was unable to get any more to Pittsburg Landing than what his men could carry. Crittenden's division loaded at Savannah with some of their artillery late Sunday and early Monday. Thomas Wood's division loaded at Savannah on Monday morning, again with only what the men could carry and a few officers' horses--less than half the division. By Monday night Nelson had left an infantry brigade and three batteries behind; Wood left an infantry brigade and four batteries; McCook left three batteries, and Crittenden got only two of his three brigades and two of his seven assigned batteries across by Monday night. The rest of Buell's army would have to wait until a path could be cleared through Savannah. Buell expected to have 24,000 men on the line by dawn and told Sherman that he planned to attack at sunup. The reports and returns of his division commanders made his strength just shy of 18,000 Monday night, but Buell later claimed he had 24,000 across the river on Monday morning; another account has all of Buell's 25,255 across, but this is unlikely.[4]

---

4. Bruce Catton, *Grant Moves South* (New York: Little, Brown and Company, 1960), 243–4; Albert Dillahunty, *Shiloh: National Military Park, Tennessee*, reprint, (Reprint 1961) (Washington, D.C.: United States Park Service, Department of the Interior, 1955), 19; Fredrick H. Dyer, *Dyer's Compendium*, reprint, (Electronic Version 1996 by Guild Press) (Des Moines, IA.: The Dyer Publishing Company, 1908), 430–1; Ulysses S. Grant, *Memoirs* (New York: Da Capo Press, 1982), 190–91; Stanley Horn, *The Army of Tennessee* (Norman, OK: University of Oklahoma Press, 1941 (Reprint 1993)), 139; Thomas Jordan, "Notes of a Confederate Staff-Officer at Shiloh," in *Battles and Leaders of the Civil War Volume 1* (New York: Thomas Yoseloff, 1956 (Electronic Edition 1997 by H-Bar Enterprises)), 603; Geoffrey Perret, *Ulysses S. Grant, Soldier and President* (New York: Random House, 1997), 198; War Department, op. cit., 302, 355–6, 377.

All Beauregard's men could do was wait for sunrise and shiver in the cold.

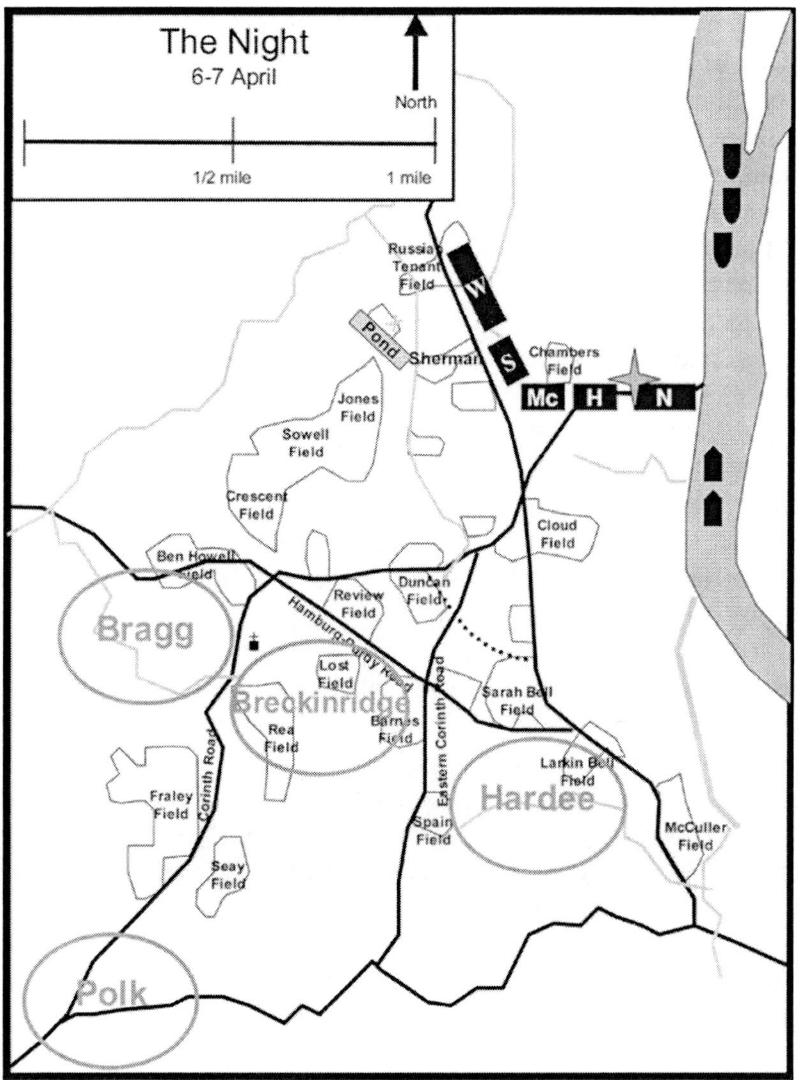

Figure 8-1 Night Positions

Under the Bluffs

Numerous accounts describe the refugees--"skulkers" to some contemporaries--packed under the bluffs, wanting to get out, threatening and bribing the steamboats to take them away, expecting that they would be captured or killed at daybreak. Grant put their numbers at about four thousand, some other observers counted up to twenty thousand. The central challenge to knowing how many people were there is that the number of noncombatants at Pittsburg Landing is unknown and unknowable; no one bothered to count them then and there's no accurate way to do it now.

If there were about three cooks, seamstresses and laundresses for every seventeen privates in a company and maybe twice as many family members attached, each regiment would have nearly a hundred civilians with men in the ranks, more with the officer's servants. Multiply this figure by 80+ regiments, and add in at least ten more for each field battery, cavalry unit, and siege artillery batteries. Then add the sutlers and other camp followers, visitors, local residents of Pittsburg Landing, and farmers passing through bringing spring piglets and lambs to market, and the number of non-combatants in the area runs into the thousands quickly. Ten thousand *people* under the bluffs may thus be low; 20,000 is possible.

Given the number of casualties Grant had suffered on the first day and the known number of prisoners taken, the civilians under the bluffs were joined by somewhere between four and six thousand soldiers. Even if there were as many as ten thousand *combatants* (25% of Grant's Sunday morning strength) under the bluffs, Grant's straggler rate was better than Louis Napoleon's 30% at Solferino just three years before Shiloh. Straggling in the Confederate ranks was just as bad as it was in the Federal, but not as visible because of the nature of the battlefield; too, there were probably large numbers of civilians following Johnston's army, though probably not near as many as Grant's.[5]

---

5. Cunningham, op. cit., 320–21, 321ff; Daniel, op. cit., 246; Grant, *Memoirs*, 179; McDonough, op. cit., 178; Gerald J.

There is a great deal of Civil War literature on the neighborhood regiments, and all of it provides a rich picture of how the soldiers often saw themselves and their units, of the collective shame of these tightly-knit communities associated with "unmanly" behavior on the "field of honor." Yet, that description denies the very nature of the one thing the front-line soldier knows he can and should be able to do that keeps his morale up in the worst firefight: run away to fight some other place, some other day. The Japanese soldier of the 20th Century was told all his life that he could neither retreat nor surrender, and tens of thousands died needlessly. The Vietnamese who "liberated" Hue in 1968 were abandoned by Hanoi because they simply could not be supported; their prolonged sacrifice are stuff of Marine Corps legends, but had no tactical military value. Unless they are sure they can get away from certain death or destruction, soldiers have a tendency destroy themselves for no sound military or patriotic reasons, or become morosely fatalistic and sacrificial. More than that, believing in "valor" above all else denies *and ignores* the shocking effect of suddenly being splattered with a childhood friend's brains or a kinsman's guts. Not every soldier is going to be able to merely think of Mom and apple pie and get past that kind of horror *during* the shock of combat. But, that is not what soldiers remember in repose, when the shooting stops and dueling memoirs crowd the shelves. These frightened citizen-soldiers described in all the histories are usually regarded as cowards and malingerers by contemporaries. We should look at these judgments with some critical reflection.[6]

The mobs under the bluffs fell into one of four distinct groups: soldiers caught up in panic who *would* return; soldiers who *might*

Prokopowitz, *All For the Regiment: The Army of the Ohio, 1861–1862* (Chapel Hill: University of North Carolina Press, 2001), 101; Ibid., 324.

6. Joseph Allan Frank, and George A. Reaves, *"Seeing the Elephant:" Raw Recruits at the Battle of Shiloh* (Chicago: University of Illinois Press, 2003), 136.

return; soldiers who *would not* return, and non-combatants. Many of the combatants were sick; 20 percent or more of Grant's army had been on sick call a week before the battle, and at least half would have been suffering from some malady or another at any time. But the first group--perhaps a third of the combatants--would make their way back to find familiar faces as soon as they could, which might have been as the last line was being formed, during the last bombardment, or perhaps just after. Buell and Nelson likely came through the refugees at their thickest and most panic-stricken, during the collapse of Grant's left between 5:00 and 6:00. Many men would later explain that units on their flanks were surprised and bolted so they had to run off to save themselves, and often they would have been truthful.[7]

The regiments needed the manpower and didn't care what their people had done before as long as they came back. The returning men would have been greeted by their weary and bloodied fellows as well as circumstances and energy levels permitted--the 1976 film version of Stephen Crane's *Red Badge of Courage* captured this scene best, where Fleming makes his way back to his unit. There would have been no recriminations since many of their messmates would have run away as well, just not stayed gone as long. The sergeants may have taken the men's stories about toting ammunition or running dispatches for the general or fighting somewhere else with generous measures of salt, but would have thought these tales plausible enough to tell the officers if they asked. The returned men would try to find some grub or coffee, a musket if they needed to, and a place to lie down for a bit with a gum blanket to get warm and some tobacco or a nip of whiskey, if any of these were to be had. We have every reason to believe that the cooks, laundresses and seamstresses also trickled back with the wives, children and other family members; they were as much a part of the regiments as the soldiers.

---

7. Cunningham, op. cit., 320–1; Ibid., 135; William S. McFeely, *Grant: A Biography* (New York: W. W. Norton & Company, 1982), 113–14.

As Crittenden's division arrived starting at about 9:00, some of those of our second group began to regain faith in the Federal position, even if a large mob had to be driven back with bayonets so the boats could land. The mob would have been thinning because they were wet, cold, tired and hungry and knew that they and stood no chance of escaping those miseries while on the run from their outfits. The cannonading from the last line was heard in Savannah, and after dark the firing from the Confederate side ended. This alone may have given many enough courage to feel as if they may have a chance of fighting it out, and their briefly suppressed sense of duty might have brought them back up the bluffs during the night to find familiar faces.[8]

The remaining men under the bluffs and in the woods must have watched Buell's men and their fellows going back to their units with some trepidation and not a little shame, and probably put some spine into the wet and frightened men under the bluffs. Getting them back to their units, or just to rejoin the fighting at all, was going to be a chore because many would have had the militia "I've done enough" attitude, which was perfectly legitimate before then. But Shiloh was different, and for the survivors of a sudden battlefield with over 20,000 casualties scattered around it, that attitude would never again be legitimate for American arms.[9]

Very large warming fires were built near the bluffs before midnight; cooking would have come soon after. Those who have been in a position of authority in any uniformed service for more than a few years know that you can get any Soldier (or Sailor, or Airman, or Marine, or Coastguardsman) to do what they're supposed to do if they get hot chow once a day. Warm feet, warm hands and a warm belly would have yielded a steady stream of men climbing the bluffs looking for their old outfits. The 15th Illinois from Veatch's brigade of

---

8. Lucius W. Barber, *Army Memoirs* (Alexandria, VA: Time Life Books, 1894 (Reprint 1984)), 55; Daniel, op. cit., 265; McDonough, op. cit., 186; Sword, op. cit., 376–7; War Department, op. cit., 355.

9. Frank, op. cit., 138–9.

Hurlbut's division started the battle with 550 men, and mustered barely two hundred by dark. Its Company D had thirteen officers and men left standing Sunday night, from fifty the night before. But in the final count Company D suffered only three dead, seventeen wounded and one deserted; nineteen men got separated in the fury of the battle and returned to the unit. Neither Alexander McCook nor Old Army Regular Lovell Rousseau, who commanded McCook's leading 4th Brigade and would have relished bashing the volunteers, reported a mob of any description by 5:00 Monday morning. Though Nelson and Crittenden spoke of having to fight through mobs of "shirkers" as they got off the boats as late as 10:00 Sunday night, no one after them did.[10]

We don't know exactly what did happen to the last refugees between 10:00 PM Sunday and 5:00 AM Monday, but we know what did not. They didn't simply melt into the countryside--the local population was too small. They weren't rounded up, court martialed and shot--someone would have written something about that.

Of the last two groups--those who would not return and the non-combatants--we know very little, but some may have formed new units under strangers. An apocryphal story goes that a general (Grant, Sherman, Buell or Lew Wallace--there's also a Confederate version) stood in front of an unknown and ragged outfit of several hundred men in loose ranks, apparently led by a haggard and hatless officer (usually a captain or a major, never a colonel) wearing an ill-fitting coat and toting a musket (or carrying a flag, or a sword, or all three), and at least one version has him in front of a cannon or two. "What regiment is that," the general asked. "Mine," the mysterious officer replied. "When we go forward can you support my flank?" "Yessir," was the answer, and that was that. These descriptions of what happened to the refugees

---

10. Barber, op. cit., 57; Cunningham, op. cit., 340–1; Grant, *Memoirs*, 188ff, 189; Prokopowitz, op. cit., 101; William T. Sherman, (Brooks D. Simpson and Jean V. Berlin, Editors), *Sherman's Civil War: Selected Correspondence of William T. Sherman, 1860–65* (Chapel Hill, NC: University of North Carolina Press, 1999), 202; Sword, op. cit., 375; War Department, op. cit., 251, 303, 307.

under the bluffs may be the stuff of stories and the product of fertile imaginations, but they make a lot more sense than a quarter of Grant's army simply cowering under the bluffs all night then suddenly disappearing with the dawn.

"We were all tyros," one Confederate general proclaimed of that Sunday morning, "Generals, colonels, captains, soldiers." These ragged "shirkers" had been militiamen on Sunday morning, citizens far more than soldiers. That day they became Soldiers. Shiloh made both armies.[11]

Sleeping on their Arms

As darkness fell, Beauregard was convinced he had won the battle, and that Grant would merely retreat come morning or be wiped out when Beauregard got around to it. At about 9:00, Jeremy Gilmer appeared at Beauregard's headquarters and told him that the Federals had fled, making the battle seem to be a complete victory. Where Gilmer got that idea is a mystery, but Beauregard sent a telegram proclaiming unqualified success to Richmond, also informing them of the death of Johnston. He sent several staff officers with Johnston's body to Corinth. The Confederate Congress spoke of a Confederate victory at Shiloh as late as May.[12]

There is said to have been something of a Confederate staff meeting that night, though it's not clear where it may have been or who was present. Beauregard is said to have instructed his senior officers to designate bivouac areas for the men, but only Polk, a trained amateur, managed to get Cheatham's division anywhere near assembled and moved to where they could at least eat a few crackers. During the long

---

11. Bruce Catton, *U.S. Grant and the American Military Tradition* (New York: Grosset & Dunlap, 1954), 87; Joan Waugh, *U.S. Grant: American Hero, American Myth* (Chapel Hill, NC: University of North Carolina Press, 2009), 58.

12. Cunningham, op. cit., 327; Daniel, op. cit., 262; McDonough, op. cit., 181; Sword, op. cit., 377.

night on that horrible battlefield most Confederates simply rested where they could find a place.[13]

Beauregard was a generous host to his most senior captive, Benjamin Prentiss. During his visit, Beauregard questioned his prisoner about this and that. This was when Beauregard learned that Smith had been ill and that Grant had been absent from the field early in the battle. Prentiss told them that Buell had arrived on the eastern side of the river the evening before, but the Confederates laughed at the idea. Why, Buell was near Decatur, they said. Grant, his captors assured him, was finished. It seems clear that a sizable number of the Confederate rank-and-file wanted to believe, like their commander and senior officers, that Grant was done and would either be gone in the morning or be swept off the field like flies off a sugar cake.[14]

But some in the Confederate army knew better. Nathan B. Forrest sent a scouting party to the river dressed in Federal overcoats. They made watched part of Buell's army unloading from steamboats sometime between 9:00 and midnight. But every bit of good intelligence yields a bad idea as to what to do with it. The lieutenant commanding the squad averred that the Federal line was so badly organized that a night attack would drive them into the river. Night infantry attacks were rare in the 19th Century, restricted to fixed points like fortifications. With only one brigade in contact, any Confederate attack on the Federal line certainly would have been somewhere between impossible to organize and suicidal to execute.

Nonetheless, the information in the report was important. After the scouts reported back, Forrest went out looking for Beauregard's headquarters. He found Chalmers, Hardee and Breckinridge, warning them that the army should either prepare for a major attack or a withdrawal. Only Beauregard had the authority to order either, but no

---

13. Daniel, op. cit., 251; Perret, op. cit., 197–8; Sword, op. cit., 372.

14. Cunningham, op. cit., 331–3; Daniel, op. cit., 251–2; Jordan, op. cit., 602–3; McDonough, op. cit., 192; Sword, op. cit., 377–8.

one by then had the troop control to prepare for much. The generals told Lieutenant Colonel Forrest to find Beauregard, but none could say where the head shed was. Another Confederate patrol at about 2:00 Monday morning confirmed the earlier report of troops arriving at the Landing.[15]

While we have no reason to doubt this account (Forrest was a very aggressive horse soldier, and was not known to exaggerate), it does put some doubt on claims that Beauregard communicated with all his corps commanders that night. If he had, Hardee and Breckinridge would certainly have known where to find him, and Forrest would have been able to deliver his report without difficulty. But Forrest apparently never did find Beauregard that night.[16]

Preston Pond, lacking any instructions, bedded his remnants down Sunday night within musket shot of the Federal lines. He could hear Crittenden's and McCook's divisions moving into position, and their bands playing. He and his men were under no illusions as to what would happen in the morning. Robert Trabue rode over the field until 11:00 Sunday night, looking for a senior officer to tell him what he should do. He gave up and delegated the job to a subordinate with an escort, who didn't have any luck either. Most studies of the battle conclude that there was no attempt at Confederate reorganization, no orders given for the next morning's fighting, not even redistribution of ammunition, though one scholar claims that Beauregard's staff officers tried vigorously but failed abysmally. The truth is almost certainly somewhere in between, where staff officers may have done what they could (which may not have been a great deal), but it was like bailing out an ocean. Beauregard may have shifted corps commander sector

---

15. Cunningham, op. cit., 333–4; Daniel, op. cit., 263–4; McDonough, op. cit., 191–92, 194; Sword, op. cit., 378–9.

16. Thomas L. Connelly, *Army of the Heartland: The Army of the Tennessee, 1861–62*, reprint, 1995 Edition (Baton Rouge: Louisiana State University Press, 1967), 173; Sword, op. cit., 378; War Department, op. cit., 387, 569–70, 613.

responsibilities Sunday night on paper, but when the senior officers may have learned of these changes is an open question. Given what Hardee and Breckinridge knew of Forrest's intelligence, and since Beauregard never mentioned being told of it, how Beauregard informed his subordinates about their changed responsibilities is a mystery. One might wonder how many circles all these couriers, scouts and staff officers rode around in...in unfamiliar territory...at night...in the rain...on the wreckage-strewn field.[17]

There must have been a scene similar to the trickle of Union soldiers returning to their fellows on the Confederate side. They would have been far more desperate for manpower and trying to rest on a battlefield strewn with the dead, dying, burning, and drowning--and with an occasional explosion overhead. The "shirkers" who rejoined the Confederate ranks may have been less numerous, but they had a bigger space to hide in. They too would have sought familiar faces, but they didn't have the reassurance of fresh troops joining their line. Instead they had the dull banging of *Tyler*'s and *Lexington*'s guns all night. The real physical effect the gunboats had was negligible, but the psychological effect was devastating, especially galling because the Confederates could do nothing about them. To them the Tennessee River was a taunting water barrier that emitted sixty-odd pounds of spherical case shot every quarter hour. The booming of the Federal gunboats all night hurt few physically, but certainly kept many awake.[18]

By midnight on the 6th the 47th Tennessee could go no further than the southern edge of the battlefield. Beauregard's last reinforcements stopped to rest in the mud and rain, with no food and no tents.[19]

---

17. Connelly, op. cit., 171; Cunningham, op. cit., 334–7; William C. Davis, *The Orphan Brigade: The Kentucky Confederates Who Couldn't Go Home* (Garden City, NY: Doubleday & Company, 1980), 90–92; Dillahunty, op. cit., 15, 16; McDonough, op. cit., 190; Sword, op. cit., 386; Williams, op. cit., 382.

18. Daniel, op. cit., 263.

19. Ibid., 264.

In the Rain

When the shooting stopped, Grant found a dry spot under a tree to stretch out while painfully hobbling around the Landing on a crude crutch as Gwin's gunboats thundered from the river. As the rain continued he conferred with his surviving division commanders (who likely came to him) and his staff. Since he could not mount a horse by himself, any meetings likely took place wherever it was he spent the night. The cabin designated as his headquarters by the river had been taken over by the surgeons and was packed with wounded men. Grant couldn't stay there since couldn't stand the sight and smell of blood: youthful experience in his father's tanning yard had so revolted him his meat always had to be well-done.

He is said to have told McPherson that he was going to "attack at daylight and whip them:" while he may have been thinking this, no written orders to that effect survive. One account has Grant giving his division commanders instructions to go on the attack at sunup, and to leave no reserve. The first claim is credible (though only Sherman mentioned it in his report), the other is not. Grant would have wanted even a small reserve for exploiting a complete collapse or covering a retreat; any experienced officer would have.[20]

One exchange between Grant and Sherman stands on shaky ground but, like other legends, may contain a kernel of truth. This is the story of when Sam Grant met Billy Sherman on Sunday night. One version finds the shadowbox scene at a fire, another in a small clearing, another on a steamboat (the least likely), others in a cabin or tent. Inevitably, Grant is puffing on a cigar. Traditionally, the conversation went like this:

Sherman: "Well, Grant, it's been the devil's own day."

Grant: "Yes. We'll whip them tomorrow, though."

---

20. Brisbin, op. cit., 58; Ulysses S. Grant, "The Battle of Shiloh," in *Battles and Leaders of the Civil War Volume 1* (New York: Thomas Yoseloff, 1956 (Electronic Edition 1997 by Guild Press)), 476; Grant, *Memoirs*, 181; Sword, op. cit., 379; War Department, op. cit., 250.

There are several versions of this, and there's no way of knowing which is right or if all are made up; different versions exchange "whip" with "lick," but Grant was a man of few words and was not known for such colorful speech, so the whole thing may be a flight of fancy. In his memoirs, Sherman wrote that Grant talked about Fort Donelson that night, using it to explain that the Confederates weren't very good at recovering from reverses, and could be bluffed by a strong front. As dull as it may be, this is far more likely all Grant had to say, rather than "whip them tomorrow."[21]

Buell was determined to attack in the morning, with or without Grant's help. One would think that two senior officers could at least exchange banalities and ideas for a few moments before attacking a common foe, but Buell considered his command to be independent and could therefore do what he wanted. While true, Halleck had told Grant to take command if he joined with Buell and came under attack. Buell may have known of these instructions (we don't know for certain), but was in no mood to be cordial, and apparently made no effort to meet with Grant on Sunday night. Grant probably lacked the desire to quibble with, or even seek out, Buell.

Buell did meet with Sherman Sunday night and managed to get a map that helped to position his army. Sherman told Buell that Grant intended to attack in the morning, and it was from this conversation that Buell apparently understood that his army would work to the east of the Corinth Road while Grant attacked on the west side. Regardless of who

---

21. Brisbin, op. cit., 58; Catton, *Grant Moves South*, 242; Daniel, op. cit., 266; Grant, "Shiloh," 476; McDonough, op. cit., 183; Perret, op. cit., 197; William T. Sherman, *Memoirs of General William T. Sherman* (New York: Literary Classics of the United States, Inc., 1990), 288; Brooks D. Simpson, *Ulysses S. Grant: Triumph Over Adversity, 1822–1865* (New York: Houghton Mifflin Company, College Division, 2000), 134–5; Sword, op. cit., 379.

commanded what, Beauregard was going to get hit with a very large force at sunrise.[22]

Finding the Answer

As teamsters wrangled ammunition wagons to the line and ordnancemen struggled with broken guns; with his army in tatters, and his reputation in question after telling his boss that he had suffered an attack that he thought was unlikely just days before, Useless Sam Grant nestled under a tree with his sore leg and took a snooze, according to what he wrote twenty years after the event.[23]

How? By nightfall Grant had been disabused of his earlier estimate of a hundred thousand attacking Confederates. His army had held off a terrible onslaught, suffering the highest casualty count that any American army had ever seen, and Lew Wallace had arrived to reinforce him. His tens of thousands of survivors were sitting on a stack of ammunition that was likely twice again what they had already expended. He had heard that Johnston was dead and that Beauregard was in charge. Grant knew that Beauregard would not expect the Federals to attack in the morning because he knew how Beauregard thought; every antebellum US Army Regular officer knew that Pierre Gustave Toutant Beauregard, the "Little Napoleon," expected battles to be mechanistic set-pieces that he could always control.[24]

After the day's fighting, his men--some of whom had been on their feet for 18 hours--were covered with soot and splinters of wood and

---

22. Arnold, op. cit., 68; Daniel, op. cit., 265–6; William B. Hazen, *A Narrative of Military Service* (Boston: Tichnor & Company, 1885), 25; Cunningham, op. cit., 342; Sword, op. cit., 379–80; Williams, op. cit., 351.

23. Edward H. Bonekemper, *A Victor, not a Butcher: Ulysses S. Grant's Overlooked Military Genius* (Washington D.C.: Regenry Publishing, 2004), 52; Cunningham, op. cit., 337–8; Daniel, op. cit., 266; Grant, "Shiloh," 477; Grant, *Memoirs*, 181; McDonough, op. cit., 188–9.

24. McDonough, op. cit., 190.

metal, bone and teeth. Some had stains of green, brown, red and black on them; their mouths were dry and cracked from the powder cartridges, their upper lips caked with grime. Many were deaf for days, some for good. Few on either side gloried in their "victory," but most felt both relief and guilt that they had survived. Many would be revolted at what they had just come through, and sad that their mess fires weren't as well attended by friendly and well-known faces.

In the cold rain, Grant discovered that he knew these volunteers, these former militiamen. That night he knew what they were capable of, and the worst of their initiation was over. Their "elephant" of battle was a magnificent and horrid creature that spewed fire and hot metal, was covered in soot and blood and was washing in the pelting rain. Grant also realized that his army could run itself, that his role would be to provide them with the strategic guidance and logistical support to let them fight at their best. They were fighting on their own, more or less, all day. Grant built reserves, organized ammunition, and tried to organize panicky men. But he gave few instructions to the senior commanders who were fighting, only encouragement and his own conviction that they would win. He didn't need to tell them how to fight, just where to be when they had to do it.[25]

Useless Sam Grant had the cold, dead eye of a man who knew how to win mid-19th Century wars between industrialized nations--ruthless and grudgingly accepting of hideous casualties. He was grimly willing to pay the price so that he and the survivors could just go home. He had found the tools he needed to end the war and restore the republic. He knew that this army could attack Beauregard with or without Buell's support and retake their camps. He was as certain of winning as he was that the sun would come up in the east.

Sunrise

Even if Grant and Buell did not make any joint plans during the night, the brigade and division commanders likely made some passing

---

25. Bonekemper, op. cit., 53–4; Grant, *Memoirs*, 187–8; McFeely, op. cit., 110, 114; Williams, op. cit., 364–5, 381–2.

arrangements between themselves, even if they didn't mention them later. We know Sherman and Buell conferred. William Hazen, commanding the 19th Brigade in Nelson's division, made a vague reference to the units of Grant's army adjacent to his (probably Tuttle's), a clue that Buell's subordinates were at least aware of who their adjoining units were. If sleep in the cold rain among the horrors of the battlefield was uneasy, any constructive thought or planning for anything would have been cursory at best.[26]

Beauregard had perhaps 20-25,000 men under command Monday morning; one scholar's head count of 28,000 is improbable but not impossible. Of the corps commanders only Breckinridge knew where all his units were at sunrise and had control of them; the other three simply took charge of whatever units they found in their crudely defined zones. There was no real Confederate planning for Monday other than move north and take charge of whatever Grant was expected to have left behind. The Confederates were not quite as ready for a Union attack Monday as the Union had been ready for a Confederate attack the previous morning.[27]

In his official report, Beauregard would later claim that his ragged band of brave Confederate survivors faced 33,000 fresh Union troops Sunday morning. While Grant and Buell had more than Beauregard they did not number 33,000, nor were they all *fresh* troops by any standard. Writing a week after the fighting, he also surmised from newspaper sources that Grant had lost 20,000 men, or about 50%, while his aggregate of casualties at the time were a little over 10,000, about 25%. Saying this in his "official" report makes it look more accurate than it almost certainly was.[28]

---

26. Williams, op. cit., 374.

27. Bonekemper, op. cit., 54.

28. Catton, *Grant Moves South*, 243; Cunningham, op. cit., 345; Daniel, op. cit., 263, 267; John Keegan, *The American Civil War: A Military History* (New York: Alfred Knopf, 2009), 133; Sword, op. cit., 380.

By 3:00 Monday morning the rain stopped, but it was still bone-chilling cold. Nelson was out checking his men at that hour, telling them to attack as soon as they could see ahead of them. Very early Monday morning, Grant is said to have met with Lew Wallace behind Morgan L. Smith's 1st Brigade that had spent the night facing west along the Hamburg-Savannah Road. The story goes that Grant pointed vaguely west and perhaps south, and that was pretty much that. Grant gave no special instructions other than to show his subordinate the direction he wanted him to advance. There were no recriminations, no rehashing of Sunday, just a simple order to move.[29]

At about 6:00, the sun came up.

---

29. Catton, *Grant Moves South*, 244; Cunningham, op. cit., 343; Daniel, op. cit., 266–7, 278, 280; McDonough, op. cit., 196; McFeely, op. cit., 115; War Department, op. cit., 149.

CHAPTER 9
ANTICLIMAX: FEDERAL COUNTERATTACK AND CONFEDERATE WITHDRAWAL, 7-8 APRIL 1862

As the sun rose Monday, Noah S. Thompson's 9th Indiana Battery from Lew Wallace's division spotted William Ketchum's Alabama Battery (attached to Preston's Pond's brigade to the north of the Hamburg-Purdy Road) about 400 yards to its front. Lew Wallace's 5,800 men had deployed precariously close to the Confederates Sunday night and didn't know it until that moment. Thompson's four 6-pounder smoothbores and two 12-pounder howitzers took Ketchum's gunners under fire as soon as they could lay the guns, but Ketchum's gunners gave as good as they got for about a half-hour. Wallace was alert to the firing and moved Buell's Independent Battery of the 1st Missouri Light Artillery[1] under James E. Thurbur up to help. Within moments Wallace's division was moving in column behind a heavy skirmish line. Pond, without any support on his flanks, realized his brigade was as exposed as a virgin bride on her wedding night. He pulled his infantry back, leaving Ketchum and John A. Wharton's Texas Rangers to cover his rear. Quickly, S.A.M. Wood's survivors joined Pond's in trying to hold Wallace back. Thurbur's four 6-pounder smoothbores and two more 12-pounder howitzers far outgunned Ketchum, who took his guns a hundred yards

---

1. Not to be construed as being under Don C. Buell, but an independent organization organized in St. Louis in July 1861 with a moniker that was obviously intended to confuse future historians and their readers.

south for better cover before horse losses immobilized him. Now it was the Confederate's turn to be surprised: Sam Grant was on the attack.[2]

Buell began his advance even before sunrise. Hazen's brigade was on their feet by 5:20; Crittenden's division was pushing south by 6:00. Hazen brushed past Hurlbut's old headquarters, shoving Bedford Forrest's skirmishers and the 6th Kentucky from Robert Trabue's brigade aside, driving on to the Wicker field and the pond. Felix Robertson may have had three guns of his Alabama battery posted in the area, but Hazen's 9th Kentucky and 6th Indiana flushed them out. Jones Withers, aware of the movement almost as soon as it began, told William Chalmers to pull his brigade back from the south side of the Spain field to better cover. Chalmers was on the move south when he spotted Hazen chasing Ketchum's gunners, and also saw Sanders Bruce's heavy skirmish line moving up alongside.[3]

Chalmers chose to stand for a while in the tree line while he waited for the 19th Alabama and 2nd Texas of Jackson's brigade to join him,

---

2. Larry J. Daniel, *Shiloh: The Battle That Changed the Civil War* (New York: Simon & Schuster, 1997), 264, 278; James L. McDonough, *Shiloh--in Hell Before Night* (Knoxville: University of Tennessee Press, 1977), 199; Wiley Sword, *Shiloh: Bloody April* (New York: Morrow, 1974), 381–2, 403; War Department, "Shiloh, Corinth: Series I, Volume X, Part 1," in *War of the Rebellion: Official Records of the Union and Confederate Armies* (Washington, D.C.: U.S. Government Printing Office, 1911 (Electronic version 1999 by Guild Press, Indianapolis, IN)), 170, 518, 528, 626; George F. Witham, *Shiloh, Shells and Artillery Units* (Memphis, TN: Riverside Press, 1980), 13, 65.

3. Daniel, op. cit., 267–9; William C. Davis, *The Orphan Brigade: The Kentucky Confederates Who Couldn't Go Home* (Garden City, NY: Doubleday & Company, 1980), 92; William B. Hazen, *A Narrative of Military Service* (Boston: Tichnor & Company, 1885), 25; Gerald J. Prokopowitz, *All For the Regiment: The Army of the Ohio, 1861–1862* (Chapel Hill, University of North Carolina Press, 2001), 102–3; Sword, op. cit., 383–4, 385.

hastily brigading with the 21st Alabama under Joseph Wheeler (Jackson himself spent the night at the Church, and was absent from the battle Monday). Chalmers volleyed at the Federal skirmish line as it crossed the Spain field. The Federal skirmishers fell back but Buell, not wanting to fall into a trap in his first battle as an army commander, stopped Nelson's division where it was so Crittenden could come up alongside. Chalmers and Withers had another hour and a half to watch the regimental flags across the narrow space of the Wicker and Spain fields. Order-of-battle analysis was performed in a commander's head then: the completely new regimental colors they saw by 7:00 made it clear that the Federals hadn't pulled out, were not going to wait for a Confederate attack, and had been reinforced: not one of the assumptions the Confederates went to bed with was true.[4]

Trabue was up and about before sunup, sending an officer off looking again in vain for someone to give him orders. While he heard Chalmers' fighting, the officer returned with orders from Beauregard to go where the shooting was. Armed with this helpful instruction (little better than evidence in a court-martial) and with a picket regiment already engaged and pushed back, Trabue got his men off in Chalmers' direction.[5]

Coming up from Pittsburg Landing just then was John Mendenhall's consolidated Batteries H and M of the 4th US Artillery, with two 3-inch ordnance rifles (also called Rodman guns) and two 12-pounder howitzers. Though they were assigned to Crittenden, Buell redirected them to Nelson's front since Nelson was more closely engaged. Mendenhall opened fire with his Rodman gun section firing case shot (a nine and a half pound can of musket balls with a powder chaser) on a

---

4. O. Edward Cunningham, (Gary D. Joiner and Timothy B. Smith, Eds.), *Shiloh and the Western Campaign of 1862* (New York: Savas Beatie, 2008), 342; McDonough, op. cit., 201; David W. Reed, *The Battle of Shiloh and the Organizations Engaged* (Knoxville, TN: University of Tennessee Press, 2008), 73–4; Sword, op. cit., 384.

5. Davis, op. cit., 92; Sword, op. cit., 386.

Confederate battery that he could barely see through the brush at about 200 yards. Alexander McCook's division was right behind Crittenden's. Leading the way, Lowell Rousseau's brigade double-quicked up to Crittenden's right on the northern corner of the Duncan field, but McCook held the brigade back. Buell's entire line was at the Hornet's Nest by 8:00 Monday. The three Regular Army battalions in Rousseau's brigade were each larger than a volunteer regiment, and were separately commanded by John King. This was an awkward but necessary arrangement; awkward because a Regular Army major commanded half a brigade where three Volunteer colonels and three lieutenant colonels (technically) outranked him; necessary because the Regular's ammunition was almost certainly different (and they carried more of it) than the Indiana, Kentucky and Ohio volunteers they were brigaded with. Though few of the Regulars had any more time in uniform than the volunteers around them, their chief advantage was that it's likely that they were all armed with rifled muskets and thus had greater range. King's Regulars were the only troops in Buell's army that showed no great deal of caution.[6]

The Confederate leadership probably only half-believed what Beauregard did about their success on Sunday. If nothing else Grant was known by reputation: the former Regulars among the Confederates knew there was nothing on God's Earth more consistently persistent than Sam Grant. Few believed he would simply retreat; Hardee, Forrest, Pond and Breckinridge all knew he had been reinforced. Even Braxton Bragg could not have earnestly believed that Grant had just gone away.[7]

---

6. Cunningham, op. cit., 347; McDonough, op. cit., 201; Harold L. Peterson, *Notes on Ordnance of the American Civil War: 1861–1865* (Washington, D. C.: American Ordnance Association, 1959); Reed, op. cit., 29; Sword, op. cit., 384–5, 387; Witham, op. cit., 41.

7. Sword, op. cit., 385.

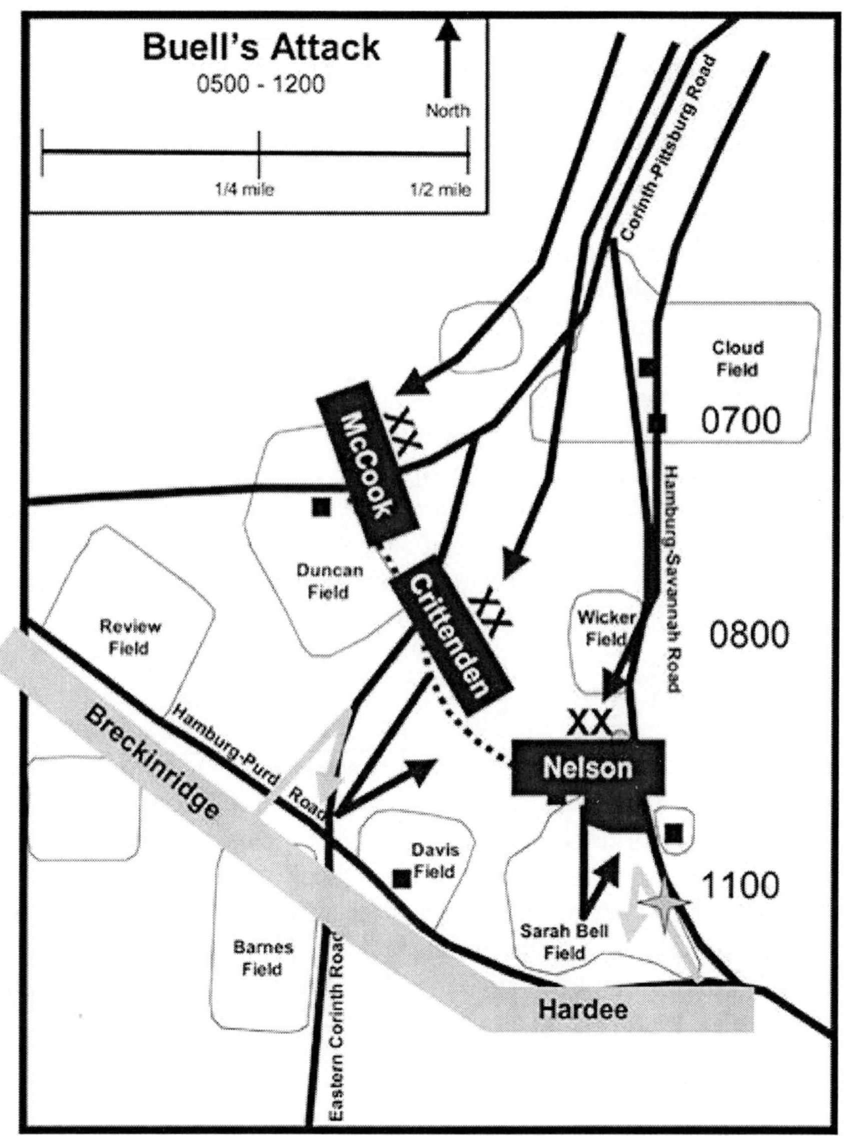

Figure 9-1 Buell's Morning Attack

Tradition holds that Beauregard was thunderstruck by the counterattack, but also that he sprang into action, sending a staff officer to fetch Polk up from the Corinth Road where he had spent the night, and sent Bragg to the front to find out what was going on. His health was still not good and may have been near exhaustion, but he must have made himself a reasonable explanation for his sudden change of fortune and got ready to destroy the combined Federal army. He gave his chief engineer, Samuel Lockett, command of a regiment scraped together from whatever troops he could find without regard to anything other than the ability to pull a trigger. For the moment, Beauregard replaced his fantasies of the night before with two others: this was Grant's last hurrah and was otherwise done, and Earl Van Dorn's army would be marching up the Corinth Road at any moment.[8]

At Des Arc, Arkansas, on the Black River some 250 air miles due west of Pittsburg Landing, Van Dorn's 20,000 man Army of the Trans-Mississippi were waiting for steamboats as the Federals attacked. They got news of a great Confederate victory in Tennessee from a passing riverboat, and saluted the triumph with thirteen guns.[9]

Flying to the Colors

The Confederate soldiers seem to have expected to take an easy hike in the woods Monday morning, and many were startled to be under attack. By 8:00 Chalmers was about out of ammunition and was still facing a fresh division at uncomfortably close range. With no ammunition or relief in sight, he pulled back across the Bell farm to Stuart's old camps, where he might at least loot Federal ammunition if there was any left. Jones Withers managed to pick up a sizable group of stragglers and marched up to the Barnes field. Confederate ordnancemen hastened to arm the 47th Tennessee with captured

---

8. Daniel, op. cit., 277–8; McDonough, op. cit., 192–4; Reed, op. cit., 21; Ibid., 402.

9. Daniel, op. cit., 301; Albert Dillahunty, *Shiloh: National Military Park, Tennessee*, reprint, (Reprint 1961) (Washington, D.C.: United States Park Service, Department of the Interior, 1955), 17.

weapons before they joined Pond's disintegrating command at about 8:00. Munson Hill's green and weary 600 men may have doubled Pond's firepower, if only for a short time. By 9:00 Withers got orders from Bragg to form a line on the Hamburg-Purdy Road joined by Felix Robinson's Florida Battery. Soon John Bowen's old brigade under John Martin was blazing away from the edge of the cotton field and peach orchard. Irving Hodgson's battery joined this line with their surviving guns, rerouted on their way to Patton Anderson. Though a bit worn around the edges, Confederate command control still worked Monday morning.[10]

Irving Hodgson's battery, supported by remnants of Stratham's brigade that included the 20th Tennessee, was outranged and probably low on ammunition, but dueled with the Federal gunners for about a half an hour. At about 9:00 the Confederate gunners were positioning their guns in the southwest corner of the cotton field when Sanders Bruce's Kentuckians broke through the tree line into the Wicker field, offering the Confederate artillery and infantry a perfect enfilade target. Startled by the sudden fire, Bruce pulled his men back to the pond. The 9th Indiana of Hazen's brigade continued to march south to the cotton field.[11]

The Federal advance wasn't a well-oiled machine, but moved in unsure fits and uncoordinated starts that needed the occasional kick from senior officers. Grant's survivors started the day a generally nervous lot that bolted at the slightest picket fire. The 53rd Ohio of Jesse Hildebrand's old command once ran for the rear after taking a scattered volley, disordering McClernand's already shaky outfit and resisting recall. C. Carroll Marsh, disgusted by the display, compared their flight to that of John Floyd from Fort Donelson. But the pace and ferocity of the fighting on Monday was unexpected. Sherman later said the firing Monday morning was the most intense he ever heard. They

---

10. Cunningham, op. cit., 351; Daniel, op. cit., 279; McDonough, op. cit., 197; Sword, op. cit., 386–8.

11. Reed, op. cit., 88; Sword, op. cit., 388.

were gun-shy at sunrise, but as the day went on Grant's army regained its feet.[12]

Most of Grant's combat power was coming from his infantry; only about half his batteries still had horses to function. Wallace's men were joined in the attack by Sherman's and parts of McClernand's and Hurlbut's commands by about 9:00; Tuttle's command was in reserve behind Buell. Wallace was cautious in the advance, but the Confederates were so thin to his front that it didn't much matter. Sherman waited for Buell's advance to catch up until about 10:00, and then continued west by south alongside Wallace. McClernand pushed due south for the Review field and his old camps. The Federals wanted their old camps back not because they wanted their stuff back (that was long gone and they knew it), but because they were more familiar with that terrain, and stood a better tactical chance on familiar ground. When Daniel Ruggles attacked Thompson's battery on Wallace's left, Thompson was running low on ammunition, having dueled with Ketchum's for hours. Thurbur shifted his guns to enfilade Ruggles, and was joined by Peter Wood's three surviving guns. McAllister's gunners took Gibson under fire while Charles Whittlesey's all-Ohio 3rd Brigade of Wallace's division moved up to join Thayer, putting Gibson and Ketchum in a bad spot. Ketchum pulled out, and Beauregard ordered Gibson to pull back with S.A.M. Wood's and Wharton's survivors.[13]

Hardee was near this action, and got word from Beauregard to counterattack at about 10:00. John C. Moore of the 2nd Texas pulled together his men and what was left of two of Stratham's Alabama regiments into something resembling a brigade that Hardee sent across the cotton field and into Bruce's men at the peach orchard at about 10:30, by which time Martin was rushing Mendenhall's guns. Hazen ordered his brigade to the rescue only to find part of the 6th Kentucky scattering in confusion. Bruce's men found their feet again and maneuvered to meet the threat. As Hazen's 41st Ohio and 9th Indiana

---

12. McDonough, op. cit., 200; Sword, op. cit., 403, 407–8.

13. McDonough, op. cit., 197; Sword, op. cit., 403–6, 407; War Department, op. cit., 149.

slammed into the fragile thrust and Bruce's men regrouped the Confederates, outnumbered, began to break for the rear, much to Hardee's fury. Hodgson lost two 6-pounders and a 12-pounder to the onrushing Federal infantry, and Hardee was dismounted when his horse was shot. Hazen's men barely stopped to take prisoners.[14]

Beauregard was aware that his army had very little fight left in it. Many of his men had discarded their non-edible trophies and were using up the captured medical supplies and ammunition at a prodigious rate. Many more were refusing to obey orders or were hiding out in the woods. On Bragg's orders Patrick Cleburne's 800-odd survivors, supported by Isadore Girardey's battery, made an advance against McClernand's and McCook's advance. It was an attack almost worth making if King's men hadn't come to aid McClernand by 11:00 after refilling their ammunition pouches. The Regulars took Cleburne in flank while Sherman's and part of Hurlbut's command hit him in front; at the same time Cleburne was enfiladed by artillery that included George Nispel's surviving guns. Cleburne's remnants broke and Girardey make a quick exit. Cleburne's brigade was done for the day, and mustered less than a hundred men by the next.[15]

B. L. Hoge led the Louisiana Crescent regiment in an impetuous charge to rescue Hodgson at about 11:00, while steady Federal pressure was wearing on the Confederate's defense. Another Confederate battery caught Hazen in enfilade, and his brigade made for the rear. In the ensuing chaos Hazen's men couldn't pull their trophy cannons back, ineffectively spiking them with mud. Hazen managed to gather some of his men together, including most of his own 9th Indiana, but his brigade was out of the major fighting. He spent the rest of the day edging the battlefield, mostly unengaged. To add insult to injury,

---

14. Cunningham, op. cit., 349; Daniel, op. cit., 281; Hazen, op. cit., 26; Sword, op. cit., 389–91.

15. Cunningham, op. cit., 357; McDonough, op. cit., 199–200; Sword, op. cit., 406–8.

confusion made William Smith's brigade of Crittenden's division fire into Nelson's rear.[16]

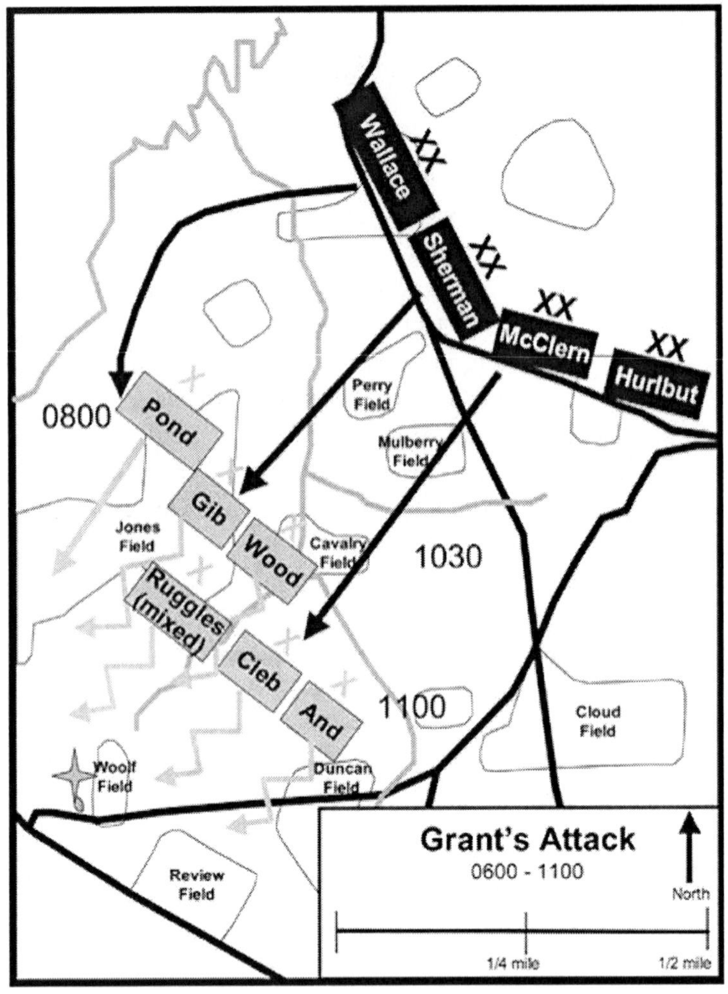

Figure 9-2 Grant's Retribution, Morning

16. Daniel, op. cit., 269–72; Hazen, op. cit., 27–8; McDonough, op. cit., 202; Sword, op. cit., 391.

Chalmers and Withers put together what men they could to hold the Confederate front together. Though they defeated a fairly green Federal brigade, they knew that there were many more where they came from. At about 11:00 Amman was ordered into the peach orchard, where his men came under fire from Robertson's battery. Robertson's guns were joined by William Harper's Mississippi battery, then under the command of Putnam Darden. This 80-man "flying" artillery unit, assigned to S.A.M. Wood's brigade in Hardee's corps (but that never caught up to them Sunday, though their battery commander was wounded) consisted of two 6-pounders and two 12-pounders. Chalmers led an advance on Amman's stationary brigade on the eastern end of Nelson's line. Plagued by wet muskets and depleted ranks, Chalmers' counterattack had little chance of success; the 26th Alabama had only 150 men in ranks, and not a single dry and functioning musket nor a ball screw (a tool used to extract bad loads) among them. Well-intentioned but feeble, Chalmers fell back again and Amman pushed south. William R. Terrill's Battery H of the 5th US Artillery arrived in support of Amman, using their two 10-pounder Parrots and two 12-pounder Napoleons to blast Chalmers' retreating ranks on the Hamburg-Purdy Road ridge, destroying one of Robertson's caissons.[17]

By noon it was clear that Chalmers was in a lot of trouble. Withers grabbed Preston Smith's and George Maney's men and hit Amman around the Sara Bell cabins to keep Chalmers from being overrun. Startled by the reverse, Amman stepped back again, exposing Terrill's guns. In the ensuing melee Terrill pulled one section out but lost a caisson to the oncoming Confederates due to personnel and horse casualties. Terrill himself served one of the Napoleons while one gun section was withdrawn to cover the other. Nelson himself rushed forward with a detail from the 6th Ohio to help; the battery was saved, and the Confederates could go no further. But Nelson's western flank

17. David G. Martin, *The Shiloh Campaign: March - April 1862*, Great Campaigns (Pennsylvania: Combined Books, 1996), 53–4; Sword, op. cit., 392–3; Witham, op. cit., 72.

was not moving and became disconnected from Crittenden's advance while Crittenden was making steady headway.[18]

This Confederate counterattack after Hazen's mauling made a mess of Nelson's line, but it was worse for the Confederates. Sanders Bruce's Kentuckians ran headlong into Robert Trabue's Kentuckians with horrible results for the Confederates just as Barrett's battery found Trabue's men easy marks for canister at about 200 yards. Edward P. Byrne's Kentucky battery of five 6-pounder guns and two 12-pounder howitzers had been firing into the Federals from the south end of the Duncan field for hours, their ranks thinning by the moment but aided by men from the 6th Kentucky. With ammunition running short, Byrne packed up his battery and followed Trabue's brigade as it pulled back. Jeremiah T. Boyle's 11th Brigade from Crittenden's division pressed through the shell-torn thickets south of the Duncan field, breaking into the open in a great mass of confusion. The green Federals were surprised by Hodgson's remnants and some Confederate cavalry and fell back again to the Duncan field.[19]

Bragg directed Russell's survivors to slow McCook down. Russell's attack on King's Regulars in the northern corner of the Duncan field was a desperate move, but there wasn't a lot else Bragg might have done. After 20 minutes, Russell's brigade fell back and Bragg rallied them to charge again, adding Patton Anderson's ragged command. Benjamin Cheatham arrived in front of McClernand, and with Gibson's brigade and Girardey's and Robertson's batteries managed to slow the Federal juggernaut. Old gunner Sherman himself directed two of McAllister's guns into the oncoming Confederates. This Confederate

---

18. Daniel, op. cit., 273; McDonough, op. cit., 205; William T. Sherman, *Memoirs of General William T. Sherman* (New York: Literary Classics of the United States, Inc., 1990), 259–60; Sword, op. cit., 393–4; Witham, op. cit., 37.

19. Daniel, op. cit., 275–6; Davis, op. cit., 93–96; Sword, op. cit., 395; Witham, op. cit., 77–8.

counterattack went no further than any other, but it did slow the Federals down for a few minutes.[20]

Thinking the Unthinkable

By early afternoon Beauregard knew that Grant had been heavily reinforced, and that his own army had significant problems that would only go away with rest, food and reorganization. He also knew he had to get away from Grant and Buell or lose his army for good. Though he didn't want to give up just yet, and he still expected Van Dorn to march up the road at any time, this hope must have been fading by late morning. By 1:00 he issued orders to begin evacuating whatever surplus equipment and supplies could be moved down the road to Corinth.[21]

Bragg too began to realize that, green or not, these fresh Federals were a serious threat to the weary Confederate army. Officers spent the morning trying to find troops that could stand for a few minutes. Though well-experienced Confederate batteries kept popping up in every clearing and field, there could never be enough of them. Many Confederate brigades had been decimated; most "divisions" could pull no more than a full-strength regiment together. Some regiments were commanded by sergeants. But neither McCook nor Crittenden had any artillery with them, which meant their muskets had to match the Confederates shot-for-shot, except where Grant's guns were. Musket balls were often deflected by trees and brush that artillery blasted through. Still, Buell's new divisions pressed south and west. Perversely, it rained off and on all day.[22]

As green as they were, Buell's division commanders had veterans to back them up: the survivors of William Wallace's 2nd Division under Tuttle who gained confidence with every forward step. Calling up a regiment or two at a time, Tuttle's Illinois and Iowa boys flushed Confederates out of the trees at will, and his Missourians were happy to

---

20. Daniel, op. cit., 283–4; Sword, op. cit., 395–6, 408.
21. Sword, op. cit., 403.
22. McDonough, op. cit., 208; Ibid., 396.

chase refugees with a whoop. They may not have had much firepower left as they had on Sunday, and they may have been short of officers, but by then they had nerves of steel and reason to be angry.[23]

By early afternoon, Withers' command was spent by casualties, desertions, withdrawal for ammunition, and simple exhaustion. Gathering what he could, he pulled back to Prentiss' camps. The 2nd Kentucky from Bruce's brigade and part of the 9th Indiana from Hazen's charged Harper's battery, which had been dueling with Terrill's guns. Harper's gunners, already slashed severely, got their guns limbered and pulled back what they could, but the Federals were so close that they lost two guns for lack of horses. Martin's brigade countercharged and threw the 2nd Kentucky back.[24]

By 1:00 Cobb's battery was blazing away at Rousseau, who was just north of the Review field with Boyle and Smith on his left flank and Mendenhall in support. When the Boyle and Smith broke through the trees on the eastern edge of Prentiss' camps in wild rush, Cobb's gunners were surprised and lost a gun section (2 guns and their caissons), 68 horses and over 40 men. King's Regulars had to pull back for ammunition again by 1:30. Anderson, and Russell, then Cheatham and Gibson joined Withers, the odd surviving gun section and Bragg himself to stop McCook again and push Boyle and Smith back. Morgan's cavalry made a try for Mendenhall's guns but were stopped by a fence. Iit was getting harder by the moment for the Confederates to rally their men.[25]

---

23. Cunningham, op. cit., 361; War Department, op. cit., 149; Kenneth P. Williams, *Lincoln Finds a General: A Military Study of the Civil War. Volume Three: Grant's First Year in the West* (New York: The McMillan Company, 1952), 384–5.

24. McDonough, op. cit., 203; Sword, op. cit., 414.

25. Daniel, op. cit., 287.

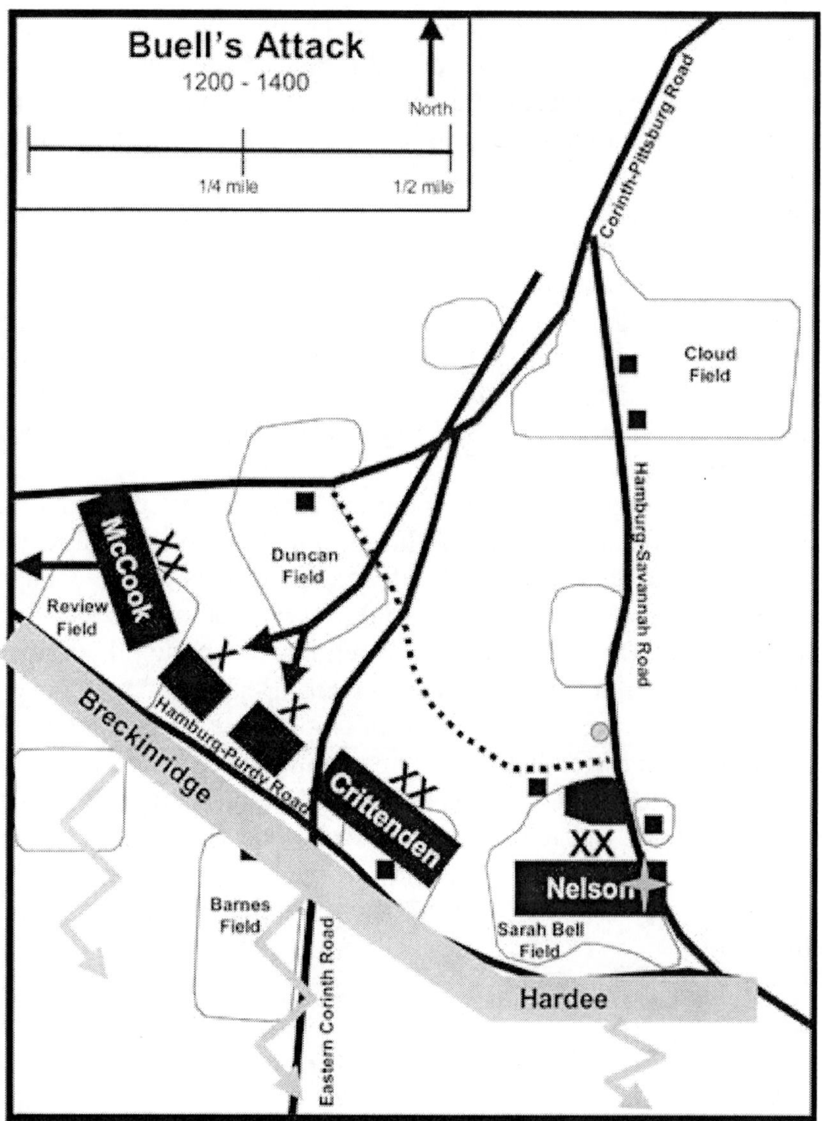

Figure 9-3 Buell's Attack, Afternoon

Another scratch outfit under Beauregard himself clashed with George Wagner's 21st Brigade from Thomas Wood's just-arrived division at about 2:00. At about 2:30 Beauregard and Bragg led a charge on William Gibson's 6th Brigade of McCook's division in the vicinity of McClernand's camps by the Water Oaks Pond through waist-deep water. Taken in flank, Gibson shifted his lines as fast as he could. Edward Kirk's 5th Brigade to the west of Gibson was nearly overwhelmed by fire and loss of field officers; Kirk himself was hit and nearly killed, and his senior colonel gravely wounded twice. But, there was so little energy in this desperate Confederate assault that it, too, was doomed to fail. Enfilading Federal artillery killed Alfred Mouton, and the colonel of the 20th Tennessee was later captured by the 77th Pennsylvania (the only "eastern" regiment in either army) at the Lost field while this was going on.[26]

By 3:00 the Confederates, running out of ammunition and had long before run out of energy, were fighting in sight of the Shiloh Church. By 3:30 what remained of the Confederate defenders were collapsing from exhaustion, and many who could were heading for Corinth on their own hook. By then Grant and Buell had not quite 30,000 men in eight divisional organizations between them; Beauregard may have had as many as 15,000 still on their feet, but most were headed south. Most of the pressure on Monday, from most Confederate's accounts, was in the sectors where Grant's survivors were fighting. There is no reason to doubt this tribute, but it refutes what Buell and Beauregard both said after the war: that Grant was saved by Buell's arrival, and the counterattack the next day was all Buell's doing, with some mopping up by Grant.[27]

---

26. Cunningham, op. cit., 360; Ibid., 289–90; Dillahunty, op. cit., 17; John J. Hollister, *Shiloh on Your Own* (Battlefield Guide Publishers, 1973), 14; Reed, op. cit., 65, 87; Sword, op. cit., 416.

27. McDonough, op. cit., 205.

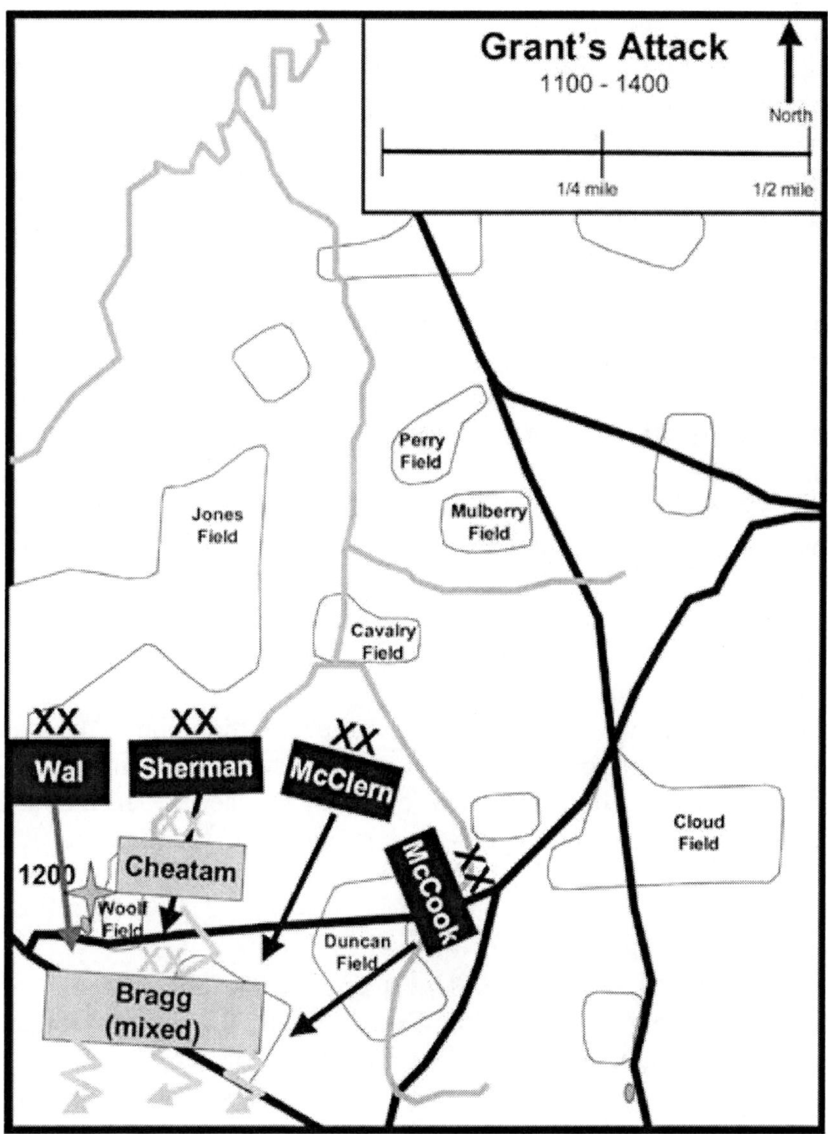

Figure 9-4, Grant's Retribution, Afternoon

Beauregard realized that the grand gamble had failed: Van Dorn wasn't coming and staying to fight was pointless. As chief of staff Bragg issued the official order to pull out for Corinth with Beauregard's acceptance; they knew they had little choice if they wanted to save anything at all. A rear guard consisting of S.A.M Wood's remnants (with fewer than 650 men), Trabue's (with no more than a thousand), and Ketchum's battery was cobbled together near the Shiloh Church, to hold out as long as they could. Behind them, Joe Wheeler took command of the fighting end of the retreating army, a small Louisiana/Alabama brigade from Russell's and Jackson's commands. Martin's brigade and the 2nd Texas were posted to watch the junction of the Bark and Corinth roads. Efforts were made to destroy or fire off everything that could not be withdrawn. The Army of Mississippi began its exodus.[28]

By about 5:00 in the afternoon Grant was at the front, ordering James Veatch's 2nd Brigade of Hurlbut's division and the 1st Ohio from Rousseau's brigade to attack Trabue's command just north of the Shiloh Church. This quickly ran out of steam because the Confederates were, for the most part, already gone. With dark coming on, going further was not in the cards.[29]

Federal cavalry operations were hampered throughout the battle. Grant started with four companies of cavalry in William Wallace's division, two battalions in each of Lew Wallace's, Hurlbut's and Sherman's divisions, another eight companies in Prentiss' outfit and two independent companies in McClernand's; probably 2,500 troopers

---

28. Daniel, op. cit., 290; Davis, op. cit., 95; Ibid., 205–6; Cunningham, op. cit., 362–3, 365; Davis, op. cit., 97; Thomas Jordan "Notes of a Confederate Staff-Officer at Shiloh," in *Battles and Leaders of the Civil War Volume 1* (New York: Thomas Yoseloff, 1956 (Electronic Edition 1997 by H-Bar Enterprises)), 603; Sword, op. cit., 396–401, 411–13; Witham, op. cit., 77.

29. Bruce Catton, *Grant Moves South* (New York: Little, Brown and Company, 1960), 245; Daniel, op. cit., 291; Grant, "Shiloh," 478; Ulysses S. Grant, *Memoirs* (New York: Da Capo Press, 1982), 185.

altogether. Lew Wallace's cavalry was commanded by an infantry officer. They had never worked together; the independent volunteer companies were little better than camp guards and scouts; there was no overall cavalry commander. The smaller cavalry units likely broke up early for reinforcements as needed. Despite this, the 4th Illinois Cavalry from Sherman's division apparently tried to charge the Confederates several times on Monday but was checked by the terrain and heavy fire.

On Monday there was little opportunity to consolidate the Federal mounted force--worn down by horse losses and straggler-wrangling work--into an effective mounted striking arm. Artillery horse losses would have been made up with cavalry mounts where possible. Broken terrain in the area and the state of the roads further complicated mounted operations. After three days out of four of rain the horse feed supply was going to be short. Most of what was available would go to the artillery, ammunition haulers and ambulances. No fresh or dry forage would have been delivered Sunday. Feeding a horse wet fodder--or allowing it to crop all night in wet grass--then putting it to work is a sure way to kill it.[30]

Vigorous Napoleonic pursuit was never contemplated by either Union army commander, and in fact was unknown in American armies. They frankly barely had a grasp of where their people were; most of Grant's units were barely organized and hungry mobs; Buell's were

---

30. Edward H. Bonekemper, *A Victor, not a Butcher: Ulysses S. Grant's Overlooked Military Genius* (Washington D.C.: Regenry Publishing, 2004), 50; Ulysses S. Grant, "The Battle of Shiloh," in *Battles and Leaders of the Civil War Volume 1* (New York: Thomas Yoseloff, 1956 (Electronic Edition 1997 by Guild Press)), 474; Grady McWhiney, and Perry D. Jamieson, *Attack and Die: Civil War Military Tactics and the Southern Heritage* (University, AL: University of Alabama Press, 1982), 133; Brent Nosworthy, *Bloody Crucible of Courage: Fighting Methods and Combat Experience of the Civil War* (New York: Carroll and Graf Publishers, 2003), 290–1, 303; War Department, op. cit., 169.

rather scattered and half-strength dead on their feet. Grant himself was unable to mount his horse on his own because of his bum leg. Buell wasn't interested in following Beauregard because his cavalry, extra ammunition and most of his artillery was on the other side of the river and needed days to get across. Not knowing the roads, and uncertain how badly Beauregard was hurt, he didn't want to get trapped in unfamiliar territory without adequate force and scouting capability.

Besides, the troops were completely spent. McCook appealed to Grant to let him stop, for his troops had been on their feet for two days and a night. Wood, too, likely told his old West Point roommate Grant that going on would be a trial: his two brigades hadn't fired a shot by Monday night but had been on the move for nearly sixty hours out of the past eighty while the officers had been on their feet or in the saddle most of that time. Of Grant's division commanders only Lew Wallace, whose outfit had suffered less than three hundred casualties, was game for a chase. A steady, cold rain returned at sunset, not quite as hard as Friday night but more than Sunday night. It turned cold and the rain mixed with hail that turned roads into ribbons of cold, slick muck.

On top of pursuit being physically improbable, there was also the prickly issue of who might be in charge of it. Grant knew he was supposed to be, but Buell could easily avoid meeting the weary and hurt Grant and do as he wished with his "independent command." Yet, later he insisted that Grant was in charge, and the matter of pursuit was Grant's decision, not his. Further, there was an order to Grant from Halleck dated 7 April to "avoid another battle--if you can," an order that Grant likely did not get before Lew Wallace started the ball Monday morning.[31]

The men had been awake for days, and many had bellyaches. Modern Civil War reenactors complain of digestive difficulties after major black powder shooting events. Biting off the end of the cartridge, one inevitably swallows powder. In addition to being dehydrating, the charcoal, sulfur and saltpeter plays havoc with the digestive tract,

---

31. Catton, op. cit., 245–7; Cunningham, op. cit., 368; Daniel, op. cit., 293–4.

resulting in what could be called the Tennessee Two-Step because the sufferer doesn't want to be more than two steps from a toilet. We can guess, a century and a half later, that many Civil War battles may have been thus affected.

James A. Garfield's 20th Brigade from Wood's division proceeded gingerly down the road to Corinth just to see what was down there on Tuesday, 8 April. They didn't get very far before they found a hospital packed with casualties. The Confederates left seriously wounded prisoners--and many of their own men--for the Union because they could neither care for nor evacuate them. A skirmish near Fallen Timbers between some of Forrest's rear guards, the 4th Illinois Cavalry and Garfield's brigade ended the minor chase.[32]

The Confederates got away, but it was anything but clean. The road back to Corinth, after the rain and traffic and hail, was a river of ice cream-like mud. The army that left Corinth on 3 April had a spring in its step; the one that left Pittsburg Landing four days later abandoned spare equipment on the battlefield for want of horses, and small knots of its wounded at homes along the way. They converted every wheeled vehicle, including forge wagons, limbers and caissons, into ambulances, but it wasn't enough to take them all. Units got lost in the rain and muck, forced to march even further. The Army of Mississippi hadn't issued rations in more than a week by the time it got back to Corinth, the last units sloughing in Thursday 10 April. Van Dorn and his army reached Corinth 18 April.[33]

---

32. James R. Arnold, *The Armies of U.S. Grant* (New York: Arms and Armor Press, 1995), 70; Cunningham, op. cit., 373–5; Daniel, op. cit., 291–2, 296–7; Dillahunty, op. cit., 19; Grant, *Memoirs*, 184 ff; McDonough, op. cit., 208; Prokopowitz, op. cit., 110; Sword, op. cit., 418–9; Williams, op. cit., 388–90.

33. Cunningham, op. cit., 370–1; Daniel, op. cit., 294–5, 302; Grant, *Memoirs*, 184–5; Stanley Horn, *The Army of Tennessee* (Norman, OK: University of Oklahoma Press, 1941 (Reprint 1993)), 142.

Beginning Monday, Dr. B.J.D. Irwin, medical director of Nelson's division, scrounged tents and equipment to establish the first-ever tent hospital amid Stuart's camps that was eventually able to handle 2,500 patients. Although the Federals had about 8,400 Union and somewhere near 1,000 Confederate casualties to care for when the shooting stopped, the medical personnel left on the field quickly organized a system to evacuate the severely wounded for better care elsewhere. The Confederates established hospitals in Corinth on Sunday, where civilian doctors and volunteers from all over the South converged. *City of Memphis* and other steamboats evacuated casualties to Savannah, which had been converted to a hospital during the battle. On Tuesday 8 April, *City of Memphis* departed for Mound City, Illinois with 700 wounded aboard, and many other steamboats followed.

William H.L. Wallace, in Confederate hands until Monday afternoon, lingered at Cherry Mansion with his wife by him until 10 April. Julius Raith, McClernand's default 3rd Brigade commander Sunday morning who was captured Sunday afternoon, was also left behind: his leg was amputated on a hospital boat but he died 11 April. The crusty Charles Smith, who taught both Grant and Sherman at West Point, died of tetanus at Cherry Mansion on 25 April.[34]

The aggregate of Federals killed outright, died of wounds, drowned/blasted to smithereens, run away, taken prisoner, and just misplaced was--depending on how one counts--about 13,000; the Confederates around 10,000. The Confederates suffered slightly fewer dead (just over 1,700 each), and wounded (about 8,000 each); the Federals suffered more missing. These figures represent nearly 15% of Grant's and Buell's combined forces and in the neighborhood of 24% of Beauregard's. Since the Army of Mississippi was a little over a quarter of all Confederate troops under arms, about an eighth of the

34. Jeffry J. Gudmens, *Staff Ride Handbook for the Battle of Shiloh, 6–7 April 1862* (Ft. Leavenworth, KS: Combat Studies Institute Press, n.d. [Electronic version downloaded 2008]), 40–41.

Confederacy's total combat strength in April 1862 became casualties in less than a week.[35]

Cleaning up the battlefield was left to the Northern "winners" of this fight. Most of the casualties fell within cannon shot of the Bloody Pond. Thousands of the dead, fearful, dying, dazed and given up littered a charnel house "field of honor" of some eight square miles of pine barrens and hardscrabble fields. The two Union armies had to contend hospitals and steamboats jammed with broken and mangled people; fields, trees and thickets blasted to splinters; homes riddled with holes and dismantled for cover; fields ruined of crops and produce, littered with broken equipment; family members searching the fields and woods for loved ones; animals panicking and suffering and bleeding and feeding in the ghastly horror; every imaginable structure and shelter crammed with the suffering and those beyond it. Perhaps the worst they saw were the wildfires creeping through the fields despite the rain and hail, fueled by precious tintype photographs, shredded uniforms and unsent letters home, feeding on the hurt and unable to escape, and on the dead and unable to care.[36]

Were there Highlanders left with wind and spit to pipe the dead through Saint Peter's gates?

---

35. Richard E. Beringer, Herman Hattaway, *Why the South Lost the Civil War* (Athens, GA: University of Georgia Press, 1986), 460; Cunningham, op. cit., 371–3; Daniel, op. cit., 297–300; Dillahunty, op. cit., 19–20; Catton, op. cit., 248; Earl J. Hess, *The Union Soldier in Battle: Enduring the Ordeal of Combat* (Lawrence, KS: University of Kansas Press, 1997), 42; William S. McFeely, *Grant: A Biography* (New York: W. W. Norton & Company, 1982), 114; Brooks D. Simpson, *Ulysses S. Grant: Triumph Over Adversity, 1822–1865* (New York: Houghton Mifflin Company, College Division, 2000), 135.

36. John Keegan, *The American Civil War: A Military History* (New York: Alfred Knopf, 2009), 132.

CHAPTER 10
THE ROAD AHEAD

To get the dead buried (which took about two days) and the horse carcasses disposed of (buried or burned, which took another week), few were concerned about identification: The Federals had to clean up quickly to control disease.[1] Once this was done, the "ration strength" of the units became a priority.

The fog of war has as much to do with what happens after a battle as it does during. Counting heads for both armies was a gruesome but necessary task, and any such work was necessarily hasty and inexact. About 8,600 men from both sides were tallied as dead a week after the battle. Exact numbers are difficult to obtain since the surgeon's logs (when they were kept) couldn't keep up with the work, so how many died waiting for succor or after having received it is unknowable. No two postwar works agree on casualty figures for any battle, and Shiloh is certainly no exception: the "missing" have to be accounted for somehow; those who "died of wounds" may have lingered for months or even years; the "wounded" might have been reclassified as non-battle by one writer and removed but still be included on another list; the "died in prison of wounds" added even more confusion. Most of the "missing" end up listed simply as deserters, but other fates were as likely: some may have drowned in a stream or a pond and stuffed under a log until decomposition made them unrecognizable as even human; others might have been buried in a mudhole and run over until there was nothing left but hog chow; no doubt some were struck by multiple

---

1. It is likely that there were a number of women and other non-combatants among the dead that haste and bloating hid from plain view. How many non-soldiers were buried in the mass graves is unknowable.

missiles and blown to fragments; many were incinerated in the fires; a few were knocked on the head hard enough that they simply forgot who they were for a while and no one knew them, but they soldiered on with no corrections ever made to the headcount. Plus, the Confederates took about 2,000 Federal prisoners back to Corinth; the Federals held nearly a thousand Confederates by Monday night. There were many ways to get lost on a 19th Century battlefield, and these were just a few of the possibilities.[2]

Given everything else that happened in April 1862, tiny Pittsburg Landing and an obscure Quaker meeting house in southwest Tennessee were of little moment to the salons and meeting rooms of both the North and the South until the butcher's bill arrived. The Northern press hauled most of the Union leadership over the coals for getting so flatfootedly surprised. Newspapers across the Union demanded Grant's dismissal from the service, but Lincoln thought better of it. Grant was one of the few Union generals at that stage of the war who did what he said he would do when he said he'd do it.

Events elsewhere soon overshadowed the clash on the Tennessee. Even while Shiloh was ongoing, George McClellan's Army of the Potomac was moving up the Virginia Peninsula, exciting the press on both sides of the Atlantic and both sides of the Mason-Dixon Line. The day after Beauregard began his retreat saw the fall of Island Number 10 to John Pope's land/water force, driving the Confederates down the Mississippi as far as Memphis. But even that was subdued by the North's elation on 25 April, occasioned by the fall of the largest city in the Confederacy, New Orleans, to the US Navy.

---

2. John Keegan, *The American Civil War: A Military History* (New York: Alfred Knopf, 2009), 133; William T. Sherman, *Memoirs of General William T. Sherman* (New York: Literary Classics of the United States, Inc., 1990), 267; Wiley Sword, *Shiloh: Bloody April* (New York: Morrow, 1974), 370–1.

Traditionally, Shiloh killed more American soldiers than every battle they had fought from April 1775 to April 1862 combined.[3] Twenty-three thousand total casualties dashed the dearly held ideas of a short, friendly war. Before Shiloh the North expected a fairly bloodless conflict when the Confederates rejoined the family like runaway children, having seen the errors of their ways in the Great Big World. The South wanted to believe that the war would be a bloodless misunderstanding between brethren, and they would soon be allowed to go their own way. Neither vision survived Shiloh. But as horrified as the public was about the casualties at Shiloh, there were soon others just as profligate of blood: George B. McClellan and Robert E. Lee killed more men in one day at Antietam than Shiloh did in two, and Ambrose Burnside expended more men at Fredericksburg than all the armies between the Alleghenies and the Mississippi combined in March and April of 1862.

The Battle in the Books

Memories of Shiloh have been colored by the usual forces that work on any historical event. Regionalism, sectionalism, and blatant partisanship have influenced interpretations of army performance, leadership, the effects and the aftermath of the war to paint an uneven picture. Civil War habitués and the war's survivors speak of the avalanche of memoirs and personal narratives that followed the war, including the *Official Record*, as a "Battle of the Books." In their cacophony of claims and counterclaims, survivors, observers and non-participants carefully dissect battles and campaigns, soldiers and leader performances for avid audiences. Battles outside the Washington-Richmond corridor are not particularly popular subjects of commemoration, and film practically ignores Shiloh. Nearly every Civil War film--and many westerns--mention or depict Gettysburg or Robert E. Lee, but only two sound-era "talkies" give any importance to Shiloh; one only spends about five minutes on Sunday night; the other

---

3. In America's early wars, especially the Revolution, the distinction between "soldier" and "civilian" was a matter of taste.

that even has Shiloh in the title, spends about 20 minutes on the battle itself but about an hour getting there. A four-reel silent film entitled "Battle of Shiloh" released in 1913 has no known surviving copies. Images of Sherman, Beauregard or Johnston in popular films are rare to nonexistent; Bragg appears but once. Images of Buell or Halleck, Hardee or Cheatham in 20th Century artworks are nearly unknown.[4]

The 150 volumes (with a one volume Index) entitled *War of the Rebellion: A Compilation of the Official Records of the Union and Confederate Armies*, known as *Official Records*, or *OR* in Civil War circles, were put together by the War Department over the course of fifty years beginning in 1861, compiled from order books, official archives and personal papers. There was plenty of room for embellishment, redaction and editing in the preparation of this record. Some "reports" were recreated from memory and from other sources, and some items are conspicuously missing (including George Pickett's report of Gettysburg). Some of these reports, including Hardee's and Prentiss' on Shiloh, were written long after the battle. And the *OR* is incomplete: a 100-volume supplement to the *OR* was published in 1996, containing other contemporary papers that somehow never made it into the first 148 volumes or into the supplementary two volumes first published in 1911. There are 229 official reports in the *OR's* Shiloh "Reports" volume alone (another volume contains the "Correspondence" or message traffic), another score of reports are found in a supplementary volume, and three more reports are in the *Official Records of the Union and Confederate Navies*, the *ONR* compiled by the Navy Department. These reports make it apparent that the senior officers at Shiloh had differing versions of Sunday's events. By habit--because there were no medals to be had in early 1862--these documents were lavish with praise for officers who had little to do with the battle, since "mentioned in dispatches" was the only awards most of

---

4. Gary W. Gallagher, *Causes Won, Lost and Forgotten: How Hollywood and Popular Art Shape What We Know About the Civil War* (Chapel Hill, NC: University of North Carolina Press, 2008).

them were going to get. While valuable, the *OR* and the *ONR* have to be read with care and something of a jaundiced eye.[5]

In their official reports after the *battle* the Confederate leaders, for the most part, conceded that the army was incapable of further offensive action by Sunday night. After the *war,* however, former Confederate generals held that Beauregard stopped the battle prematurely. Because the Confederate leadership didn't say this in the *Official Records*, confusion in early battle narratives has colored subsequent works.[6]

Two major themes prevail in Civil War historiography: the Lost Cause, and Save the Republic. The popular image of Shiloh, for better or ill, fits only vaguely in the first, and, because of geography and the political importance of the national capitols, has to be force-fit into the second. The evidence points to an unready and green Confederate army striking an unprepared and green Union army early on a Sunday morning on the banks of the Tennessee River. By dark both were beaten to a frazzle; with the help of another green and weary army the Union forces managed to get their camps back the next day. All books on the battle agree on these points. After that, they all diverge somewhat.

Three popular historical models for Shiloh are seen in general Civil War histories. The first model holds that Grant was caught flatfooted, that he neglected his men and his army was nearly destroyed. This view is typified by spurious claims that have Prentiss captured early Sunday by Confederate troops routing him from his bunk, and the claim that only Buell's timely arrival saved the remnant of Grant's shattered army

---

5. O. Edward Cunningham, (Gary D. Joiner and Timothy B. Smith, Eds.), *Shiloh and the Western Campaign of 1862* (New York: Savas Beatie, 2008), 377; James L. McDonough, *Shiloh--in Hell Before Night* (Knoxville: University of Tennessee Press, 1977), 154, 175–6.

6. Thomas L. Connelly, *Army of the Heartland: The Army of the Tennessee, 1861–62*, reprint, 1995 Edition (Baton Rouge: Louisiana State University Press, 1967), 169–70; T. Harry Williams, "Beauregard at Shiloh," *Civil War History* 1, no. 1 (March 1955): 33–4.

from being pushed into the river. This "Buell Saves the Day" model, first promulgated by Buell's supporters, is often used by Southern writers in whole or in part.

The second popular model maintains that Grant was surprised by a wily Johnston, whose premature death and Beauregard's timidity robbed the Confederacy of its chance at victory. This "Martyr of the Lost Cause" model sometimes uses parts of the "Buell Saves the Day" model as filler, and is common in the South, and with Northern writers who wish to appeal to Southern audiences. It also appeals to Northern audiences (especially Buell fans) because it also allows for a tipsy, indifferent, and incompetent Grant.

The last and least seen model can be simply called "Grant the Military Genius." In it, Grant was surprised on Sunday, but was recovered enough by midmorning to point every cannon and musket in the right direction, and that at no time did anyone near the Landing even hear any shooting. In this model Grant maintained a continuous battle line all Sunday, and merely marched forward back to his camps on Monday morning. The stragglers under the bluffs, when mentioned at all, were small in number and mostly non-combatants. This model is seen primarily in 19th Century and early 20th Century biographies of Grant. Grant's and Sherman's memoirs present a watered-down version of this model.

The common thread among Civil War scholars in articles, essays and analyses of Union and Confederate strategy specifically on Shiloh is more nuanced. Serious writers don't suggest that Grant was drunk. Most scholars agree that before Shiloh Johnston had an impossible mission to fulfill; that he came as close to success at Shiloh as he did is remarkable, but no Confederate victory there would have saved the Confederacy in the long term. Most writers hold that the Confederates achieved complete strategic surprise on officers who should have known better. Much of the debate about Shiloh in academic circles hinges around the question of whether or not Johnston could have succeeded with more manpower, a different plan, or any one of a number of other variables. Nearly all hold that Grant was simply on the wrong side of the river, and believed what he wanted to believe about Confederate capabilities and plans.

For both scholars and popular readers, Shiloh suffers from the unforgivable sin of strategic and perceptual unimportance. It was a geographic backwater, an accidental battlefield that went forgotten for years after the battle. No one had to fight over the same ground again or camp on it for more than a month or so, and indeed no one ever had to go back after Corinth and Memphis were in Union hands. It decided the fate of no cities, though arguably it did decide that of Tennessee. A month after the battle Pittsburg Landing and the lower Tennessee went back to relative obscurity. The titanic events on the Virginia Peninsula, much closer to the media outlets of the day, were of much greater perceived importance than Shiloh. Finally, it was a little embarrassing since few knew much about that part of the world, and the huge casualty list over a riverboat landing was a perceptual leap few could make.

The Hornet's Nest: Did It Matter?

A great deal of ink has been spilled since the battle about the intensity, the value and the real effects of the Hornet's Nest. Beauregard may have earnestly believed that the Hornet's Nest was all Grant had Sunday afternoon, and may have been mildly surprised that Grant wasn't captured or killed there. In reducing the Prentiss-Wallace-Hurlbut Bullet Magnet and Magic Show at least half of all the Confederate artillery and parts of 12 of 16 brigades to reduce less than 5,000 Union effectives, leaving the remnants of four weakened infantry brigades to entertain two Federal divisions Beauregard knew were on the field. How did Grant's militiamen manage that trick?

Southern notions of honor may have seen the Hornet's Nest as a challenge that in the *Code Duello* had to be answered regardless of the cost. This might fit Southern notions of war that would have been readily understood by all Southerners without spelling it out, negating the need for later discussion or debate. That Gibson failed to appreciate this later may explain Bragg's rage at him for reporting on the futility of the repeated attacks. The casualty count, the horrific storm of cannon that blasted the thing loose, the ragged bands of survivors that accepted the surrender of other ragged bands of survivors in a chaos of blood and splintered trees, and the wisdom of needing 18,000 men to neutralize less than 5,000 is pretty compelling evidence that this was an important piece of real estate that Grant needed on Sunday because the Confederates *thought* they had to take it. Beauregard and the other senior Confederate officers may have ignored the rest of Grant's army because they *wanted* to believe Grant was on the ropes.

The battle ended in such a way that both sides could proclaim victory, and ever since 8 April 1862 both sides have. With respect to his predecessors, this writer submits that after two days of fighting the Confederates retreated under Union pressure, and it was the Union in full possession of the battlefield when the shooting stopped. The Confederate attack achieved none of its objectives, which included saving the Mississippi Valley, destroying Grant's force and preventing a juncture between him and Buell. Beauregard later claimed success because--he said--all he wanted to do was acquire supplies so he could save Corinth. But his army was nearly destroyed and Corinth fell in six weeks--not especially compelling evidence to support a claim of "victory."[7]

Shiloh in Myth and Legend

Shiloh's sheer scale and remoteness would have made for a number of legends, and the death of Johnston would have added poignancy, but Grant's reputation and the needs of news reporting early in the war combined to create a whole mythos around it. "News" reports filed within hours of the battle suggesting that Federal soldiers killed in their tents have been repeated for generations; tales of panicky and unlikely conversations between generals are still commonplace in lore. Grant

---

7. Richard E. Beringer, Herman Hattaway, *Why the South Lost the Civil War* (Athens, GA: University of Georgia Press, 1986), 128; Connelly, op. cit., 152; Cunningham, op. cit., 375–7; Stanley Horn, *The Army of Tennessee* (Norman, OK: University of Oklahoma Press, 1941 (Reprint 1993)), 138.

wrote that Shiloh has been the most "consistently misunderstood" battle of the Civil War.[8]

Whitelaw Reid filed the first major news story on the battle dated 9 April under his "Agate" penname. It was likely written on steamboat *City of Memphis* en route to Cairo and on a train to Cincinnati, while he was swapping notes with Henry Villard of the *New York Herald*. Reid's *Cincinnati Daily Gazette* ran the story on 14 April, and the *Herald* picked it up somewhat later, probably with some changes by Villard. Reid had managed to scoop every other reporter, but his was a breathtaking mix of fact, fallacy and outright fabrication combined with details that he could not have possibly known without a crystal ball when he left Pittsburg Landing.

Reid's story began with an account of his arrival which, if the battle was the way he described it at that moment, could not have been before 11:00 Sunday. Some popular histories accept the Reid "surprise" version of the first contact almost without blinking because it included a breathtakingly detailed and accurate order of battle for both Johnston's and Grant's armies, and a creditable description of Johnston's approach march. Some of these details, unknown to the Union immediately, had to have been added to the original by helpful editors, but add cachet to the dubious "accuracy" of the story's more blatant fictions.[9]

Reid's dispatch started the "killed in their tents" myth about Grant's men that has been repeated by respected military historians into the 21st Century. But the only Federals still in tents by the time the Confederates reached the Federal camps were either very sick or newly

---

8. Ulysses S. Grant, "The Battle of Shiloh," in *Battles and Leaders of the Civil War Volume 1* (New York: Thomas Yoseloff, 1956 (Electronic Edition 1997 by Guild Press)), 465; Sherman, op. cit., 265–8.

9. Without the original manuscript it would be difficult to say now that it was printed the way he wrote it. Between editorial embellishment and telegraphic garbling it may have been altered considerably.

hurt. Second, while the idea of bayoneting sick or wounded men may have occurred to some of the more bloodthirsty Confederates, it seems unlikely to have been acted on amid the cornucopia of food and drink that they found after days of short rations and hard marching. Finally, critics often say that the bayonet rarely drew blood in the Civil War, a claim that finds no argument here.[10]

Demonization of the enemy is an ages-old psychological warfare tool makes beasts of people to explain and justify the chaotic cruelty of war. While this kind of ploy has been around for as long as war has, this may have been one of those instances where false reporting became the stuff of history. That the more hurtful elements of the story were not refuted in the media of the day may have been a calculated act intended to hurt Grant. Reid worked for Horace Greely, the media titan who detested Grant and his political patrons. While neither Greely nor Reid politically or privately wished Grant any good will, they didn't editorially or publicly wish any fortune on the Confederates either. Greely used his newspaper and political connections to repeat the innuendoes about Grant's abilities as often and as loudly as he could. Reid or any one of several others along the way may have taken advantage of a confused and deadly situation to make the Confederates look even worse than they really were.[11]

---

10. Keegan, *American Civil War*, 129.

11. James R. Arnold, *The Armies of U.S. Grant* (New York: Arms and Armor Press, 1995), 60; Ibid.; Whitelaw Reid, (James G. Smart, Editor,), *A Radical View: The "Agate" Dispatches of Whitelaw Reid, 1861–65 Vol 1.* (Memphis, TN: Memphis State University Press, 1976), 105, 120–71; W. A. Swanberg, *Pulitzer* (New York: Charles Scribner's Sons, 1967), 28; Joan Waugh, *U.S. Grant: American Hero, American Myth* (Chapel Hill, NC: University of North Carolina Press, 2009), 57; Kenneth P. Williams, *Lincoln Finds a General: A Military Study of the Civil War. Volume Three: Grant's First Year in the West* (New York: The McMillan Company, 1952), 391.

Another legend of Shiloh finds great currency among Civil War buffs.[12] It describes a meeting between Grant and Buell, said to have taken place sometime Sunday. The exchange between them was supposed to have gone something like this:

Buell: General, can you hold out for a day?
Grant: No.
Buell: Can you hold out for an afternoon?
Grant: No.
Buell: Can you hold out for an hour?
Grant: No. I can't hold out another minute. I have no army left!
Buell: Then get the hell out of my way!

There are several versions, all unclear as to who was present and when or where the exchange took place. All are quite clear, however, that Buell arrived just in time to save the battle for the Union, and that Grant was beaten like a red-headed stepchild. Though Buell himself would have relished such an exchange he was not known to have acknowledged such a conversation, and Grant certainly didn't. Other than the hurried conference on Sunday afternoon that probably took about a hundred words from each (at most), the two didn't meet again for days. Buell's *Century Magazine* article wasn't fulsome in praise of Grant, but it didn't condemn him directly. This fanciful "meeting" story fits the common perception of Grant the bloodletting drunk, and suits the viewpoint that Buell was an unrecognized and underutilized military genius who was unlucky enough to have never been in the right place at the right time. Buell's fans are without exception Grant-haters, and Shiloh has always been their favorite place to condemn Grant.

Aside from that, there's the fact that anyone who has read anything definitive about Shiloh or Buell or Grant would realize that it simply

---

12. A buff knows how many cartridges were in an ammunition pouch; a scholar knows the effect of that number on infantry training and doctrine.

doesn't sound like either one of them, but it does sound like something Ambrose Bierce might come up with. Bierce, an NCO with Hazen's brigade of Nelson's division in April 1862, was an avid Buell fan and a venomous Grant hater. His *What I Saw of Shiloh*, published in 1881 when he was well established as an all-around curmudgeon, contains flavors of the Whitelaw Reid version of the battle, alleging that the Landing was nearly taken by the time Grant arrived from Cherry Mansion, and that Buell's army saved the day. Bierce spent the first part of his essay describing that which he had no way of seeing, namely all of Sunday's battle. The death of Buell in 1898 gave Bierce yet another platform on which to pile scorn on Grant (who by then had been dead for over a decade), claiming that Buell saved Grant's army from "the consequences of its commander's fatuity." In his eulogy Bierce repeats the claim that only nightfall and Buell's timely arrival saved Grant's army from certain destruction. Bierce goes on to praise Buell over both Sherman and Grant, treating Buell as if he were the equal of Robert E. Lee in word, thought and deed. If a single post-battle source might have concocted the "get out of my way" meeting, it was Bierce.[13]

A story Buell refuted in his *Century Magazine* article has Grant telling Buell at their meeting Sunday that he wouldn't need steamboats to evacuate more than 10,000 men on Sunday afternoon. This story, like the "get out of my way" meeting, could have been created by someone who may not have been at the battle or long afterwards by someone who was. Buell mentioned it only in passing to dismiss it.[14]

The reasons why at least some of these myths and legends were created, and are still believed, have a great deal to do with Grant

---

13. Ambrose Bierce, (Russell Duncan and David Klooster, eds.), *Phantoms of a Blood-Stained Period: The Civil War Writings of Ambrose Bierce* (Boston: University of Massachusetts Press, 2002), 93–112.

14. Don C. Buell, "Shiloh Reviewed," in *Battles and Leaders of the Civil War Volume 1* (New York: Thomas Yoseloff, 1956 (Electronic Edition 1997 by Guild Press)), 493ff.

himself. By his own admission Grant was a failure at almost everything when he was out of uniform. He was something of a melancholy homebody, and early in his adult life he, like many of his peers, may have sought solace in drink when he was isolated from his family. Since Grant was small in stature even for the times (he was five foot five inches tall and never weighed more than 140 pounds) he didn't need much to get him tipsy.

But he also suffered from blinding headaches and "ague" -- a 19th Century name for a number of conditions, including recurring malaria--most of his life. These "spells" or attacks, whichever they were, might have been both alleviated and aggravated by the only analgesic other than opiates available at the time: alcohol. They might also have been mistaken for benders and hangovers.

The charge is frequently laid by non-historians that Grant was drunk at Shiloh, but there is no evidence to support it, and indeed there is testimony from civilian eyewitnesses to refute it. John Rawlins insisted that Grant not touch alcohol as long as he was around, and there are numerous accounts of Rawlins so stating, with Grant agreeing before witnesses. Grant had only a few real friends, and Rawlins was one of them. Grant would likely not have risked losing his association by drinking recreationally. If he imbibed at all it might have been laudanum (opium in an alcohol solution) or just enough medicinal (diluted) brandy or whiskey to take enough of the edge off his chronic pain.[15]

Finally, he didn't behave like an oiler. Slurred speech and clumsiness can have many causes, but mistakes in judgment, occasional paranoia, unconsciousness at critical times, forgetfulness, prevarication, procrastination and neglect of duties--just a few of many other well-documented behaviors of alcoholics--simply were not present in

---

15. Edward H. Bonekemper, *A Victor, not a Butcher: Ulysses S. Grant's Overlooked Military Genius* (Washington D.C.: Regenry Publishing, 2004), 56; Editors of Time-Life Books, *Voices of the Civil War: Shiloh* (Alexandria, VA: Time-Life Books, 2000), 106; Waugh, op. cit., 39–41.

Grant's wartime life. But regardless of behavior, the specter of Grant as a drunkard would follow him all his adult life, a ready charge to whisper into a listening ear whenever anything went wrong and Grant was connected to it.[16]

Many legitimate sources picked up on other rumors and whisperings about Shiloh, some that don't make any sense. One Iowa newspaper article stated that the wife of the 11th Iowa's colonel, William Hall, had slept in camp with her husband Saturday night, and that her garments were "perforated by several stray bullets" before she put them on Sunday morning.

There had to have been a good deal of embellishment to Mrs. Hall's account. It would require that McClernand's camps were under fire before Sherman was displaced, which is contrary to every other description. It also requires that the 11th Iowa's camps at the Cloud field were under fire before 8:00, which is also refuted by other evidence, including Hall's official report. The Confederates weren't in musket range of the Cloud field until at least 10:00.[17]

By the time her story appeared in May 1862, the fact-and-fancy Reid story was the popular version of Shiloh, so her story was probably enhanced to mesh with that. Though women with the armies were the norm they were not *expected* to be in harm's way. While Mrs. Hall may have been at the battle, and it is entirely possible that her garments were pierced by something, it seems unlikely that she was under fire before she got up, unless both she and her husband were REAL sound sleepers who stayed abed most of the morning and the Colonel later fudged his report. But someone would have noticed the colonel's absence from his regiment, and no evidence has been found of that.

---

16. Waugh, op. cit., 38–40.

17. War Department, "Shiloh, Corinth: Series I, Volume X, Part 1," in *War of the Rebellion: Official Records of the Union and Confederate Armies* (Washington, D.C.: U.S. Government Printing Office, 1911 (Electronic version 1999 by Guild Press, Indianapolis, IN)), 130.

Finally, Mrs. Hall was reputed to have quipped that she was not "properly prepared to receive company," in a homey, Iowa newspaper fashion meant to make light of a deadly situation. In a sea of unfamiliar men, how "unprepared" could *or should* she have been? Given the other accounts (including her husband's report), we can safely say that the details of Mrs. Hall's story were almost certainly altered to suit needs other than news reporting, with a dash of plucky courage added for entertainment.[18]

Absolute historical certainty backed by irrefutable and unfalsifiable evidence is impossible, but the reader is free to resort to a time machine if one can be found. Even the best documented news story in human history--the moon landing of 20 July 1969--now has some controversial elements (aside from the deniers): did Neil Armstrong say "one small step for man," or "one small step for *a* man"? Even he couldn't remember in an interview in 2010, and the broadcast that more people heard than have heard Elvis is distorted at the crucial instant. It is up to the users of history to decide what to believe.

Did Buell Save Grant?

This question rests on three suppositions:

- Grant needed saving;
- The Confederates were able to destroy Grant or take Pittsburg Landing;
- Buell was able to save Grant.

The situation at Shiloh was stabilized before full dark Sunday. Grant was well emplaced behind substantial artillery reserves, had enough muskets on the line to support the guns and protect the ammunition stores, Lew Wallace's division would show up eventually, and Grant still had the gunboats if he needed them. Grant was in no danger when Beauregard stopped the attack near dark.

As for Pittsburg Landing as a geographic target, there was nothing to save because the Confederates could neither take nor hold it, and

---

18. Larry J. Daniel, *Shiloh: The Battle That Changed the Civil War* (New York: Simon & Schuster, 1997), 177.

Union naval dominance of the upper Tennessee negated its importance to them other than to deny it to Grant. Beauregard's first report on the battle, penned sometime Sunday night and sent off by courier to Corinth, boasted of a battle gloriously won, complete with Johnston the martyred hero breathing his last at the cusp of victory. In his second report of 11 April Beauregard lamented that he had been sick for months and, though amply supported by senior officers, he was just not up to a "pursuit" of Grant after the collapse of the Hurlbut-Prentiss-Wallace Magic Show. He went on to blame the Federal "ironclad" gunboats for his army's inability to finish Grant Sunday:[19]

> By a rapid and vigorous attack on General Grant it was expected he would be beaten back into his transports and the river, or captured, in time to enable us to profit by the victory, and remove to the rear all the stores and munitions that would fall into our hands in such an event before the arrival of General Buell's army on the scene. It was never contemplated, however, to retain the position thus gained and abandon Corinth, the strategic point of the campaign.[20]

The "never contemplated" phrase is telling: it likely was not retrospective cover for defeat because the strategic situation was increasingly grim. Union advances since the beginning of the war had cost the Confederacy an area roughly the size of France. The Union would have the Mississippi Valley under direct attack from both ends before summer. The largest city in the Confederacy, New Orleans, had been practically stripped of its garrison (many of whom were captured at Fort Donelson) while a considerable Union fleet had been cruising between the mouth of the Mississippi and Mobile, and had been shelling Biloxi. It would take them at most two days to reach the Mississippi. Though the Confederate forts near the river mouth were strong, their fleet below New Orleans was a floating Potemkin village

---

19. War Department, "OR I/X/1," 384–92.
20. Ibid., 385.

short on men, guns, armor and machinery. With John Pope investing Island Number 10 a day's steaming above Memphis before Johnston left Corinth, the Confederate commanders knew that it would only be a matter of time before Memphis fell to the Union, negating the strategic importance of the upper Tennessee River for the defense of the Mississippi Valley. Holding the Mississippi Valley depended on a mobile and well-supplied force close to transportation, and Pittsburg Landing wasn't the place for it. Supplying the Army of Mississippi around Pittsburg Landing by road from Corinth was improbable, so a bulk of the army would have returned regardless if they won or lost. Though staging a large-scale raid as the Southern Confederacy's first strategic offensive with 10% of its combat power seems unlikely after the events of the first quarter of the year, especially for officers with Johnston's and Beauregard's reputations, in the best of all possible worlds Shiloh could have been nothing more than that.

Several battle reports and post-war articles say Buell showed up just in the nick of time to blunt the Confederate attack Sunday. Nelson's and Amman's contemporary reports, and the realities of the river operation, make this claim questionable (see Appendix, "Steamboats of Shiloh"). Many factors make it unlikely that Nelson's division could have crossed any faster or in any larger numbers than they did. The final barrage, which Buell dismissed as being no more than perhaps a dozen guns, had already done its work by the time Buell had enough firepower on the line to have any influence at all: the Army of the Ohio had only about 4,500 men across the river by dark on Sunday, and no artillery of its own. Grant's report gives Buell's army some credit for blunting the attack, but like the rest of the reports it was for the consumption of a Congress that gave rewards for participation where there was not really a lot. The maps used to support the "Buell saved Grant at Shiloh" contention were made from memory long after the battle. Embellished reports and questionable maps are the probable origins of the version of Shiloh that has followed the battle ever since.[21]

---

21. Buell, op. cit., 506–36; Horn, op. cit., 135–6.

Then again, did Buell want to save Grant? There seems to be some evidence that he may have been ambivalent on that point, and that he crossed the river for reasons other than to support a general he openly disliked. Sherman wrote that on Sunday Buell acted as if he did not trust Grant's army to still be around in the morning, and Sherman feared that Buell would not bring any of his army at all. Buell's generals left at least half their strength behind and brought only two batteries of artillery across by dawn Monday (though other factors influenced this). If he had wanted to help Grant, new, full divisions with their artillery would have dwarfed Grant's ragged survivors and provided him with enough power to perhaps pursue. So why did Buell's division commanders leave much of their strength and supply behind? One traditional reason is that Buell's army wanted in on the fighting, and the faster they could get there, the better the chance they have at glory. This explanation goes to the heroic vision most readers have of the Civil War, and fits well with the tone and style of other writings. But still: why leave so much behind? The four unblooded yet incomplete divisions, hungry and weary as they were, extended Grant's line considerably and gave it more stability, but probably weren't necessary to push Beauregard back. Two of Buell's huge (most of his divisions were twice the size of Grant's), complete divisions would have done the same thing.[22]

What the steamboats did manage to deliver was about all they were in a position to deliver. Buell may have had it in his head that he would need as many maneuver units as he could get to do whatever he wanted to do without having to accept orders from Grant. Fewer (if larger) divisions would have made Buell's "independence" an impossible fiction to maintain. It's likely that Buell knew it would be difficult to get the guns across, so he settled for the apparent strength of multiple divisions. Buell's attitude on Sunday afternoon was that of a peevish child, snapping at others for doing what they thought best at the time. But, this might have been the attitude of a general who was technically under the command of someone he saw as inferior. We don't know for

22. Sherman, op. cit., 266.

certain what passed between Buell and Grant in their Sunday meeting, but among the formalities that such meetings would have had included Grant showing Buell Halleck's telegram that put Grant in charge if their joint force was attacked. For Buell any subordination to Grant, even if temporary, would have been unacceptable. This might explain why they didn't meet again until well into Monday or after: Buell simply didn't want to have to take Grant's orders.[23]

The answer to the question "did Buell save Grant?" is: unlikely. Grant didn't need saving; the Confederates couldn't stay and fight for more than another day; Pittsburg Landing and the steamboats were safe; Buell was unable to bring enough forces across the river Sunday to save anything, and he may not have wanted to.

The Mystery of the Confederate Attacking Order

Does anyone really know how the Confederate forces were deployed when the fighting started? General Orders #8, Beauregard's outline for the attack, described waves of corps led by Hardee, followed a thousand yards apart by Bragg, Polk and Breckinridge. This kind of formation had fallen into disuse before the French and Indian War, in part because it required terrain that resembled a parade ground to control. Beauregard's General Orders #8 also give a great deal of latitude to the corps commanders to adjust their deployments "according to the extent of the ground;" in other words, as they saw fit.[24]

---

23. Kenneth P. Williams, op. cit., 351.

24. Brent Nosworthy, *Bloody Crucible of Courage: Fighting Methods and Combat Experience of the Civil War* (New York: Carroll and Graf Publishers, 2003), 400; Geoffrey Perret, *Ulysses S. Grant, Soldier and President* (New York: Random House, 1997), 190; War Department, "Shiloh, Corinth: Series I, Volume X, Part 2," in *War of the Rebellion: Official Records of the Union and Confederate Armies* (Washington, D.C.: U.S. Government Printing Office, 1911 (Electronic version 1999 by Guild Press, Indianapolis, IN)), 392–5; Ibid., 355.

The legion of maps and descriptions made since then has several variations, including:

- All four corps spread out into a single wide front line;[25]
- Hardee in front, with Bragg behind him, both in lines of brigades (where units are spread out across the front), with Polk and Breckinridge following them in columns of brigades (brigades stacked one behind the other);[26]
- Hardee on the left and part of Bragg on the right in the first line, the rest of Bragg making up the center line, followed by Polk and Breckinridge in a third line;[27]
- A Napoleonic column of corps with divisions and brigades in line.[28]

Given the way the battle unfolded, parts of all of these descriptions may have been correct at one time or another on Sunday. The most likely starting formation is Hardee and one brigade of Bragg in the first line in brigade columns with Bragg following in line of divisions, and Polk making up a rough third line followed by Breckinridge--neither in any discernible order.

---

25. John Keegan, *The Mask of Command* (New York: Viking-Penguin, 1987), 123–4; David G. Martin, *The Shiloh Campaign: March - April 1862*, Great Campaigns (Pennsylvania: Combined Books, 1996), 103.

26. James R. Arnold, *Shiloh 1862: The Death of Innocence* (Oxford, England: Osprey Publishing, LTD., 1998), 23; Cunningham, op. cit., 139; David W. Reed, *The Battle of Shiloh and the Organizations Engaged* (Knoxville, TN: University of Tennessee Press, 2008), xxiii.

27. Pierre G. T. Beauregard, "The Campaign of Shiloh," in *Battles and Leaders of the Civil War Volume 1* (New York: Thomas Yoseloff, 1956 (Electronic Edition 1997 by H-Bar Enterprises)), 587; Albert Dillahunty, *Shiloh: National Military Park, Tennessee*, reprint, (Reprint 1961) (Washington, D.C.: United States Park Service, Department of the Interior, 1955), 9; Horn, op. cit., 127.

28. Daniel, op. cit., 119–20.

Regardless of that, the Confederate deployments outlined in General Orders# 8 were based on a false premise: they surmised that Grant's camps were further south of Shiloh Church than they were. That scale compression gave Johnston a poor impression of the size of the encampment and Grant's army. But, Johnston may have never seen General Orders #8. Jefferson Davis would later claim that Beauregard changed Johnston's simpler plan without consultation, and too late for Johnston to change it back. Johnston's son claimed the battle was fought just as his father planned it, and that Beauregard subsequently made false claims for the plan.[29]

Thomas Jordan said he used Napoleon's orders for Waterloo as a model in creating General Orders #8, basing specifics on notes Beauregard gave him. What he used the 1815-vintage orders for is unclear. None of the descriptions of Shiloh fit any known versions of the initial French deployment at Waterloo, so it wasn't used for the attack plan. Perhaps, in using Waterloo order as a guide, the expectation was to hit Grant first then Buell as he came up, just as Napoleon wanted to fend off the Prussians and other allies before hitting Wellington south of Brussels. Perhaps...but we really can't know. It is odd that the Confederates selected Napoleon's most spectacular defeat to follow.[30]

---

29. Beringer, op. cit., 131–32; Connelly, op. cit., 153–4; Horn, op. cit., 124; William P. Johnston, "Albert Sidney Johnston at Shiloh," in *Battles and Leaders of the Civil War Volume 1* (New York: Thomas Yoseloff, 1956 (Electronic Edition 1997 by H-Bar Enterprises)), 559; T. Harry Williams, op. cit., 20.

30. *Thomas Jordan, "Notes of a Confederate Staff-Officer at Shiloh," in Battles and Leaders of the Civil War Volume 1* (New York: Thomas Yoseloff, 1956 (Electronic Edition 1997 by H-Bar Enterprises)), 595 ff; John Keegan, *The Face of Battle: A Study of Agincourt, Waterloo and the Somme* (New York: Random House, 1977), 124–5; Stephen Pope, Editor, "Map 29: Waterloo, Morning Positions," in *Dictionary of the Napoleonic Wars* (New York: Facts on

Planning for this battle depended on maps that were best used to wrap fish. Studying them a century and a half later, we can conclude that Beauregard's maps were based on incomplete or nonexistent information: Bragg's chief engineer didn't start his survey of the ground until 4:00 in the morning of the 6th, and no first-hand reconnaissance of the area was conducted before then.

Neither Clausewitz nor Jomini would have thought highly of the dispositions for the attack. Though there was a plan for a turning movement by the river flank, the area next to the Tennessee had to be clear for such a sweep to work: if the Federals found cover to organize behind near the river, any assault was going to bog down. The rest of the area was too restricting and broken for anything but a brutal frontal attack. This should have been quite clear to Johnston in planning the attack if he used local sources of information on the nature of the target area. We are told he did have such information, but we don't know what it was because he didn't seem to be aware of conditions around the Landing.

The lack of information on Federal forces, despite an allegedly abundant supply of reports from local residents, is exemplified by the fact that the Confederates seemed unaware that William Wallace and Stephen Hurlbut and their divisions were at the Landing, even if Johnston's officers estimated Grant's strength fairly accurately. Worse, their impression of Buell's army was way off the mark: Ormsby Mitchell's 10,000 men, mentioned in the telegram of 3 April, were a week's march away under the best of conditions. Buell's main body of about 40,000 men altogether reached Grant on Saturday night, and was completely opaque to the Confederates.[31]

File, 1999), 597; Geoffrey Wooten, *Waterloo 1815: The Birth of Modern Europe* (Oxford, UK: Osprey Publishing, 1992), 54–55.

31. Bruce Catton, *Grant Moves South* (New York: Little, Brown and Company, 1960), 238; S. H. Lockett, "Surprise and Withdrawal at Shiloh," in *Battles and Leaders of the Civil War Volume 1* (New York: Thomas Yoseloff, 1956 (Electronic Edition 1997 by H-Bar Enterprises)), 604; McDonough, op. cit., 106.

The Confederates made three grievous errors on Sunday that they never recovered from. The first was trying to fight a linear battle on terrain that prohibited it. The second was in not knowing about the terrain. His last was trying to reduce the Hornet's Nest instead of bypassing it. All pointed to unpreparedness in planning, a lack of coordination and tactical reconnaissance, but worse, more than a little hubris. They could not imagine that they could be defeated.[32]

No plan survives contact with the enemy, and Beauregard's was certainly no exception. As Grant said, Shiloh is consistently misunderstood. It was misunderstood even while it was happening.

The Road Ahead: Because of Shiloh

Two pathetically untrained armies stumbled into each other like feuding paraplegics, unable to run away but committed to win. Though ultimate responsibility for training and dispositions belonged to Grant and Johnston, strategic decisions were foisted on both. Lincoln's glib "both green together" phrase with which he scolded McClellan ignores the fact that untrained soldiers die at a much higher rate regardless of who they are fighting simply because they have no battle sense--and both armies were short on situational awareness at Shiloh. To be fair it is hard to imagine how anyone other than Grant and Johnston would have done better at training in those circumstances. Because of Shiloh Grant concluded that he, his army, and his generals had a great deal to learn. No doubt other officers felt the same way--it is difficult to imagine that they did not--but few of them said as much.

Grant, uncomfortable about not being on the offensive all the time, was confident to the point of arrogance before the battle. While his confidence remained afterwards, it was leavened with a dose of caution and a sense of long-term mission. In the aftermath of Shiloh he started to believe that the war was to be won by breaking the power of slaveholding societies in the United States. He resolved that if the South didn't give up its peculiar institution willingly, he would destroy

32. Perret, op. cit., 193–4.

its capacity to maintain it. Shiloh thus was instrumental in changing the fabric of American society.[33]

The artillery suffered greatly at Shiloh in large part due to draft animal casualties. Polk's corps alone reported that they lost 139 of 347 animals in just four batteries. Chronic horse shortages made the situation even worse for the Confederacy: after Shiloh's enormous horse losses, Confederate field artillery was reorganized into four gun batteries and four battery battalions. Shiloh was also the beginning of the end for the 6-pounder batteries in most American artillery parks that pre-war doctrine treated like small infantry battalion that shot across the flanks. The 6-pounders were effectively outranged by even inferior infantry muskets by 1862, exposing their chronically overworked horses to small arms fire. Even the Confederacy melted most of the smaller pieces down and recast them into larger guns, but at a cost: the larger guns needed more draft animals that the South could only barely provide. The James rifles, as much as a third of Grant's artillery strength, were unreliable and inadequate compared to the Parrots and Rodmans that were available in larger numbers as the war went on, and were almost entirely replaced by the end of 1863 in Union service. The 24-pounders and the big siege guns were left behind for most of the rest of the war. Though a few 6-pounders were kept double-charged with canister "just in case," and the larger guns were available for sieges, the field batteries gradually moved to a 10- and 12-pounder/three inch standard.[34]

Tactically, Shiloh demonstrated that "Napoleonic" maneuvers with masses of infantry in easy view of artillery were as dead as the Emperor

---

33. Bonekemper, op. cit., 56–7; Keegan, *American Civil War*, 133; Waugh, op. cit., 60–1.

34. Jeffry J. Gudmens, *Staff Ride Handbook for the Battle of Shiloh, 6–7 April 1862* (Ft. Leavenworth, KS: Combat Studies Institute Press, n.d. [Electronic version downloaded 2008]), 14; Spencer Jones, "The Influence of Horse Supply upon Field Artillery in the American Civil War," *The Journal of Military History* 74, no. 2 (April 2010); War Department, "OR I/X/1," 413.

himself. Shiloh was the first time that American infantry supported by large numbers of rifled artillery pieces clashed in open battle. The rifled gun's range and the threefold increase in the reliability of infantry fire increased the size of the battlefield as it decreased the density of formations. Given the primitive state of tactical communications, this made it nearly impossible to command more than a few score men in the tangled wilderness of most Civil War battles: senior officers came to depend on subordinates who knew what they had to do. Grant's ability to let the army fight while he just pointed in the right direction and fed them made him something of a pioneer on this new land battlefield.[35]

If "the South never smiled after Shiloh," as the expression put it, it was because it made the Confederacy realize, in private at least, that they could not win a military victory against the Union that would result in lasting and meaningful political and economic independence. As brave as the 4th Tennessee may have been, McAllister's guns had more ammunition, other batteries and more infantry to support them: there are only so many heroes. The depth of resources, or their scarcity, determined far more than spirited yells, beautiful flags and thundering speeches.

In every battle and campaign from 1861 through 1865 the Confederacy came up just short enough for the weight of Northern numbers and gun power to either succeed or not fail completely. In late 1862 a partly realized, multi-front Confederate plan to invade the Union ended at Antietam and Perryville, foundering on the capacity of the Union's armies to spread themselves out more than the Confederacy could take advantage of. Shortages in manpower and industrial output--the raw material of the brutal business of war--doomed the Confederacy to military incapacity: more men and more guns really did matter.

They also needed men who knew what they were doing. By mid-morning Sunday large parts of Johnston's army were acting like teenagers on summer vacation: looking for something to do. Thomas

---

35. Keegan, *American Civil War*, 135.

Jordan, Johnston's adjutant general, described groups of Confederate soldiers at Shiloh simply standing around for want of orders, their commanders having forgotten about them. Staff officers wore out horses scouring the rear areas to get men moving who didn't know to march to the sound of the guns. Want of battle experience also deprived the Confederates of much-needed manpower, and by mid-afternoon Sunday that was all too plain.[36]

Southern armies destroyed only one Northern army beyond repair during the war, whereas the North destroyed at least four Southern armies. Even apparent Northern disasters like Chancellorsville were territory-neutral fights where the Southern victory was just another geographic repulse of one of several Northern armies: the South wouldn't get any stronger for winning. Gettysburg, in the best of all possible worlds a raid like Shiloh, could demonstrate nothing as long as Lee had to go back south to rebuild his army. Even if he bested George Meade in Pennsylvania and further pillaged southeastern Pennsylvania, the Army of Northern Virginia did not have the resources to seize and hold a major city for an extended period. Only one major Southern city, Galveston, was recaptured by the Confederacy after the Union occupied it, and the Confederacy took no Northern towns for more than a few days.

The green solders of Shiloh performed better than anyone could have hoped for before the battle. No one expected the ferocity of the Confederate attacks at Shiloh, and no one expected two furious bombardments Sunday afternoon. The Confederate attacks impressed Grant even decades later. "Disregard of losses" was the phrase he would use in his *Century Magazine* article. That volunteers would rush the unholy terror of McAllister's great guns was breathtaking, and no prewar Regular could imagine them doing it time and again. Just as important, that green volunteers would stand up to the attacks for so long without relief was new. The men fell in when threats became clear, mostly obeyed orders, fell back, and went into attacks that beat

36. Jordan, op. cit., 599–600; McDonough, op. cit., 104–5; Reed, op. cit., 41–2.

back forces twice their strength. As one officer said after the war, green troops will either run away at once or not at all. That worthy left out, however, that green American troops run until they get tired and they turn around to fight again.[37]

While Lexington Green started a fight for the independence of an infant nation that had suffered abuse at the hands of its homeland, Shiloh was a part of a fight for the survival for the American Experiment, an ideal that went beyond slavery and the rights of states. Grant's resolve and the recasting of the role of the citizen-soldier to the state also meant a permanent break with the ideals of warfare held so dearly by Jomini. Though France is credited with the concept of a nation-at-arms (that included citizen-soldiers in uniform and out, of all ages and genders) those revolutionary ideas of entire societies dedicated to war weren't formalized. The Americans, crude, nasty and without an understanding of cavalry in 1861, would transform France's nation-at-arms into "We Are Coming, Father Abraham," followed by the Arsenal of Democracy. That the men stayed together to fight, that they drifted back to the campfires after running away, that the steamboatmen risked their lives and livelihoods in the dark rain and raging river was especially important. They were militia who for generations had known only one formula: hold until the Regulars come.

At Shiloh the militias and the civilians that followed them *became* the Army, and would be the Army to the end of their enlistments, their conflicts, their health or their lives. The Professionals provided the brains and the bones: the muscle and blood came from the Volunteers. The citizen-soldiers became self-organizing communities far more cohesive than the neighborhood regiments from which they sprang. They became a brotherhood of blood and noise, of smoke and toil, forging bonds between themselves and their enemies that non-combatants only stare at in wonder. After sunrise on Sunday, 6 April 1862 these citizen-soldiers fought not for an exalted ideal of state's rights or Union, but for themselves and for each other. These armies

---

37. Grant, "Shiloh," 472; Ulysses S. Grant, *Memoirs* (New York: Da Capo Press, 1982), 177.

were, for the first time since Washington's Continentals, the real citizen-soldiers, and there was no going back to colorful parades and blaring bands. The old militias would gradually split to become National Guards, eventually more a part of the Army than of their communities. This was the raw stuff that would shape the armies of 1898, 1917 and 1941, and would, however reluctantly and for good or ill, take up the slack in the Berlin Airlift, in Korea, in the crisis with Cuba, in Southeast Asia, in the Persian Gulf, and after 9/11. Before the war the militias and National Guards were an influential source of amusement and political power in the United States, and the civilians that served them were barely thought of at all. After Shiloh shopkeepers and farmers, debutantes and homemakers became soldiers and sailors, interrogators and helicopter pilots from the deep wells of national power.

The Army and the country were leaving their childhoods behind in the smoky woods of Shiloh. A dozen conflicts would be won by the power of the descendants of the frightened and sick citizen-soldiers roused in their wrath to fight at impossible odds barely knowing what they were doing, and doing it simply because it needed doing. The dull booming of the gunboats Sunday night was the death knell of any chance for peaceful settlement between the two distinct societies that the Founding Fathers inadvertently left behind them. The Southern Confederacy's genteel, insulated aristocracy of landed "gentlemen of affairs" who expected to settle their differences in secluded meadows at dawn was going to end. Grant could smash the Southern political economy, and the law would change to forbid the keeping of slaves, but he could not fight his way to full of legal and social "all men are created equal" status in hearts and minds. Both Shiloh and Grant had a hand in the beginning of the transformation of the American military and its public policy from simply keeping the peace and patrolling the wilderness to enabling a world-striding power of projection.

Shiloh was where the transformation of America to world power status began. But that is another story.

APPENDIX
THE STEAMBOATS OF SHILOH: A STUDY IN CIVIL WAR RIVER LOGISTICS AND PRIVATE WARFARE

The number of vessels available for transport duties on Sunday, their cargo capacity, the size and state of the loading and landing sites, and the availability of pilots needed to get the Army of the Ohio to Pittsburg Landing are important. Because the soldiers were so new to the business and the fighting on Sunday such a desperate business, few records were kept on exactly what happened with the cross-river movement. From what we know of steamboat operations on the western rivers, that Buell's army got as much as they did across in twenty-four hours (about 18,000 men and 22 guns) is remarkable given the realities of river steamboat logistics.

The most cost-effective way to get bulk material, heavy items or large volumes of anything from one place to another is by water. Before the coming of the railroads in the 1850's river steamboats had been essential to the economy of the Mississippi valley and the Ohio country. River steamboats grew to rival the carrying capacity of oceangoing coastal ships. They were of shallow draft, with flexible and flat-bottomed hulls, and uniquely flexible drive trains to accommodate the bending of the hulls over snags and sandbars, so they had little in common with their salt water or Great Lakes cousins other than they were nearly all wood. They also had the most deck space imaginable to maximize cargo capacity, and tiny holds if they had any at all, thus tending to be top-heavy. By 1860 the "average" river steamboat could carry about 650 tons of bulk cargo at roughly nine knots.[1] Sidewheel boats (those with their paddlewheels on the side of the vessel) had been the most popular style until the 1850s when sternwheelers (with wheels astern) began to gain ground. Sternwheelers had more complex drive linkage, but fouled their paddles less often in flotsam on the river and drew less water, making them able to work more months of the year; sidewheelers were more stable and mechanically simpler, generally speedier, and easier to turn.

To work with the steamboats, the US Army had to work with some of the contrariest creatures on two legs that, for all their faults, were of the militia just as most of the soldiers were. The American rivermen (or steamboatmen, collectively called "men" regardless of gender or age) on the rivers fought the unpredictable waterways, often dangerous boats, crooked merchants, each other, the odd Indian, ruthless bandits, troublesome revenuers, greedy farmers, conniving contractors and anyone or anything else who got in the way of their profits and pleasures--and they did so with equal measures of enthusiasm and fatalistic dedication.

It would appear as if the logistical backbone of the Army in 1862 was outsourced to civilian contractors. But like the Sea Fencibles of Britain, the Union rivermen, merchant sailors, whalers and fishermen provided trained manpower and logistical support to both branches of service. Though they never assembled as units, seagoing militia had the same responsibilities to their states and societies and dedication to their jobs as the landward militias. The specialized skills and craft of the rivermen--especially the pilots who guided the vessels through the ever-changing rivers--were at a premium, and were the backbone of logistics west of the Alleghenies. These steamboats were run by civilians, especially the engine room gangs who tended the unique drive linkages. Many were family operations with spouses and children

---

1. "Average" is an estimate at best. The history of western river steamboats is so vague that few deck plans or hull elevations survive, let alone fuel consumption figures.

living on board during the working season; some were business assets owned by others or by combines with hired crews; a few were both.

The Tennessee River is a tempestuous stream that was only tamed in the 20th Century after a civil engineering project second only in the western hemisphere to the building of the Panama Canal. Most Tennessee River cargo was floated downstream on flatboats--rafts built by farmers that came downriver with the spring and fall floods. In some years as many as 350 flatboats a month reached the Ohio. The commercial length Tennessee River is 250 miles between Muscle Shoals, Alabama and the Ohio River--not far enough, and the area was not wealthy enough, for the average steamboat's risks. Less than a dozen steamboats worked the Tennessee with any regularity before the war, which meant there were few pilots who knew the hazards of the stream, and family owned small vessels tended to be risk-averse.

Contracts to haul troops, ammunition and equipment into combat zones in large steamboats on an unfamiliar stream might have been lucrative, but they were risky, and few owner/operators would do it lightly regardless of cause. But because the war disrupted trade, early 1962 was a desperate time for a profession and a way of life that was already being marginalized by railroads. The larger steamboats at Shiloh would have been either in very bold hands, or very well paid ones, or were operated by those who earnestly believed that the war wouldn't last long.[2]

---

2. Charles Dana Gibson, *Dictionary of Transports and Combatant Vessels, Steam and Sail, Employed by the Union Army, 1861–66*, The Army's Navy Series (Camden, Maine: Ensign Press, 1995); Charles Dana Gibson, *Assault and Logistics: Union Army in Coastal and River Operations 1861–6*, The Army's Navy Series (Camden, ME: Ensign Press, 1995); Louis Hunter, *Steamboats on the Western Rivers: An Economic and Technological History* (New York: Dover Publications, Inc., 1993); Fredrick Way, *Way's Packet Directory, 1848–1994* (Athens, OH: Ohio University Press, 1983).

Wood and Coal

Fueling steamboats on the inland rivers was a challenge met by American ingenuity before the war. The average river steamboat consumed 50-75 cords of wood and 3-4,000 bushels of coal every thousand miles (consumption for each steam plant and grade of fuel varied widely). An average steamboat sucked up about four bushels of coal (roughly 350 pounds) and at least a half cord of wood (another 2-400 pounds) every mile steamed. Most steamboats carried only a few days' worth of fuel, and expected to take on wood at least once a day. Independent contractors and farmers clearing land felled trees along the rivers, stacked the wood on the banks, and got paid in cash, provisions, or tools. The professionals moved on when the trees were too far away from the water to make a profit; farmers sometimes built landings for trading with and for launching flatboats.

Woodcutting for a living in all weathers is hard work, and not one many would choose if they didn't have to. Combat action, irregular boat traffic and squads of recruiters depleted the itinerant woodcutters' numbers by 1862 and the system that had a tendency to be fragile anyway became erratic. There were efforts to preposition wood and coal barges along the rivers that enterprising businessmen had begun before the war, but this required time and manpower that the Union simply didn't have at hand. Steady money, shelter and food while working in a factory, a farm or an army probably attracted many away from this hit-or-miss occupation.

Most of the coal on the Tennessee River came from the Ohio and Cumberland River mine system of the Appalachians. Coal was first barged out of Pennsylvania collieries in 1845, and thereafter traffic in it became more profitable and common. Production of anthracite (hard) coal in the region was at about 16 million tons a year by the time the war broke out. Petroleum fuels were known in the 1860s, but were not used for river steamboats until well after the war.

Steamboats arriving at Pittsburg Landing would have been low on fuel, and both wood *and* coal was the fuel mixture of choice by 1850. All could buy or cut wood locally, but coal would have had to have been brought in. All could burn wood, but because their engines were designed for both larger steamboats would consume wood-only fuel faster and without generating as much heat, which translated into less steam pressure and thus less power.[3]

Geography of the Tennessee River in Hardin County

The Tennessee flows from south to north in Hardin County, and is walled by steep bluffs for much of its length. Non-natural thruways had to be arduously cut and maintained. Because the river's level was so variable, docks, piers, and seawalls were rare on the Tennessee, making beaches and shallows valuable for commerce. Savannah, on the Tennessee's eastern shore, grew where it was because it was by one of the only reasonably flat beaches with gradual inclines from the river. It is two miles downriver from the smaller of two streams flowing around a land feature called Wolf Island. This two and a half mile long shovelful of sand grasping a ribbon of rock begins a mile and a half north (downstream) from Crump's Landing, on the western shore of the Tennessee. Wolf Island created a slackwater at Savannah during part of the year, a welcome steamboat respite from the Tennessee's strong current.

Between Crump's Landing and Pittsburg Landing is Diamond Island, a mile and a half long prominence treacherous with flotsam and snags. Of the two streams flowing around it, the western channel is the widest and deepest. Wolf Island made a slackwater for Crump's, but Crump's beach is small. Pittsburg Landing, on the western side of the river, wasn't blessed with any slackwater from Diamond Island at all, but numerous creeks fed into the Tennessee from there that kept any backed-up silt moving. The eastern side was closest to the shallower channel around Diamond Island that made mud flats across from Pittsburg Landing for several hundred yards upstream in most seasons. Because of the mud flats upstream of Diamond Island, the river bank opposite Pittsburg Landing was not suitable as a commercial landing. The main road that Buell's army had to use to get to Savannah looks

---

3. Gibson, *Army's Navy II*; Hunter, op. cit., 264.

like it might come to a point across from Pittsburg Landing, but it turned north towards Savannah a mile from the river.[4]

The Number of Steamboats Available at Shiloh

In July 1919 T.M. Hurst listed 152 transport steamers involved in some way with Shiloh, a figure used in Shiloh books and articles ever since. J. Haden Aldridge's *A History of Navigation on the Tennessee River System* reproduced this list and added twenty more. Henry Dana Gibson in his estimable "Army's Navy Series," builds on this combined list and adds two more. Combined, the three provide names for 205 vessels that were said to be on the Tennessee in the spring of 1862. Some steamboat names may be redundant because several vessels in the consolidated list were known to have more than one name, but the nature of the sources encourage the careful researcher to include all possibly relevant data. Given this, the original Hurst list is almost certainly wrong.

There's no real record of which boats were in the area on Sunday and Monday. Among the things we do know is that larger boats known to have been in the Shiloh area during the battle mostly came from the Ohio, Missouri and Mississippi River routes, many from the lucrative St. Louis-New Orleans circuit.

The three tables that follow are composites of many sources and lists. All the steamboats that were known to have been at Shiloh and are in several accounts, which also includes rated capacity in tons, and routes before the war (where known) and are mentioned in several reliable sources *and* at least one of the lists. Though river steamboats often shared names, some have names unique to the records such that their status in April 1862 is beyond dispute.

---

4. ---, *Navigation Charts for the Tennessee River* (Washington, D.C.: U.S. Government Printing Office, 2003), 28, 29.

NAME	TONS	ROUTES
ALECK SCOTT		STL-NO
AMERICUS	205	PIT-NAS; STL-PEO
ANGLO-SAXON	400	CIN-NO
ARGYLE	319	CIN-NO-STL
AUGUSTUS MCDOWELL	451	STL-MEM
BAY CITY		PIT-CIN
CITY OF ALTON		STL-ALTON
CITY OF MADISON	419	CIN-NO
CLARA POE		PIT-CIN
COMMERCIAL	266	CIN-STL
CONTINENTAL		STL-NO
DENMARK		STL-ST PAUL
DUNLEITH	155	
EMPRESS	854	STL-NO
GLADIATOR		STL-NO
HANNIBAL	497	STL-NO
HIAWATHA	767	STL-NO
JESSE K BELL	325	LOU-STL
JOHN J ROE	691	STL-NO
JOHN RAMM		
JOHN WARNER	391	
PLANET	604	STL-NO
MINNEHAHA	351	MISSOURI R.
TIGRESS	321	
WAR EAGLE	446	MISSOURI R
WHITE CLOUD	345	MISSOURI R

Table 1, Steamboats at Shiloh

The steamboats listed on Table 2 are "probable," those appearing other sources and lists. There are two *City Belles* of greatly different size listed.

NAME	TONS	ROUTES
AUTOCRAT		LOU-NO
BELLE CREOLE		LOU-PITTSBURG LANDING
CITY BELLE	153	
CITY BELLE	215	GALENA-ST PAUL
DA JANUARY	440	STL-STJ
DILIGENT	140	
EH FAIRCHILD	496	LOU-NO
EMERALD	686	
EMMA 2		MEM-WHITE RIVER
EUGENE	298	LOU-HENDERSON
FORT WAYNE	321	
GLENDALE	394	CIN-MEM
IMPERIAL	907	STL-NO
JEWESS		CIN-MEM
JS PRINGLE	307	TENNESSEE R
JW HAILMAN	267	
LANCASTER 4	218	CIN-NEW RICHMOND
NASHVILLE	497	NAS-NO
POLAND	161	LOU-NASH
POST BOY	348	
ROCKET	176	PIT-CIN
SUNSHINE	354	STL-STP
TYCOON	321	PIT-CIN
UNIVERSE	399	CIN-NO

Table 2, Steamboats Probably at Shiloh

Steamboats listed in Table 3 are mentioned in one or two accounts, on at least one list and not contradicted by other accounts.

NAME	TONS	ROUTE
BALTIC		LOU-NO
CHANCELLOR	392	LOU-NO
CRESCENT CITY		
DJ TAYLOR		
EMMA DUNCAN		
FANNY BULLITT		LOU-NO
GOODY FRIENDS	195	STP-MEM
IATAN		MOB-NO
IZETTA	301	
JOHN H DICKEY	403	
JW CHEESMAN	215	CINCINNATI
METEOR	417	NO-NATCHEZ
PLATTE VALLEY		STJ-KC; STL-VIC
ROB BOY		
SPITFIRE		
TECUMSEH	418	CIN-NO
WILSON		

Table 3, Steamboats Possibly at Shiloh

Several of these vessels were not acting as transports. At least one steamboat (probably *Tigress)* was sent to Fort Henry sometime Sunday night to telegraph Halleck about the battle. *Rocket* of 176 tons (the first vessel to negotiate Muscle Shoals into the upper Tennessee) had two barges and was herself was loaded with ammunition as late as mid-afternoon; she was probably chosen as an ammunition ship because her master was familiar with the stream and less likely to get into trouble. *Fort Wayne,* unknown to the Tennessee, was laden with pontoons, and James Webster, Grant's Chief of Staff, made sure that she stood well off from shore. The river was moving too fast to use the little canvas boats as ferries, and it would have taken too much time and manpower to build a bridge. There were also at least three hospital ships at Pittsburg Landing when the battle began.[5] *Empress* of 854 tons, *Nashville* of 497 tons, and *City of Alton* are called "casualty boats;" *Continental,* the steamer that shipped Ann Wallace (William Wallace's wife) was crammed with casualties by afternoon. When these vessels became loaded with wounded men is a good question, but without reliable and detailed first-hand accounts of the Pittsburg Landing rear area we won't be able to tell, but *Continental* is out because Ann Wallace's account excludes her. Lew Wallace's headquarters boat (*John Warner*) and Grant's (*Tigress,* even though she may have gone to Fort Henry) are included as possible transports (for at least one trip) because there were no special modifications for their nominal roles, and they would have been perfectly capable of carrying men.

Eliminating the known or suspected hospital and casualty boats, and those that couldn't have been transports, 40 steamboats were probably available to transport Buell by midday Sunday or so. Those 40 boats were going to have to be able to haul six hundred men each to get all of Buell's purported 24,000 across by dawn Monday, and that is unlikely; the 18,000 that were crossed by dark Monday requires each steamboat to carry 450, more probable but still high. Building a bridge was not a consideration because of a shortage of time, labor, materials and talent.[6]

---

5. Wiley Sword suggests there was only one, other sources count as many as five.

6. Gibson, *Army's Navy II*, 78–79, 179; Gibson, *Army's Navy I*; Navy Department, "West Gulf Blockading Squadron from January 1, 1865 to January 31 1866; Naval Forces on Western Waters from May 8, 1861 to April 11, 1862; Series 1 Volume 22," in *Official Records of the Union and Confederate Navies in the War of the Rebellion*, reprint, 1987 (Washington, D.C. (reprint Harrisburg, PA): Government Printing Office (reprint National Historical Society), 1908); War Department, "Shiloh, Corinth: Series I, Volume X, Part 1," in *War of the Rebellion: Official Records of the Union and Confederate Armies* (Washington,

Table 4 lists 85 boats that appear on at least one list as being in the "Shiloh campaign," but are unconfirmed by other sources. This is an unfortunate description because it wasn't known as the "Shiloh campaign" until the early 20th Century, so 19th Century accounts that would said that were few. Some of these vessels may have been contracted for a single run up the river at any time, may have only been involved with operations against Fort Henry or Fort Donelson. Their presence is therefore undetermined and, because of many factors, unlikely.

D.C.: U.S. Government Printing Office, 1911 (Electronic version 1999 by Guild Press, Indianapolis, IN)); Way, op. cit.

ATHY WATHAM	EMPIRE CITY	JOHN BELL	NW THOMAS
AURORA	EVANSVILLE	JOHN D ROE	OHIO 3
BEN J ADAMS	FAIRCHILD	JOHN RAINE	PRARIE ROSE
BEN SOUTH	FANNIE BARKER	JONAS POWELL	ROSE HAMBLETON
BLACK HAWK	FOREST QUEEN	JW CHAPMAN	RUTH
BOSTON	GRAY EAGLE	JW HILLMAN	SALINE
BOSTONIA 2	HAZEL DELL	JW KENNET	SALLIE LIST
CHAMPION 1	HD BACON	LADY JACKSON	SHENANGO
CHAMPION 2	HENRY CHOUTEAU	LADY PIKE	SIR WILLIAM WALLACE
CHARLEY BOWEN	HENRY CLAY	LENORA	SOUTH WESTER
CHARLEY MILLER	HENRY FITZHUGH	LIBERTY	SPREAD EAGLE
CHARLIE	HORIZON	MARENGO	SUNNY SOUTH
CHOUTEAU	INDIANA	MARY E FORSYTH	SUPERIOR
CLARIONET	IOWA	MASONIC GEM	SW THOMAS
CORONET	JACOB MUSSLEMAN	METROPOLITAN	TELEGRAM 3
DANIEL G TAYLOR	JACOB POE	MUSSLEMAN	TELEGRAPH 3
DIAMOND	JAMES H TROVER	NASHVILLE	THOMAS E TUTT
DUETT	JB DICKEY	NEBRASKA	TJ PATTEN
EDWARD WALSH	JB FORD	NEW ERA	TL MCGILL
EMILIE	JC SWAN	NEW UNCLE SAM	WESTMORELAND
EMMA	JJ SWAN	NIAGRA	WILD CAT

Table 4, Steamboats not likely to have been at Shiloh

None of the names on Table 5 could have been present because reliable sources tell us they could not have been. Some were in Confederate registry throughout the war, some were elsewhere, a few hadn't been built yet, and a few more had been out of service or destroyed years before. Others were serving as Army gunboats, though they hadn't been entered in the records as such, a few were with Pope.

ADAM JACOBS	FALLS CITY	LIZZIE SIMMONS	SCOTIA
ARMADA	GOLDEN GATE	LOUISIANA	SILVER MOON
BELLE OF THE WEST	GOLDEN STATE	MANHATTAN	SILVER WAVE
BOSTONIA 1	GOSSAMER	MARBLE CITY	SPITFIRE
CAIRO	HAVANA	MEMPHIS	ST CLAIR
CHARLES MILLER	JOHN GAULT	OHIO	ST JOHN
COMMERCE	KATE B PORTER	OHIO BELLE	TRIBUNE
COUNTESS	LAKE ERIE	ORIENTAL	VF WILSON
ELENORA	LANCASTER 3	PHANTOM	WISCONSIN
EMPIRE	LENI LEOTI	PINK VARBLE	WISCONSIN 2
EQUINOX	LEWELLYN	REBECCA	YORKTOWN

Table 5, Steamboats that were Not at Shiloh

The Capacity of the Boats

How much the steamboats available could carry is an open question. We aren't certain, for instance, how many "average" boats a "typical" infantry regiment needed to be transported. We know *Minnehaha,* a 586 ton sidewheeler that plied the Missouri and Mississippi Rivers before the war, disembarked the 15th Iowa's 760 men on Sunday morning, but we don't know if the description is of most of the outfit or just of the headquarters element. How long it took to load and unload them, how much of their equipment, baggage and ammunition they had on that steamboat is unclear. The 15th Iowa had to be issued ammunition after they unloaded, but that does not mean that *Minnehaha* had no ammunition on board. We know that there were at least three other Federal regiments still afloat and that unloaded during the battle Sunday morning, but we don't know a great deal more than that. Much of the following, therefore, is based on informed guesswork and crude calculations derived from sources that are not intended to tell us much about steamboats in military logistics.

In the spring of 1862 there was little inclination to convert steamboats into exclusive troop transports on the Western rivers since "everyone knew" that the war wouldn't last long. Given that, the Army had to rely on civilian guidelines for boat capacity for what logistical planning there was at the time. In the mid-19th Century steamboat displacement (cargo capacity), an important commercial consideration, was calculated measuring the available space for cargo, performed mostly by rule-of-thumb and was dependent on deck arrangements. An "average" steamboat of 650 tons *could* have deck space for about six to eight hundred men without their extra ammunition, rations, camp equipment, surgeons' kits, officer's horses, camp followers, and the thirty pounds of grain and hay that each horse needed every day. The baggage alone for a unit this size (about a regiment) required at least one other boat of similar size.

A field artillery battery of six guns (without their hundred and more horses) might fit on one boat of 650 tons, but another two or three boats would be needed for their limbers, caissons, ammunition, forge wagons, gunner's baggage, and of course forage, horses, cooks and seamstresses. It could have taken as many boats to move an entire battery as it might an infantry brigade. Ammunition, fodder and even artillery pieces could be stacked on a weather deck, but ammunition loaded that dense would be a deadweight hazard few skippers would take on in the changing waters of the Tennessee. Enough general supplies to last an army of Grant's size about a month, rations for a week or fodder for about a day could fit onto one boat capable of handling 650 tons of cargo. But all the boats would have had to be of "average" size for the entire river system for any of these assumptions to be valid, and that is unlikely. Based on the named boats we have dimensions for, a bulk of the steamers working Pittsburg/Crump's/Savannah were smaller and middling size sidewheelers of about 300 tons. *JS Pringle,* at 307 tons, is the only vessel we have dimensions for that frequented the Tennessee, and she may not have even been there.

Boats that were already loaded with cargo or troops Sunday morning would have had to have been unloaded to be used as ferries. Though the troops and horses could unload themselves, their baggage was another issue, and getting dead cargo off steamboats on an unimproved landing is time-consuming and back-breaking labor. We know it was done; Reilly Madison's siege battery was unloaded during the battle, and each of his five guns weighed five tons and needed ten horses to draw. This was a Herculean task of unimaginable proportions that had to have been done with muscle power alone (most steam capstans of the time weren't that powerful, if there were any around) while panicked, armed men were running around shouting doom and defeat.

River current was another issue. The Tennessee was running high and fast in exactly the opposite direction that the Federals needed to come from Savannah. Gunboat *Lexington,* rated at 7 knots, needed at least three hours to make the round trip between Crump's Landing and Pittsburg Landing, a trip she made at least three times during the battle. But *Lexington* didn't have to run in to the beach, unload, or take on fuel.

But there was also going to be a critical shortage of pilots. Most boats would not have had local pilots familiar with the local conditions. Only *JS Pringle* and *Belle Creole* were known to have frequented Pittsburg Landing, and they only *may* have been present at Shiloh. Other skippers might have been familiar enough with the waters because they had been coming and going to Pittsburg Landing for weeks in daylight and good weather, but not in the dark and rain. There would have been few pilots with confidence enough to guide steamboats around the two islands at night during a rainstorm with the river at flood, so most of the steamboats were probably moving slowly.[7]

---

7. Hunter, op. cit., 270; William Fox, *Fox's Regimental Losses* (Albany, NY: Randow Printing Company, 1889 [Electronic version 1997 by Guild Press of Indiana]), 410; Gibson, *Army's Navy I*, 61, 226;

The Crossing of the 4th Division

The Army of the Ohio's 4th Division under William H. Nelson was closest to the river on the morning of 6 April. The record is spotty on exactly how Buell's crossing worked, so the 4th Division's experience isn't a good guide for how the rest of the army got across, but it is the only one we have brigade and regiment level details for.

The lead elements of Jacob Amman's 10th Brigade made the ten miles from near Savannah to the firing line in about four and half hours. By Nelson's report it took half an hour to get the leading elements of Amman's brigade across the river--less than a thousand men in two regiments to Pittsburg Landing before dark Sunday night (just over a hundred minutes from when he started to sundown). The boats probably needed a minimum of a half hour to load and unload, using all the boat ramps and ingenuity at their disposal. The maximum number of men that could be got across the river on an average single boat available to get Buell across from the eastern side of the Tennessee River opposite Pittsburg Landing was likely somewhere between two and six hundred. If four boats could get in to drop their ramps (most had two) to load simultaneously opposite Pittsburg Landing, the rate at which Buell's army could get across from the eastern side of the river would have been from eight hundred to 2,400 men every hour. But on the Pittsburg Landing side they also had to work their way through refugees and (before dark, anyway) duck under fire, which took more time. The record shows that a thousand or so fully equipped infantrymen needed an hour and six boats to get from the eastern shore to Pittsburg Landing. William Hazen's 19th Brigade followed Amman's at about 6:30 (Ambrose Bierce, in *What I Saw of Shiloh*, said it was raining when he disembarked with the 9th Indiana; rain didn't start before 9:00 Sunday night, so either he or his 9th Indiana were delayed or he got it wrong).

The boat skippers weren't going to push off without putting as many fighting men aboard as they felt they could. They probably realized that

---

Wiley Sword, *Shiloh: Bloody April* (New York: Morrow, 1974), 329; War Department, op. cit., 290, 371; Way, op. cit., 152, 400.

the Union needed as many muskets on the western shore as they could possibly get, as fast as they could get them there. They also knew that overloading their vessels and getting them stuck in the mud wasn't going to help anyone. Though they may have been capable of carrying more men, they may not have been able to get on and off the beach carrying more. The Federals needed firepower around Pittsburg Landing *now*, and that meant getting infantrymen across the river as fast as they could be moved. Wagons or artillery could not have been loaded across from Pittsburg Landing. Buell may have been a pompous ass but he was not such a fool that he would risk grounding steamboats or losing equipment, men and horses trying to load Nelson's batteries: getting artillery to the battle was only physically realistic from Savannah.

At Savannah, steamboats available to make the trip would probably need an hour (minimum) to load and get all the fuel aboard that they possibly could, more time back off from the beach, steam upriver and unload at Pittsburg, longer to back off the beach again and likely loaded with casualties, head downstream and run in to Savannah, unload the hurt and helpless, then start the process again. It probably took every steamboat carrying infantry at least four hours to make a round trip, probably longer to load and unload litter patients. With this fairly long transit time (though we don't really know how long it was) it would have been remarkable if any of them made more than two trips, especially those large enough to carry artillery.

Each of Buell's three batteries brought across Sunday night would have required at least two steamboats for guns, men, caissons, and horses alone, leaving the baggage, forge wagons, rations, fodder and other accoutrements behind. Getting artillery unloaded on the unimproved landing of Pittsburg was another challenge that only time and labor could solve, but solved it was. Each battery would have needed at least two hours to load their burdens on and off their transports, tying up a beach spot on each end. Given the fuel requirements, the time needed to perform a transit, the loading and unloading capacity of the known beaches, and other fudge factors, it seems unlikely that every one of the boats available was going to make more than one trip Sunday night with an average of four hundred men each. None of these rough guesses take into account the boat traffic in the two narrow channels around the islands, snags, non-catastrophic accidents, equipment breakdowns, fueling stops or any other technical mishaps that doubtless occurred.

The fighting was over before Buell's men were numerous enough to influence the battle. By Monday night the steamboats had moved just under 18,000 men and four batteries,[8] and given what we know of the conditions and limitations it is remarkable that they managed that. Under modern conditions the gunboat officers would have been directing this operation, but civilian seamen rarely cotton to taking orders from brass hats. Even though some boats were idle by 9:00 Sunday night (either for want of fuel or pilots or both, or because they were simply spending the Sabbath ashore), and Alexander McCook's staff had to "compel the captains out of their beds" at Savannah to get his 2nd Division upriver Sunday night, the operation seems to have been without major mishap. [9]

The glory of Buell's arrival lay not with his army, but with the riverine militiamen that carried it. This was the rivermen's operation, and they handled it with as much skill and speed as could be asked for,

---

8. Battery A of the 1st Ohio Light Artillery arrived on the battlefield at about 2:00 Monday afternoon. They were probably loaded at Savannah Monday morning.

9. Larry J. Daniel, *Shiloh: The Battle That Changed the Civil War* (New York: Simon & Schuster, 1997), 248; Jeffry J. Gudmens, *Staff Ride Handbook for the Battle of Shiloh, 6–7 April 1862* (Ft. Leavenworth, KS: Combat Studies Institute Press, n.d. [Electronic version downloaded 2008]), 37; James L. McDonough, *Shiloh--in Hell Before Night* (Knoxville: University of Tennessee Press, 1977), 178–9; Geoffrey Perret, *Ulysses S. Grant, Soldier and President* (New York: Random House, 1997), 189; David W. Reed, *The Battle of Shiloh and the Organizations Engaged* (Knoxville, TN: University of Tennessee Press, 2008), 100, 102; Sword, op. cit., 358–9; War Department, op. cit., 302, 324, 328, 337, 339, 348; George F. Witham, *Shiloh, Shells and Artillery Units* (Memphis, TN: Riverside Press, 1980), 11.

a logistical miracle of the first order that compares to the French taxicab army of 1914, the Berlin airlift of 1948-49, the reinforcement of Korea in 1950, and the buildup in Saudi Arabia in 1990-91. The steamboats and their crews are the unsung heroes of Shiloh.

SOURCES

---. *Navigation Charts for the Tennessee River*. Washington, D.C.: U.S. Government Printing Office, 2003.

Answers.com. "Breckinridge, John Cabell." Http://www.answers.com/topic/john-c-breckinridge, Accessed October 2008.

———. "Polk, Leonidas." Http://www.answers.com/topic/leonidas-polk, Accessed 22 October 2008.

Arnold, James R. *The Armies of U.S. Grant*. New York: Arms and Armor Press, 1995.

———. *Shiloh 1862: The Death of Innocence*. Oxford, England: Osprey Publishing, LTD., 1998.

Axelrod, Alan. *Chronicle of the Indian Wars: From Colonial Times to Wounded Knee*. New York: Prentice-Hall, 1993.

Barber, Lucius W. *Army Memoirs*. Alexandria, VA: Time Life Books, 1894 (Reprint 1984).

Beauregard, Pierre G. T. "The Campaign of Shiloh." In *Battles and Leaders of the Civil War Volume 1*. New York: Thomas Yoseloff, 1956 (Electronic Edition 1997 by H-Bar Enterprises).

Beringer, Richard E., Herman Hattaway. *Why the South Lost the Civil War*. Athens, GA: University of Georgia Press, 1986.

Bierce, Ambrose, (Russell Duncan and David Klooster, eds.). *Phantoms of a Blood-Stained Period: The Civil War Writings of Ambrose Bierce*. Boston: University of Massachusetts Press, 2002.

Black, Jeremy. "A Revolution in Military Cartography? Europe 1650–1815." *The Journal of Military History* 73, no. 1 (January 2009): 49–68.

Black, Robert C. *The Railroads of the Confederacy*. Chapel Hill, NC: University of North Carolina, 1998.

Boatner, Mark M. "Brevet Rank." In *The Civil War Dictionary*. New York: David McKay & Company, 1988.

———. "Clark, Charles." In *The Civil War Dictionary*. New York: David McKay & Company, 1988.

———. "Smith, Charles Ferguson." In *The Civil War Dictionary*. New York: David McKay & Company, 1988.

———. "Wallace, Lewis." In *The Civil War Dictionary*. New York: David McKay & Company, 1988.

———. "Wallace, William Harvey Lamb." In *The Civil War Dictionary*. New York: David McKay & Company, 1988.

———. "Wood, Thomas John." In *The Civil War Dictionary*. New York: David McKay & Company, 1988.

Bonekemper, Edward H. *A Victor, not a Butcher: Ulysses S. Grant's Overlooked Military Genius*. Washington D.C.: Regenry Publishing, 2004.

Brisbin, James S. "The Battle of Shiloh." In *New Annals of the Civil War*. New York: Stackpole Books, 2004.

Buell, Don C. "Shiloh Reviewed." In *Battles and Leaders of the Civil War Volume 1*. New York: Thomas Yoseloff, 1956 (Electronic Edition 1997 by Guild Press).

Carmichael, Peter S. "New South Visionaries: Virginia's Last Generation of Slaveholders, the Gospel of Progress, and the Lost Cause." In *The Myth of the Lost Cause and Civil War History*. Indianapolis: Indiana University Press, 2000.

Catton, Bruce. *Grant Moves South*. New York: Little, Brown and Company, 1960.

———. *Reflections on the Civil War*. Norwalk, CT: Easton Press, 1987.

———. *U.S. Grant and the American Military Tradition*. New York: Grosset & Dunlap, 1954.

Chisholm, Alexander R. "The Shiloh Battle Order and the Withdrawal Sunday Evening." In *Battles and Leaders of the Civil War Volume 1*. New York: Thomas Yoseloff, 1956 (Electronic Edition 1997 by H-Bar Enterprises).

Civilwarhome.com. "Bragg, Braxton." Http://www.civilwarhome.com/braggbio.htm, Accessed January 2009.

———. "Buell, Don C." Http://www.civilwarhome.com/buellbio.htm, Accessed October 2008.

———. "Cheatham, Benjamin Franklin." Http://www.civilwarhome.com/ CMHcheathambio.htm, Accessed December 2008.

———. "Halleck, Henry Wager." Http://www.civilwarhome.com/halleckbio.htm, Accessed October 2008.

———. "Hardee, William." Http://www.civilwarhome.com/hardeebio.htm, Accessed October 2008.

———. "Johnston, Albert Sidney." Http://www.civilwarhome.com/asjohnstonbio.htm, Accessed October 2008.

———. "Pierre Gustave Toutant Beauregard." Http://www.civilwarhome.com/beaubio.htm, Accessed October 2008.

———. "Sherman, William T." Http://www.civilwarhome.com/sherbio.htm, Accessed October 2008.

———. "Wallace, Lew." http://www.civilwarhome.com/wallacebio.htm, Accessed October 2008.

Citino, Robert M. *The German Way of War: From the Thirty Year's War to the Third Reich*. Lawrence, KS: University of Kansas Press, 2005.

Connelly, Thomas L. *Army of the Heartland: The Army of the Tennessee, 1861–62*. 1995 Edition. Baton Rouge: Louisiana State University Press, 1967.

Cooling, B. Franklin. "Henry and Donelson Campaign." In *Encyclopedia of the Confederacy, Volume 2*. New York: Simon and Shuster, 1993.

Cunningham, O. Edward, (Gary D. Joiner and Timothy B. Smith, Eds.). *Shiloh and the Western Campaign of 1862*. New York: Savas Beatie, 2008.

Daly, John Patrick. "Holy War: Southern Religion and the Road to War and Defeat, 1831–1865." *North and South*, September 2003.

Daly, R.W. *How the Merrimac Won: The Strategic Story of the CSS Virginia*. New York: Thomas Y. Cromwell, 1957.

Daniel, Larry J. *Shiloh: The Battle That Changed the Civil War*. New York: Simon & Schuster, 1997.

Davis, William C. *The Orphan Brigade: The Kentucky Confederates Who Couldn't Go Home*. Garden City, NY: Doubleday & Company, 1980.

De Pauw, Linda Grant. *Battle Cries and Lullabies: Women in War from Prehistory to the Present*. Norman, OK.: University of Oklahoma Press, 2000.

Diamond, Jared. *Guns, Germs and Steel: The Fates of Human Societies*. New York: W.W. Norton & Company, 1999.

Dickison, J.J., Clement A. Evans, (Editor). *Confederate Military History Volume XI (Florida)*. Confederate Military History. New York: Thomas Yoseloff, 1962.

Dillahunty, Albert. *Shiloh: National Military Park, Tennessee*. (Reprint 1961). Washington, D.C.: United States Park Service, Department of the Interior, 1955.

Dyer, Fredrick H. *Dyer's Compendium*. (Electronic Version 1996 by Guild Press). Des Moines, IA.: The Dyer Publishing Company, 1908.

Editors of Time-Life Books. *Voices of the Civil War: Shiloh*. Alexandria, VA: Time-Life Books, 2000.

Eicher, John H. and David E. *Civil War High Commands*. Stanford, CA: Stanford University Press, 2001.

Ellis, John. *Founding Brothers: The Men of the Revolutionary Generation*. Cambridge: Yale University Press, 2004.

Faust, Patricia L. (Editor). "Clark, Charles." In *Historical Times Illustrated Encyclopedia of the Civil War*. New York: Harper and Row, 1986.

———. "Department No. 2, Confederate." In *Historical Times Illustrated Encyclopedia of the Civil War*. New York: Harper and Row, 1986.

———. "McClernand, John A." In *Historical Times Illustrated Encyclopedia of the Civil War*. New York: Harper & Row, 1986.

———. "Prentiss, Benjamin Mayberry." In *Historical Times Illustrated Encyclopedia of the Civil War*. New York: Harper and Row, 1986.

———. "Ruggles, Daniel." In *Historical Times Illustrated Encyclopedia of the Civil War*. New York: Harper & Row, 1986.

———. "Smith, Charles Ferguson." In *The Historical Times Illustrated Encyclopedia of the Civil War*. New York: Harper& Row, 1986.

———. "Wallace, Lewis." In *Historical Times Illustrated Encyclopedia of the Civil War*. New York: Harper & Row, 1986.

———. "Wallace, William Harvey Lamb." In *Historical Times Illustrated Encyclopedia of the Civil War*. New York: Harper and Row, 1986.

———. "Withers, Jones Mitchell." In *Historical Times Illustrated Encyclopedia of the Civil War*. New York: Harper and Row, 1986.

———. "Wood, Thomas John." In *Historical Times Illustrated Encyclopedia of the Civil War*. New York: Harper & Row, 1986.

Farrand, Max. *Fathers of the Constitution: A Chronicle of the Establishment of the Union*. New Haven, CT: Yale University Press [Project Gutenberg], 1921 [Electronic edition 2006].

Feis, William B. *Grant's Secret Service: The Intelligence War from Belmont to Appomattox*. Lincoln, NE: University of Nebraska Press, 2002.

Floyd, Dale E. "Brevet Rank." In *Historical Times Illustrated Encyclopedia of the Civil War*. New York: Harper & Row, 1986.

Force, M.F. *From Fort Henry to Corinth*. Campaigns of the Civil War. New York: Charles Scribner's Sons [Guild Press of Indiana], 1881 [electronic edition 1999].

Fox, William. *Fox's Regimental Losses*. Albany, NY: Randow Printing Company, 1889 [Electronic version 1997 by Guild Press of Indiana].

Frank, Joseph Allan, and George A. Reaves. *"Seeing the Elephant:" Raw Recruits at the Battle of Shiloh*. Chicago: University of Illinois Press, 2003.

Gallagher, Gary W. *Causes Won, Lost and Forgotten: How Hollywood and Popular Art Shape What We Know About the Civil War*. Chapel Hill, NC: University of North Carolina Press, 2008.

Gibson, Charles Dana. *Assault and Logistics: Union Army in Coastal and River Operations 1861–6*. The Army's Navy Series. Camden, ME: Ensign Press, 1995.

———. *Dictionary of Transports and Combatant Vessels, Steam and Sail, Employed by the Union Army, 1861–66*. The Army's Navy Series. Camden, Maine: Ensign Press, 1995.

Gootch, Rex A. "Prentiss, Benjamin." Http://members.aol.com/rexagooch/ prentissbiography.html, Accessed October 2008.

Grant, Ulysses S. "The Battle of Shiloh." In *Battles and Leaders of the Civil War Volume 1*. New York: Thomas Yoseloff, 1956 (Electronic Edition 1997 by Guild Press).

———. *Memoirs*. New York: Da Capo Press, 1982.

Griffith, Paddy. *Battle Tactics of the Civil War*. Mansfield, England: Fieldbooks, 1986.

Gudmens, Jeffry J. *Staff Ride Handbook for the Battle of, 6–7 April 1862*. Ft. Leavenworth, KS: Combat Studies Institute Press, n.d. [Electronic version downloaded 2008].

Hankinson, Alan. *First Bull Run 1861: The South's First Victory*. London: Osprey Publishing LTD., 1990.

Hattaway, Herman. "Cheatham, Benjamin Franklin." In *Historical Times Illustrated Encyclopedia of the Civil War*. New York: Harper and Row, 1986.

Haites, Erik F., James Mak and Gary M Walton. *Western River Transportation: The Era of Internal Development, 1810–1860*. Baltimore: Johns Hopkins University Press, 1975.

Hagerman, Edward. *The American Civil War and the Origins of Modern Warfare*. Indianapolis: University of Indiana Press, 1992.

Hazen, William B. *A Narrative of Military Service*. Boston: Ticknor & Company, 1885.

Hess, Earl J. *The Union Soldier in Battle: Enduring the Ordeal of Combat*. Lawrence, KS: University of Kansas Press, 1997.

Hollister, John J. *Shiloh on Your Own*. Battlefield Guide Publishers, 1973.

Holton, Woody. *Unruly Americans and the Origins of the Constitution*. New York: Hill and Wang, 2007.

Horn, Stanley. *The Army of Tennessee*. Norman, OK: University of Oklahoma Press, 1941 (Reprint 1993).

Hunter, Louis. *Steamboats on the Western Rivers: An Economic and Technological History*. New York: Dover Publications, Inc., 1993.

James, Brian. "Allies in Disarray: The Messy End of the Crimean War." *History Today* 58 (March 2008).

Jensen, Les D. "Hardee, William Joseph." In *Historical Times Illustrated Encyclopedia of the Civil War*. New York: Harper & Row, 1986.

Johnson, Robert U., Buel, Editors. "The Opposing Forces at New Madrid, Fort Pillow and Memphis." In *Battles and Leaders of the Civil War Volume 1*. New York: Thomas Yoseloff, 1956 (Electronic Edition 1997 by H-Bar Enterprises).

Jordan, Thomas. "Notes of a Confederate Staff-Officer at Shiloh." In *Battles and Leaders of the Civil War Volume 1*. New York: Thomas Yoseloff, 1956 (Electronic Edition 1997 by H-Bar Enterprises).

Johnston, William P. "Albert Sidney Johnston at Shiloh." In *Battles and Leaders of the Civil War Volume 1*. New York: Thomas Yoseloff, 1956 (Electronic Edition 1997 by H-Bar Enterprises).

Jones, Archer. *Civil War Command and Strategy: The Process of Victory and Defeat*. New York: The Free Press, 1992.

———. *Confederate Strategy from Shiloh to*. Baton Rouge, LA: University of Louisiana Press, 1991.

Jones, Spencer. "The Influence of Horse Supply upon Field Artillery in the American Civil War." *The Journal of Military History* 74, no. 2 (April 2010).

Jordan, Thomas. "Notes of a Confederate Staff-Officer at Shiloh." In *Battles and Leaders of the Civil War Volume 1*. New York: Thomas Yoseloff, 1956 (Electronic Edition 1997 by H-Bar Enterprises).

Katcher, Philip. *American Civil War Artillery 1861–65*. Oxford, UK: Osprey Publishing, 2001.

———. *The Confederate Artilleryman*. Chicago: Raintree/Reed Elsevier, 2003.

Keegan, John. *The American Civil War: A Military History*. New York: Alfred Knopf, 2009.

———. *The Face of Battle: A Study of Agincourt, Waterloo and the Somme*. New York: Random House, 1977.

———. *The Mask of Command*. New York: Viking-Penguin, 1987.

King, Duane H. "Cherokee." In *Encyclopedia of North American Indians*. New York: Houghton Mifflin Company, 1996.

Latin Library, The. "Hurlbut, Stephen." Http://www.thelatinlibrary.com/chron/ civilwarnotes/hurlbut.html, Accessed October 2008.

Lanier, Robert S., (Editor). *The Opening Battles*. Photographic History of the Civil War. New York: The Review of Reviews Company, 1911 (Electronic version 1998 by H-Bar Enterprises).

Lewin, J. G., and P. J. Huff, Compilers. *Witness to the Civil War: First-Hand Accounts from Frank Leslie's Illustrated Newspaper*. New York: HarperCollins, 2006.

Lockett, S. H. "Surprise and Withdrawal at Shiloh." In *Battles and Leaders of the Civil War Volume 1*. New York: Thomas Yoseloff, 1956 (Electronic Edition 1997 by H-Bar Enterprises).

Lord, Francis Alfred. *They Fought for the Union*. Harrisburg, Pa.: Stackpole Co., 1960.

Luragi, Raimondo. *A History of the Confederate Navy*. London: Chatham Publishing, 1996.

Martin, David G. *The Shiloh Campaign: March - April 1862*. Great Campaigns. Pennsylvania: Combined Books, 1996.

McDonough, James L. *Shiloh--in Hell Before Night*. Knoxville: University of Tennessee Press, 1977.

McFeely, William S. *Grant: A Biography*. New York: W. W. Norton & Company, 1982.

McIntosh, Kenneth W. "Creek (Muskogee)." In *Encyclopedia of North American Indians*. New York: Houghton Mifflin Company, 1996.

McPherson, James M. *Battle Cry of Freedom : The Civil War Era*. New York: Oxford University Press, 1988.

McWhiney, Grady, and Perry D. Jamieson. *Attack and Die: Civil War Military Tactics and the Southern Heritage*. University, AL: University of Alabama Press, 1982.

Miller, William J. *Great Maps of the Civil War*. Nashville, TN: Rutledge Hill Press, 2004.

Miskimon, Christopher. "The Multiple Launch Rocket System." *Military Heritage Magazine*, December 2008.

Musicant, Ivan. *Divided Waters: The Naval History of the Civil War*. Edison, New Jersey: Castle Books, 1995.

Navy Department. "West Gulf Blockading Squadron from January 1, 1865 to January 31 1866; Naval Forces on Western Waters from May 8, 1861 to April 11, 1862; Series 1 Volume 22." In *Official Records of the Union and Confederate Navies in the War of the Rebellion*. 1987. Washington, D.C. (reprint Harrisburg, PA): Government Printing Office (reprint National Historical Society), 1908.

Nevin, David. *Road to Shiloh: Early Battles in the West*. Time-Life's The Civil War. Alexandria, VA: Time-Life Books, 1983.

Nicolay, John G. *Outbreak of the Rebellion*. Campaigns of the Civil War. New York: Charles Scribner's Sons [Guild Press of Indiana], 1861 [electronic edition 1999].

Nofi, Albert A. "The American Civil War, 1861–1865." *Strategy and Tactics Magazine #43* (1974).

NNDB.com. "McClernand, John Alexander." Http://www.nndb.com/people /289/000050139/, Accessed November 2008.

Nosworthy, Brent. *Battle Tactics of Napoleon and His Enemies*. London: Constable and Company, Ltd., 1995.

———. *Bloody Crucible of Courage: Fighting Methods and Combat Experience of the Civil War*. New York: Carroll and Graf Publishers, 2003.

Parker, William H., Clement A. Evans, (Editor). *Confederate Military History Volume XII (Confederate States Navy)*. Confederate Military History. New York: Thomas Yoseloff, 1962.

Perret, Geoffrey. "ANACONDA: The Plan That Never Was." *North and South* Vol. 6 # 4 (May 2003).

———. *A Country Made By War: From the Revolution to Vietnam--The Story of America's Rise to Power*. New York: Random House, Inc., 1989.

———. *Ulysses S. Grant: Soldier and President*. New York: Random House, 1997.

Peterson, Harold L. *Notes on Ordnance of the American Civil War: 1861–1865*. Washington, D. C.: American Ordnance Association, 1959.

Pincus, Steve. *1688: The First Modern Revolution* New Haven: Yale University Press, 2009.

Pope, Stephen, Editor. "Austerlitz, Battle Of." In *Dictionary of the Napoleonic Wars*. New York: Facts on File, 1999

———. "Map 29: Waterloo Morning Positions." In *Dictionary of the Napoleonic Wars*. New York: Facts on File, 1999.

Porter, David D. *Naval History of the Civil War*. Secaucus, NJ: Castle Books, 1984.

Porter, James D., Clement A. Evans, (Editor). *Confederate Military History Volume VIII (Tennessee)*. Confederate Military History. New York: Thomas Yoseloff, 1962.

Prokopowitz, Gerald J. *All For the Regiment: The Army of the Ohio, 1861–1862*. Chapel Hill: University of North Carolina Press, 2001.

Reed, David W. *The Battle of Shiloh and the Organizations Engaged*. Knoxville, TN: University of Tennessee Press, 2008.

Reid, Whitelaw, (James G. Smart, Editor,). *A Radical View: The "Agate" Dispatches of Whitelaw Reid, 1861–65 Vol. 1.* Memphis, TN: Memphis State University Press, 1976.

Ringle, Dennis J. *Life in Mr. Lincoln's Navy*. Annapolis, MD: Naval Institute Press, 1998.

Ripley, Warren. *Artillery and Ammunition of the Civil War*. New York: Promontory Press, 1970.

Robertson, James I. "Ruggles, Daniel." In *Encyclopedia of the Confederacy Volume 3*. New York: Simon & Shuster, 1993.

Roland, Charles P. "Albert Sidney Johnston." In *The Confederate General*, vol. 3. Harrisburg, PA: National Historical Society, 1991.

Sherman, William T., (Brooks D. Simpson and Jean V. Berlin, Editors). *Sherman's Civil War: Selected Correspondence of William T. Sherman, 1860–65*. Chapel Hill, NC: University of North Carolina Press, 1999.

———. *Memoirs of General William T. Sherman*. New York: Literary Classics of the United States, Inc., 1990.

———. "We Do Our Duty According To Our Means." In *Eyewitnesses to the Indian Wars, 1865–1890* (Peter Cozzens, Ed). New York: Stackpole Books, 2005.

Silverstone, Paul H. *Civil War Navies, 1855–1883*. Annapolis, MD: Naval Institute Press, 2001.

Simpson, Brooks D. *Ulysses S. Grant: Triumph Over Adversity, 1822–1865*. New York: Houghton Mifflin Company, College Division, 2000.

Skates, Ray. "Clark, Charles." In *Encyclopedia of the Confederacy Volume 1*. New York: Simon & Shuster, 1993.

Stanchak, John E. "Cleburne, Patrick Ronyane." In *Historical Times Illustrated Encyclopedia of the Civil War*. New York: Harper and Row, 1986.

Sumida, Jon Tetsuro. *Inventing Grand Strategy and Teaching Command: The Classic Works of Alfred Thayer Mahan Reconsidered*. Baltimore, MD: The Johns Hopkins University Press, 1997.

Swanberg, W. A. *Pulitzer*. New York: Charles Scribner's Sons, 1967.

Sword, Wiley. *Shiloh: Bloody April*. New York: Morrow, 1974.

Tucker, Spencer. *Arming the Fleet: US Navy Ordnance in the Muzzle-Loading Era*. Annapolis, MD: Naval Institute Press, 1989.

Turner, George Edgar. *Victory Rode the Rails: The Strategic Place of the Railroads in the Civil War*. Lincoln, NE: University of Nebraska Press, 1992.

Tyson, Brian. *The Institution of Slavery in the Southern States, Religiously and Morally Considered in Connection with Our Sectional Troubles*. Washington, D.C. [Chapel Hill, NC]: H Polkinhorn, Printer [University of North Carolina at Chapel Hill], 1863 [electronic edition 2001].

U.S. Navy Historical Institute. "Gwin, William." Http://www.history.navy.mil/books/callahan/reg-usn-g.htm, Accessed December 2008.

War Department. "Shiloh, Corinth Series I, Volume VII." In *War of the Rebellion: Official Records of the Union and Confederate Armies*. Washington, D.C.: U.S. Government Printing Office, 1911 (Electronic version 1999 by Guild Press, Indianapolis, IN).

———. "Shiloh, Corinth: Series I, Volume X, Part 1." In *War of the Rebellion: Official Records of the Union and Confederate Armies*. Washington, D.C.: U.S. Government Printing Office, 1911 (Electronic version 1999 by Guild Press, Indianapolis, IN).

———. "Shiloh, Corinth: Series I, Volume X, Part 2." In *War of the Rebellion: Official Records of the Union and Confederate Armies*. Washington, D.C.: U.S. Government Printing Office, 1911 (Electronic version 1999 by Guild Press, Indianapolis, IN).

Walke, Henry. "The Gun-Boats at Belmont and Fort Henry." In *Battles and Leaders of the Civil War Volume 1*. New York: Thomas Yoseloff, 1956 (Electronic Edition 1997 by H-Bar Enterprises).

Wallace, Lew. "The Capture of Fort Donelson." In *Battles and Leaders of the Civil War Volume 1*. New York: Thomas Yoseloff, 1956 (Electronic Edition 1997 by H-Bar Enterprises).

Warren, Robert Penn. *The Legacy of the Civil War: Meditations on the Centennial*. New York: Vintage Books, 1961.

Waugh, Joan. *U.S. Grant: American Hero, American Myth*. Chapel Hill, NC: University of North Carolina Press, 2009.

Way, Fredrick. *Way's Packet Directory, 1848–1994*. Athens, OH: Ohio University Press, 1983.

Weigley, Russell F. "American Strategy from Its Beginnings through the First World War." In *Makers of Modern Strategy*; Peter Paret, Editor. Princeton, New Jersey: Princeton University Press, 1986.

———. *History of the United States Army*. New York: Macmillan, 1983.

———. *Towards an American Army: American Military Thought from Washington to Marshall*. New York: Columbia University Press, 1962.

Wherry, William M. "Wilson's Creek, and the Death of Lyon." In *Battles and Leaders of the Civil War Volume 1*. New York: Thomas Yoseloff, 1956 (Electronic Edition 1997 by H-Bar Enterprises).

Wikipedia.com. "Braxton Bragg." Http://en.wikipedia.org/wiki/Braxton_Bragg, Accessed January 2009.

———. "Charles Clark." Http://en.wikipedia.org/wiki/Charles_Clark (governor), Accessed December 2008.

———. "Daniel Ruggles." Http://en.wikipedia.org/wiki/Daniel Ruggles, Accessed December 2008.

———. "George B. Crittenden." Http://en.wikipedia.org/wiki/ George_B._Crittenden, Accessed October 2008.

———. "Jones Mitchell Withers." Http://en.wikipedia.org/wiki/ Jones_M_Withers, Accessed December 2008.

———. "Thomas Leonidas Crittenden." Http://en.wikipedia.org/wiki/ Thomas_ Leonidas_Crittenden, Accessed October 2008.

———. "William 'Bull' Nelson." Http://en.wikipedia.org/wiki/Bull_Nelson, Accessed October 2008.

———. "William Gwin." Http://en.wikipedia.org/wiki/William_Gwin_ (naval_officer), Accessed December 2008.

———. "William Harvey Lamb Wallace." Http://en.wikipedia.org/wiki/WHL_Wallace, Accessed October 2008.

———. "Wood, Thomas J." Http://en.wikipedia.org/wiki/ Thomas_J._Wood, Accessed October 2008.

Wiley, Bell Irvin. *The Life of Johnny Reb*. Baton Rouge: Louisiana State University Press, 1978.

Williams, Kenneth P. *Lincoln Finds a General: A Military Study of the Civil War. Volume Three: Grant's First Year in the West*. New York: The McMillian Company, 1952.

Williams, T. Harry. "Beauregard at Shiloh." *Civil War History* 1, no. 1 (March 1955).

———. *Lincoln and His Generals*. New York: Alfred A. Knopf, Inc., 1952.

Wilson, Harold S. *Confederate Industry: Manufactures and Quartermasters in the Civil War*. Jackson, MS: University Press of Mississippi, 2002.

Witham, George F. *Shiloh, Shells and Artillery Units*. Memphis, TN: Riverside Press, 1980.

Wood, C. E. *Mud: A Military History*. Washington, D. C.: Potomac Books, 2006.
Wood, W. J. *Civil War Generalship: The Art of Command*. New York: Da Capo Press, 1997.
Wootten, Geoffrey. *Waterloo 1815: The Birth of Modern Europe*. Oxford, UK: Osprey Publishing, 1992.
Yafa, Stephen. *Big Cotton: How a Humble Fiber Created Fortunes, Wrecked Civilizations, and Put America on the Map*. New York: Viking Press, Inc., 2005.
———. "The Man Who Made Cotton King." *Invention and Technology*, Winter 2005.

INDEX

CPSIA information can be obtained at www.ICGtesting.com
232764LV00003B/76/P

9 781609 106614